Teach Yourself Microsoft® PowerPoint 97 VISUALLY™

IDG's 3-D Visual™ Series

IDG Books Worldwide, Inc.
An International Data Group Company
Foster City, CA • Indianapolis • Chicago • New York

Teach Yourself Microsoft® PowerPoint 97 VISUALLY™

Published by
IDG Books Worldwide, Inc.
An International Data Group Company
919 E. Hillsdale Blvd., Suite 400
Foster City, CA 94404

Library of Congress Catalog Card No.: 98-75598

ISBN: 0-7645-6062-X

Printed in the United States of America
10 9 8 7 6 5 4 3 2 1

Distributed in the United States by IDG Books Worldwide, Inc.

Distributed by Transworld Publishers Limited in the United Kingdom; by IDG Norge Books for Norway; by IDG Sweden Books for Sweden; by Woodslane Pty. Ltd. for Australia; by Woodslane (NZ) Ltd. for New Zealand; by Addison Wesley Longman Singapore Pte Ltd. for Singapore, Malaysia, Thailand, Indonesia and Korea; by Norma Comunicaciones S.A. for Colombia; by Intersoft for South Africa; by International Thomson Publishing for Germany, Austria and Switzerland; by Toppan Company Ltd. for Japan; by Distribuidora Cuspide for Argentina; by Livraria Cultura for Brazil; by Ediciencia S.A. for Ecuador; by Ediciones ZETA S.C.R. Ltda. for Peru; by WS Computer Publishing Corporation, Inc., for the Philippines; by Unalis Corporation for Taiwan; by Contemporanea de Ediciones for Venezuela; by Computer Book & Magazine Store for Puerto Rico; by Express Computer Distributors for the Caribbean and West Indies. Authorized Sales Agent: Anthony Rudkin Associates for the Middle East and North Africa.
For corporate orders, please call maranGraphics at 800-469-6616.
For general information on IDG Books Worldwide's books in the U.S., please call our Consumer Customer Service department at 800-762-2974.
For reseller information, including discounts and premium sales, please call our Reseller Customer Service department at 800-434-3422.
For information on where to purchase IDG Books Worldwide's books outside the U.S., please contact our International Sales department at 650-655-3200 or fax 650-655-3297.
For information on foreign language translations, please contact our Foreign & Subsidiary Rights department at 650-655-3021 or fax 650-655-3281.
For sales inquiries and special prices for bulk quantities, please contact our Sales department at 650-655-3200.
For information on using IDG Books Worldwide's books in the classroom or for ordering examination copies, please contact our Educational Sales department at 800-434-2086 or fax 317-596-5499.
For press review copies, author interviews, or other publicity information, please contact our Public Relations department at 650-655-3000 or fax 650-655-3299.
For authorization to photocopy items for corporate, personal, or educational use, please contact maranGraphics at 800-469-6616.

Trademark Acknowledgments

Permissions

The following companies have given us permission to use their screen shots:
Discovery Channel Online
Flower Stop

The 3-D illustrations are the copyright of maranGraphics, Inc.

U.S. Corporate Sales
Contact maranGraphics at (800) 469-6616 or Fax (905) 890-9434.

U.S. Trade Sales
Contact IDG Books at (800) 434-3422 or (650) 655-3000.

Welcome to the world of IDG Books Worldwide.

IDG Books Worldwide, Inc., is a subsidiary of International Data Group, the world's largest publisher of computer-related information and the leading global provider of information services on information technology. IDG was founded more than 25 years ago and now employs more than 8,500 people worldwide. IDG publishes more than 270 computer publications in over 75 countries (see listing below). More than 90 million people read one or more IDG publications each month.

Launched in 1990, IDG Books Worldwide is today the #1 publisher of best-selling computer books in the United States. We are proud to have received eight awards from the Computer Press Association in recognition of editorial excellence and three from Computer Currents' First Annual Readers' Choice Awards. Our best-selling ...For Dummies® series has more than 25 million copies in print with translations in 30 languages. IDG Books Worldwide, through a joint venture with IDG's Hi-Tech Beijing, became the first U.S. publisher to publish a computer book in the People's Republic of China. In record time, IDG Books Worldwide has become the first choice for millions of readers around the world who want to learn how to better manage their businesses.

Our mission is simple: Every one of our books is designed to bring extra value and skill-building instructions to the reader. Our books are written by experts who understand and care about our readers. The knowledge base of our editorial staff comes from years of experience in publishing, education, and journalism - experience which we use to produce books for the '90s. In short, we care about books, so we attract the best people. We devote special attention to details such as audience, interior design, use of icons, and illustrations. And because we use an efficient process of authoring, editing, and desktop publishing our books electronically, we can spend more time ensuring superior content and spend less time on the technicalities of making books.

You can count on our commitment to deliver high-quality books at competitive prices on topics you want to read about. At IDG Books Worldwide, we continue in the IDG tradition of delivering quality for more than 25 years. You'll find no better book on a subject than one from IDG Books Worldwide.

John Kilcullen
CEO
IDG Books Worldwide, Inc.

Steven Berkowitz
President and Publisher
IDG Books Worldwide, Inc.

IDG Books Worldwide, Inc., is a subsidiary of International Data Group, the world's largest publisher of computer-related information and the leading global provider of information services on information technology. International Data Group publishes over 276 computer publications in over 75 countries. Ninety million people read one or more International Data Group publications each month. International Data Group's publications include: Argentina: Annuario de Informatica, Computerworld Argentina, PC World Argentina; Australia: Australian Macworld, Client/Server Journal, Computer Living, Computerworld, Computerworld 100, Digital News, IT Casebook, Network World, On-line World Australia, PC World, Publishing Essentials, Reseller, WebMaster; Austria: Computerwelt Osterreich, Networks Austria, PC Tip; Belarus: PC World Belarus; Belgium: Data News; Brazil: Annuário de Informática, Computerworld Brazil, Connections, Super Game Power, Macworld, PC Player, PC World Brazil, Publish Brazil, Reseller News; Bulgaria: Computerworld Bulgaria, Networkworld/Bulgaria, PC & MacWorld Bulgaria; Canada: CIO Canada, Client/Server World, ComputerWorld Canada, InfoCanada, Network World Canada; Chile: Computerworld Chile, PC World Chile; Colombia: Computerworld Colombia, PC World Colombia; Costa Rica: PC World Centro America; The Czech and Slovak Republics: Computerworld Czechoslovakia, Elektronika Czechoslovakia, Macworld Czech Republic, PC World Czechoslovakia; Denmark: Communications World, Computerworld Danmark, Macworld Danmark, PC Privat Danmark, PC World Danmark, PC World Danmark Supplements, TECH World; Dominican Republic: PC World Republica Dominicana; Ecuador: PC World Ecuador; Egypt: Computerworld Middle East, PC World Middle East; El Salvador: PC World Centro America; Finland: MikroPC, Tietoverkko, Tietoviikko; France: Distributique, Golden, Hebdo-Distributique, Info PC, Le Guide du Monde Informatique, Le Monde Informatique, Reseaux & Telecoms; Germany: Computer Partner, Computerwoche, Computerwoche Extra, Computerwoche Focus, I/M Information Management, Macwelt, PC Welt; Greece: GamePro, Multimedia World; Guatemala: PC World Centro America; Honduras: PC World Centro America; Hong Kong: Computerworld Hong Kong, PCWorld Hong Kong, Publish in Asia; Hungary: ABCD CD-ROM, Computerworld Szamitastechnika, PC & Mac World Hungary, PC-X Magazine; Iceland: Tolvuheimur/PC World Island; India: Information Systems Computerworld, PC World India, Publish in Asia; Indonesia: InfoKomputer PC World, Komputek Computerworld, Publish in Asia; Ireland: ComputerScope, PC Live!; Israel: People & Computers; Italy: Computerworld Italia, Computerworld Italia Special Editions, Macworld Italia, Networking Italia, PC Shopping, PC World Italia, PC World/Walt Disney; Japan: DTP World, HP Open World Japan, Macworld Japan, Nikkei Personal Computing, Open World Japan, OS/2 World Japan, SunWorld Japan, Windows World Japan; Kenya: East African Computer News; Korea: Hi-Tech Information/Computerworld, Macworld Korea, PC World Korea; Macedonia: PC World Macedonia; Malaysia: Computerworld Malaysia, PC World Malaysia, Publish in Asia; Mexico: Computerworld Mexico, Macworld, PC World Mexico; Myanmar: PC World Myanmar; Netherlands: Computer! Totaal, LAN Magazine, LanWorld Buyers Guide, Macworld, Net Magazine, Totaal! Beurskrant; New Zealand: Absolute Beginner's Guide, Computer Buyer, Computer Industry Directory, Computerworld New Zealand, MTB, Network World, PC World New Zealand; Nicaragua: PC World Centro America; Nigeria: PC World Nigeria; Norway: Computerworld Norge, Computerworld Privat (Datamagasinet), CW Rapport Norge, IDG's KURSGUIDE, Macworld Norge, Multimediaworld, PC World Ekspress, PC World Nettverk, PC World Norge, PC World's Produktguide, Windows World Spesial; Pakistan: Computerworld Pakistan, PC World Pakistan; Panama: PC World Panama; P. R. of China: China Computer Users, China Computerworld, China Infoworld, China Telecom World Weekly, Computer & Communication, Electronic Design China, Electronics Today, Electronics Weekly, Game Camp, Game Soft, Network World China, PC World China, Popular Computer Weekly, Software Weekly, Software World, Telecom World; Peru: Computerworld Peru, PC World Profesional Peru, PC World Peru; Poland: Computerworld Poland, Computerworld Special Report, Macworld, Networld, PC World Komputer; Philippines: Computerworld Philippines, PC World Philippines, Publish in Asia; Portugal: Cerebro/PC World, Computerworld/Correio Informático, Dealer World Portugal, Mac*In/PC*In, Multimedia World Portugal; Puerto Rico: PC World Puerto Rico; Romania: Computerworld Romania, PC World Romania, Telecom Romania; Russia: Computerworld Russia, Mir PK, Sety; Singapore: Computerworld Singapore, PC World Singapore, Publish in Asia; Slovenia: MONITOR; South Africa: Computing S.A., InfoWorld S.A., Network World S.A., Software World; Spain: Computerworld Espa-a, COMUNICACIONES WORLD, Dealer World, Macworld Espa-a, PC World Espa-a; Sweden: CAP&Design, Computer Sweden, Corporate Computing, MacWorld, Maxi Data, MikroDatorn, Nätverk & Kommunikation, PC/Aktiv, PC World, Windows World; Switzerland: Computerworld Schweiz, Macworld Schweiz, PCtip; Taiwan: Computerworld Taiwan, Macworld Taiwan, PC World Taiwan, Publish Taiwan, Windows World; Thailand: Thai Computerworld, Publish in Asia; Turkey: Computerworld Turkiye, MACWORLD Turkiye, PC WORLD Turkiye; Ukraine: Computerworld Kiev, Computers & Software, Multimedia World Ukraine, PC World Ukraine; United Kingdom: Acorn User, Amiga Action, Amiga Computing, Appletalk, Computing, GamePro, Macworld, Network News, Parents and Computers, PC Advisor, PC Home, PSX Pro UK, The WEB; United States: Cable in the Classroom, CD Review, CIO Magazine, Computerworld, Computerworld Client/Server Journal, Digital Video Magazine, DOS World, Federal Computer Week, GamePro, InfoWorld, I-Way, JavaWorld, Macworld, Multimedia World, Netscape World Online, Network World, PC Entertainment, PC World, Publish, SunWorld Online, SWATPro Magazine, Video Event, WebMaster; Uruguay: PC World Uruguay; Venezuela: Computerworld Venezuela, PC World Venezuela; and Vietnam: PC World Vietnam.

Every maranGraphics book represents the extraordinary vision and commitment of a unique family: the Maran family of Toronto, Canada.

Back Row (from left to right): *Sherry Maran, Rob Maran, Richard Maran, Maxine Maran, Jill Maran.*

Front Row (from left to right): *Judy Maran, Ruth Maran.*

Richard Maran is the company founder and its inspirational leader. He developed maranGraphics' proprietary communication technology called "visual grammar." This book is built on that technology—empowering readers with the easiest and quickest way to learn about computers.

Ruth Maran is the Author and Architect—a role Richard established that now bears Ruth's distinctive touch. She creates the words and visual structure that are the basis for the books.

Judy Maran is the Project Manager. She works with Ruth, Richard and the highly talented maranGraphics illustrators, designers and editors to transform Ruth's material into its final form.

Rob Maran is the Technical and Production Specialist. He makes sure the state-of-the-art technology used to create these books always performs as it should.

Sherry Maran manages the Reception, Order Desk and any number of areas that require immediate attention and a helping hand.

Jill Maran is a jack-of-all-trades who works in the Accounting and Human Resources department.

Maxine Maran is the Business Manager and family sage. She maintains order in the business and family—and keeps everything running smoothly.

CREDITS

Author & Architect:
Ruth Maran

Copy Development Director:
Kelleigh Wing

Copy Developers:
Roxanne Van Damme
Jason M. Brown
Cathy Benn

Project Manager:
Judy Maran

Editing & Screen Captures:
Raquel Scott
Janice Boyer
Michelle Kirchner
James Menzies
Frances Lea
Emmet Mellow

Layout Designer:
Treena Lees

Illustrators:
Russ Marini
Jamie Bell
Peter Grecco
Steven Schaerer

Illustrator & Screen Artist:
Sean Johannesen

Indexer:
Raquel Scott

Permissions Coordinator:
Jenn Hillman

Post Production:
Robert Maran

Editorial Support:
Michael Roney

ACKNOWLEDGMENTS

Thanks to the dedicated staff of maranGraphics, including Jamie Bell, Cathy Benn, Janice Boyer, Jason M. Brown, Francisco Ferreira, Peter Grecco, Jenn Hillman, Sean Johannesen, Michelle Kirchner, Wanda Lawrie, Frances Lea, Treena Lees, Jill Maran, Judy Maran, Maxine Maran, Robert Maran, Sherry Maran, Russ Marini, Emmet Mellow, James Menzies, Steven Schaerer, Raquel Scott, Jimmy Tam, Roxanne Van Damme, Paul Whitehead and Kelleigh Wing.

Finally, to Richard Maran who originated the easy-to-use graphic format of this guide. Thank you for your inspiration and guidance.

TABLE OF CONTENTS

Chapter 1

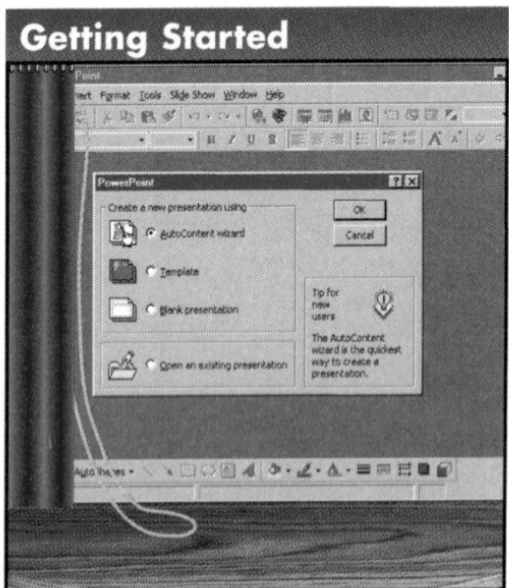

Chapter 2

Chapter 3

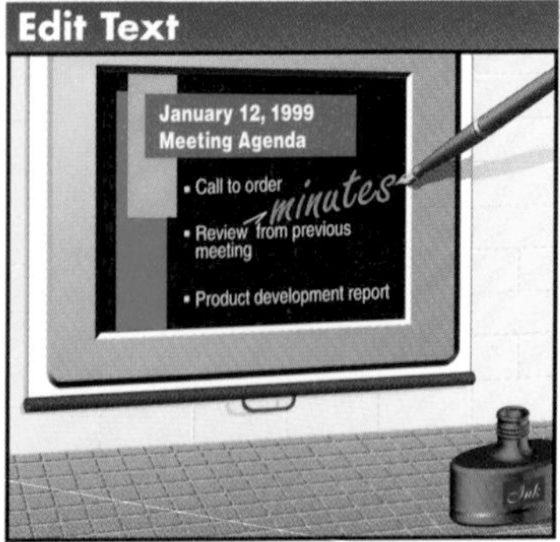

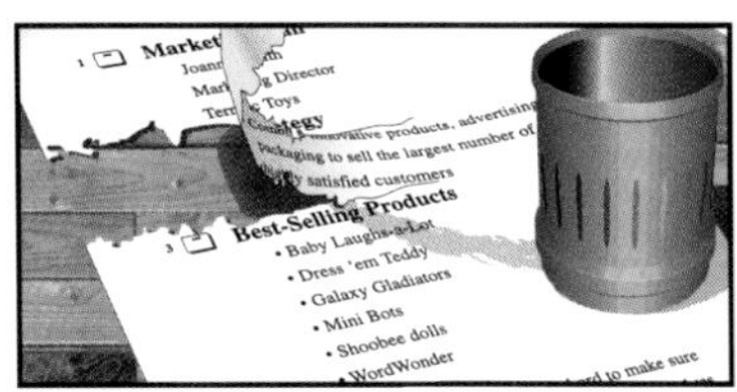

Chapter 4

Format Text

Chapter 5

Change Appearance of Slides

Chapter 6

Add Objects to Slides

TABLE OF CONTENTS

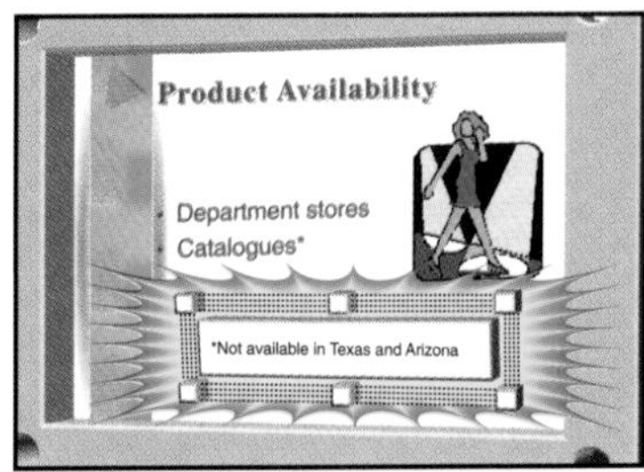

Chapter 7

Work With Objects on Slides

Chapter 8

Add Multimedia to Slides

Chapter 9

Add Special Effects to Slides

Chapter 10

Fine-Tune a Presentation

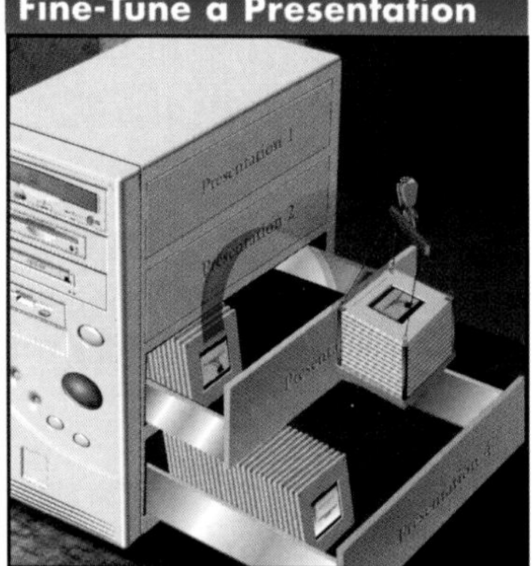

Chapter 11

Deliver a Presentation

Chapter 12

PowerPoint and the Internet

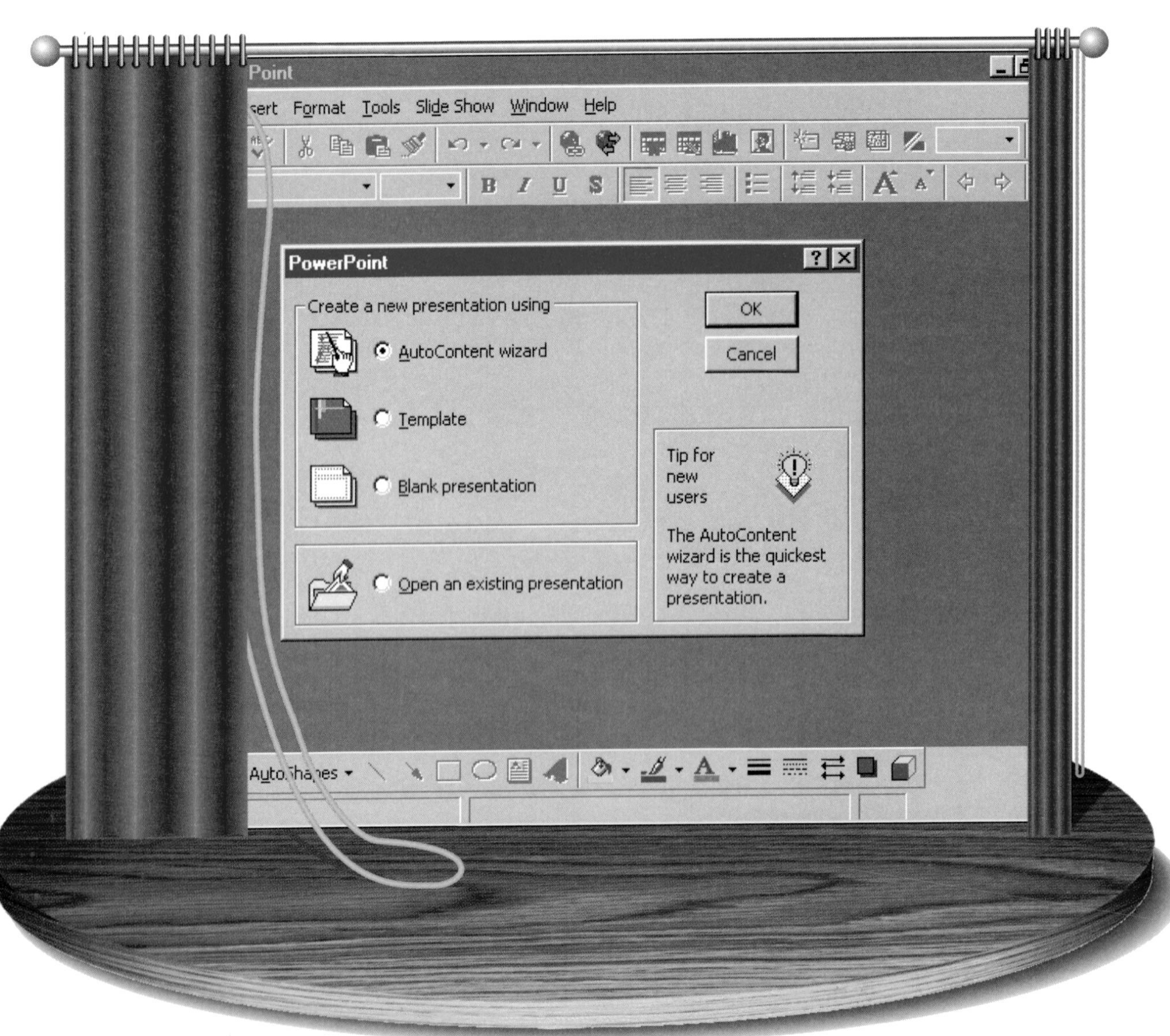
Point
sert Format Tools Slide Show Window Help
PowerPoint
Create a new presentation using
AutoContent wizard
Template
Blank presentation
Open an existing presentation
OK
Cancel
Tip for new users
The AutoContent wizard is the quickest way to create a presentation.
AutoShapes

CHAPTER 1

Getting Started

Are you ready to begin using Microsoft PowerPoint 97? This chapter will help you get started.

INTRODUCTION TO POWERPOINT

PowerPoint helps you create, design and organize professional presentations that you can deliver to colleagues and clients.

Create Presentations

PowerPoint includes a wizard and pre-designed templates to help you create presentations that you will deliver using a computer screen, overheads or 35mm slides. You can also create a presentation and save it as a collection of Web pages. You can then publish the presentation on the Web.

Edit Text

PowerPoint offers many features to help you work with the text in your presentation. You can add, delete and move text, as well as change the importance of text on your slides. You can also check for spelling mistakes, find and replace text and insert symbols.

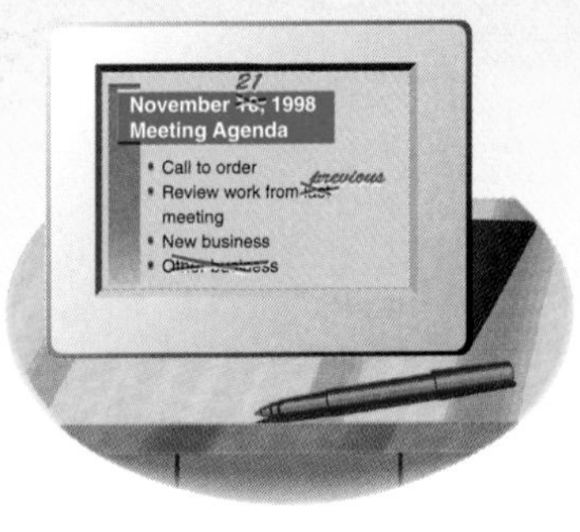

Format Slides

There are many ways you can change the appearance of text in your presentation. For example, you can change the font, color, alignment and line spacing of the text. You can also change the slide design, color scheme and background of slides to enhance the overall appearance of your presentation.

Add Objects to Slides

You can add objects to slides to illustrate important concepts and make your slides more interesting. Objects you can add include simple shapes, clip art images, pictures, text effects, charts and tables.

Add Multimedia to Slides

Adding multimedia to slides can make your presentation more entertaining. You can add sounds, movies and voice narration to slides. You can also play a music CD during a presentation to add background music to the slides.

Add Special Effects to Slides

PowerPoint includes special effects you can use to enhance your presentation and help direct the attention of the audience to important information. You can add transitions to help introduce slides in your presentation. You can also add movement and sound effects to objects on the slides.

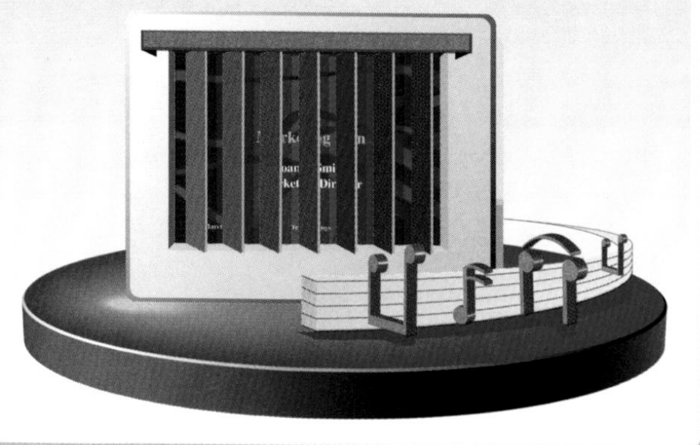

Deliver Presentations

You can rehearse and deliver a presentation on your computer screen. During a presentation, you can monitor your progress, record meeting minutes and refer to your speaker notes. PowerPoint also lets you create handouts that you can distribute to your audience.

CREATING GREAT PRESENTATIONS

TIPS FOR CREATING A GREAT PRESENTATION

Consider the Audience

You should consider your audience when developing the content and tone of your presentation. You should also make sure the level of vocabulary you use is suitable for your audience.

For example, a presentation for the engineering department of a company should be different than a presentation for the sales department.

Organize the Text

When writing the text for your slides, consider the following:

- Use uppercase and lowercase text, not ALL UPPERCASE.
- Be specific and clear.
- Discuss only one concept per slide.
- Include only main ideas on each slide, not all the information you want to present.
- Do not include more than six points on a slide.
- Each point on a slide should be no more than two lines long.
- Each slide title should be no more than two lines long.
- Spell check your presentation.

Choose Colors and Fonts

When designing your slides, consider the following:

- Choose colors that match the mood of your presentation. For example, use bright colors to convey good news.
- Choose colors and fonts that make your text easy to read.
- You should not use more than five colors per slide.
- You should not use more than three fonts per slide.

Add Visuals

Add visuals, such as pictures, charts, tables or movies, to your slides. Visual information is easier to remember than text.

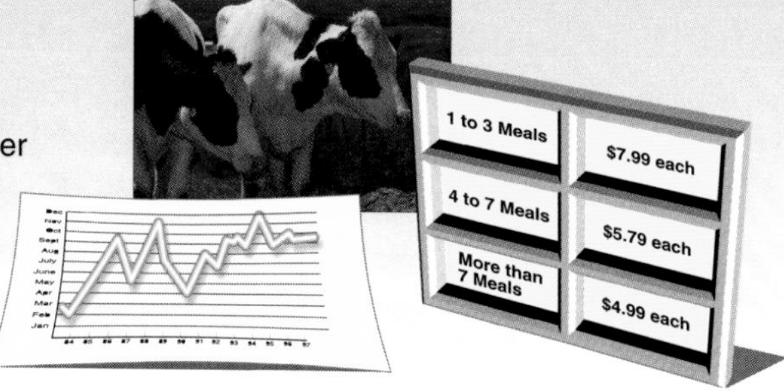

For example, displaying sales figures in a chart is more effective than displaying a list of numbers. Visuals can help enhance a presentation, but you should try to avoid cluttering your slides with visuals that have no purpose.

Create Speaker Notes

You can create speaker notes that contain copies of your slides with all the ideas you want to discuss during your presentation.

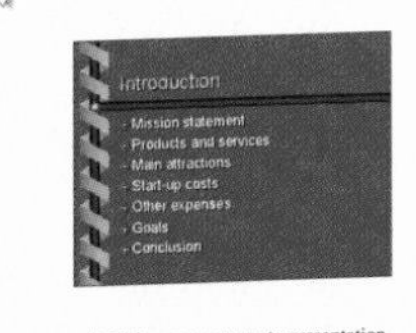

Speaker notes can include important points, statistics or additional information that will help you answer questions from the audience. When delivering the presentation, you should not read directly from your speaker notes.

Print Handouts

You can print and distribute handouts to the audience to help them follow your presentation and take notes on the slides. Handouts can include additional information about your presentation and are ideal for audience members who cannot clearly view the screen.

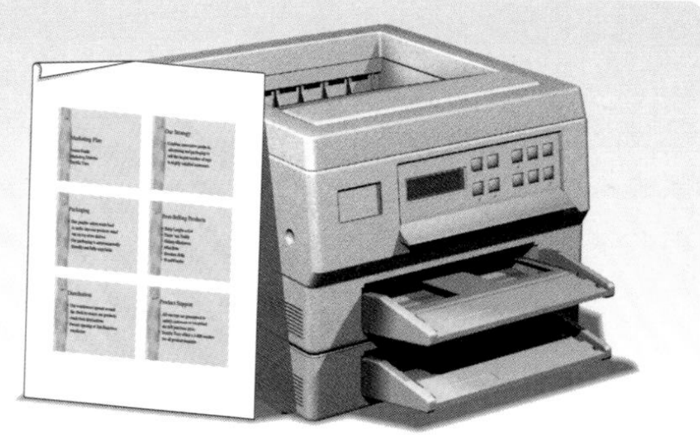

WAYS TO DELIVER A PRESENTATION

View on a Computer Screen

You can deliver your presentation on a computer screen. This method is ideal for delivering a presentation to a small audience and allows you to add multimedia, such as sounds, movies or animations, to your slides.

View on Two Screens

You can control your presentation from one computer screen while the audience views the presentation on another computer screen. For example, you can deliver your presentation from a notebook computer while the audience views the slide show on a computer with a larger monitor.

Use a Slide Projector

You can use a slide projector to deliver a presentation on 35mm slides. 35mm slides offer better color and crisper images than a presentation shown on a computer screen. A service bureau can output your presentation to 35mm slides.

Use an Overhead Projector

You can use an overhead projector to display your presentation on a screen or wall. Many office supply stores sell overhead transparencies that you can print your presentation on. A service bureau can also print your presentation on overhead transparencies.

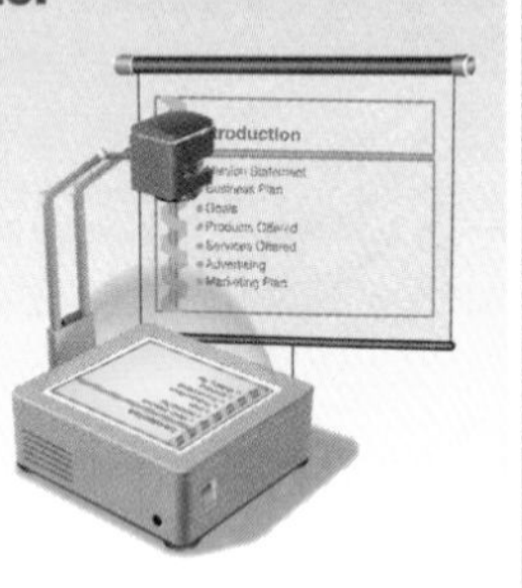

Use a Computer Projector

You can connect a computer to a projector to display your presentation on a screen or wall. Computer projectors are available at many computer stores.

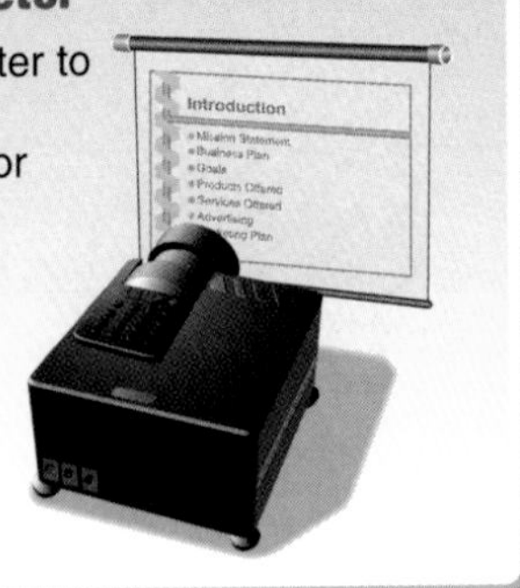

View at a Kiosk

You can create a self-running presentation that people can view at a kiosk. Kiosks are often found at trade shows and shopping malls.

TIPS FOR DELIVERING A GREAT PRESENTATION

Rehearse the Presentation

Make sure you rehearse your presentation before you deliver it in front of an audience. This will help your presentation flow smoothly and can help ensure that you will complete the presentation in the time provided. If possible, practice your presentation in front of a friend or colleague.

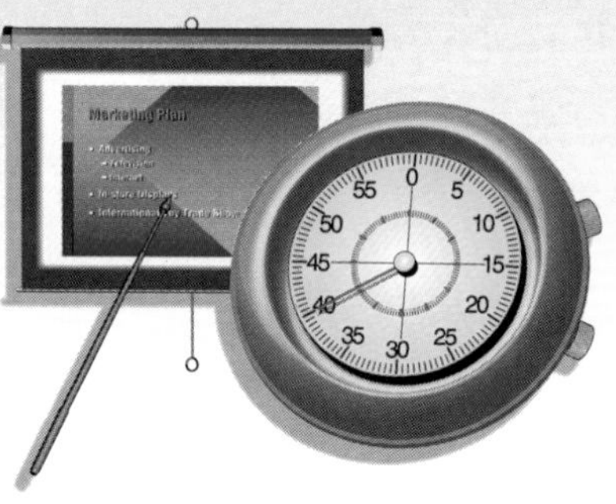

Check the Hardware

Before you deliver your presentation, check all the hardware you plan to use. Make sure you know how to operate the hardware and that you have all the parts you need, such as spare bulbs or an extension cord. In case of a hardware failure, you should always have a paper copy of your presentation with you.

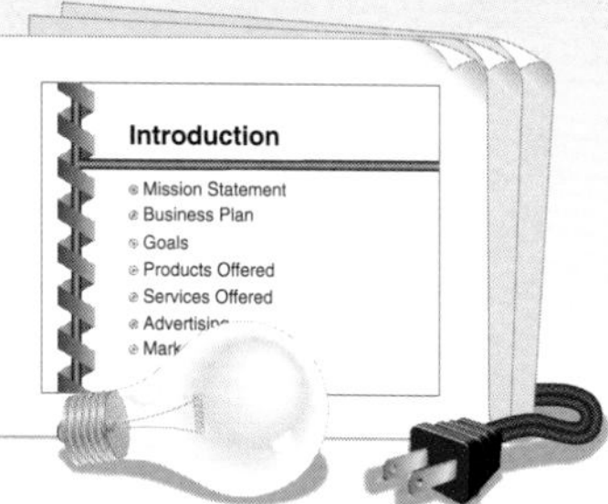

Check the Presentation Room

You should check the room you will be presenting in before the presentation. Make sure the slides are readable from all areas of the room. If necessary, determine the location of electrical outlets and light switches.

Check Your Body Language

When delivering a presentation, your posture should convey a relaxed and confident manner. Make eye contact with your audience while presenting and avoid hiding or clasping your hands.

USING THE MOUSE

A mouse is a handheld device that lets you select and move items on your screen.

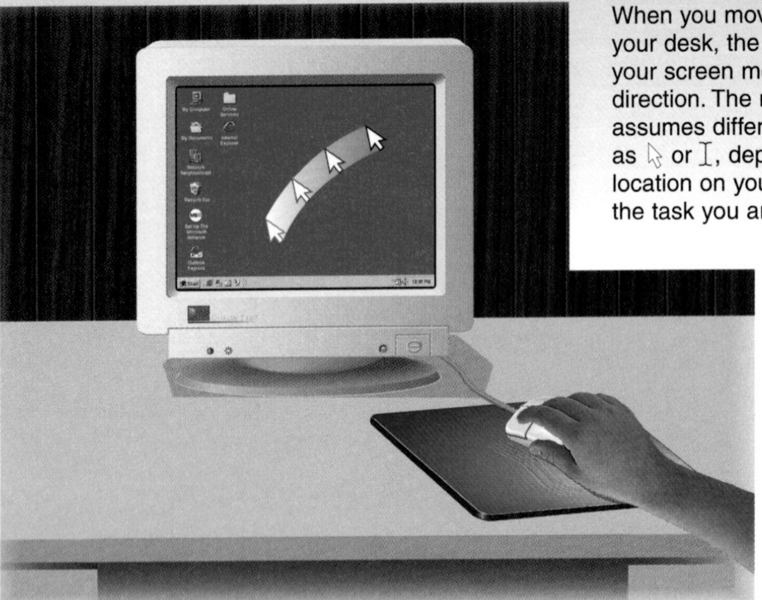

When you move the mouse on your desk, the mouse pointer on your screen moves in the same direction. The mouse pointer assumes different shapes, such as ↖ or I, depending on its location on your screen and the task you are performing.

Resting your hand on the mouse, use your thumb and two rightmost fingers to move the mouse on your desk. Use your two remaining fingers to press the mouse buttons.

MOUSE ACTIONS

Click

Press and release the left mouse button.

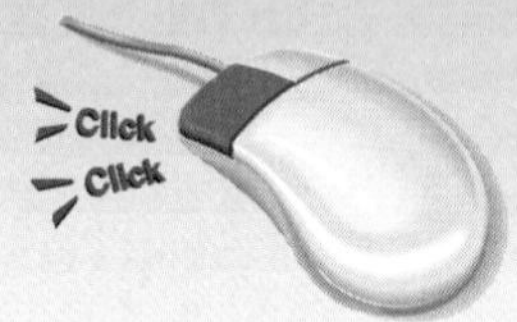

Double-click

Quickly press and release the left mouse button twice.

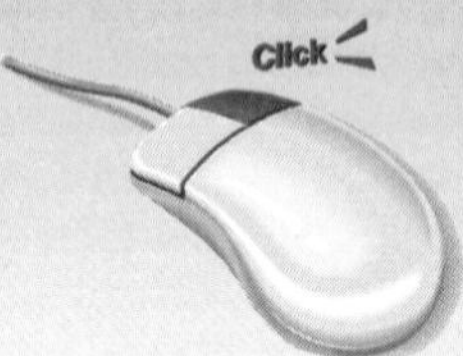

Right-click

Press and release the right mouse button.

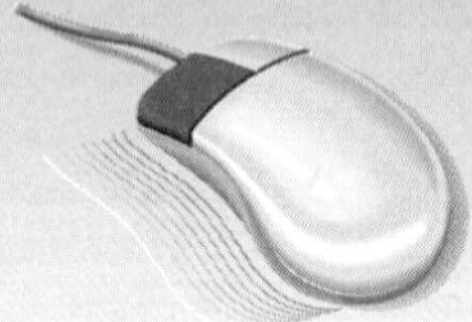

Drag

Position the mouse pointer (↖) over an object on your screen and then press and hold down the left mouse button. Still holding down the button, move the mouse to where you want to place the object and then release the button.

START POWERPOINT

You can start PowerPoint to create a professional presentation.

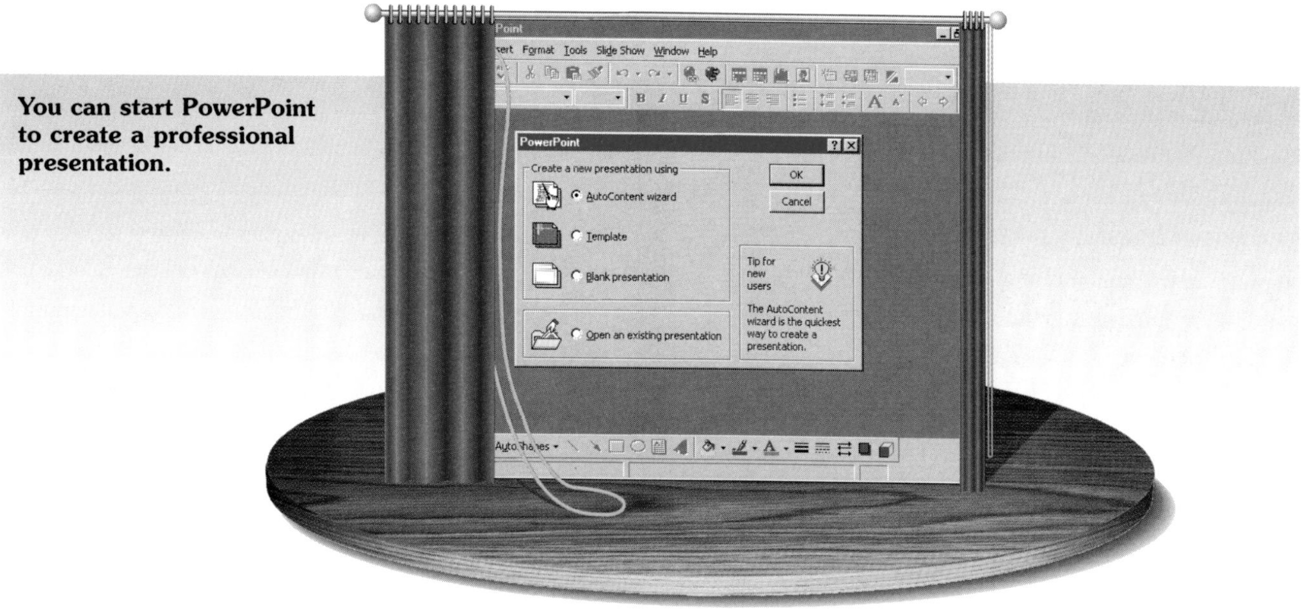

START POWERPOINT

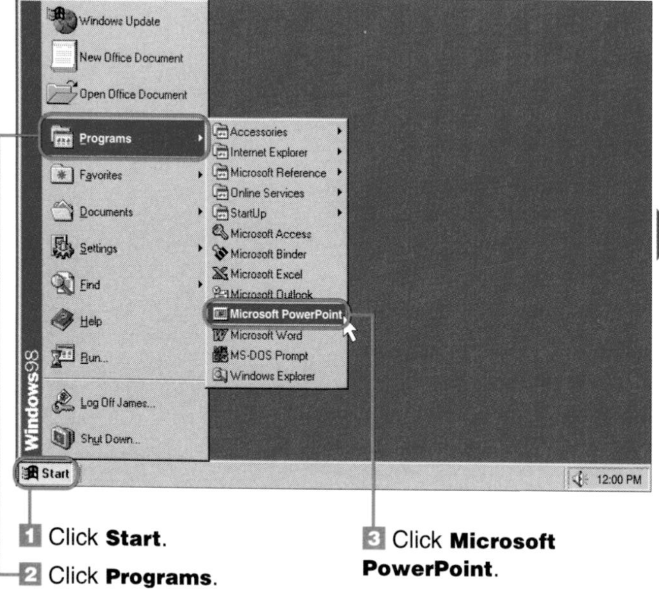

1 Click **Start**.

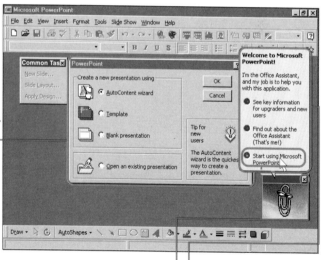

2 Click **Programs**.

3 Click **Microsoft PowerPoint**.

■ The PowerPoint dialog box appears each time you start PowerPoint, allowing you to create or open a presentation.

Note: To create a presentation, see page 12 or 16. To open an existing presentation, see page 22.

■ The Office Assistant welcome appears the first time you start PowerPoint.

4 Click this option to start using PowerPoint.

■ Click ☒ to hide the Office Assistant.

CREATE A PRESENTATION USING THE AUTOCONTENT WIZARD

You can use the AutoContent Wizard to quickly create a presentation. The wizard asks you a series of questions and then sets up a presentation based on your answers.

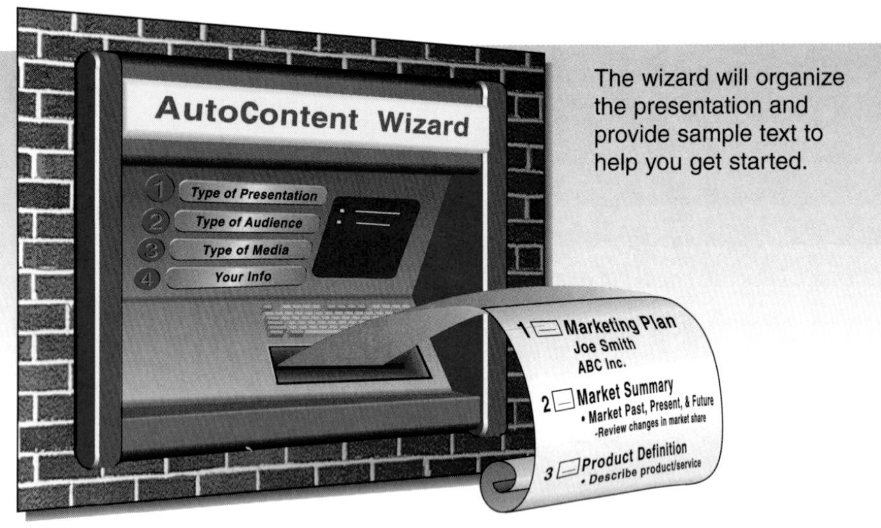

The wizard will organize the presentation and provide sample text to help you get started.

CREATE A PRESENTATION USING THE AUTOCONTENT WIZARD

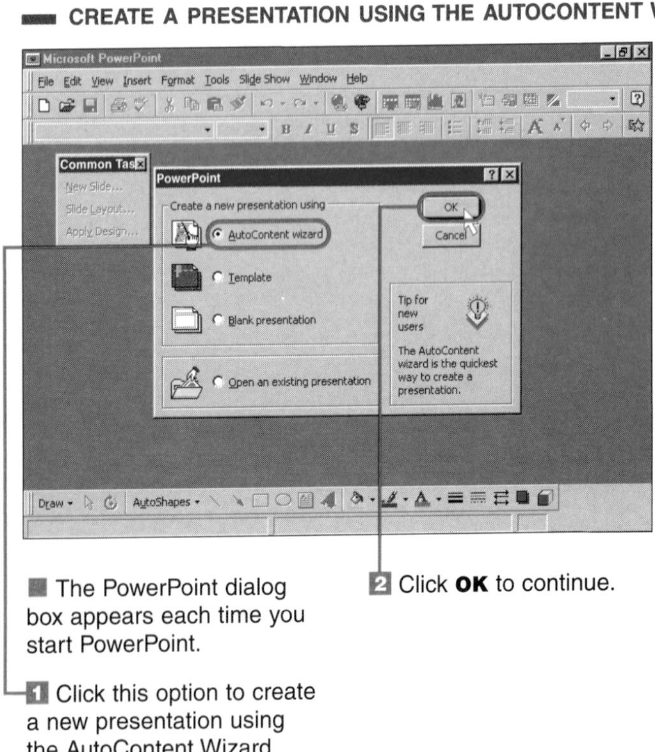

■ The PowerPoint dialog box appears each time you start PowerPoint.

1 Click this option to create a new presentation using the AutoContent Wizard (○ changes to ⊙).

2 Click **OK** to continue.

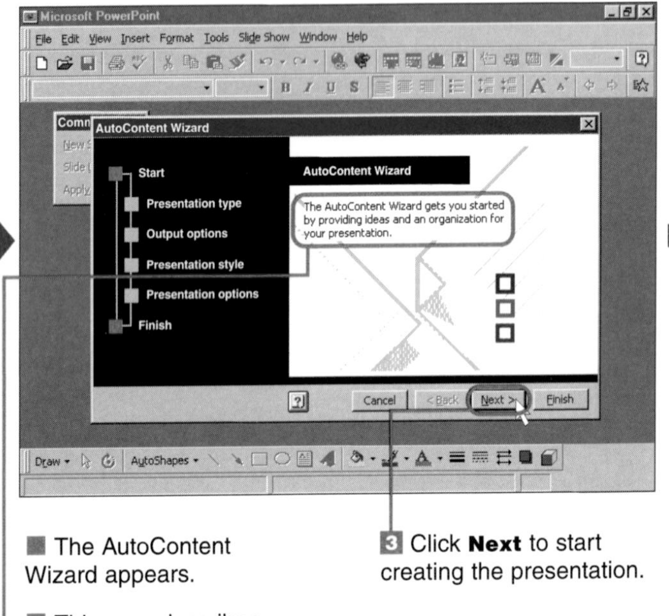

■ The AutoContent Wizard appears.

■ This area describes the wizard.

3 Click **Next** to start creating the presentation.

Which option should I select when the AutoContent Wizard asks how my presentation will be used?

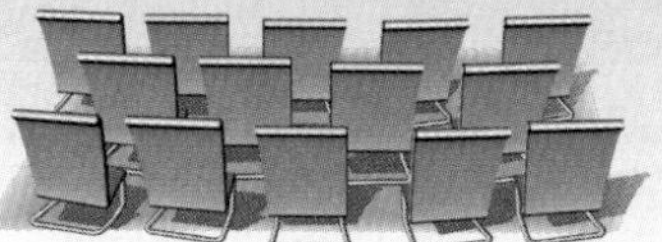

Presentations, informal meetings, handouts

Select this option if you plan to deliver the presentation to an audience. This option creates a presentation you can deliver using a computer screen, overheads or slides.

Internet, kiosk

Select this option if you plan to have others view the presentation on their own. This option creates a presentation you can publish as a Web page or display at a kiosk. Kiosks are often found at trade shows and shopping malls.

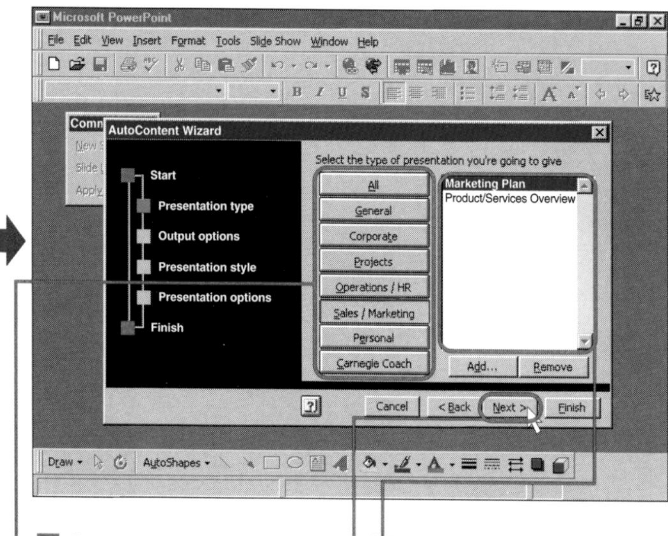

4 Click the category that best describes the type of presentation you want to create.

*Note: If you are not sure which category to select, click **All** to display all the available presentations.*

5 This area lists the presentations in the category you selected. Click the presentation that best suits your needs.

6 Click **Next** to continue.

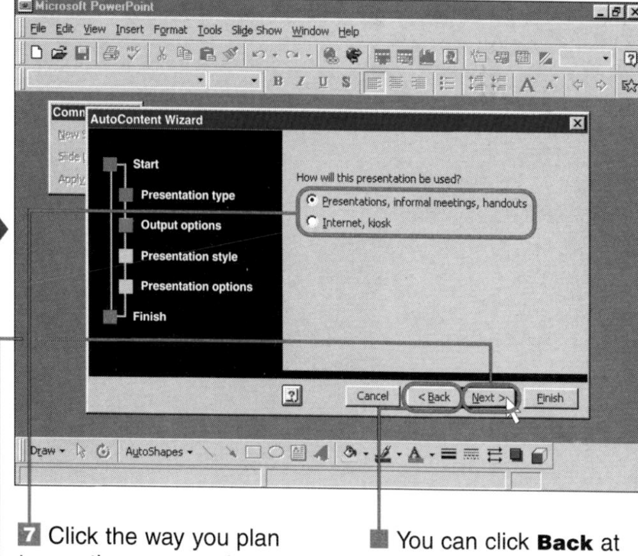

7 Click the way you plan to use the presentation (○ changes to ⊙).

8 Click **Next** to continue.

■ You can click **Back** at any time to return to a previous step and change your answers.

■ The options available in the next screens depend on the option you selected in step 7.

CONTINUED

CREATE A PRESENTATION USING THE AUTOCONTENT WIZARD

The AutoContent Wizard allows you to choose how you want to output the presentation.

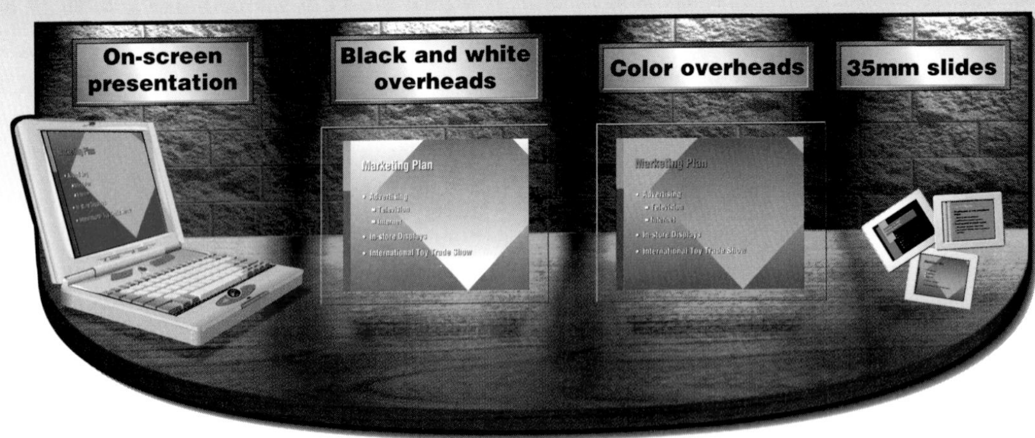

CREATE A PRESENTATION USING THE AUTOCONTENT WIZARD (CONTINUED)

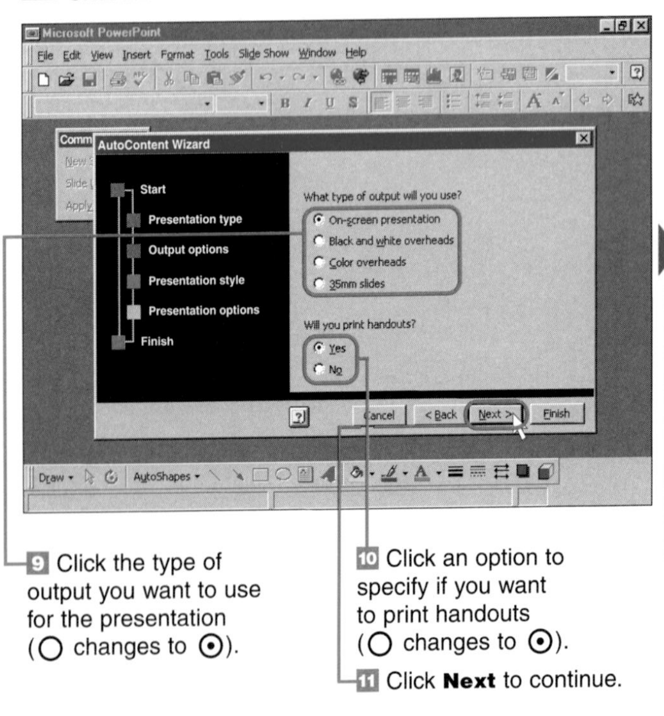

9 Click the type of output you want to use for the presentation (○ changes to ⦿).

10 Click an option to specify if you want to print handouts (○ changes to ⦿).

11 Click **Next** to continue.

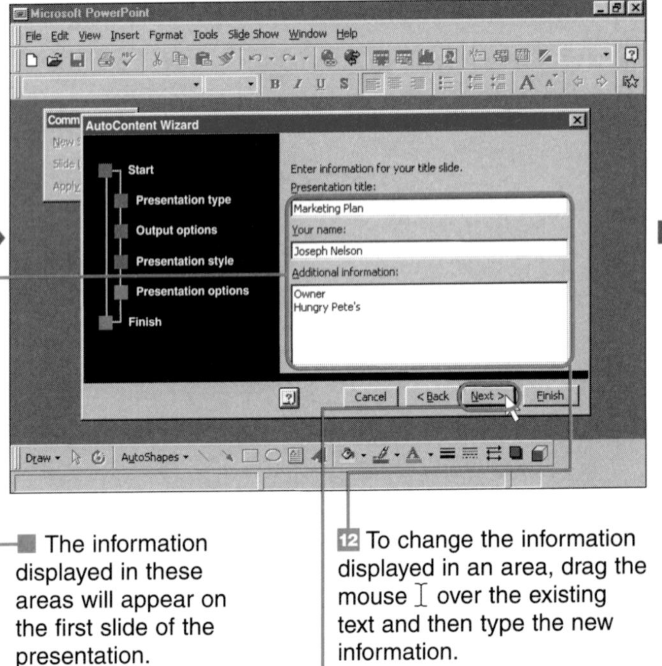

■ The information displayed in these areas will appear on the first slide of the presentation.

12 To change the information displayed in an area, drag the mouse I over the existing text and then type the new information.

13 Click **Next** to continue.

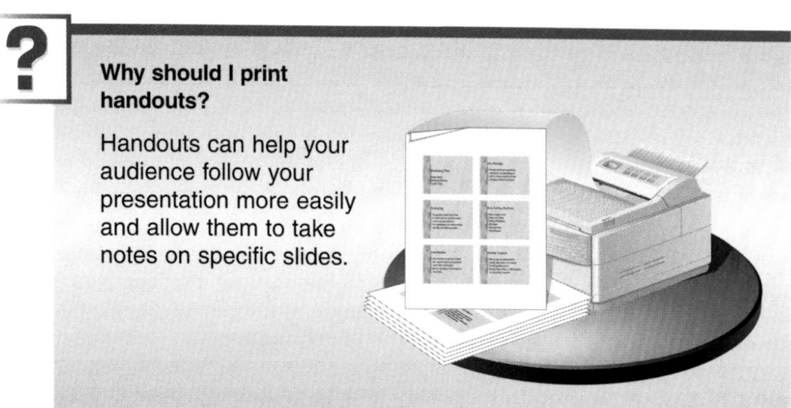

Why should I print handouts?

Handouts can help your audience follow your presentation more easily and allow them to take notes on specific slides.

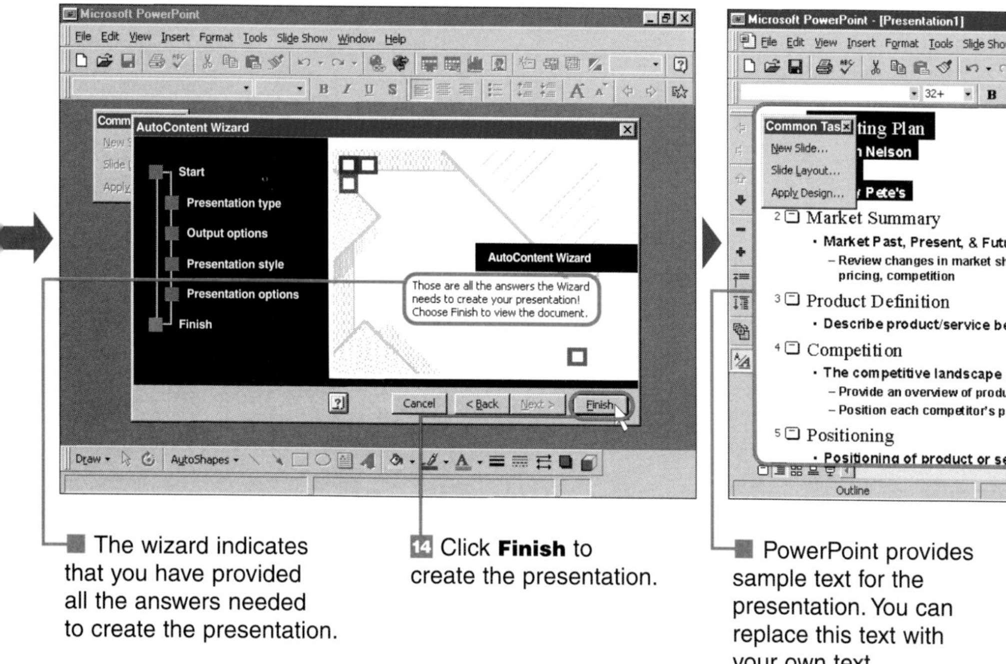

■ The wizard indicates that you have provided all the answers needed to create the presentation.

14 Click **Finish** to create the presentation.

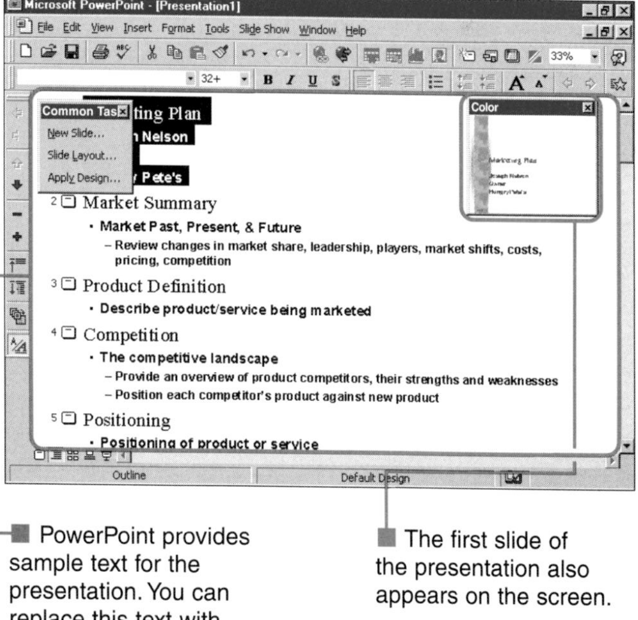

■ PowerPoint provides sample text for the presentation. You can replace this text with your own text.

■ The first slide of the presentation also appears on the screen.

CREATE A PRESENTATION USING A TEMPLATE

You can use a template to create a presentation. Each template uses fonts, backgrounds and colors to create a particular look.

When you create a presentation using a template, PowerPoint creates only the first slide. You can add additional slides to your presentation as you need them.

CREATE A PRESENTATION USING A TEMPLATE

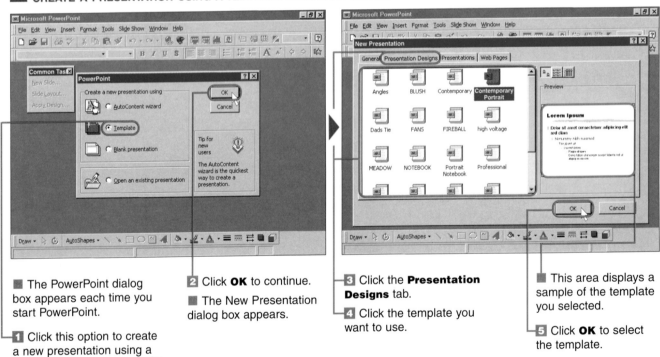

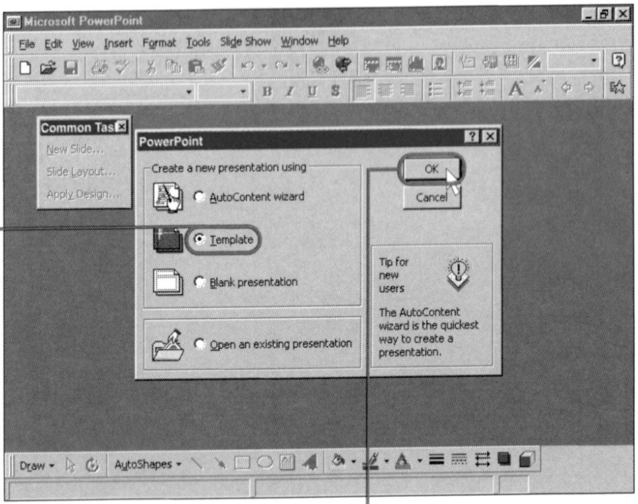

■ The PowerPoint dialog box appears each time you start PowerPoint.

1 Click this option to create a new presentation using a template (○ changes to ⊙).

2 Click **OK** to continue.

■ The New Presentation dialog box appears.

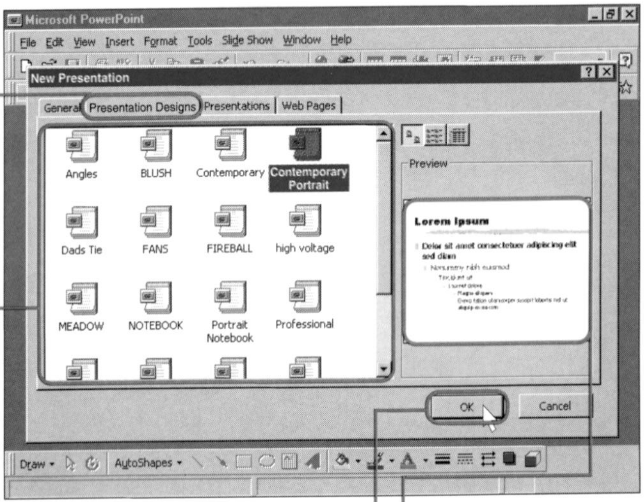

3 Click the **Presentation Designs** tab.

4 Click the template you want to use.

■ This area displays a sample of the template you selected.

5 Click **OK** to select the template.

How do I create a presentation while working in PowerPoint?

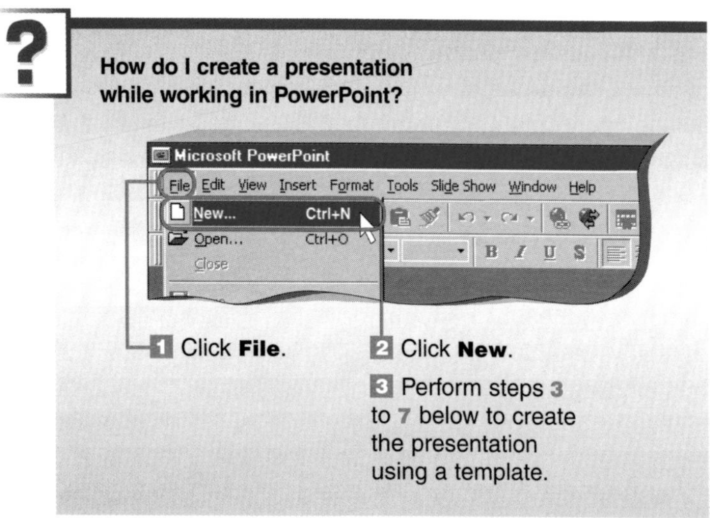

1 Click **File**.

2 Click **New**.

3 Perform steps 3 to 7 below to create the presentation using a template.

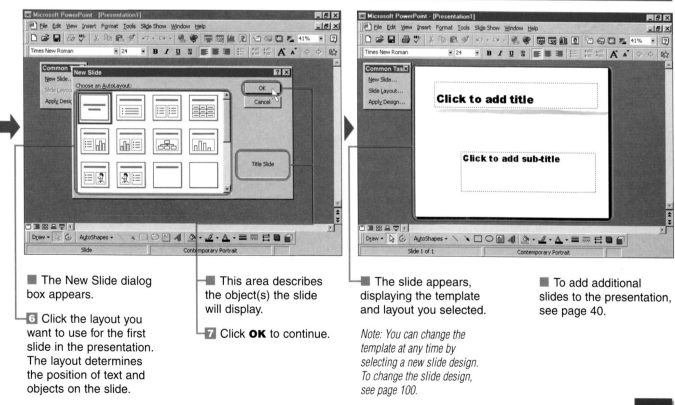

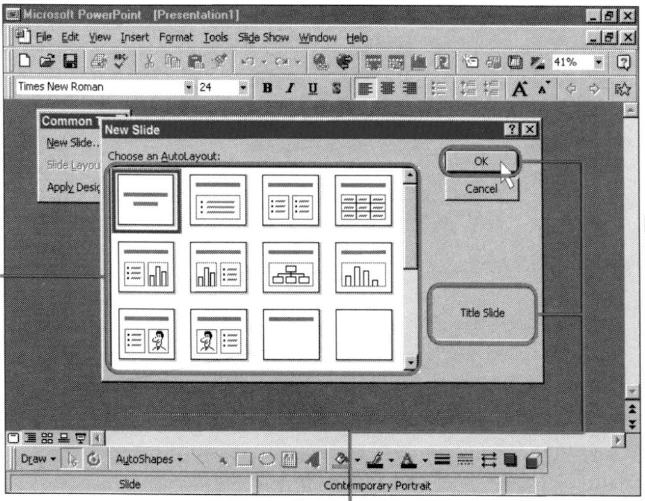

■ The New Slide dialog box appears.

6 Click the layout you want to use for the first slide in the presentation. The layout determines the position of text and objects on the slide.

■ This area describes the object(s) the slide will display.

7 Click **OK** to continue.

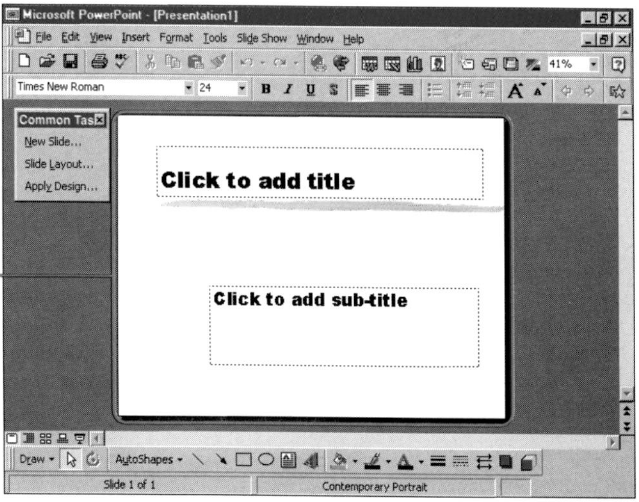

■ The slide appears, displaying the template and layout you selected.

Note: You can change the template at any time by selecting a new slide design. To change the slide design, see page 100.

■ To add additional slides to the presentation, see page 40.

SAVE A PRESENTATION

You can save your presentation to store it for future use. This allows you to later review and make changes to the presentation.

SAVE A PRESENTATION

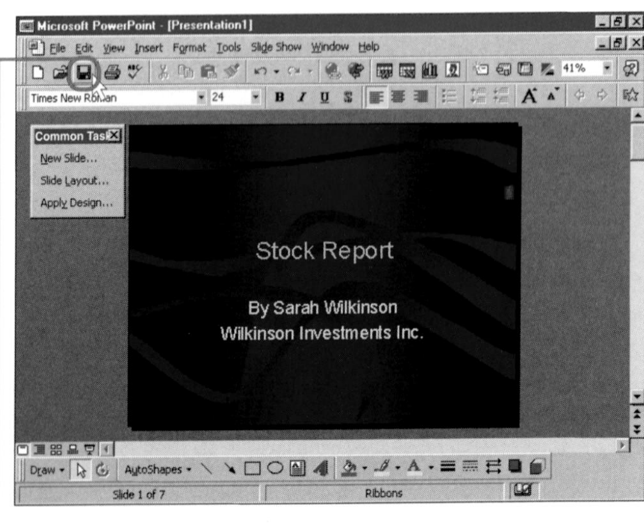

1 Click [save icon] to save the presentation.

■ The Save dialog box appears.

Note: If you previously saved the presentation, the Save dialog box will not appear since you have already named the presentation.

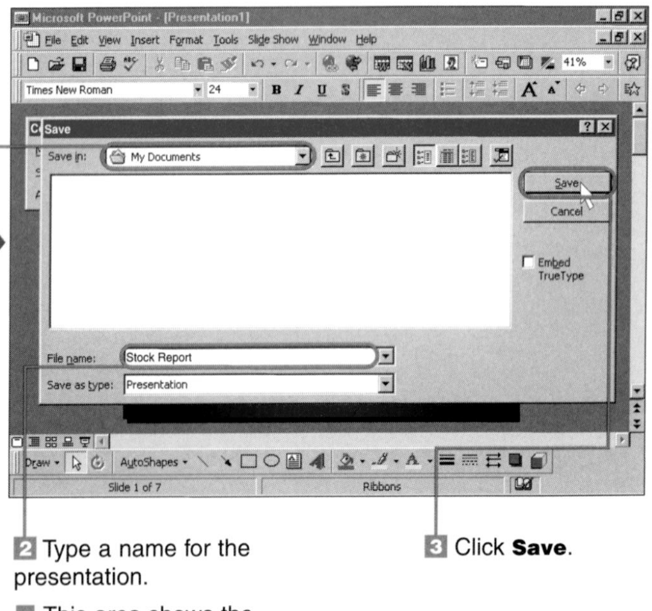

2 Type a name for the presentation.

■ This area shows the location where PowerPoint will save the presentation. You can click this area to change the location.

3 Click **Save**.

What should I name my presentation?

You should give your presentation a descriptive name that will help you later identify the presentation. You can use up to 255 characters, including spaces, to name the presentation. A presentation name cannot contain the / \ < > * " | ? : or ; characters.

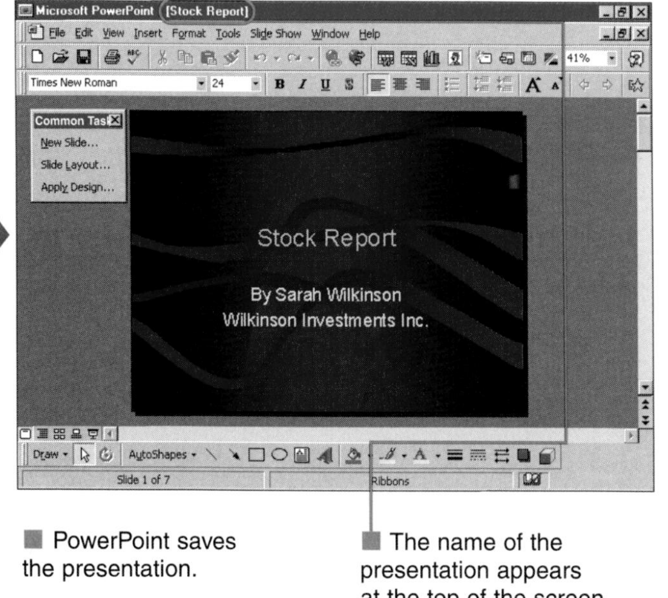

■ PowerPoint saves the presentation.

■ The name of the presentation appears at the top of the screen.

SAVE CHANGES

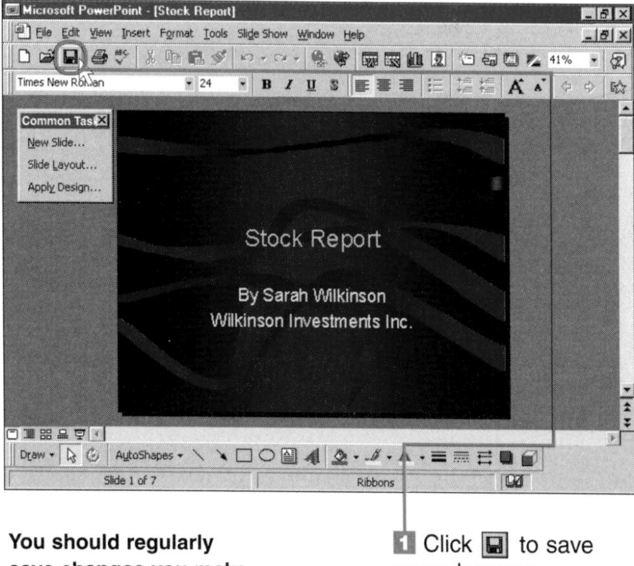

You should regularly save changes you make to a presentation to avoid losing your work.

1 Click [save icon] to save your changes.

CLOSE A PRESENTATION

When you finish working with a presentation, you can close the presentation to remove it from your screen.

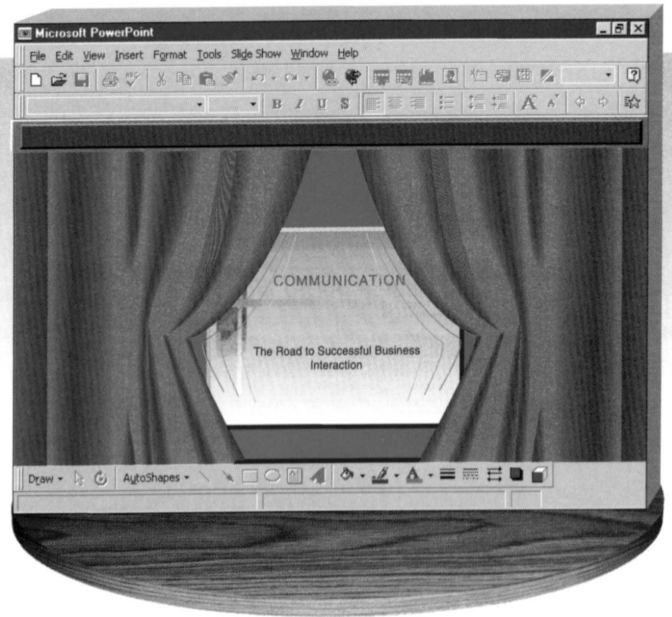

When you close a presentation, you do not exit the PowerPoint program. You can continue to work on other presentations.

CLOSE A PRESENTATION

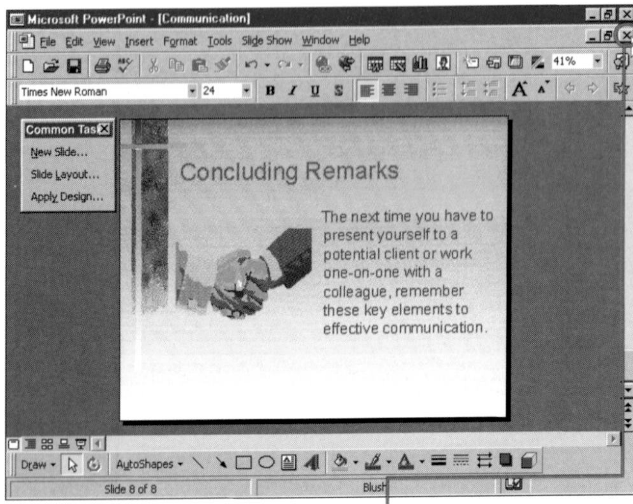

1 Save the presentation displayed on your screen before closing the presentation. To save a presentation, see page 18.

2 Click ☒ to close the presentation.

■ PowerPoint removes the presentation from your screen.

■ If you had more than one presentation open, the second last presentation you worked on would appear on your screen.

EXIT POWERPOINT

When you finish using PowerPoint, you can exit the program.

To prevent the loss of data, you should always exit all open programs and shut down Windows before turning off your computer.

EXIT POWERPOINT

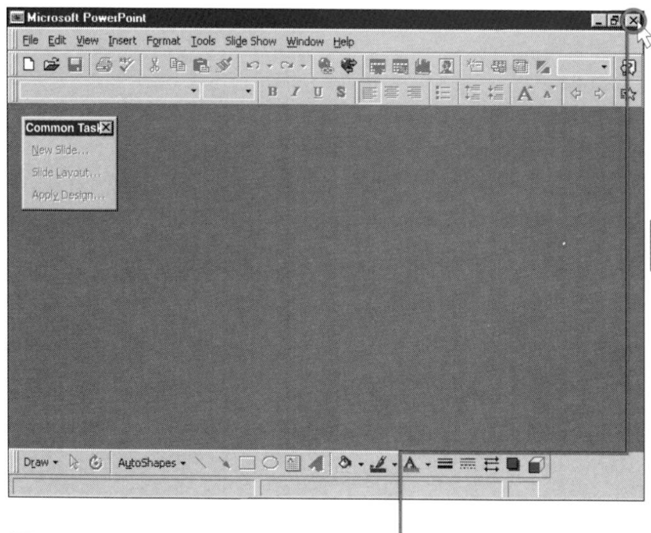

1 Save all your open presentations before exiting PowerPoint.
To save a presentation, see page 18.

2 Click ☒ to exit PowerPoint.

■ The Microsoft PowerPoint window disappears from your screen.

OPEN A PRESENTATION

You can open a saved presentation and display it on your screen. This lets you review and make changes to the presentation.

OPEN A PRESENTATION

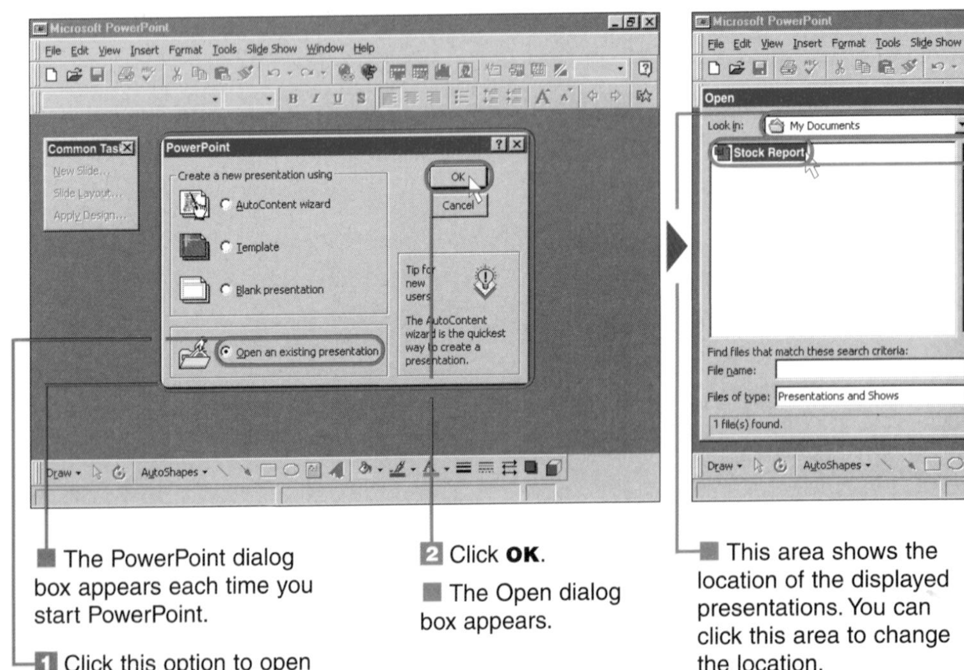

■ The PowerPoint dialog box appears each time you start PowerPoint.

1 Click this option to open an existing presentation (○ changes to ⊙).

2 Click **OK**.

■ The Open dialog box appears.

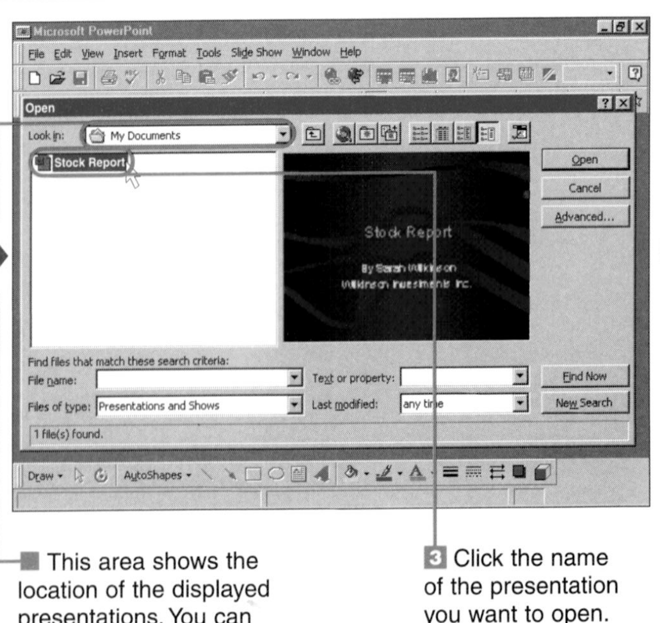

■ This area shows the location of the displayed presentations. You can click this area to change the location.

3 Click the name of the presentation you want to open.

?

While working in PowerPoint, can I quickly open a presentation I recently used?

PowerPoint remembers the names of the last four presentations you worked with. You can quickly open one of these presentations.

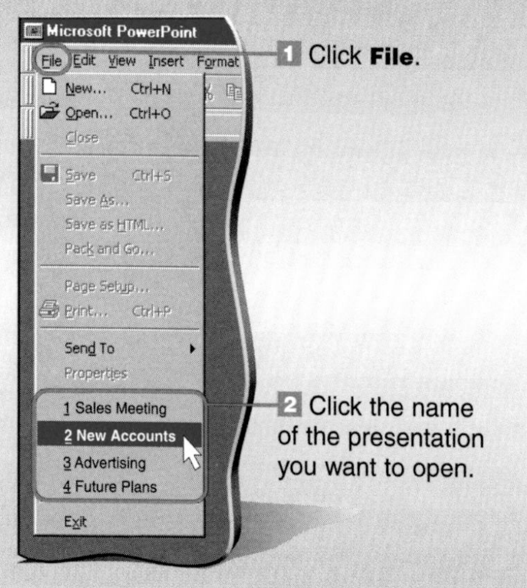

1 Click **File**.

2 Click the name of the presentation you want to open.

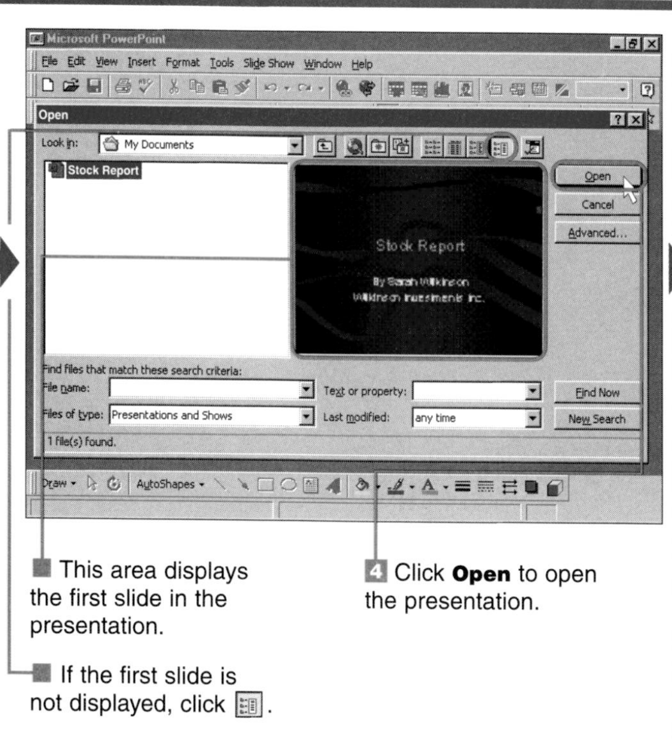

■ This area displays the first slide in the presentation.

■ If the first slide is not displayed, click ▦.

4 Click **Open** to open the presentation.

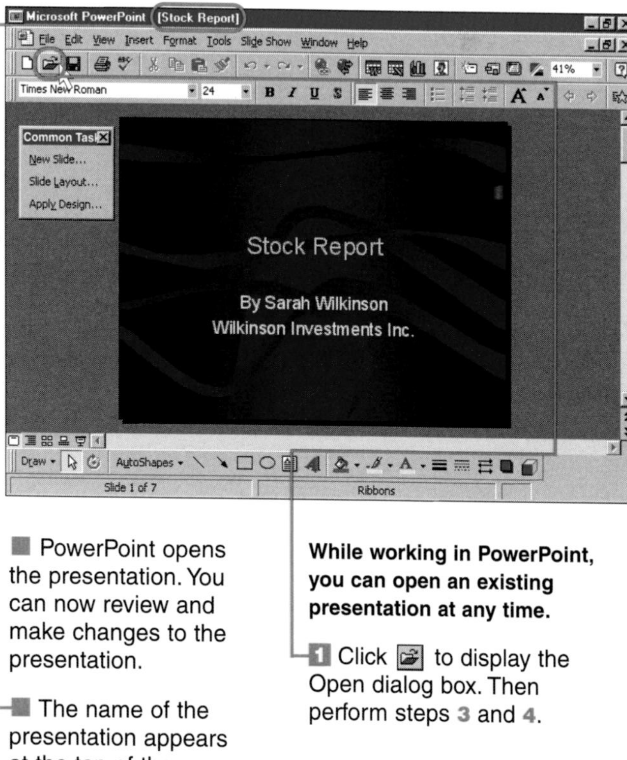

■ PowerPoint opens the presentation. You can now review and make changes to the presentation.

■ The name of the presentation appears at the top of the screen.

While working in PowerPoint, you can open an existing presentation at any time.

1 Click 📂 to display the Open dialog box. Then perform steps 3 and 4.

FIND A PRESENTATION

If you cannot find the presentation you want to open, you can have PowerPoint search for the presentation.

FIND A PRESENTATION

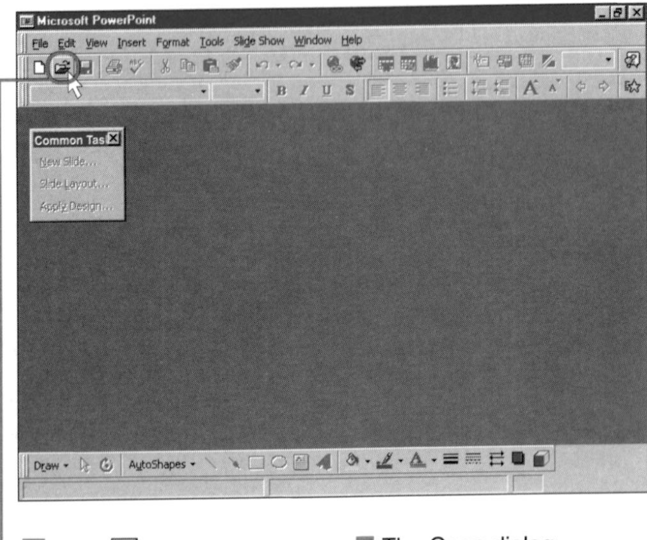

1 Click 📂.

■ The Open dialog box appears.

2 To specify where you want PowerPoint to search for the presentation, click this area.

3 Click the location you want to search.

?

Can PowerPoint find a presentation if I know only part of the presentation name?

PowerPoint will find all the presentations with names that contain the text you specify. For example, searching for **sales** will find **Sales Meeting**, **Annual Sales Report** and **Salesperson Awards**.

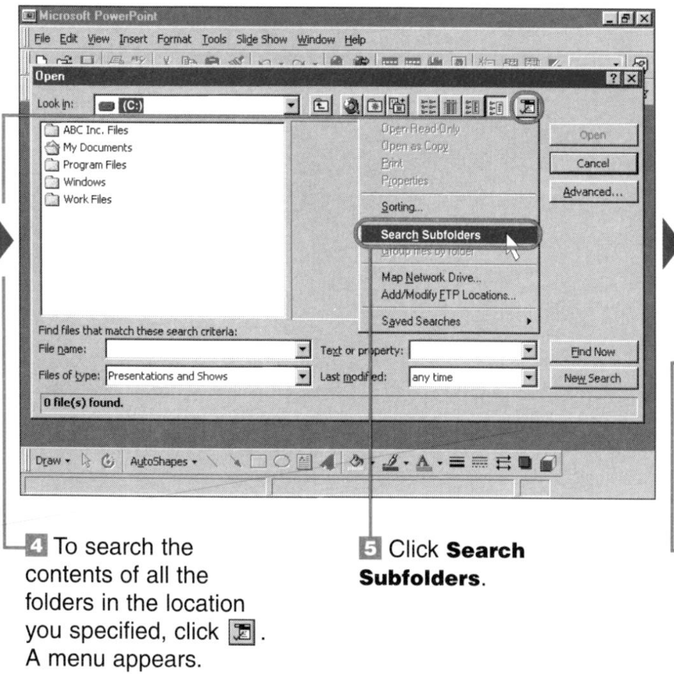

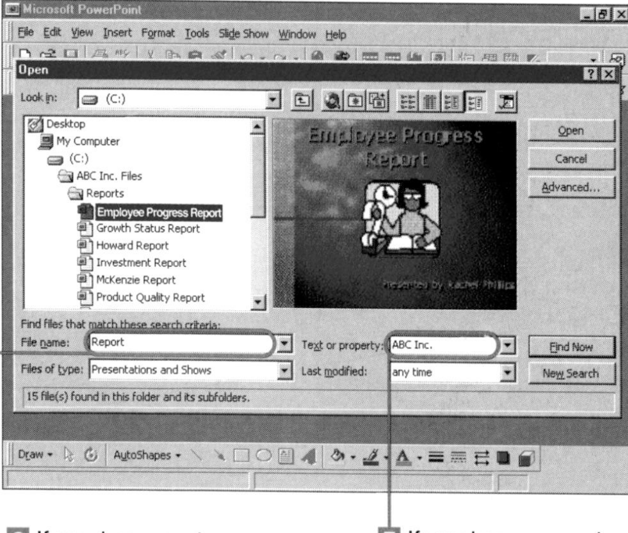

4 To search the contents of all the folders in the location you specified, click the icon. A menu appears.

5 Click **Search Subfolders**.

6 If you know part or all of the name of the presentation, click this area and then type the name.

7 If you know a word or phrase in the presentation, click this area and then type the word or phrase.

CONTINUED

FIND A PRESENTATION

When the search is complete, PowerPoint displays the names of the presentations it found.

FIND A PRESENTATION (CONTINUED)

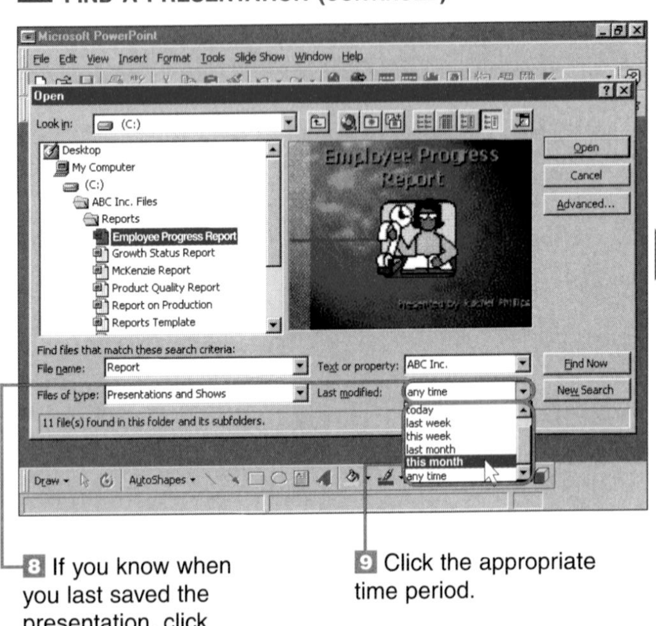

8 If you know when you last saved the presentation, click this area.

9 Click the appropriate time period.

10 Click **Find Now** to complete the search.

?

PowerPoint did not find the presentation I was looking for. What can I do?

If the search did not provide the results you were expecting, you may not have provided PowerPoint with enough information or you may have specified incorrect information.

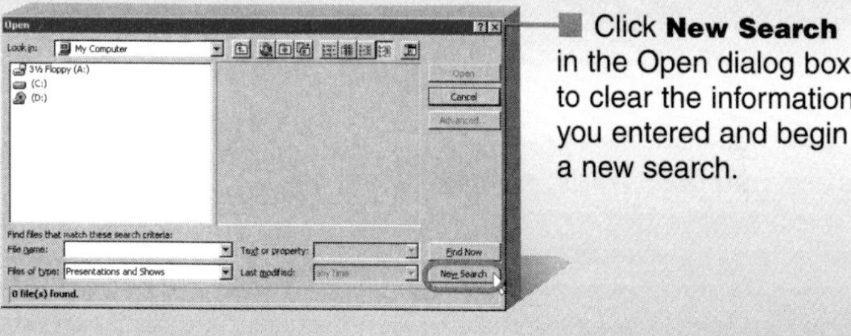

■ Click **New Search** in the Open dialog box to clear the information you entered and begin a new search.

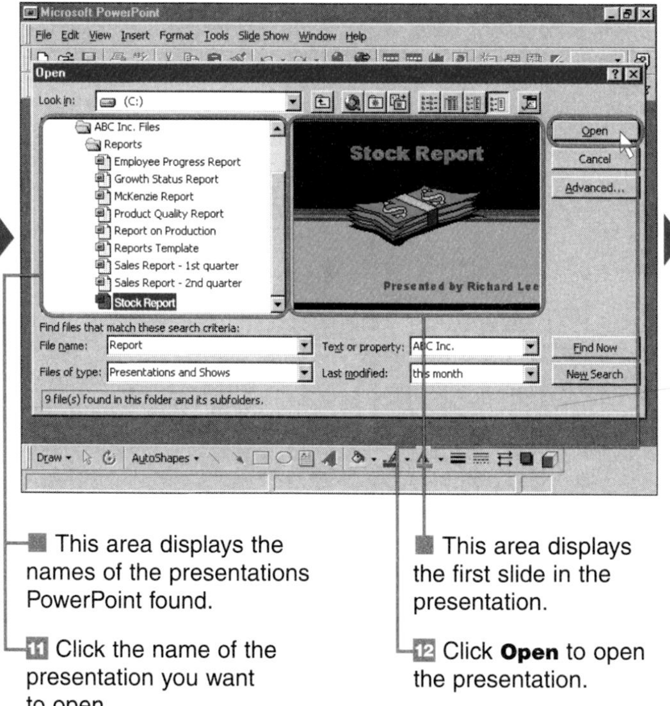

■ This area displays the names of the presentations PowerPoint found.

11 Click the name of the presentation you want to open.

■ This area displays the first slide in the presentation.

12 Click **Open** to open the presentation.

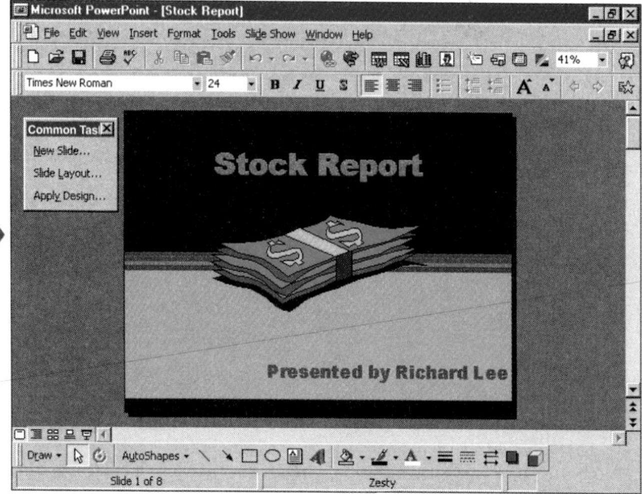

■ PowerPoint opens the presentation and displays it on your screen. You can now review and make changes to the presentation.

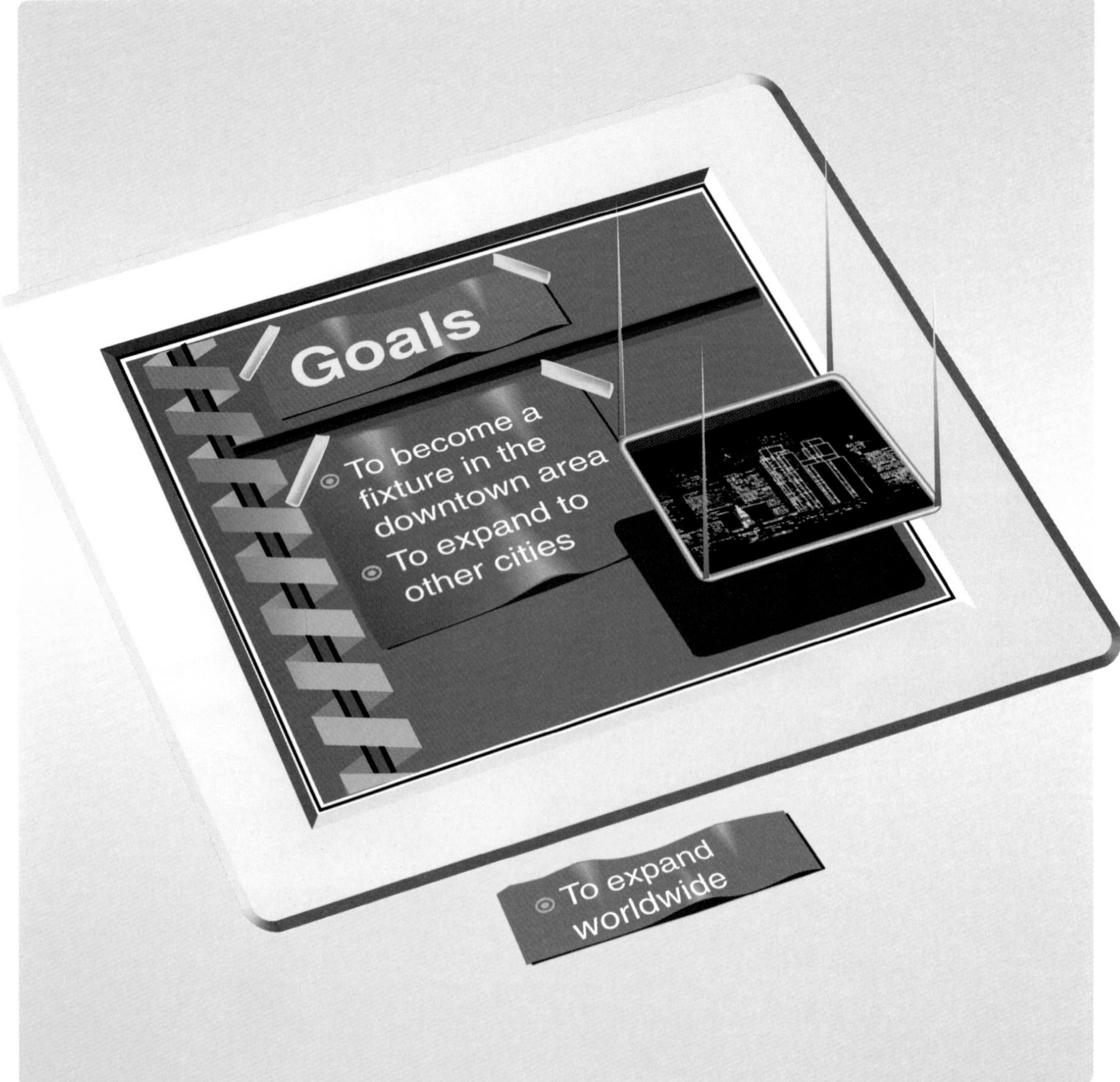
Goals
To become a fixture in the downtown area
To expand to other cities
To expand worldwide

CHAPTER 2

PowerPoint Basics

Would you like to learn some basic PowerPoint skills? This chapter teaches you how to begin working with your PowerPoint presentations.

CHANGE THE VIEW

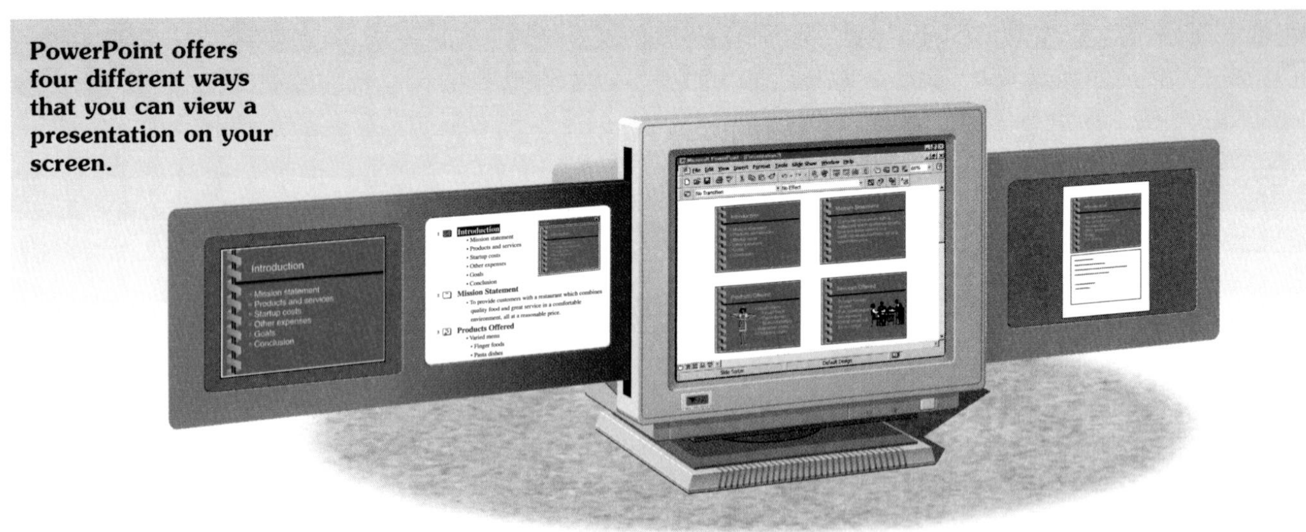

PowerPoint offers four different ways that you can view a presentation on your screen.

CHANGE THE VIEW

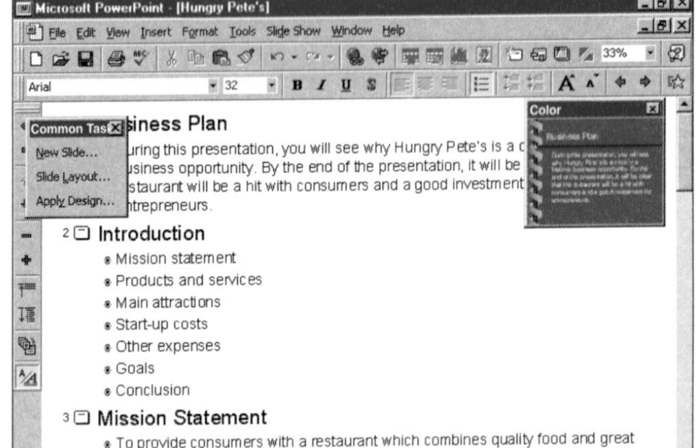

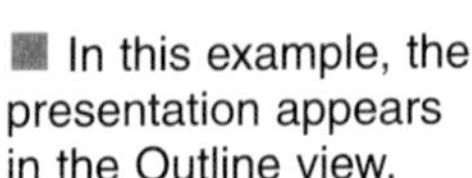

■ In this example, the presentation appears in the Outline view.

1 Click an option to display the presentation in a different view.

- Slide
- Outline
- Slide Sorter
- Notes Page

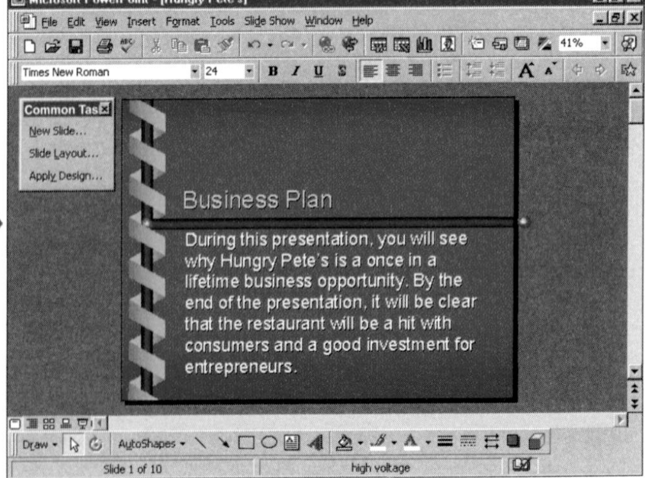

■ PowerPoint displays the presentation in the new view.

■ All views display the same presentation. If you make changes to a slide in one view, the other views will also display the changes.

THE FOUR VIEWS

Slide

The Slide view displays one slide at a time. This view is useful for adding graphics and changing the layout of individual slides.

Outline

The Outline view displays the text on all the slides in your presentation and a miniature version of the current slide. This view is useful for developing the content and organization of your presentation.

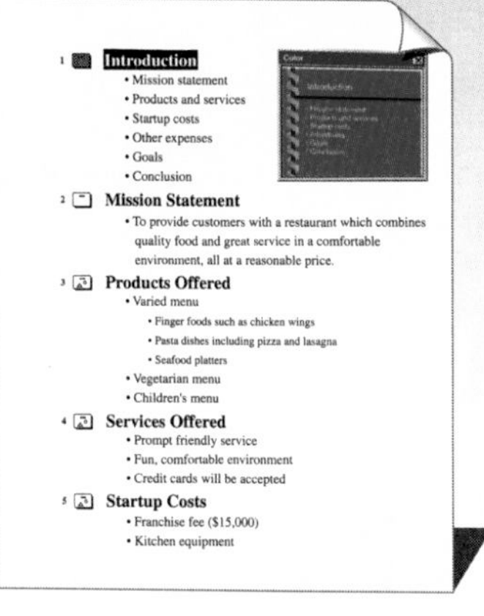

Slide Sorter

The Slide Sorter view displays a miniature version of each slide to provide an overview of your entire presentation. This view is useful for adding, deleting and re-organizing slides.

Notes Page

The Notes Page view displays one slide at a time, with space to type comments. You can use these comments as a guide when delivering your presentation.

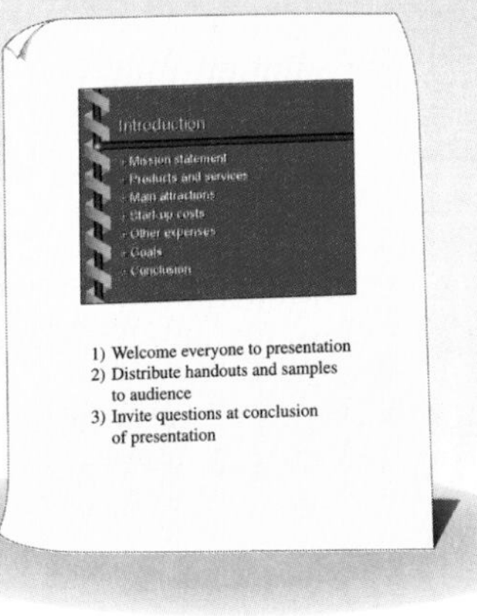

USING THE SCROLL BAR

Your computer screen cannot display your entire presentation at once. You can use the scroll bar to view a different part of your presentation.

USING THE SCROLL BAR

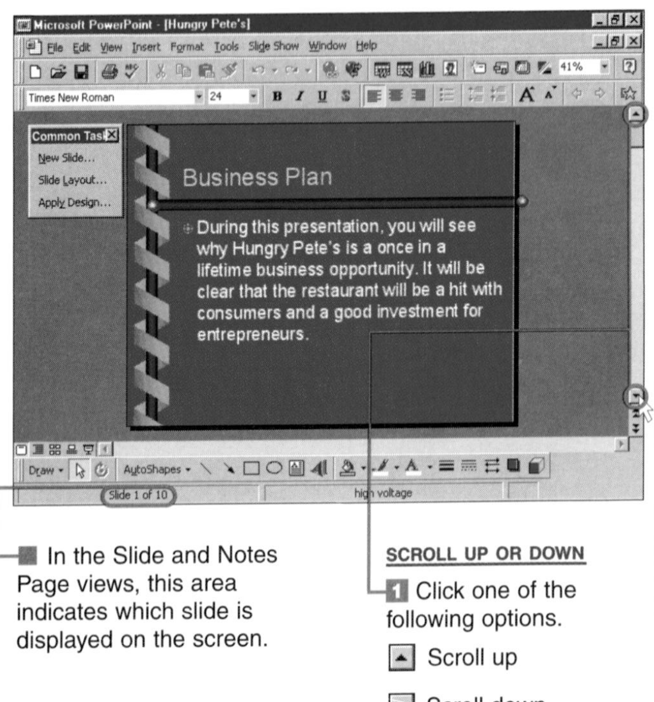

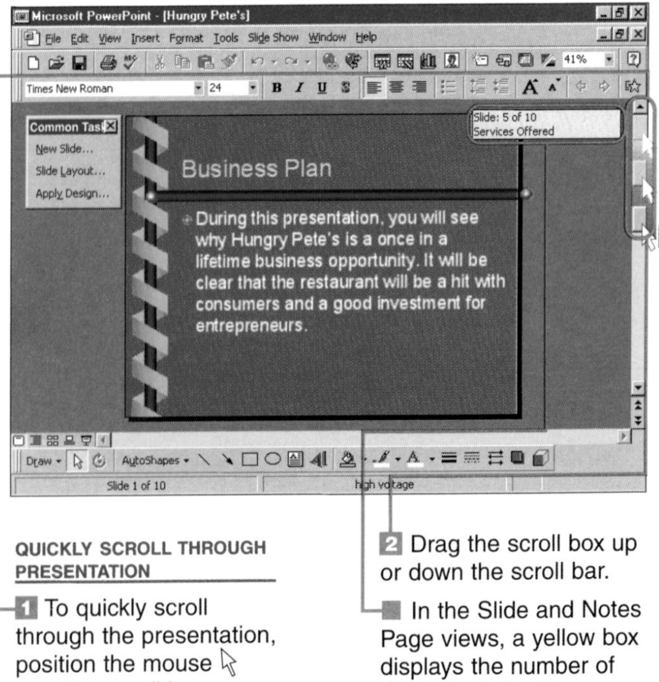

■ In the Slide and Notes Page views, this area indicates which slide is displayed on the screen.

SCROLL UP OR DOWN

1 Click one of the following options.

▲ Scroll up

▼ Scroll down

QUICKLY SCROLL THROUGH PRESENTATION

1 To quickly scroll through the presentation, position the mouse over the scroll box.

2 Drag the scroll box up or down the scroll bar.

■ In the Slide and Notes Page views, a yellow box displays the number of the slide that will appear on the screen.

?

How do I use a wheeled mouse to scroll through my presentation?

A wheeled mouse has a wheel between the left and right mouse buttons. Moving this wheel lets you quickly scroll through your presentation. The Microsoft IntelliMouse is a popular example of a wheeled mouse.

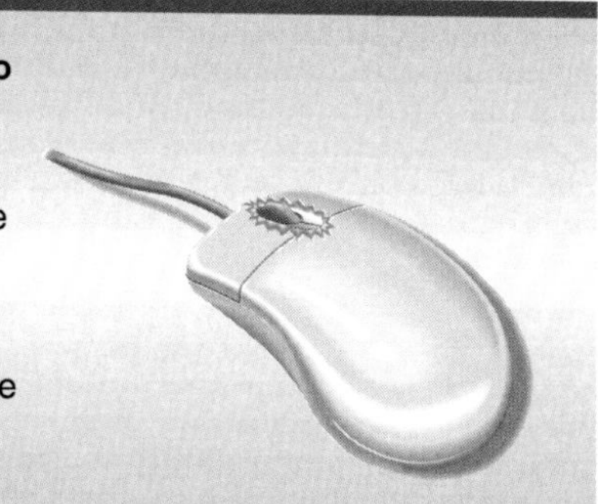

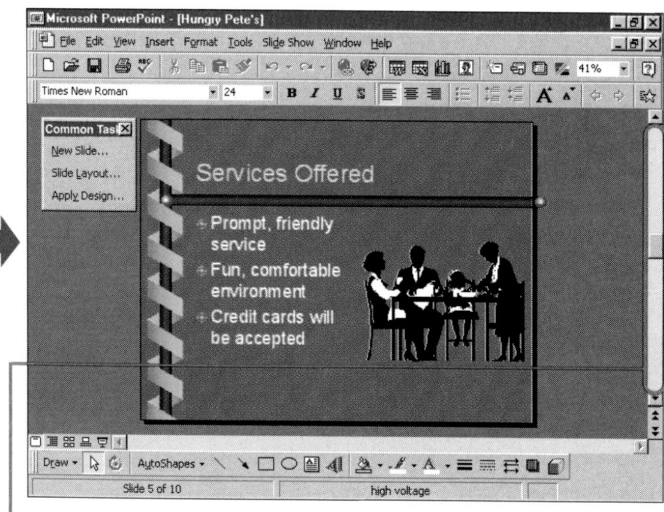

■ The location of the scroll box indicates which part of the presentation you are viewing. To view the middle of the presentation, drag the scroll box to the middle of the scroll bar.

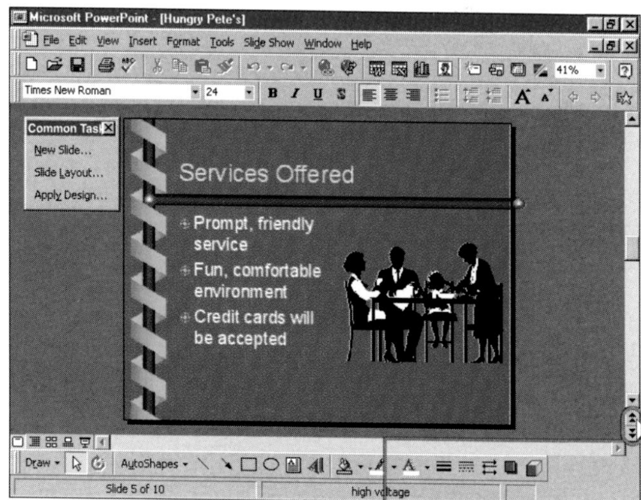

DISPLAY PREVIOUS OR NEXT SLIDE

■ The Slide and Notes Page views allow you to quickly display the previous or next slide.

1 Click one of the following options.

- Display previous slide
- Display next slide

DISPLAY OR HIDE TOOLBARS

PowerPoint offers several toolbars that you can display or hide at any time. Each toolbar contains buttons that help you quickly perform tasks.

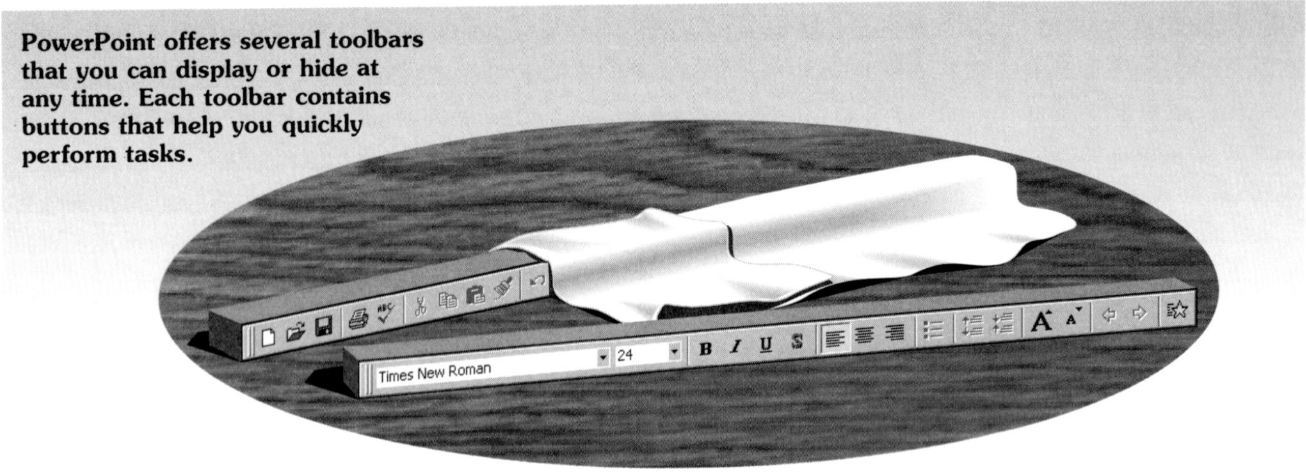

DISPLAY OR HIDE TOOLBARS

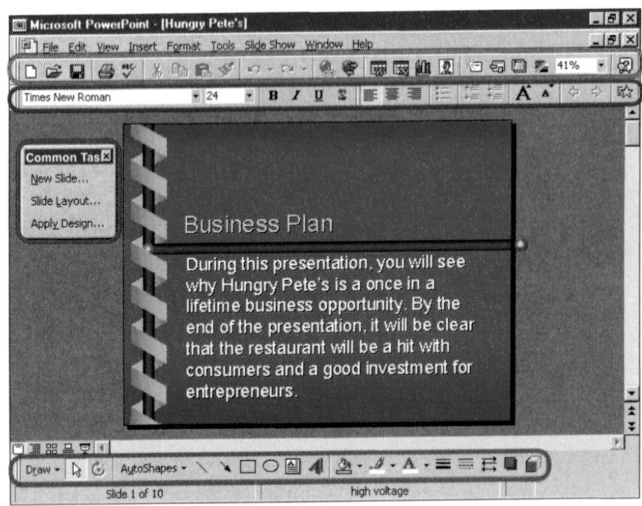

■ PowerPoint automatically displays several toolbars on your screen.

Standard toolbar

Formatting toolbar

Common Tasks toolbar

Drawing toolbar

Note: The Drawing toolbar does not appear in the Outline or Slide Sorter view.

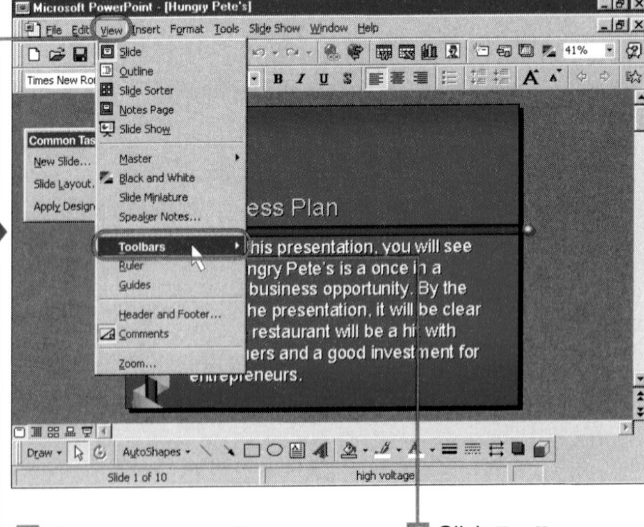

1 Click **View** to display or hide a toolbar.

2 Click **Toolbars**.

?

Why would I want to hide a toolbar?

A screen displaying fewer toolbars provides a larger and less cluttered working area.

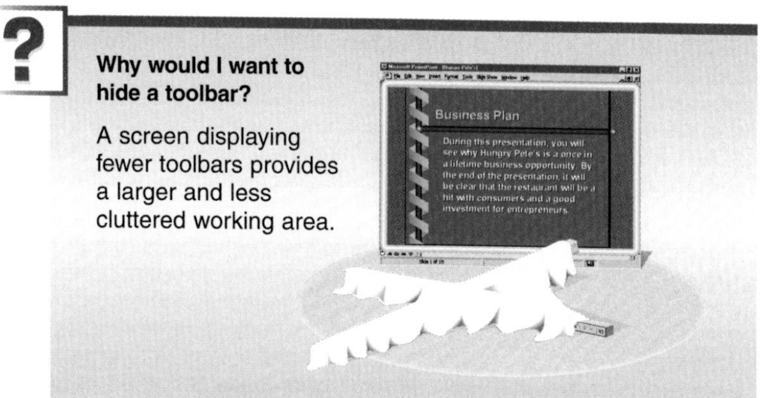

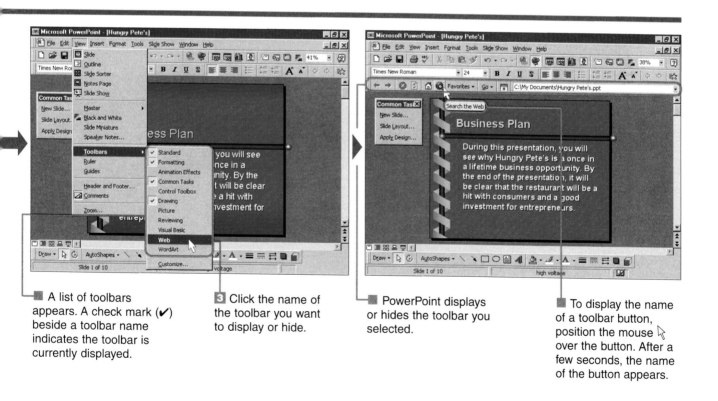

■ A list of toolbars appears. A check mark (✔) beside a toolbar name indicates the toolbar is currently displayed.

3 Click the name of the toolbar you want to display or hide.

■ PowerPoint displays or hides the toolbar you selected.

■ To display the name of a toolbar button, position the mouse over the button. After a few seconds, the name of the button appears.

ZOOM IN OR OUT

PowerPoint allows you to enlarge or reduce the display of information on your screen.

ZOOM IN OR OUT

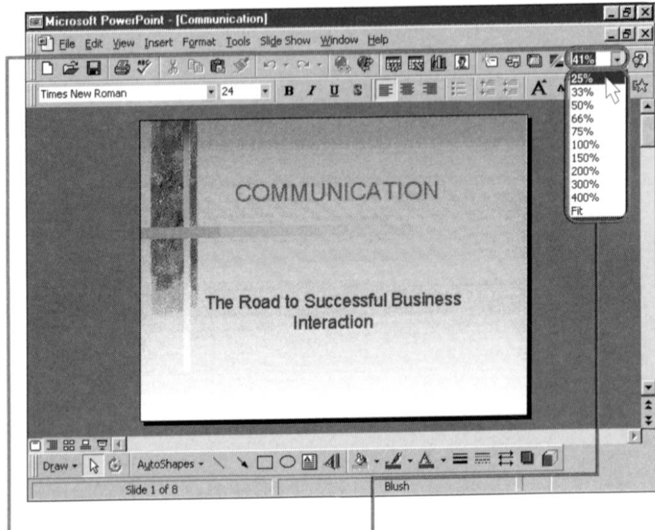

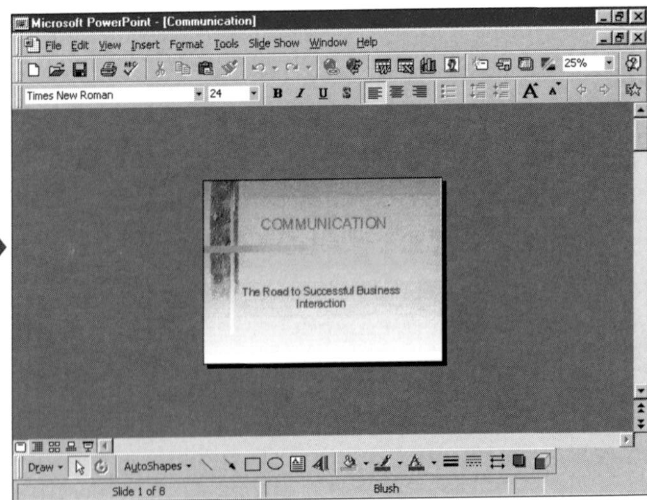

1. Click ▼ in this area to display a list of zoom settings.

2. Click the zoom setting you want to use.

*Note: In the Slide and Notes Page views, you can click **Fit** to display the entire slide in the area provided.*

■ The information appears in the new zoom setting.

SWITCH BETWEEN PRESENTATIONS

PowerPoint lets you have several presentations open at once. You can switch from one open presentation to another.

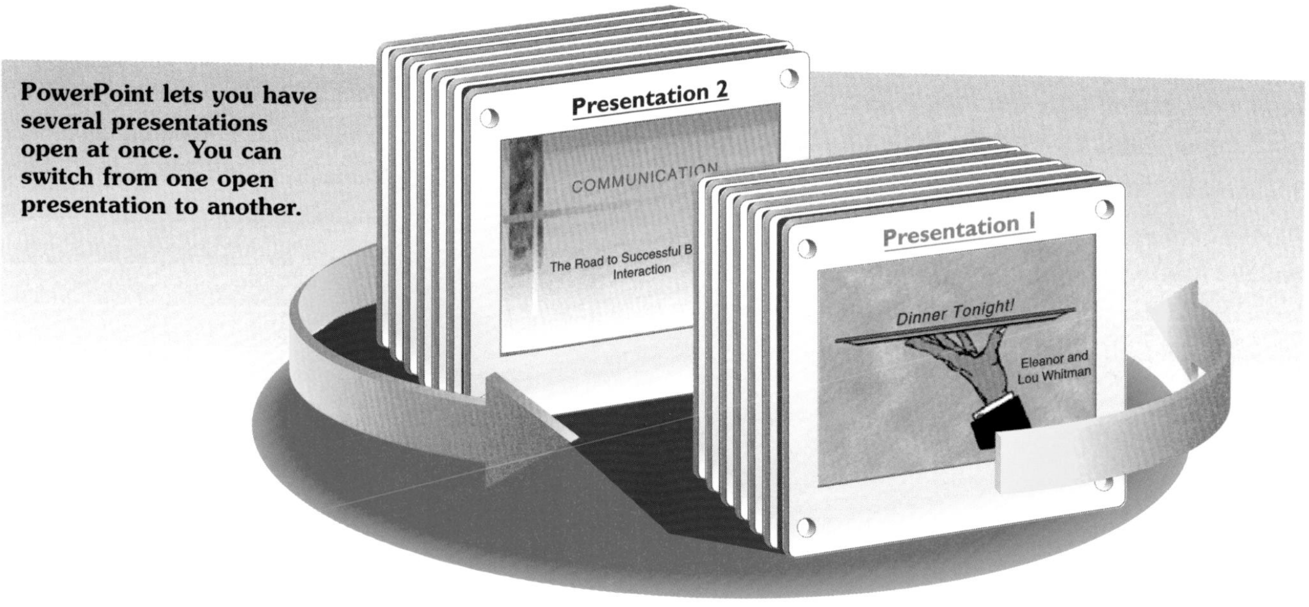

SWITCH BETWEEN PRESENTATIONS

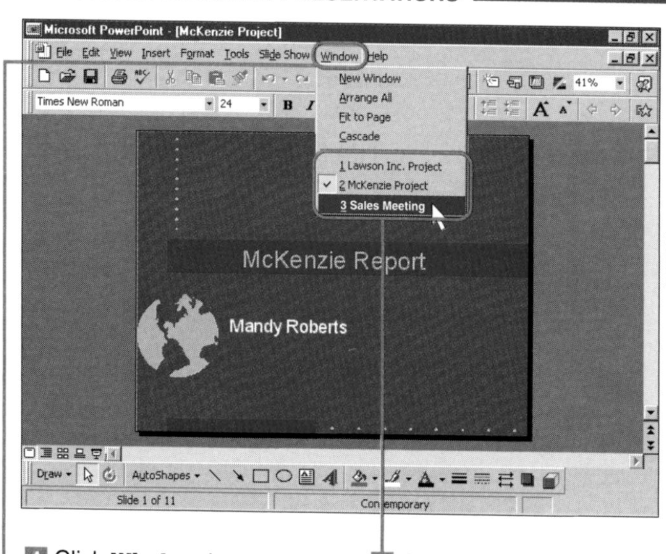

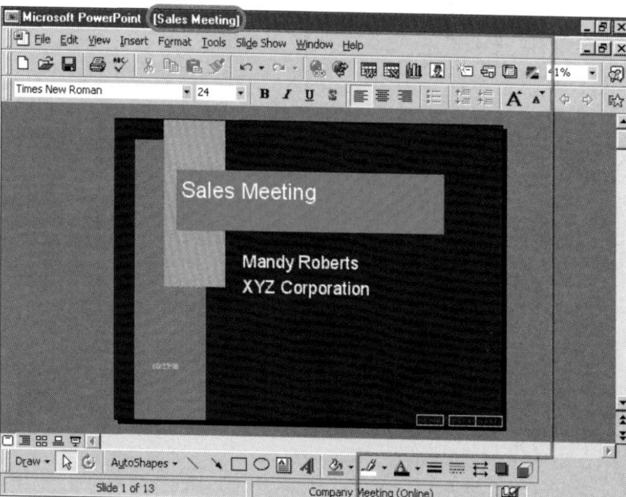

1 Click **Window** to display a list of all the presentations you have open.

2 Click the name of the presentation you want to display.

■ The presentation appears.

■ PowerPoint displays the name of the presentation at the top of your screen.

CHANGE THE SLIDE LAYOUT

You can change the layout of a slide in your presentation to accommodate text and objects you want to add.

Each slide layout displays placeholders that allow you to easily add objects, such as a chart or a clip art image, to a slide.

CHANGE THE SLIDE LAYOUT

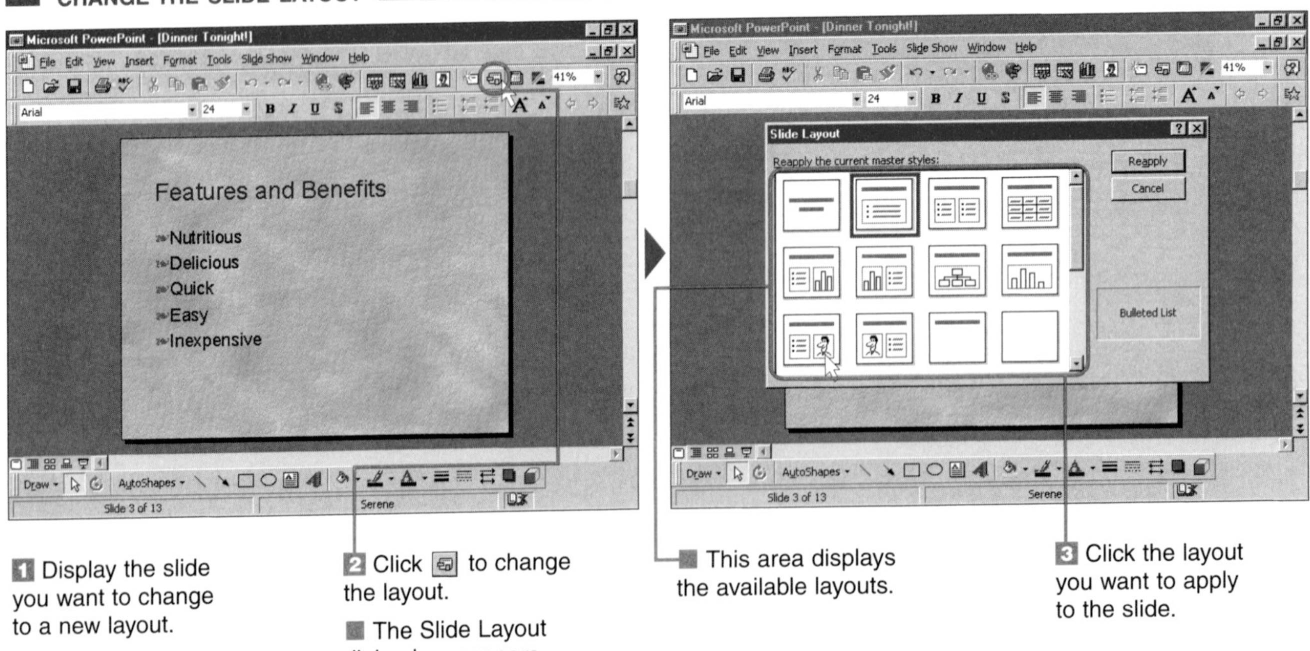

1 Display the slide you want to change to a new layout.

2 Click to change the layout.

■ The Slide Layout dialog box appears.

■ This area displays the available layouts.

3 Click the layout you want to apply to the slide.

?

Can I change the slide layout at any time?

You should not change the slide layout after you have added an object to a slide. An object you have added will remain on the slide even after PowerPoint adds the placeholders for the new slide layout. This can cause the slide to become cluttered with overlapping objects and placeholders.

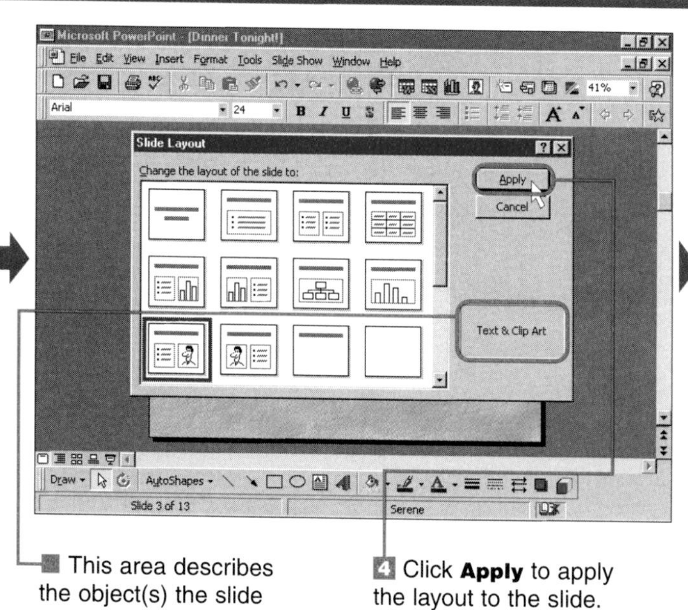

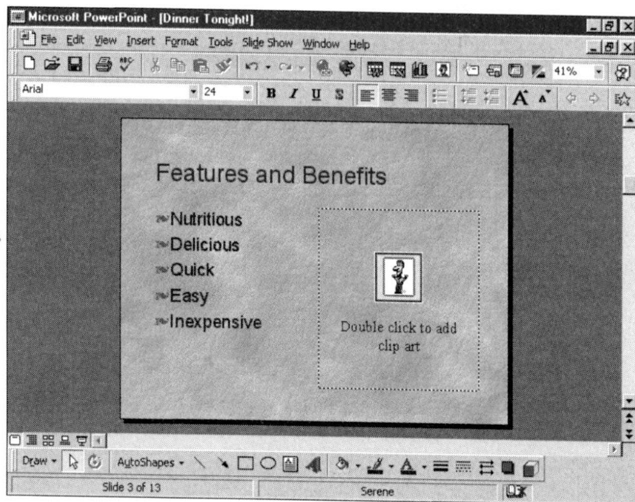

■ This area describes the object(s) the slide will display.

4 Click **Apply** to apply the layout to the slide.

■ The slide appears in the new layout.

ADD A NEW SLIDE

You can insert a new slide into your presentation to add a new topic you want to discuss.

ADD A NEW SLIDE

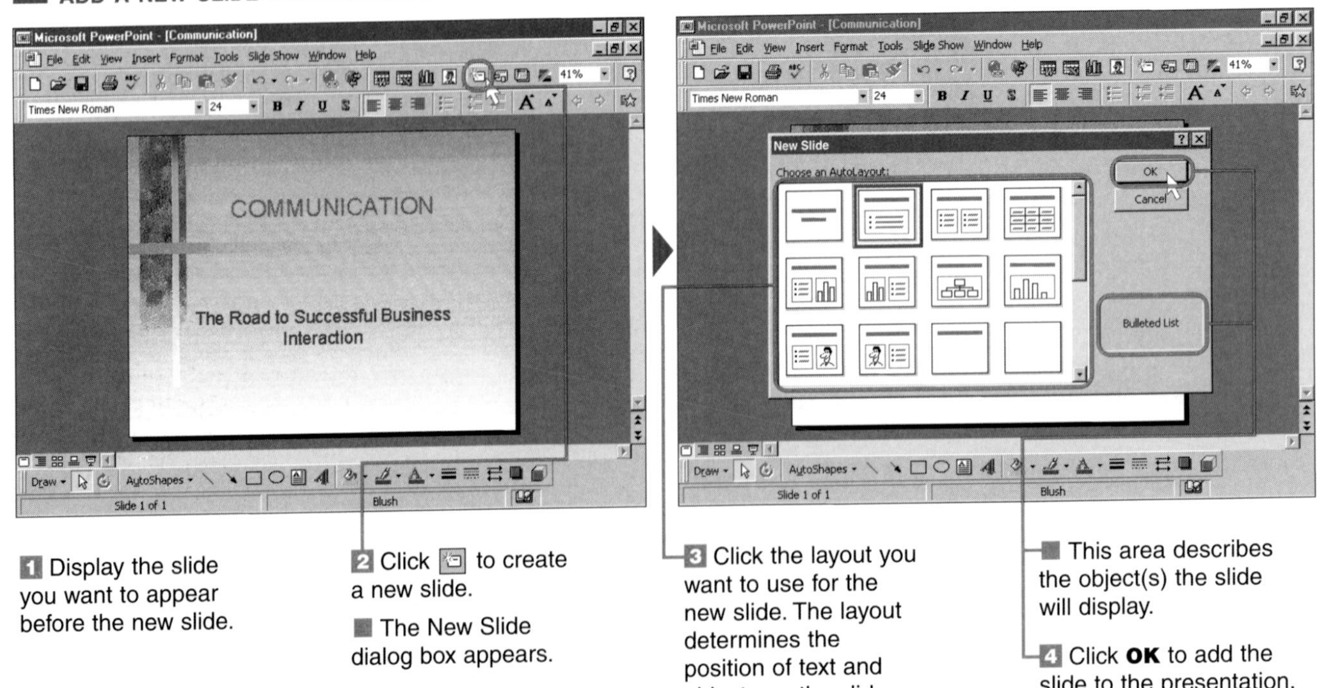

1 Display the slide you want to appear before the new slide.

2 Click [icon] to create a new slide.

■ The New Slide dialog box appears.

3 Click the layout you want to use for the new slide. The layout determines the position of text and objects on the slide.

■ This area describes the object(s) the slide will display.

4 Click **OK** to add the slide to the presentation.

?

How much text can I include on a slide?

You should be careful not to include too much text on a slide in your presentation. Too much text on a slide can make the slide difficult to read and minimize the impact of important ideas. If a slide contains too much text, you should add a new slide to accommodate some of the text.

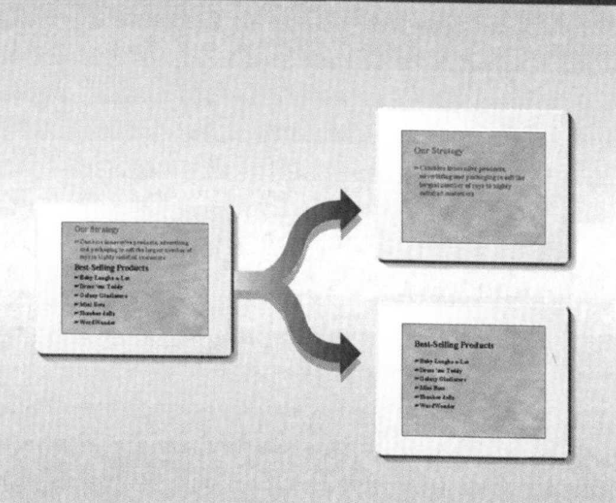

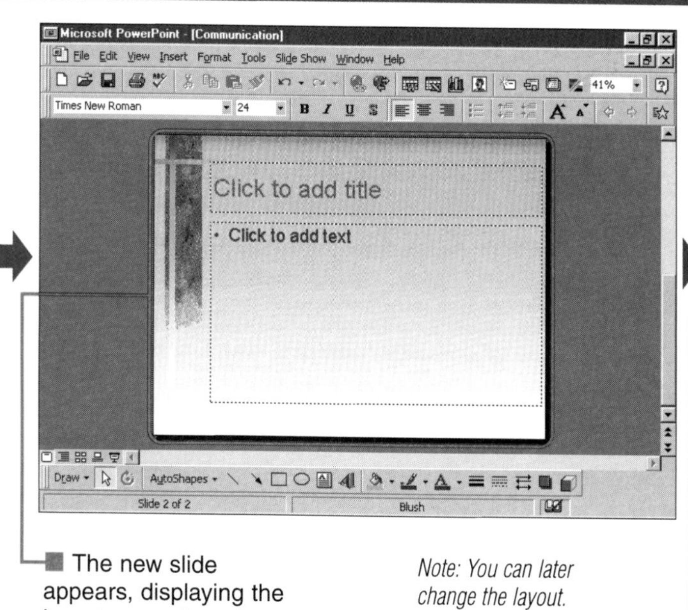

■ The new slide appears, displaying the layout you selected.

Note: You can later change the layout. To change the slide layout, see page 38.

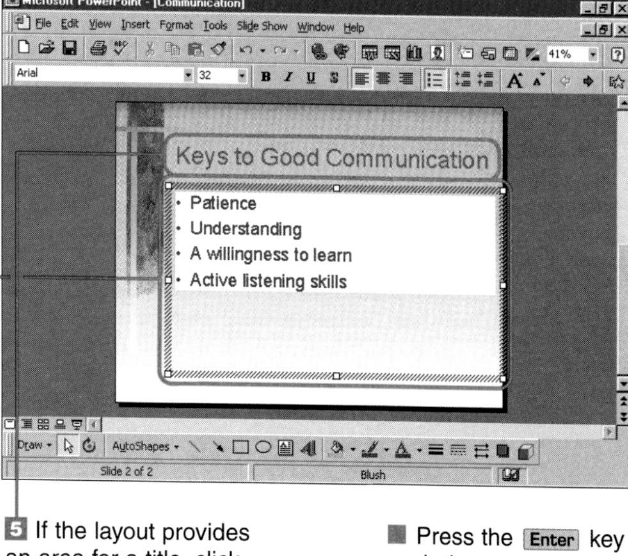

5 If the layout provides an area for a title, click the area and then type the title.

6 If the layout provides an area for a list of points, click the area and then type a point.

■ Press the Enter key each time you want to start a new point.

GETTING HELP

If you do not know how to perform a task in PowerPoint, you can ask the Office Assistant for help.

USING THE OFFICE ASSISTANT

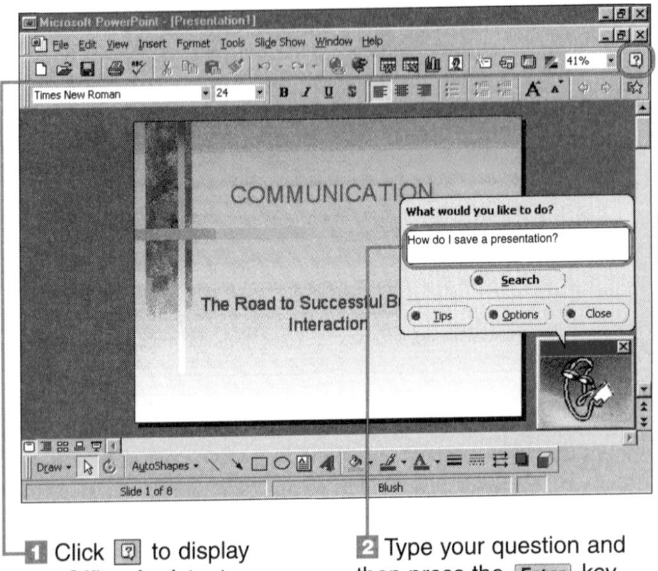

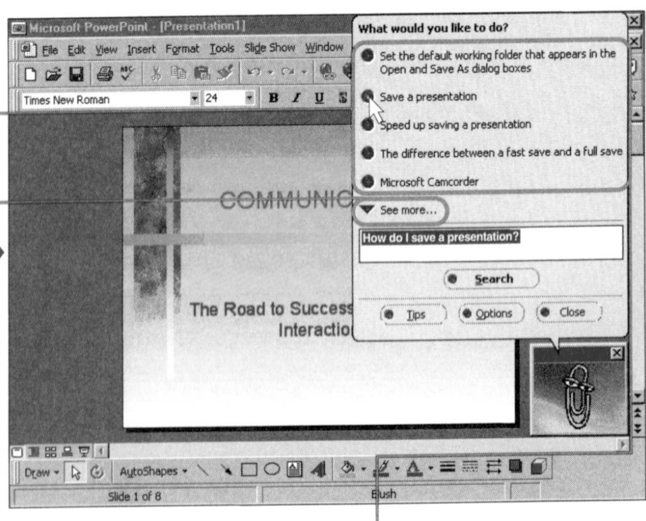

1 Click [?] to display the Office Assistant.

2 Type your question and then press the Enter key.

Note: If the question area does not appear, click the Office Assistant.

■ A list of help topics related to your question appears.

■ If more help topics exist, you can click **See more** to view the additional topics.

Note: If you do not see a help topic of interest, try rephrasing your question.

3 Click the help topic of interest.

?

Why does a light bulb appear beside the Office Assistant?

A light bulb appears when the Office Assistant has a tip about how to use a PowerPoint feature more effectively. You can click the light bulb to display the tip.

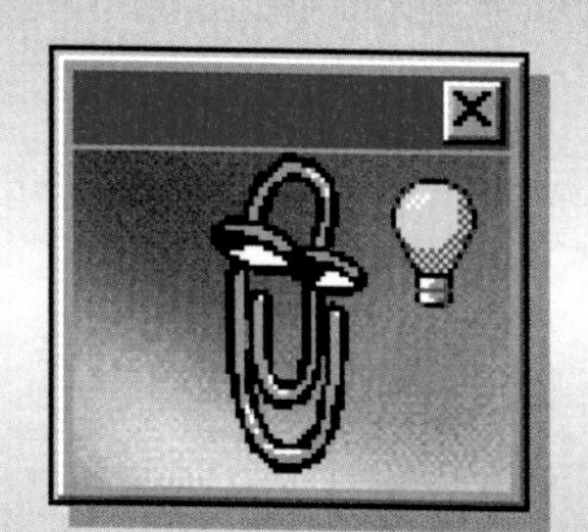

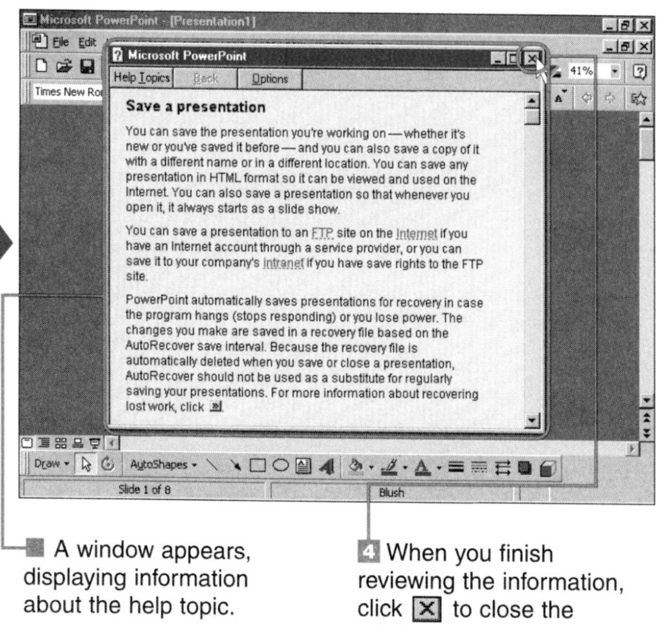

■ A window appears, displaying information about the help topic.

4 When you finish reviewing the information, click ☒ to close the window.

HIDE THE OFFICE ASSISTANT

1 Click ☒ to hide the Office Assistant.

GETTING HELP

You can use PowerPoint's help index to locate topics of interest.

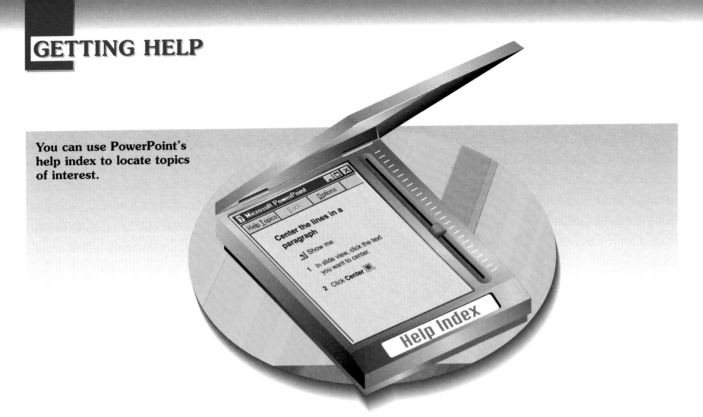

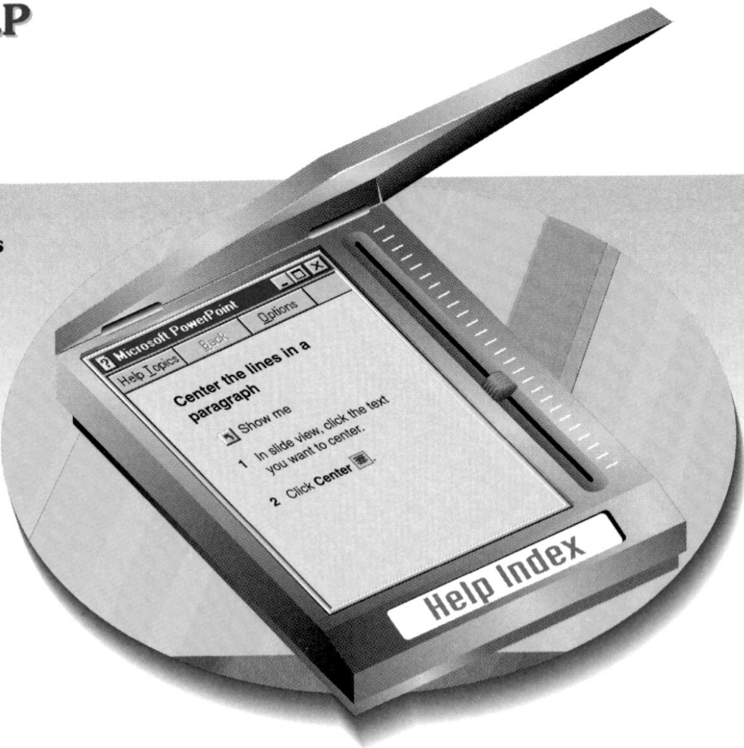

USING THE HELP INDEX

1 Click **Help**.

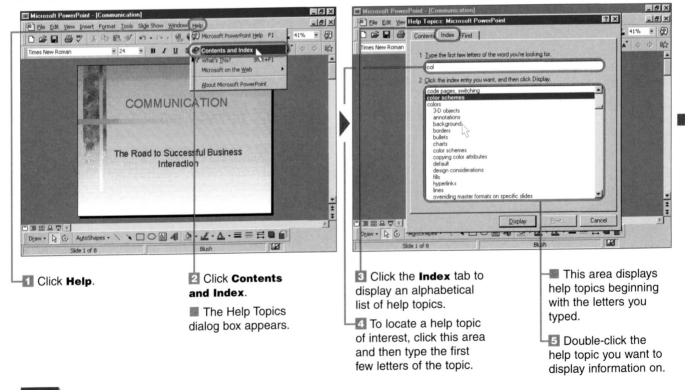

2 Click **Contents and Index**.

■ The Help Topics dialog box appears.

3 Click the **Index** tab to display an alphabetical list of help topics.

4 To locate a help topic of interest, click this area and then type the first few letters of the topic.

■ This area displays help topics beginning with the letters you typed.

5 Double-click the help topic you want to display information on.

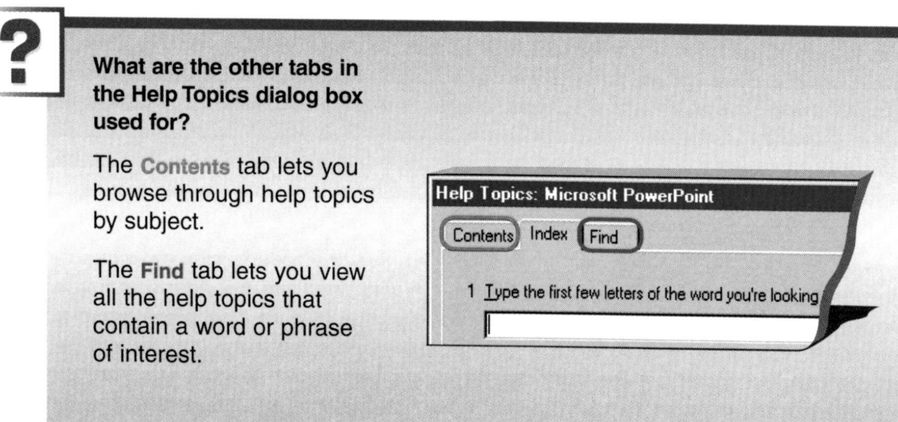

?

What are the other tabs in the Help Topics dialog box used for?

The **Contents** tab lets you browse through help topics by subject.

The **Find** tab lets you view all the help topics that contain a word or phrase of interest.

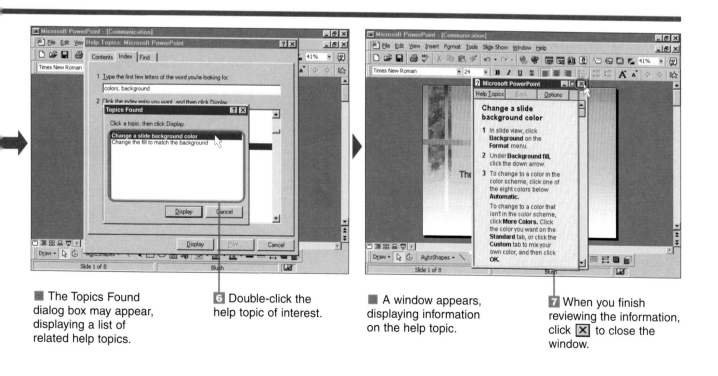

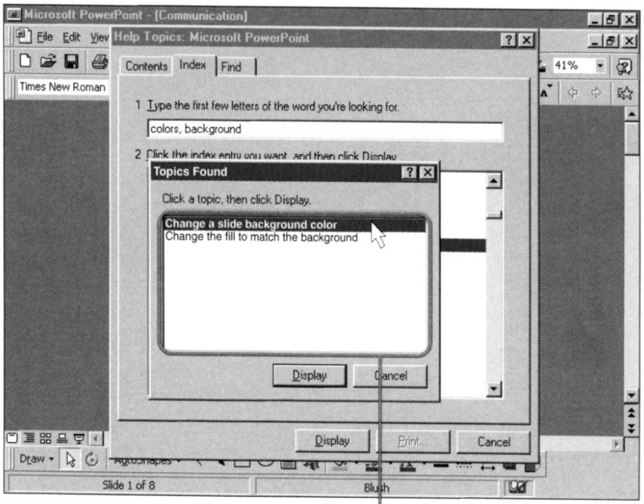

■ The Topics Found dialog box may appear, displaying a list of related help topics.

6 Double-click the help topic of interest.

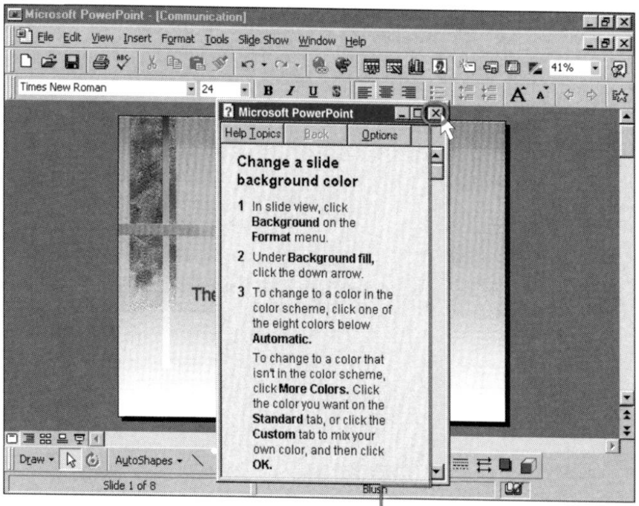

■ A window appears, displaying information on the help topic.

7 When you finish reviewing the information, click ☒ to close the window.

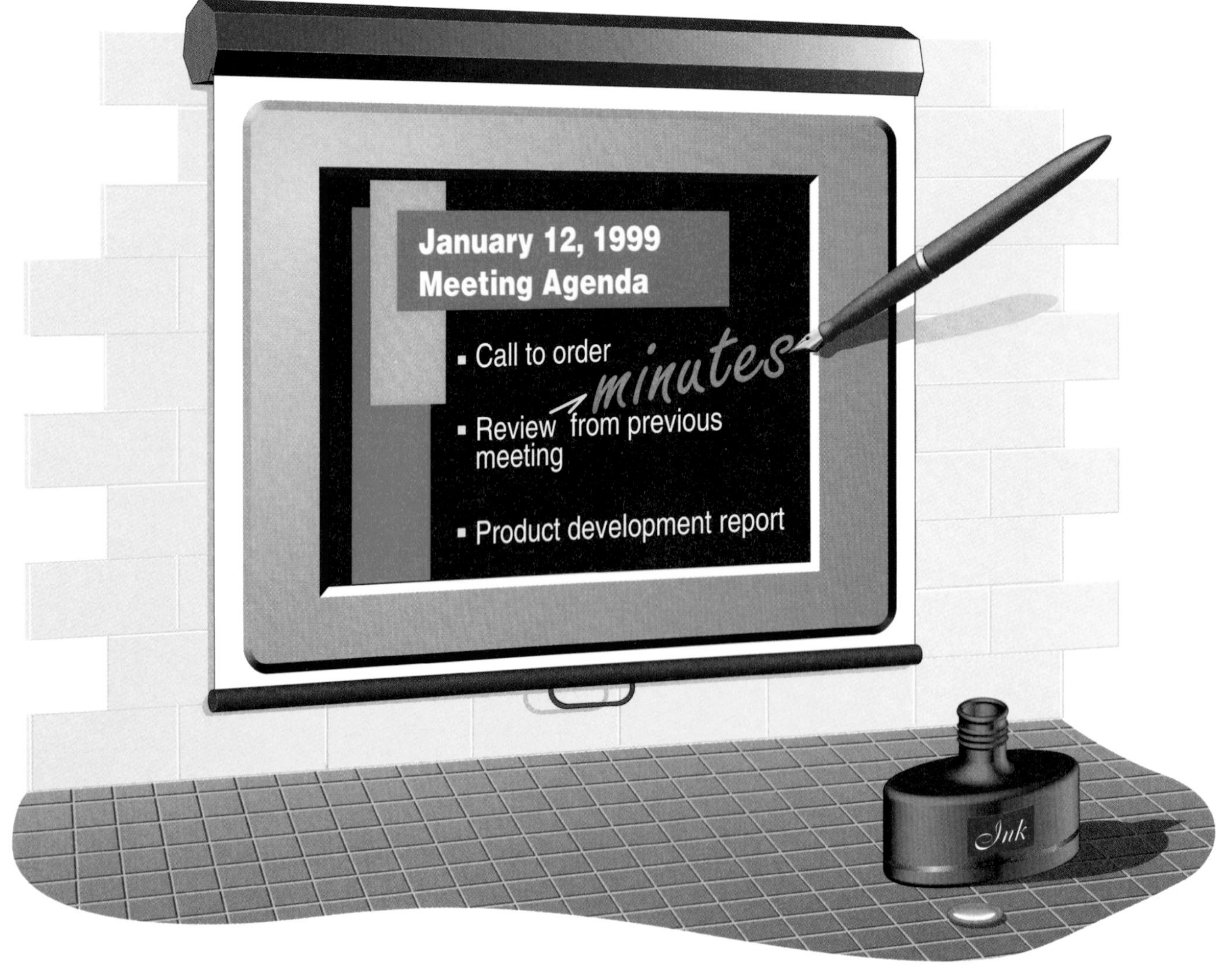
January 12, 1999
Meeting Agenda
Call to order
minutes
Review from previous meeting
Product development report
Ink

CHAPTER 3

Edit Text

Are you wondering how to edit the text in your presentation? In this chapter you will learn how to move text, check spelling, change the importance of text and much more.

SELECT TEXT

Before changing text in a presentation, you will often need to select the text you want to work with. Selected text appears highlighted on your screen.

SELECT TEXT

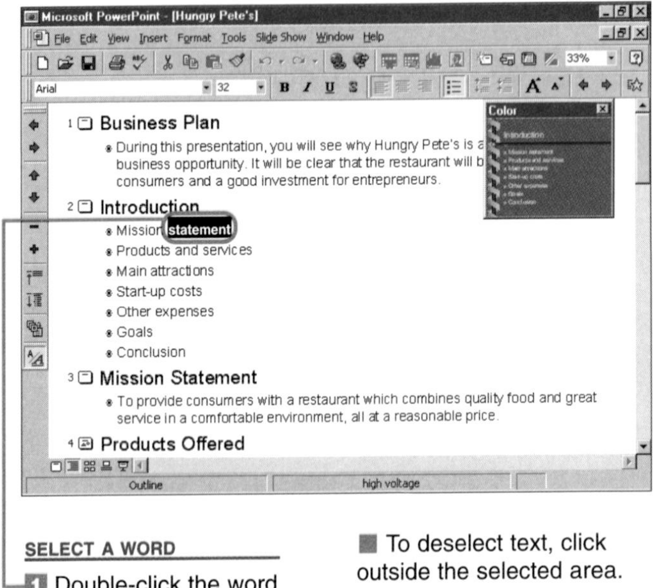

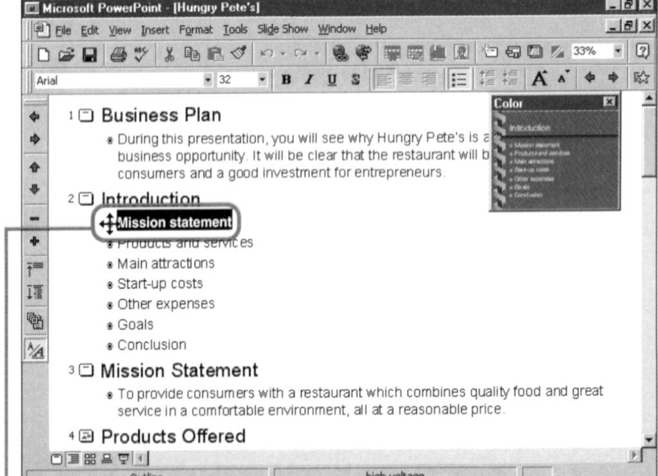

SELECT A WORD

1 Double-click the word you want to select.

■ To deselect text, click outside the selected area.

SELECT A POINT

1 Click the bullet (◉) beside the point you want to select.

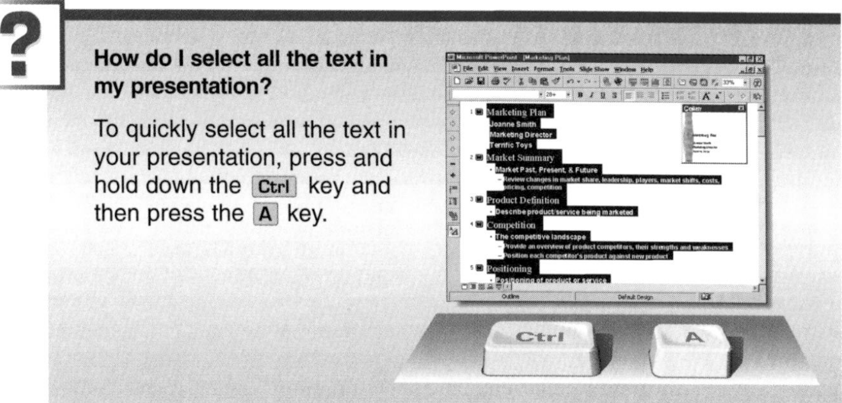

How do I select all the text in my presentation?

To quickly select all the text in your presentation, press and hold down the Ctrl key and then press the A key.

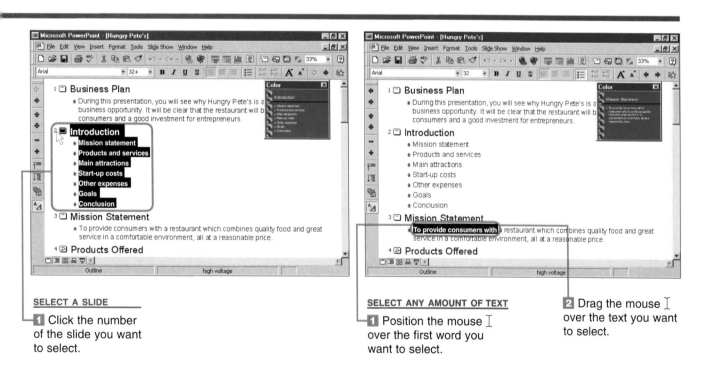

SELECT A SLIDE

1 Click the number of the slide you want to select.

SELECT ANY AMOUNT OF TEXT

1 Position the mouse I over the first word you want to select.

2 Drag the mouse I over the text you want to select.

REPLACE SELECTED TEXT

You can replace text you have selected in your presentation with new text.

When you use the AutoContent Wizard to create a presentation, you need to replace the sample text provided by the wizard with your own text. For information on the AutoContent Wizard, see page 12.

REPLACE SELECTED TEXT

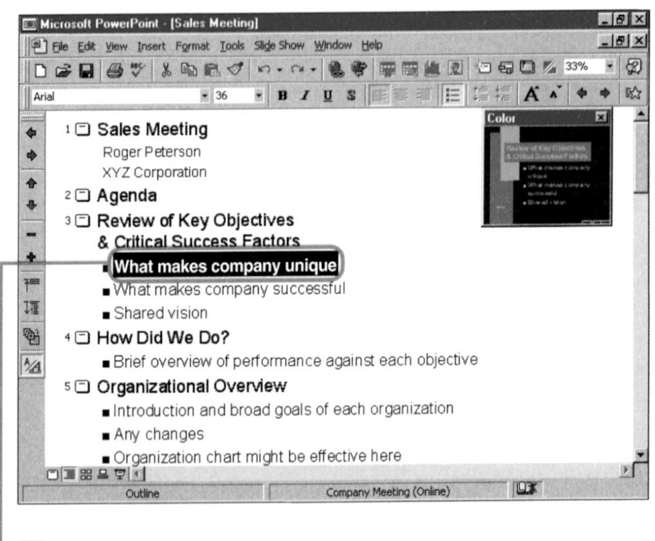

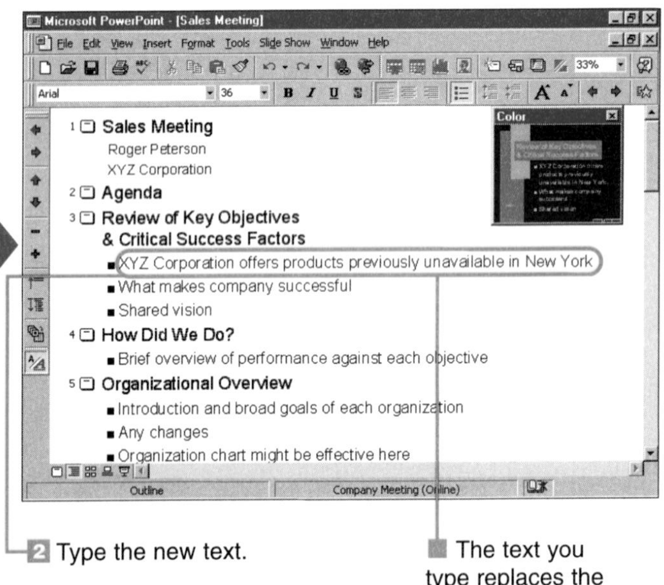

1 Select the text you want to replace with new text. To select text, see page 48.

2 Type the new text.

■ The text you type replaces the selected text.

UNDO LAST CHANGE

PowerPoint remembers the last changes you made to your presentation. If you regret these changes, you can cancel them using the Undo feature.

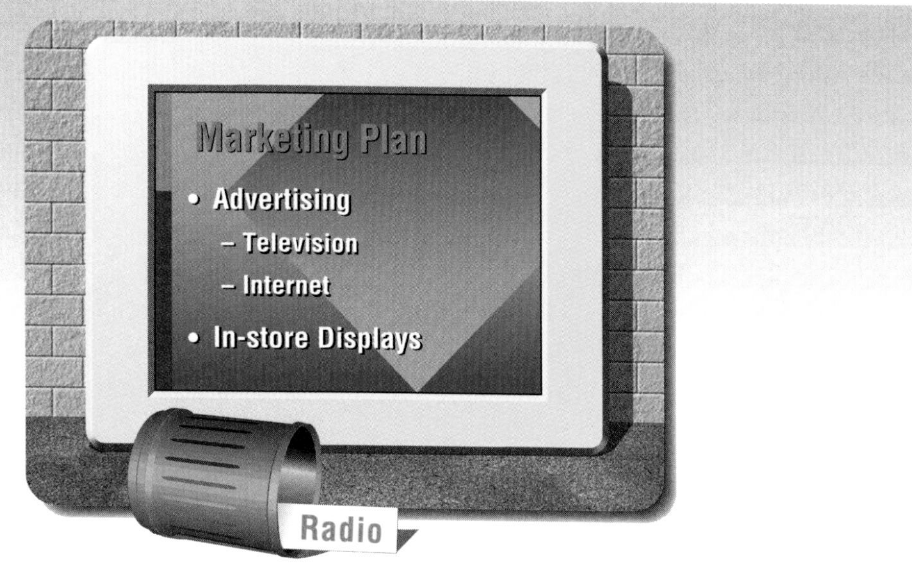

UNDO LAST CHANGE

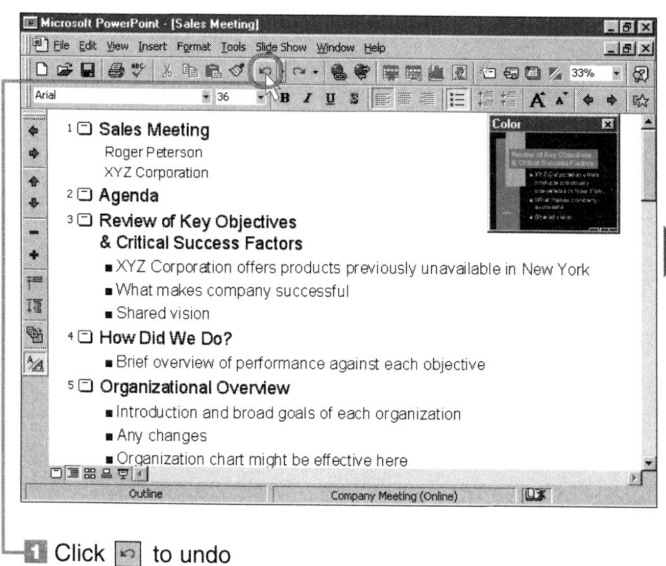

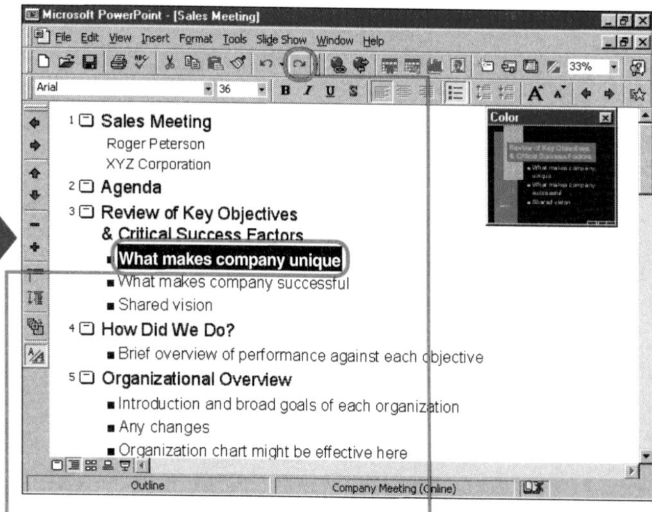

1 Click ↶ to undo your last change.

■ PowerPoint cancels the last change you made to the presentation.

■ You can repeat step 1 to cancel previous changes you made.

■ To reverse the results of using the Undo feature, click ↷.

INSERT TEXT

You can add new text to your presentation to update the presentation or include new ideas.

INSERT CHARACTERS

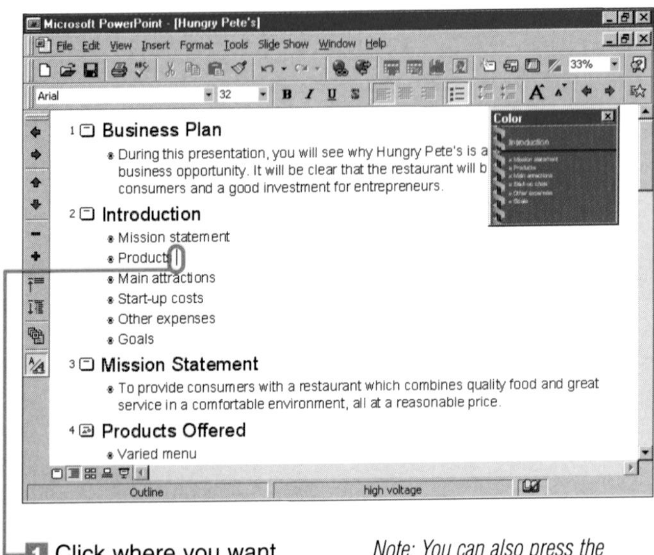

1 Click where you want to insert new text.

■ The text you type will appear where the insertion point flashes on your screen.

Note: You can also press the ←, →, ↑ or ↓ key to move the insertion point.

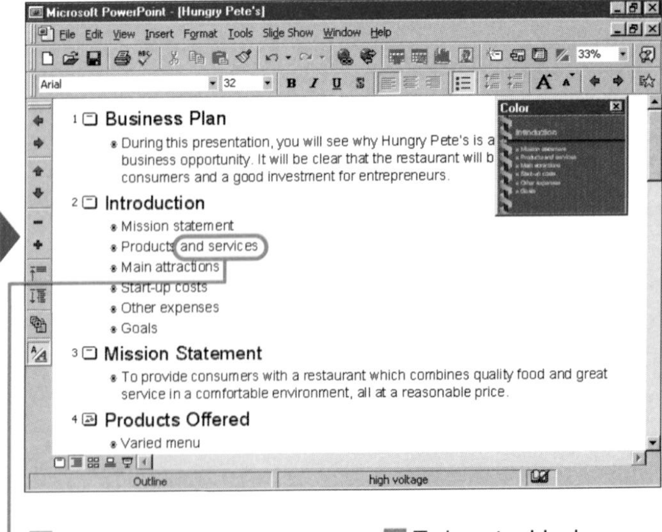

2 Type the text you want to insert.

3 To insert a blank space, press the **Spacebar**.

?

Why does a wavy, red line appear under some words in my presentation?

If PowerPoint does not recognize a word in your presentation, it considers the word misspelled and underlines the word with a wavy, red line. To spell check your presentation, see page 66.

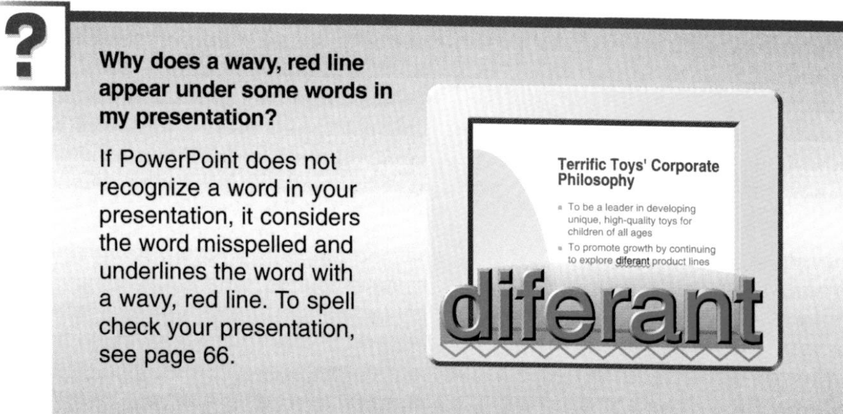

INSERT A NEW POINT

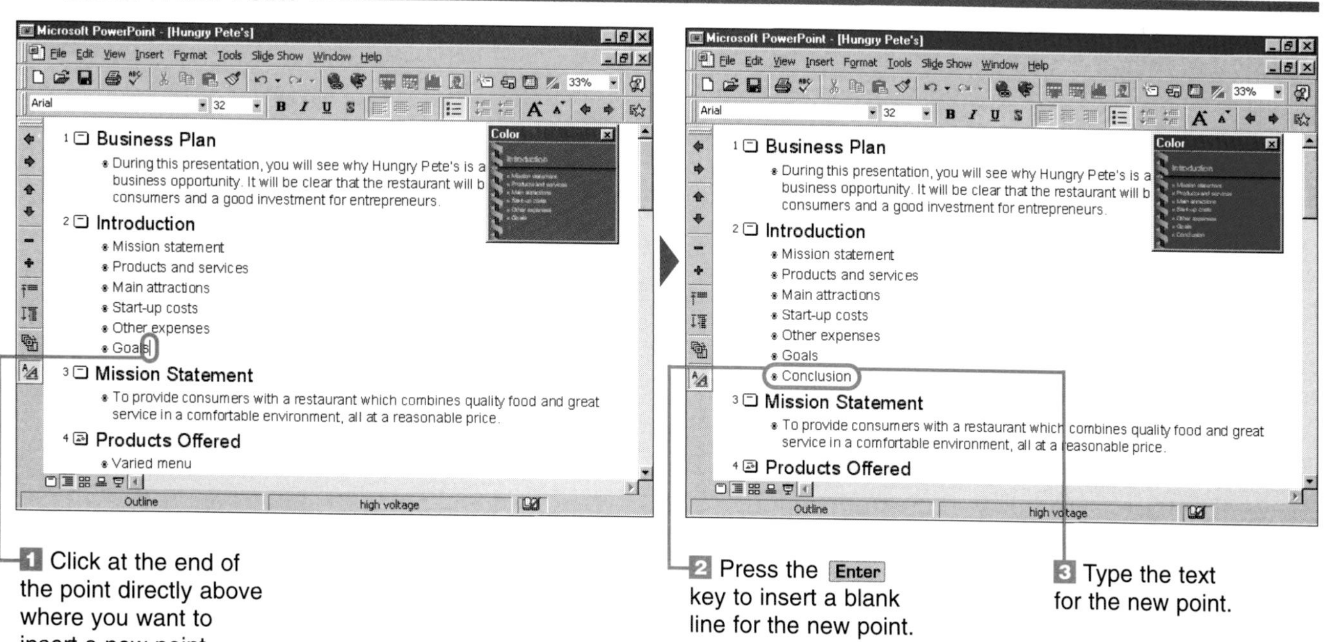

1 Click at the end of the point directly above where you want to insert a new point.

2 Press the Enter key to insert a blank line for the new point.

3 Type the text for the new point.

DELETE TEXT

You can remove text you no longer need from your presentation.

DELETE CHARACTERS

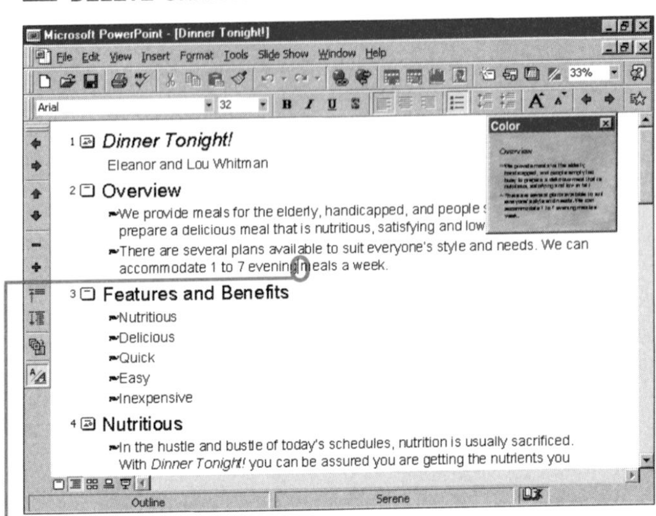

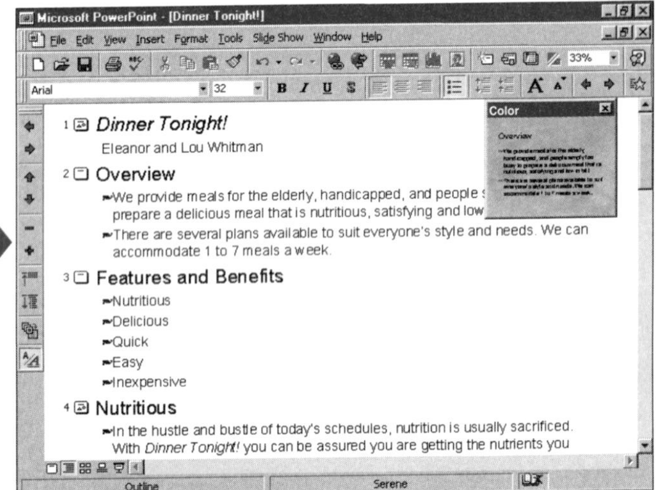

1 Click to the right of the first character you want to delete.

■ PowerPoint will delete the character to the left of the flashing insertion point.

Note: You can also press the ←, →, ↑ or ↓ key to move the insertion point.

2 Press the Backspace key once for each character or space you want to delete.

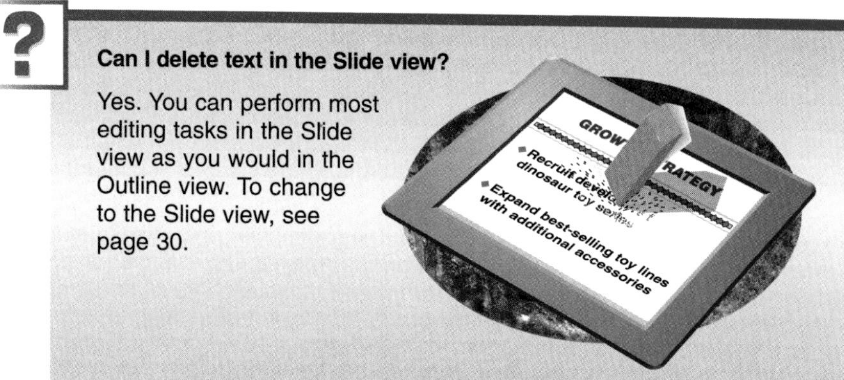

Can I delete text in the Slide view?

Yes. You can perform most editing tasks in the Slide view as you would in the Outline view. To change to the Slide view, see page 30.

DELETE SELECTED TEXT

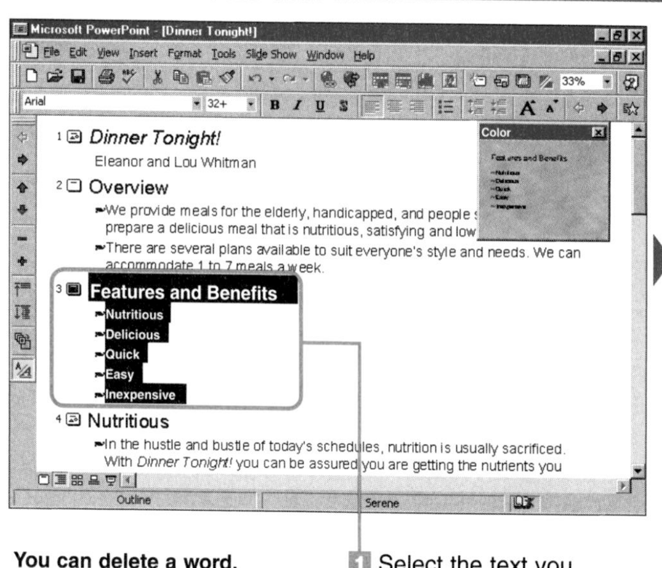

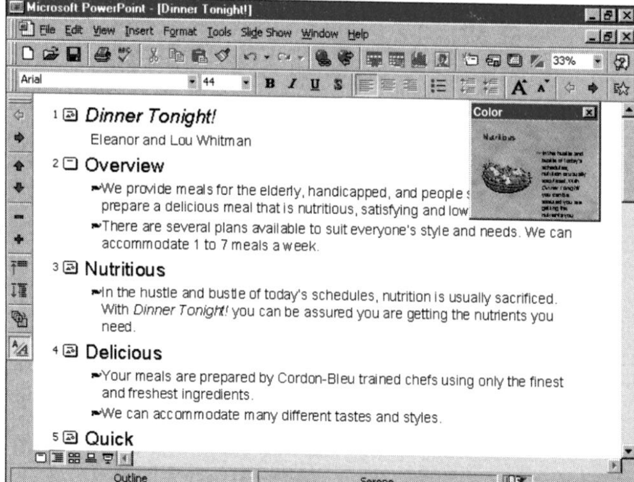

You can delete a word, point or entire slide from your presentation.

1 Select the text you want to delete. To select text, see page 48.

2 Press the Delete key to remove the text.

MOVE TEXT

You can move text in your presentation to reorganize your ideas.

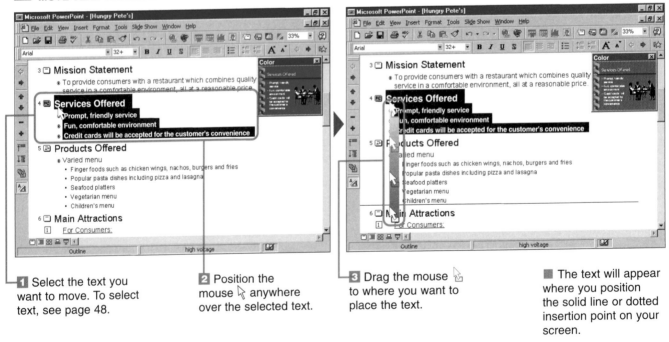

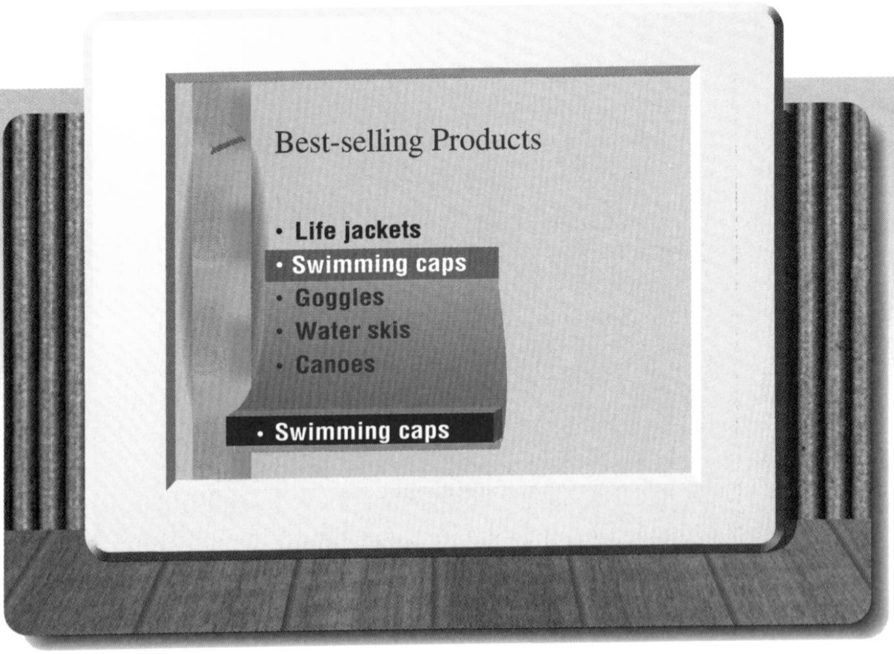

Best-selling Products

- Life jackets
- Swimming caps
- Goggles
- Water skis
- Canoes

MOVE TEXT

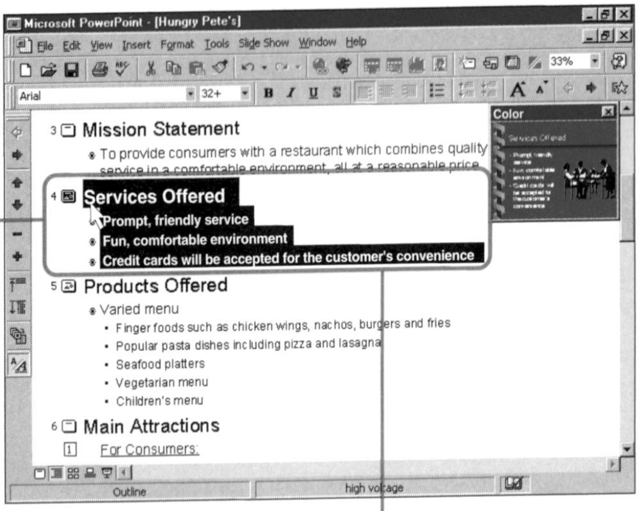

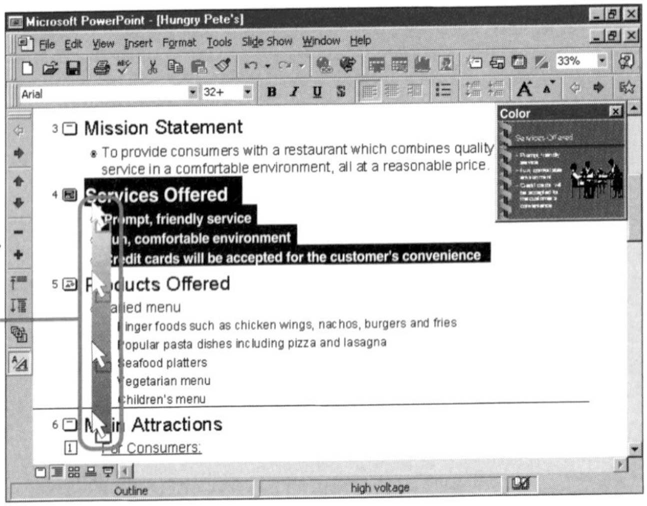

1 Select the text you want to move. To select text, see page 48.

2 Position the mouse anywhere over the selected text.

3 Drag the mouse to where you want to place the text.

■ The text will appear where you position the solid line or dotted insertion point on your screen.

?

Can I copy text from one slide to another?

If you want two slides in your presentation to contain similar points, you can copy the points from one slide to the other. This will save you time since you do not have to retype the text.

To copy text, perform steps 1 to 3 starting on page 56, except press and hold down the Ctrl key as you perform step 3.

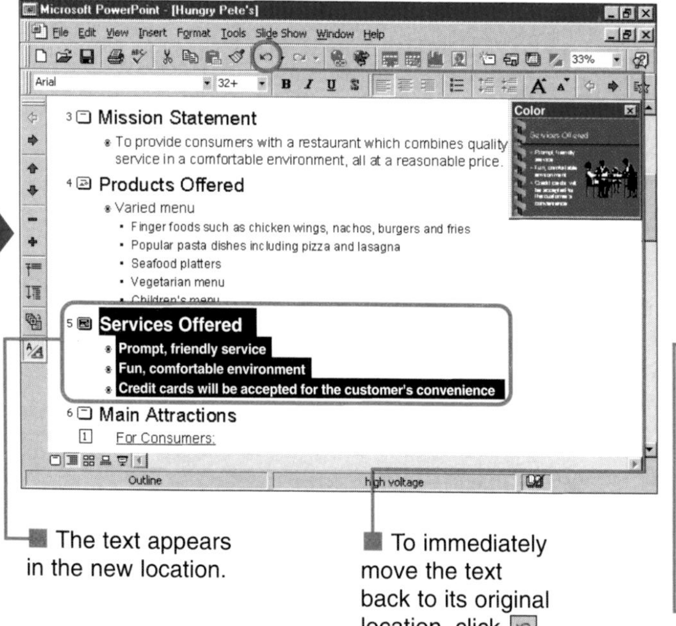

■ The text appears in the new location.

■ To immediately move the text back to its original location, click ↶.

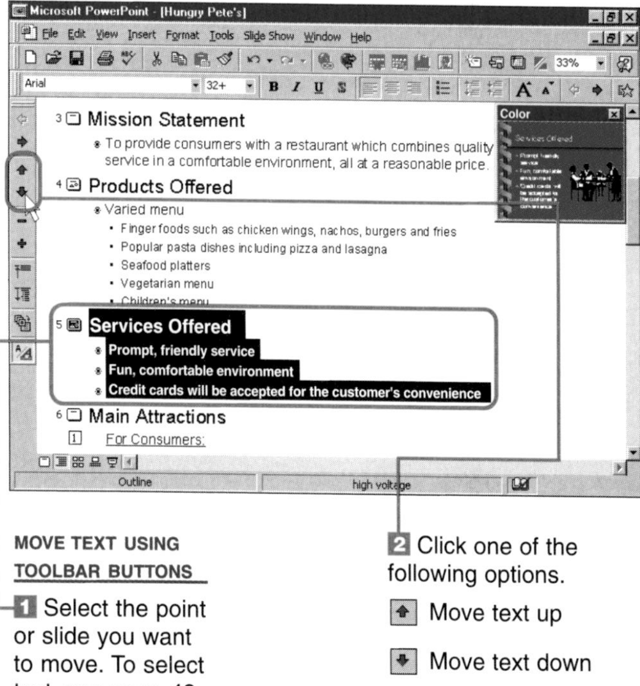

MOVE TEXT USING TOOLBAR BUTTONS

1 Select the point or slide you want to move. To select text, see page 48.

2 Click one of the following options.

🡅 Move text up

🡇 Move text down

DUPLICATE A SLIDE

You can duplicate a slide in your presentation. This is useful if you want to create a new slide based on the content and appearance of an existing slide.

DUPLICATE A SLIDE

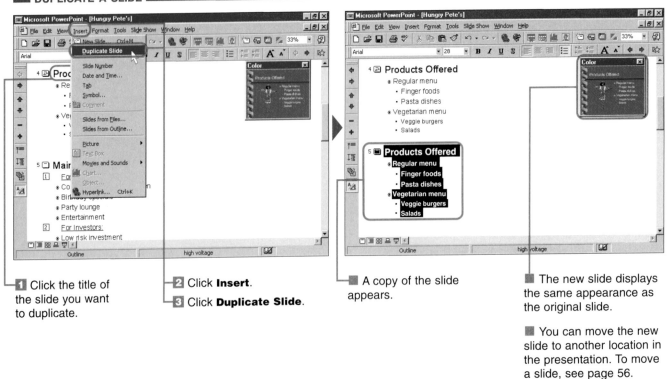

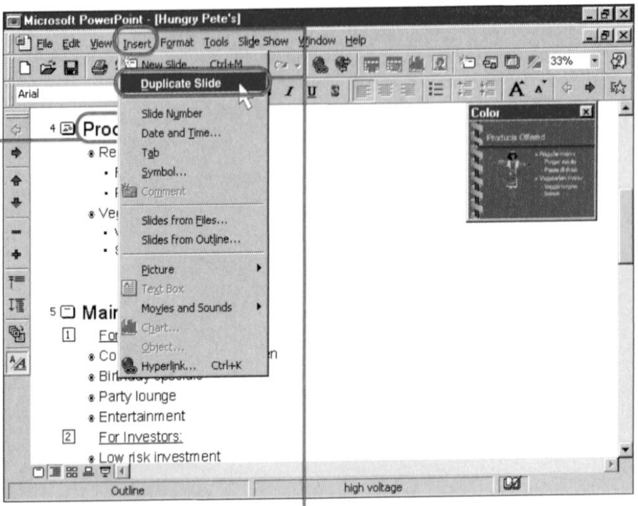

1 Click the title of the slide you want to duplicate.

2 Click **Insert**.

3 Click **Duplicate Slide**.

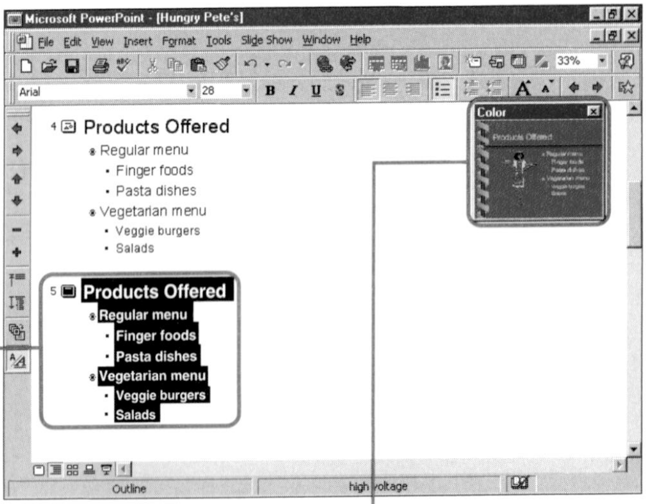

■ A copy of the slide appears.

■ The new slide displays the same appearance as the original slide.

■ You can move the new slide to another location in the presentation. To move a slide, see page 56.

EXPAND A SLIDE

If a slide contains many points, you can have PowerPoint create a new slide for each point. This is useful for breaking up information on a cluttered slide.

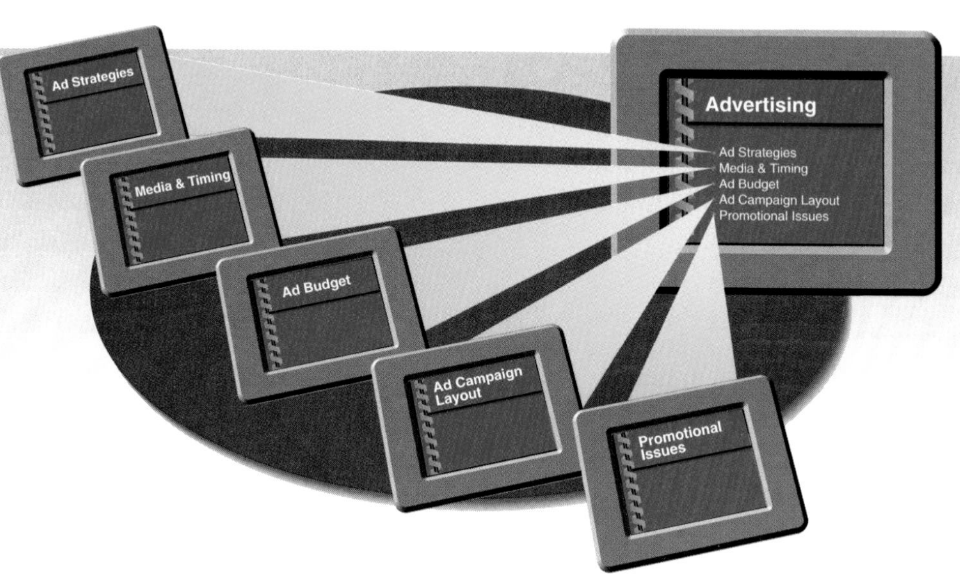

EXPAND A SLIDE

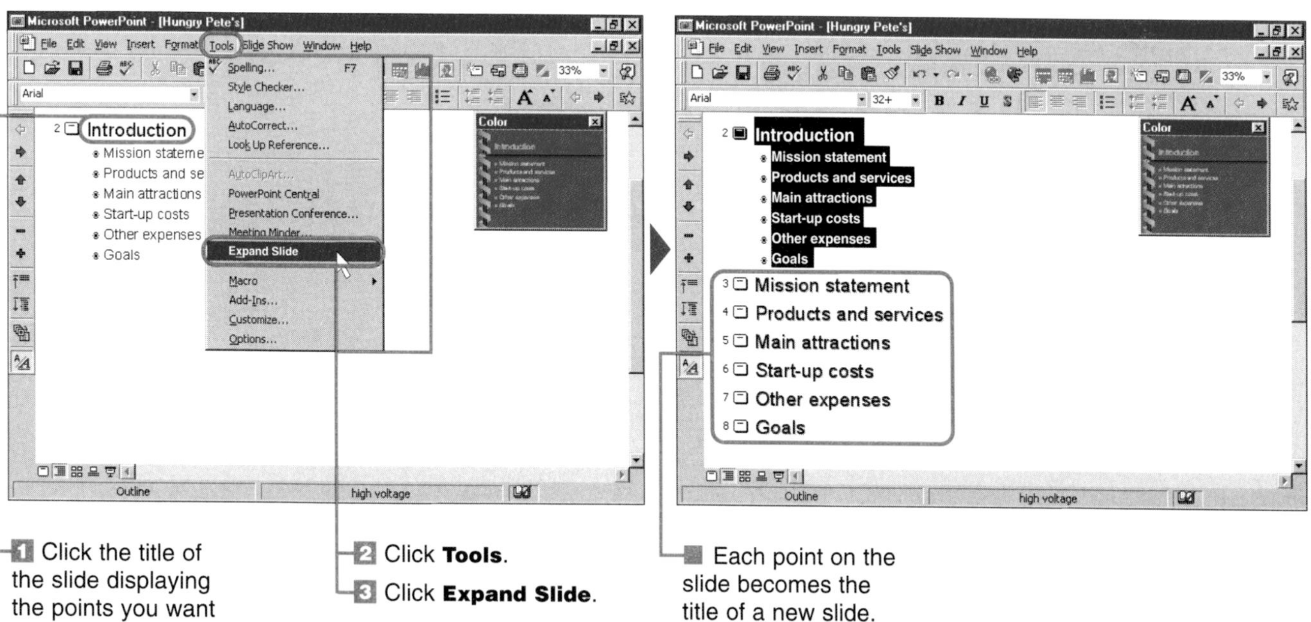

1 Click the title of the slide displaying the points you want to move to their own slides.

2 Click **Tools**.

3 Click **Expand Slide**.

■ Each point on the slide becomes the title of a new slide.

HIDE TEXT

You can hide the text for the slides in your presentation and display only the slide titles.

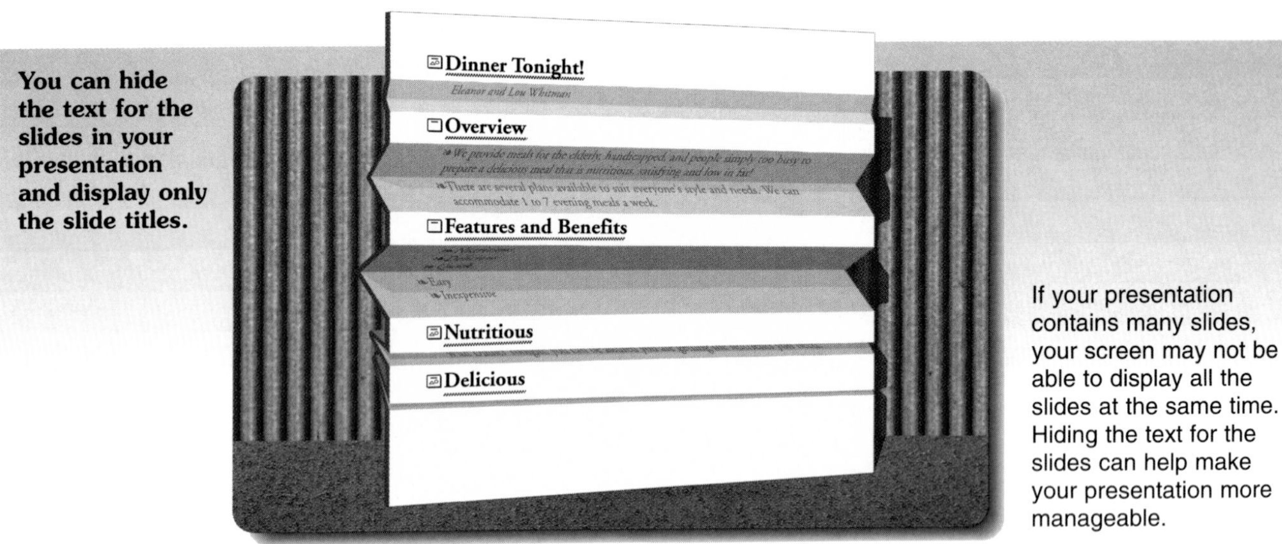

If your presentation contains many slides, your screen may not be able to display all the slides at the same time. Hiding the text for the slides can help make your presentation more manageable.

HIDE TEXT FOR ONE SLIDE

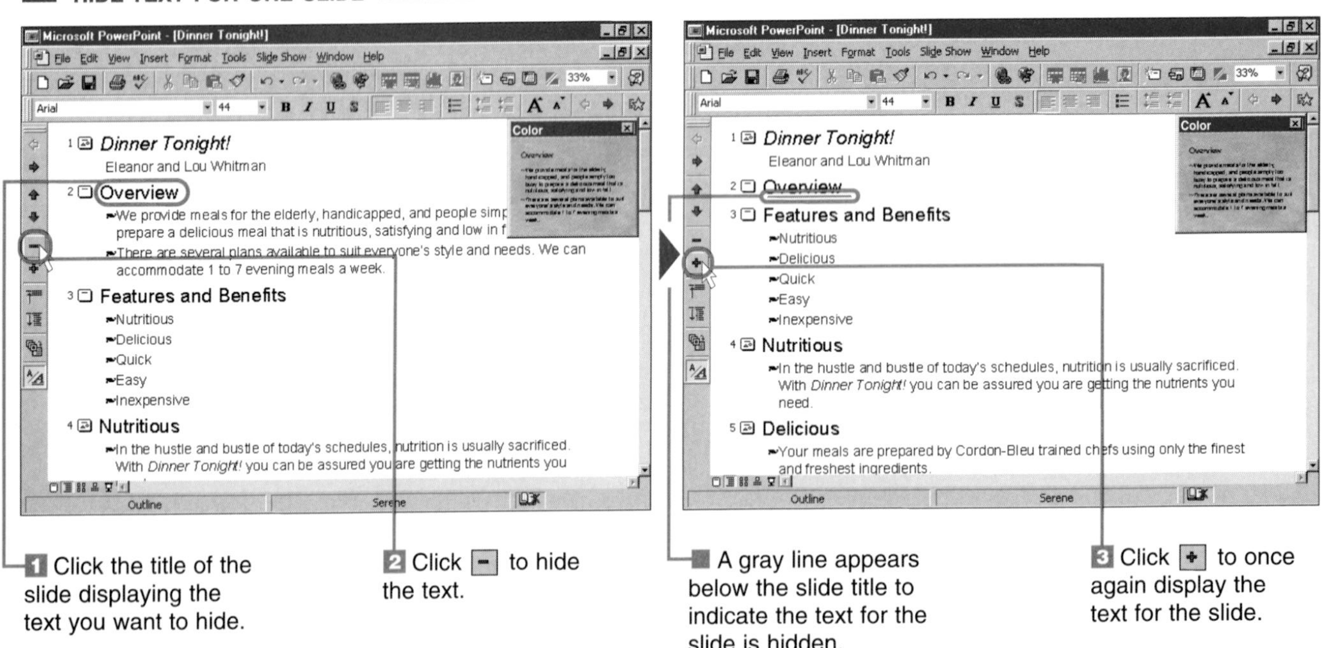

1 Click the title of the slide displaying the text you want to hide.

2 Click [−] to hide the text.

■ A gray line appears below the slide title to indicate the text for the slide is hidden.

3 Click [+] to once again display the text for the slide.

?

Can I make changes to the structure of my presentation after hiding the text for the slides?

Yes. Even when slide text is hidden, you can perform tasks such as deleting a slide you no longer need or moving a slide to a new location. For example, when you move a slide title, all the hidden text for the slide also moves.

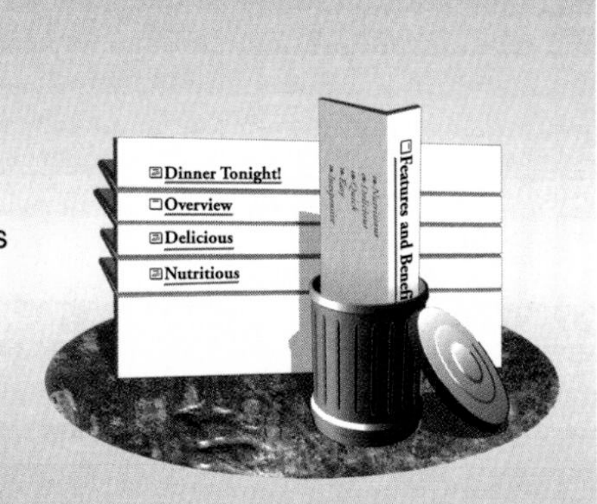

HIDE TEXT FOR ALL SLIDES

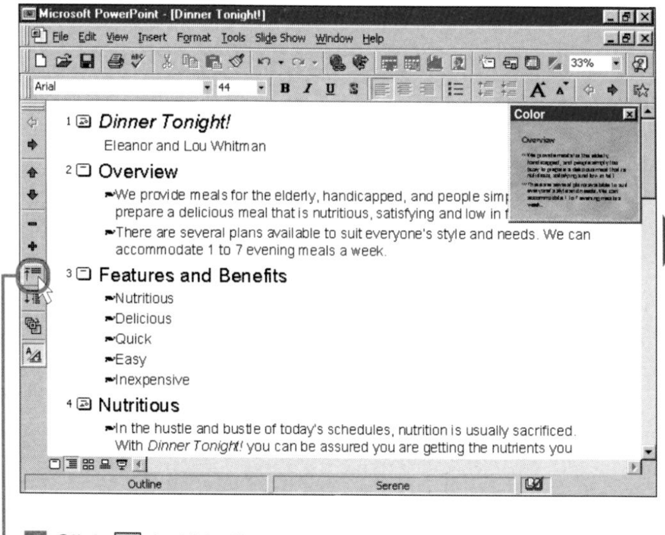

1 Click to hide the text for all the slides in the presentation.

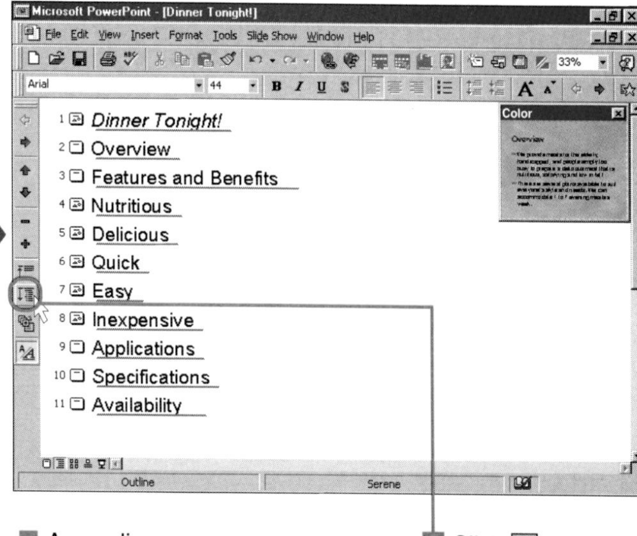

■ A gray line appears below each slide title to indicate the text for the slide is hidden.

2 Click to once again display the text for each slide.

HIDE FORMATTING

You can hide the formatting for text in the Outline view to simplify the appearance of text in your presentation.

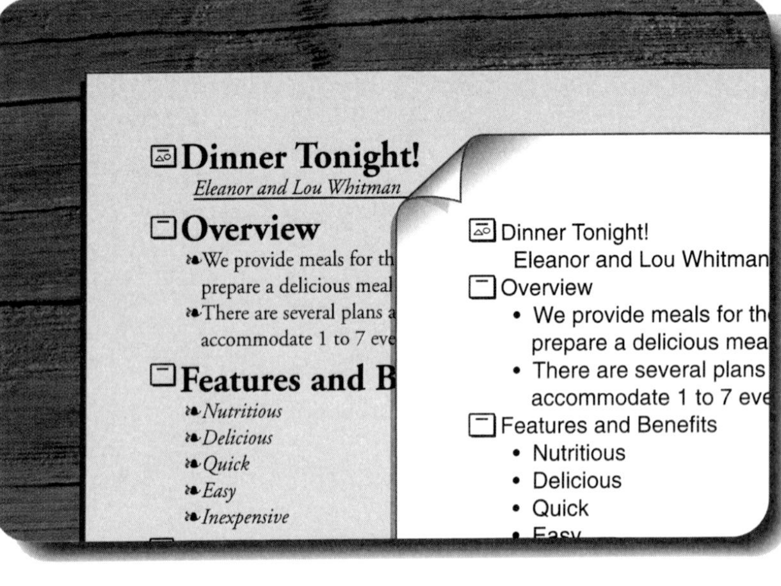

Hiding formatting can help minimize distractions while you develop the content and organization of your presentation.

HIDE FORMATTING

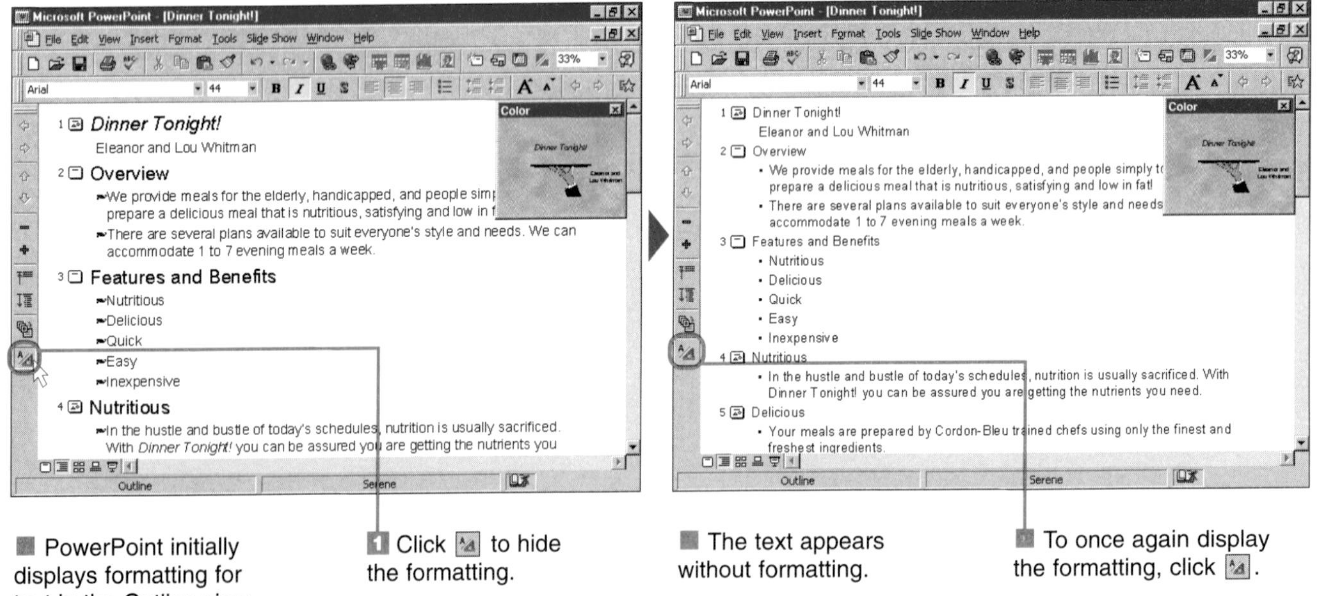

■ PowerPoint initially displays formatting for text in the Outline view.

1 Click to hide the formatting.

■ The text appears without formatting.

■ To once again display the formatting, click .

CHANGE IMPORTANCE OF TEXT

You can increase or decrease the importance of text in your presentation.

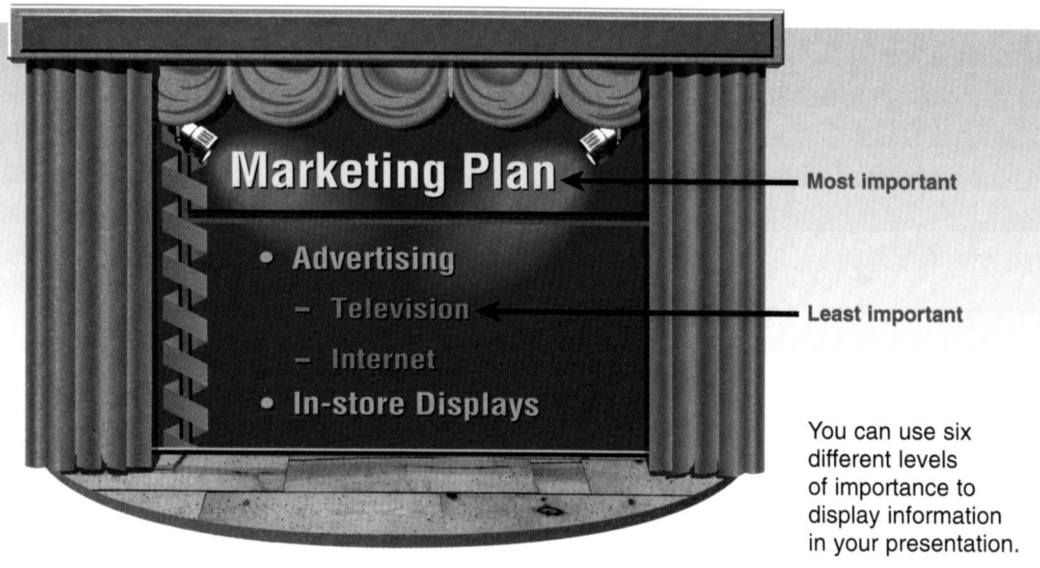

You can use six different levels of importance to display information in your presentation.

CHANGE IMPORTANCE OF TEXT

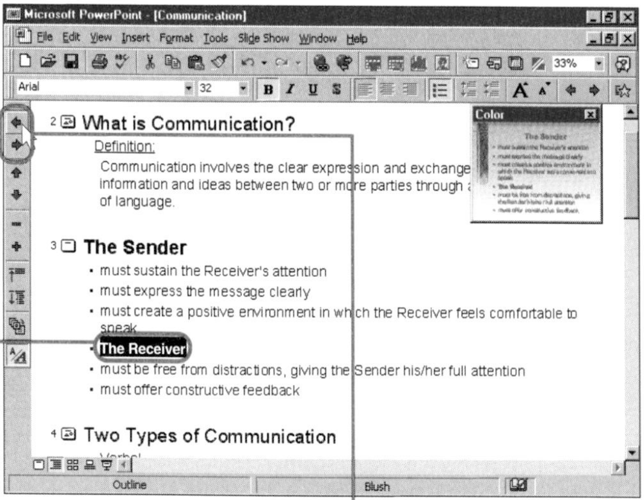

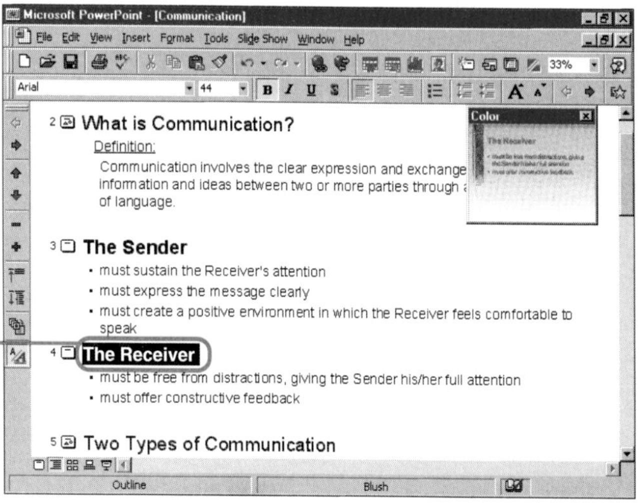

1 Select the text you want to change. To select text, see page 48.

2 Click one of the following options.

- Increase importance
- Decrease importance

■ The text displays the change.

FIND AND REPLACE TEXT

The Replace feature can locate and replace every occurrence of a word or phrase in your presentation. This is useful if you have frequently misspelled text, such as a company name.

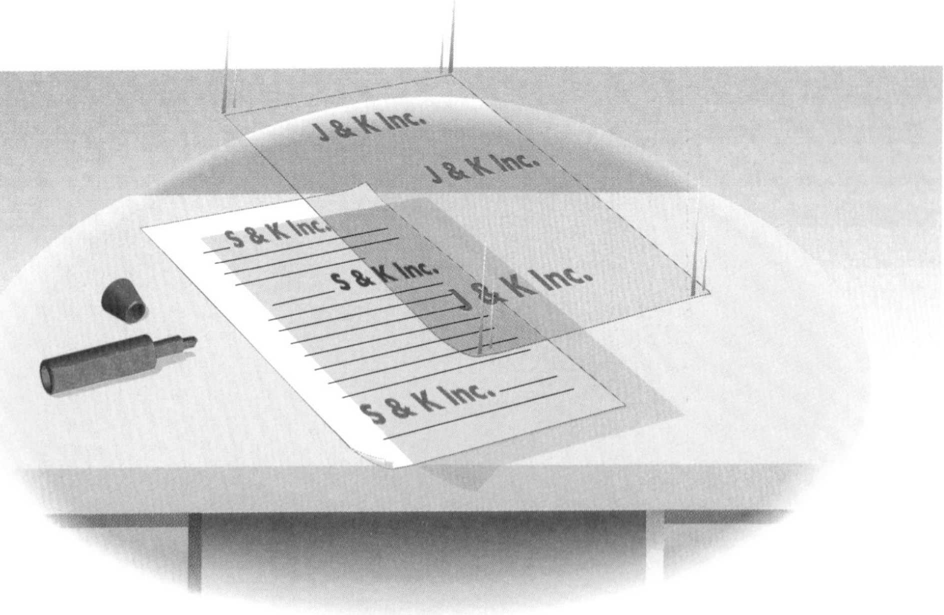

FIND AND REPLACE TEXT

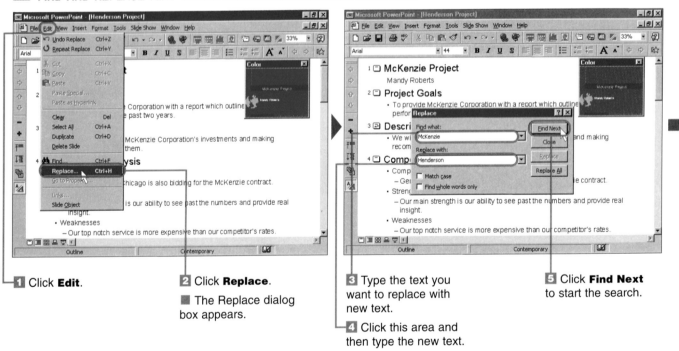

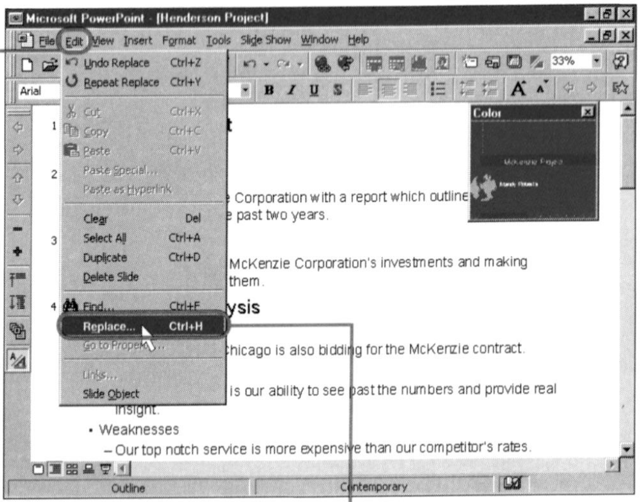

1 Click **Edit**.

2 Click **Replace**.

■ The Replace dialog box appears.

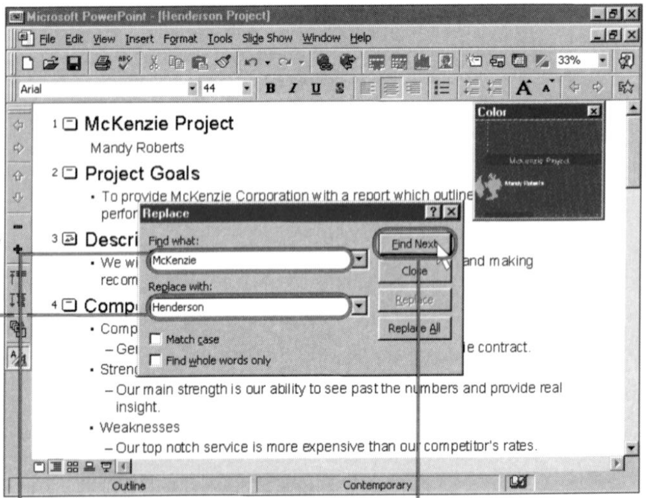

3 Type the text you want to replace with new text.

4 Click this area and then type the new text.

5 Click **Find Next** to start the search.

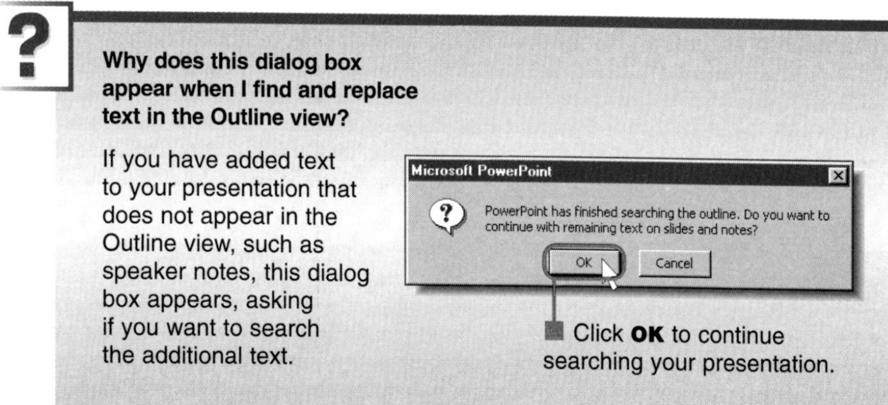

Why does this dialog box appear when I find and replace text in the Outline view?

If you have added text to your presentation that does not appear in the Outline view, such as speaker notes, this dialog box appears, asking if you want to search the additional text.

■ Click **OK** to continue searching your presentation.

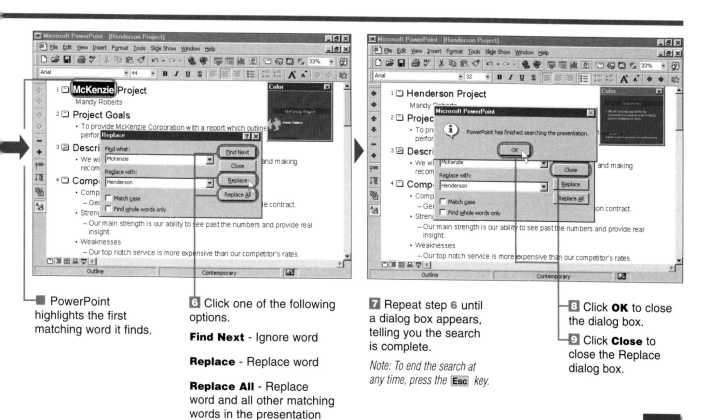

■ PowerPoint highlights the first matching word it finds.

6 Click one of the following options.

Find Next - Ignore word

Replace - Replace word

Replace All - Replace word and all other matching words in the presentation

7 Repeat step 6 until a dialog box appears, telling you the search is complete.

Note: To end the search at any time, press the Esc *key.*

8 Click **OK** to close the dialog box.

9 Click **Close** to close the Replace dialog box.

CHECK SPELLING

PowerPoint automatically checks your presentation for spelling errors as you type. You can correct an error at any time.

A wavy, red line appears under words that PowerPoint considers misspelled. The underline will not appear when you view the slide show or print the presentation.

CORRECT OR IGNORE AN ERROR

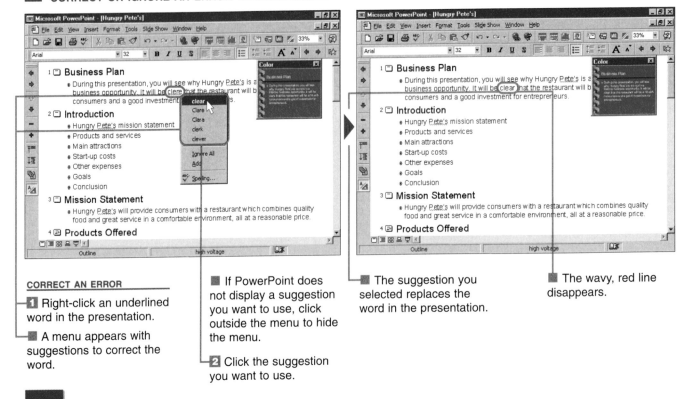

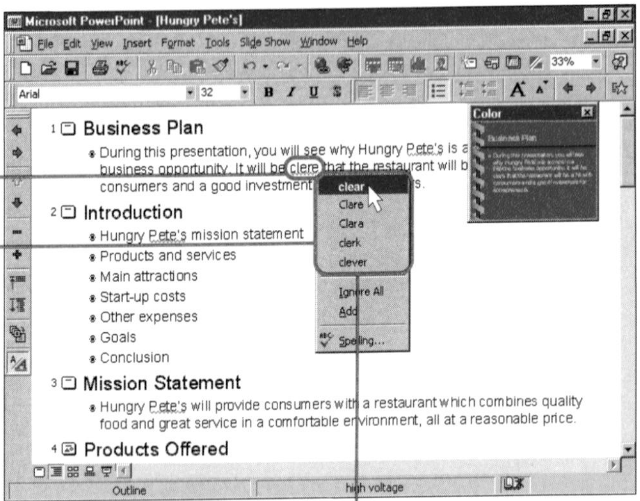

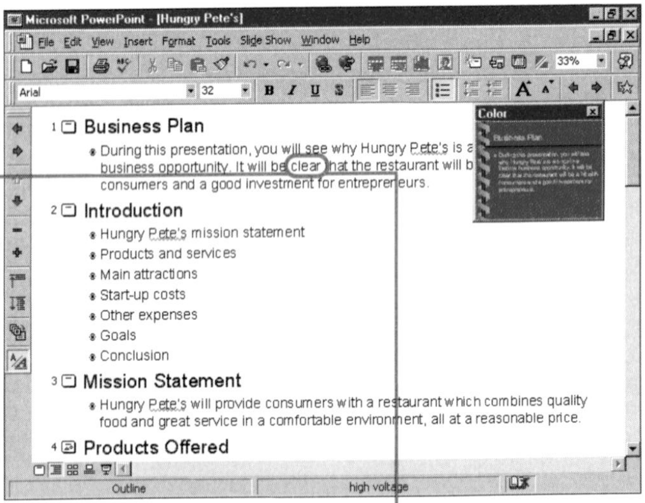

CORRECT AN ERROR

1 Right-click an underlined word in the presentation.

■ A menu appears with suggestions to correct the word.

■ If PowerPoint does not display a suggestion you want to use, click outside the menu to hide the menu.

2 Click the suggestion you want to use.

■ The suggestion you selected replaces the word in the presentation.

■ The wavy, red line disappears.

?

Why did PowerPoint underline a correctly spelled word?

PowerPoint compares every word in your presentation to words in its dictionary. If a word in your presentation does not exist in PowerPoint's dictionary, PowerPoint considers the word misspelled.

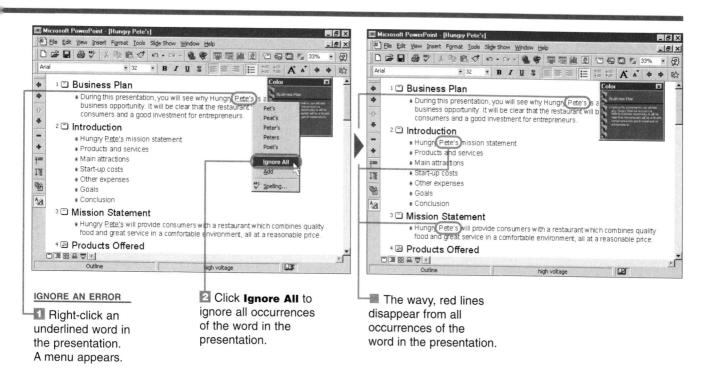

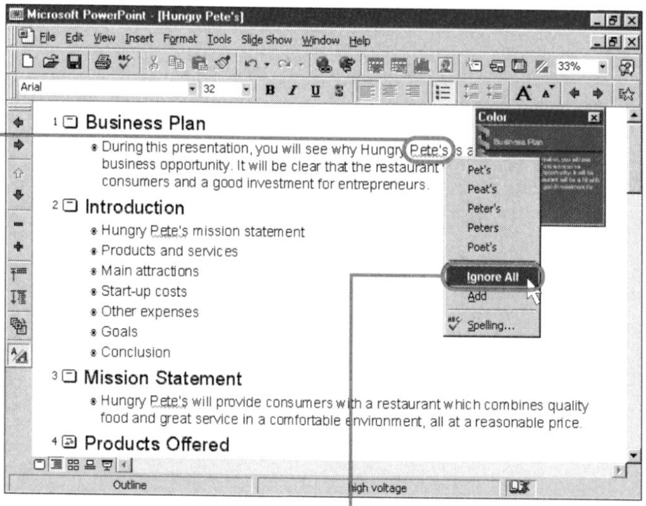

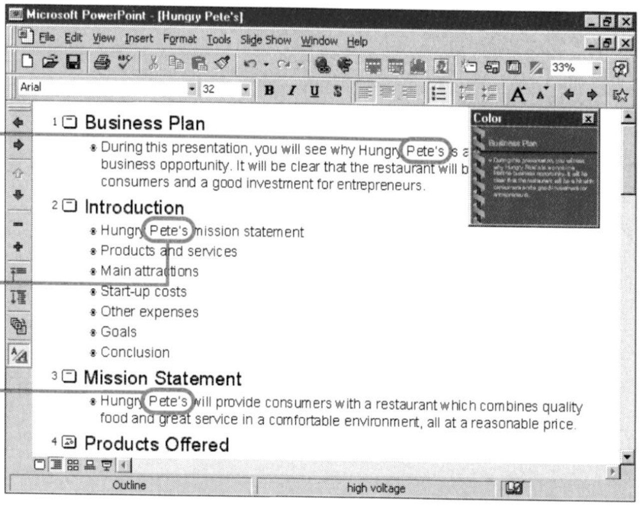

IGNORE AN ERROR

1 Right-click an underlined word in the presentation. A menu appears.

2 Click **Ignore All** to ignore all occurrences of the word in the presentation.

■ The wavy, red lines disappear from all occurrences of the word in the presentation.

CHECK SPELLING

You can find and correct all the spelling errors in your presentation at once.

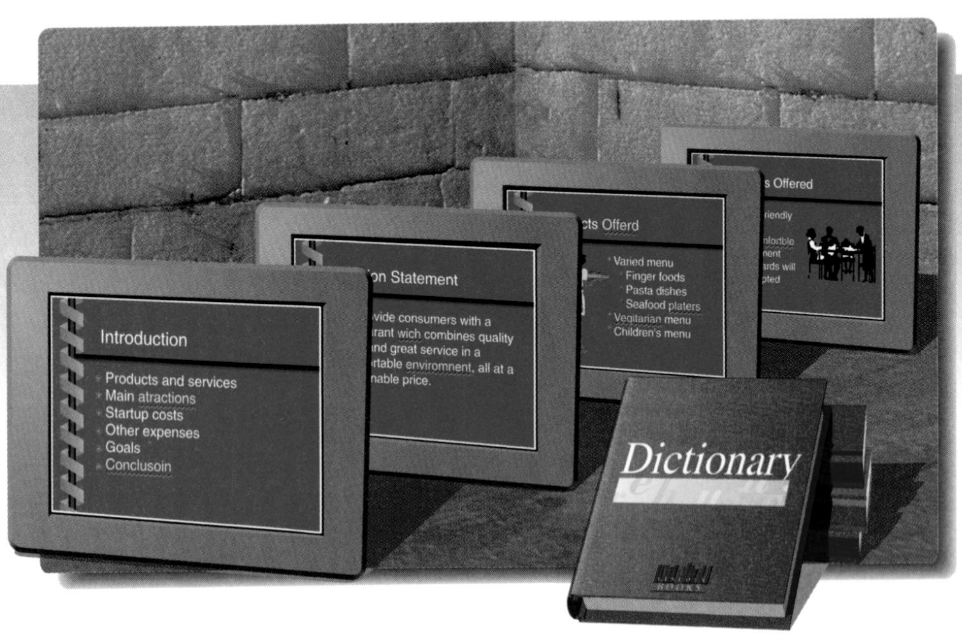

CORRECT ENTIRE PRESENTATION

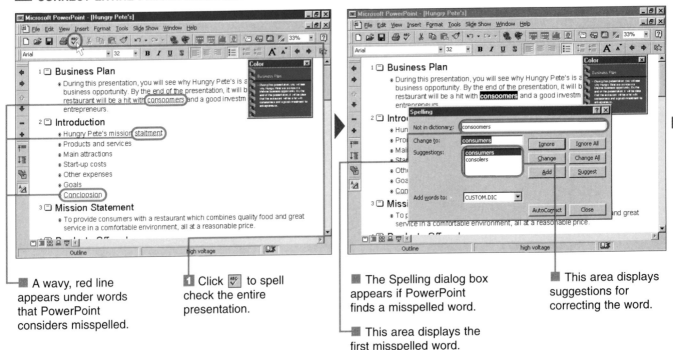

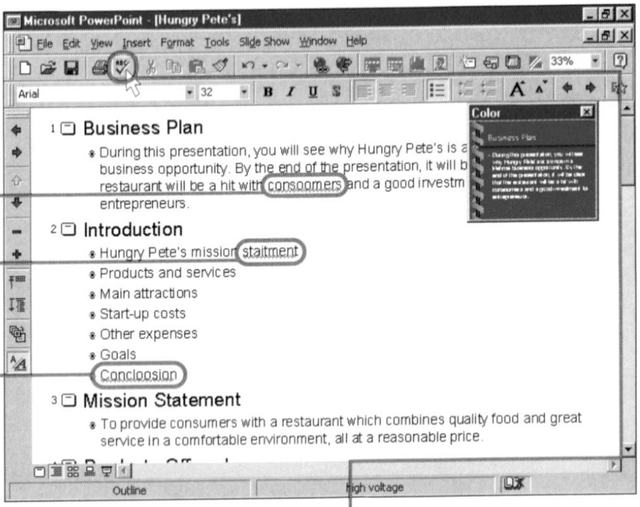

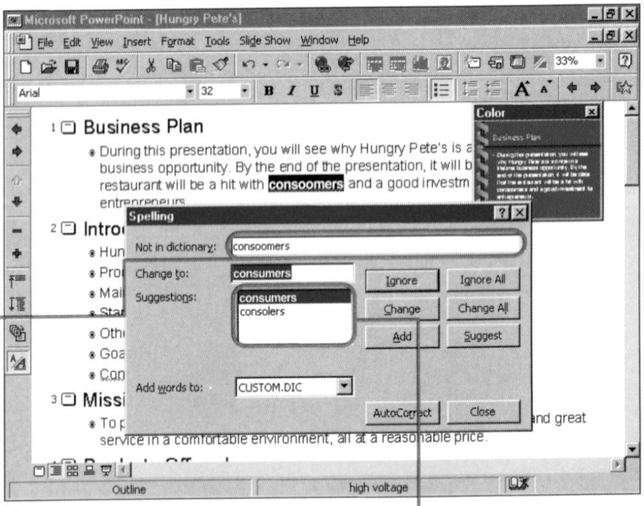

■ A wavy, red line appears under words that PowerPoint considers misspelled.

1 Click the spelling button to spell check the entire presentation.

■ The Spelling dialog box appears if PowerPoint finds a misspelled word.

■ This area displays the first misspelled word.

■ This area displays suggestions for correcting the word.

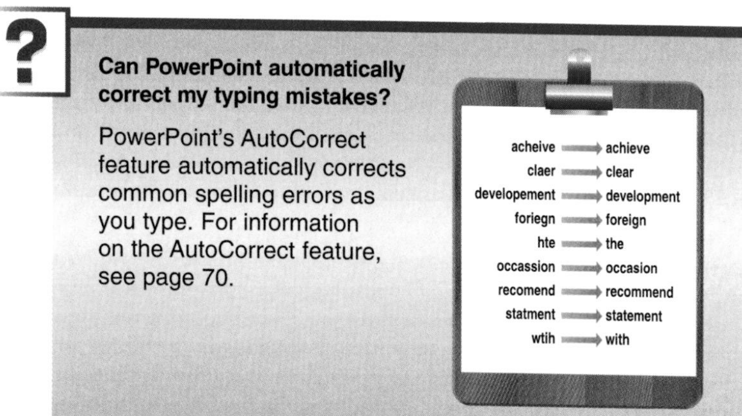

Can PowerPoint automatically correct my typing mistakes?

PowerPoint's AutoCorrect feature automatically corrects common spelling errors as you type. For information on the AutoCorrect feature, see page 70.

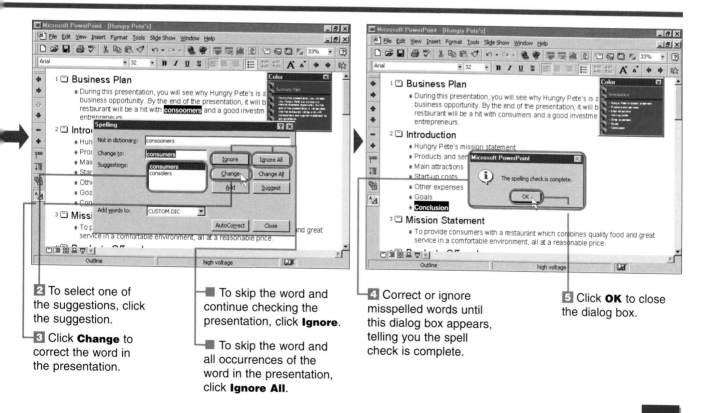

2 To select one of the suggestions, click the suggestion.

3 Click **Change** to correct the word in the presentation.

■ To skip the word and continue checking the presentation, click **Ignore**.

■ To skip the word and all occurrences of the word in the presentation, click **Ignore All**.

4 Correct or ignore misspelled words until this dialog box appears, telling you the spell check is complete.

5 Click **OK** to close the dialog box.

USING AUTOCORRECT

PowerPoint automatically corrects hundreds of common typing, spelling and grammar errors as you type. You can create an AutoCorrect entry to add your own words and phrases to the list.

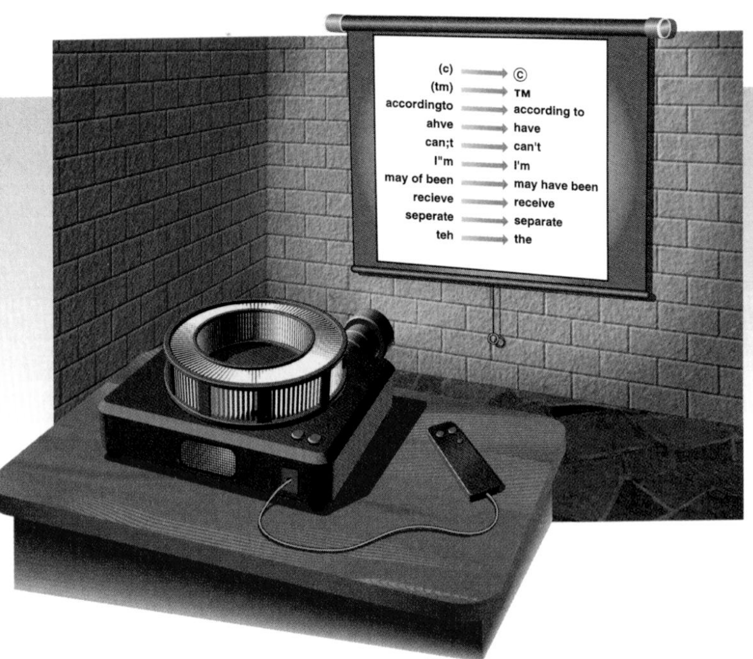

USING AUTOCORRECT

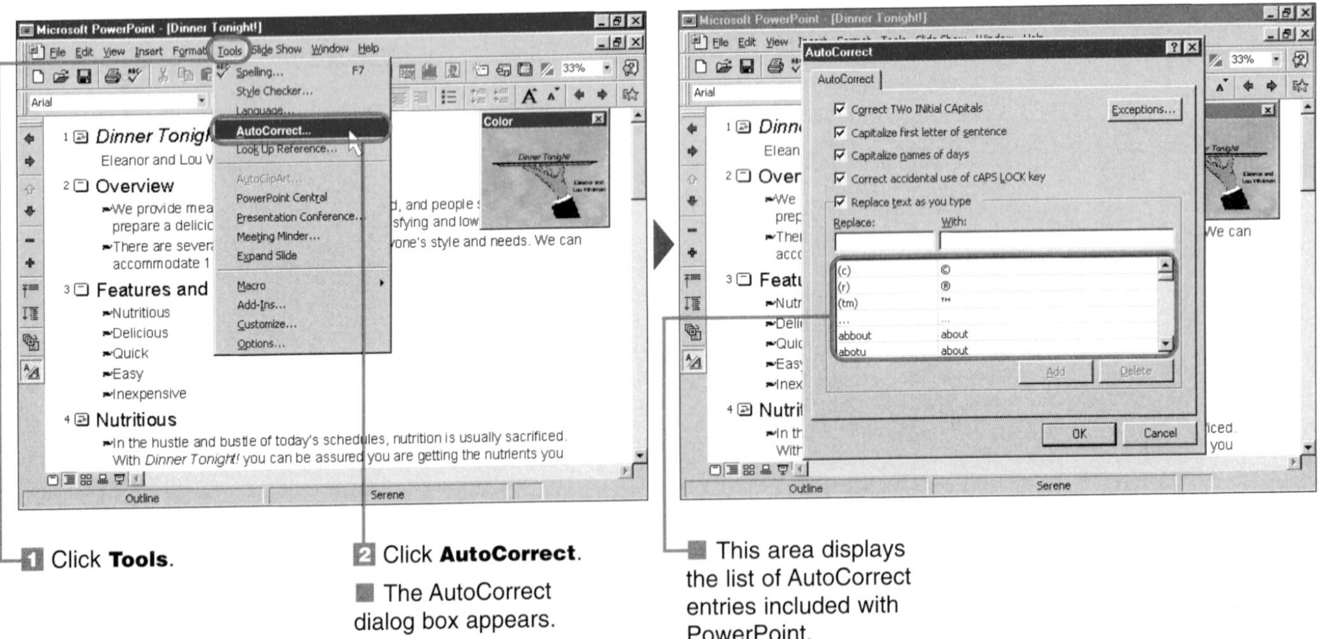

1 Click **Tools**.

2 Click **AutoCorrect**.

■ The AutoCorrect dialog box appears.

■ This area displays the list of AutoCorrect entries included with PowerPoint.

?

Can I use the AutoCorrect feature to save time typing?

Yes. You can add a short form of a long word or phrase you regularly type to the list of AutoCorrect entries. For example, you can have the AutoCorrect feature replace **mfs** with **Melbourne Financial Services.** AutoCorrect will replace every instance of the short form with the longer word or phrase, so you should make sure the short form you use is not a real word.

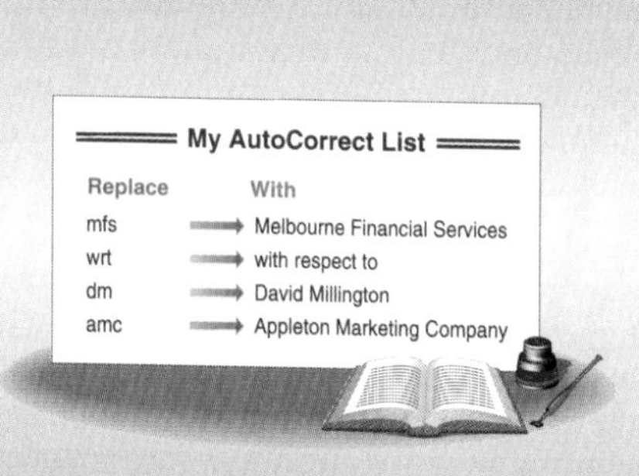

My AutoCorrect List
Replace
With
mfs
Melbourne Financial Services
wrt
with respect to
dm
David Millington
amc
Appleton Marketing Company

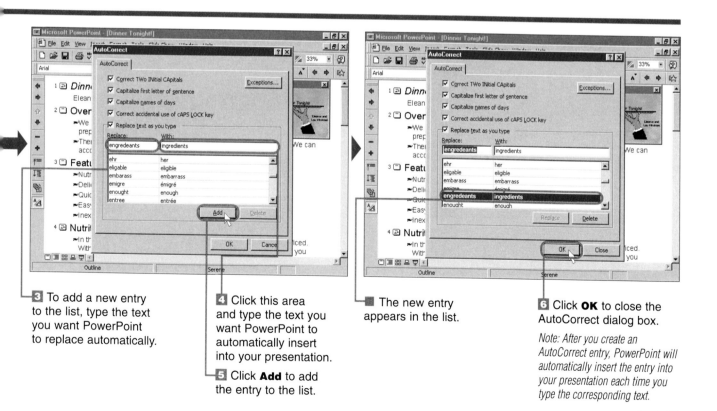

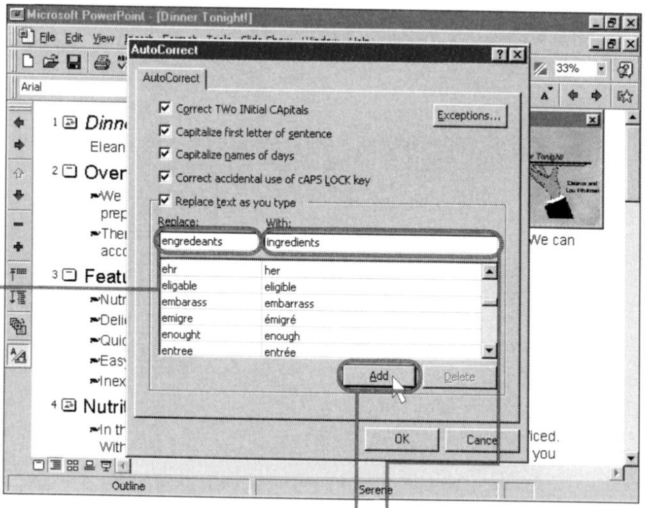

3 To add a new entry to the list, type the text you want PowerPoint to replace automatically.

4 Click this area and type the text you want PowerPoint to automatically insert into your presentation.

5 Click **Add** to add the entry to the list.

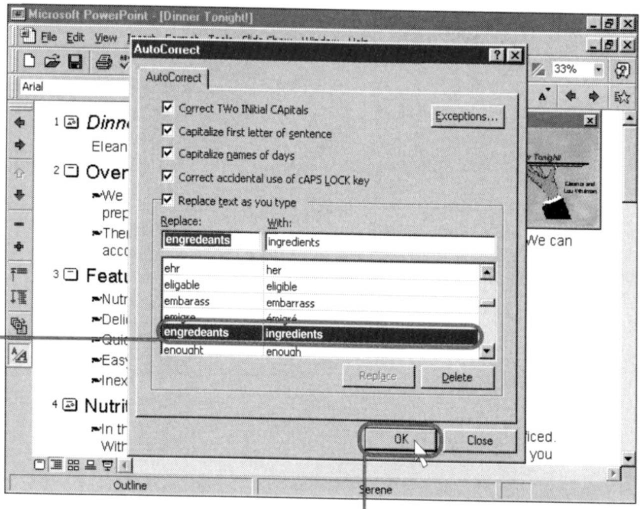

■ The new entry appears in the list.

6 Click **OK** to close the AutoCorrect dialog box.

Note: After you create an AutoCorrect entry, PowerPoint will automatically insert the entry into your presentation each time you type the corresponding text.

INSERT SYMBOLS

You can add symbols that do not appear on your keyboard to your slides.

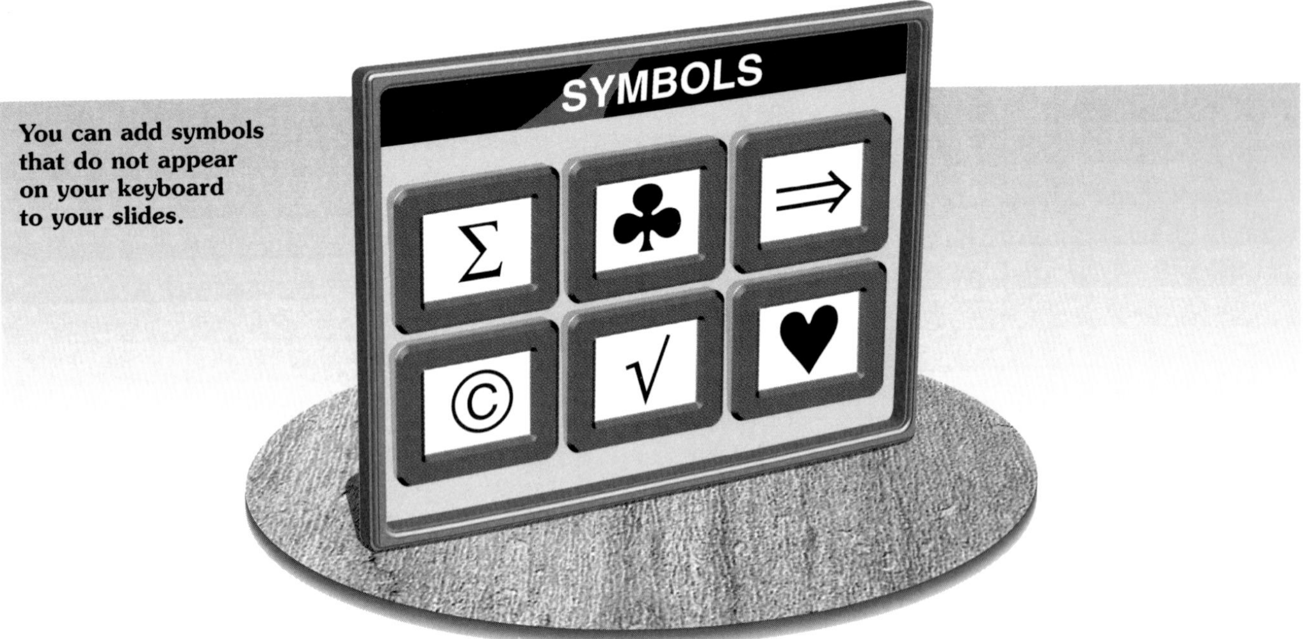

INSERT SYMBOLS

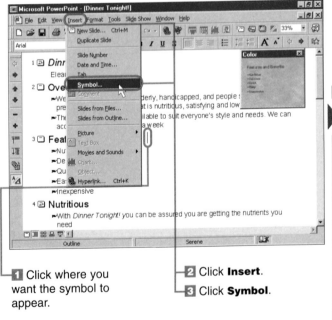

1 Click where you want the symbol to appear.

2 Click **Insert**.

3 Click **Symbol**.

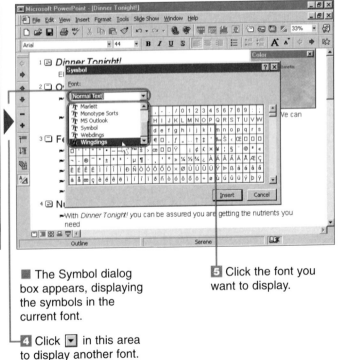

■ The Symbol dialog box appears, displaying the symbols in the current font.

4 Click ▼ in this area to display another font.

5 Click the font you want to display.

Which font should I select in the Symbol dialog box?

The Symbol and Wingdings fonts are two popular fonts available in the Symbol dialog box. The Symbol font contains a selection of symbols for mathematical equations. The Wingdings font contains a variety of bullet and arrow symbols.

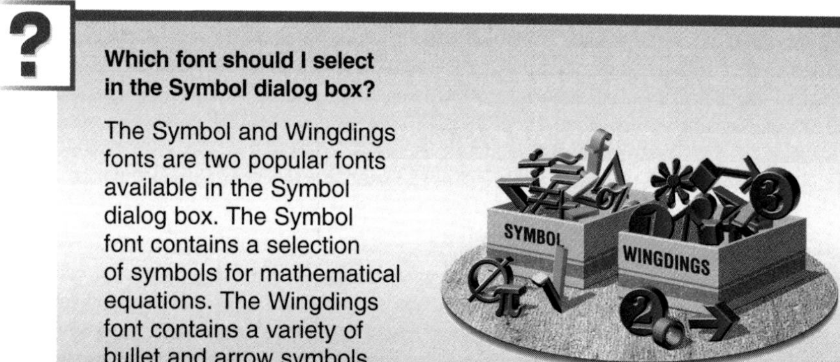

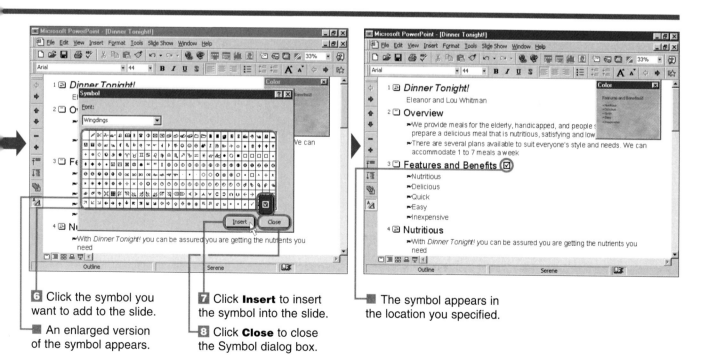

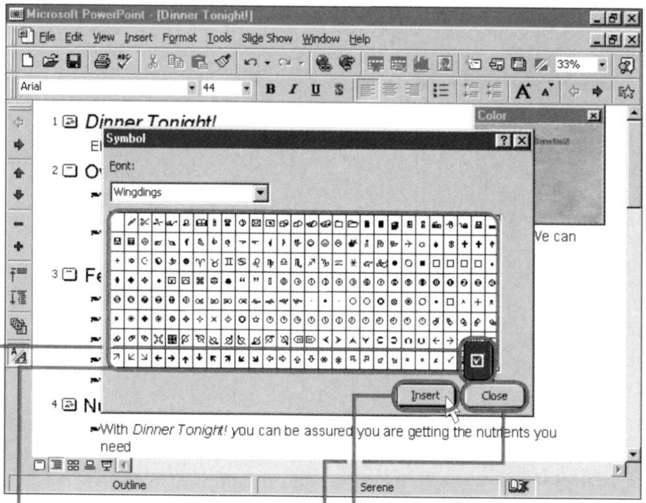

6 Click the symbol you want to add to the slide.

- An enlarged version of the symbol appears.

7 Click **Insert** to insert the symbol into the slide.

8 Click **Close** to close the Symbol dialog box.

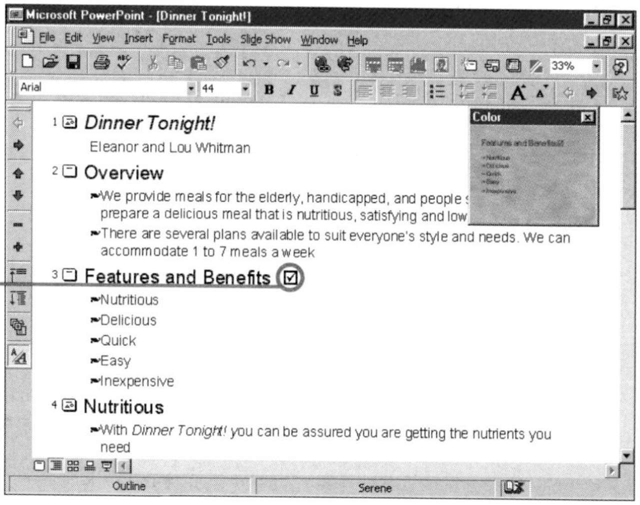

- The symbol appears in the location you specified.

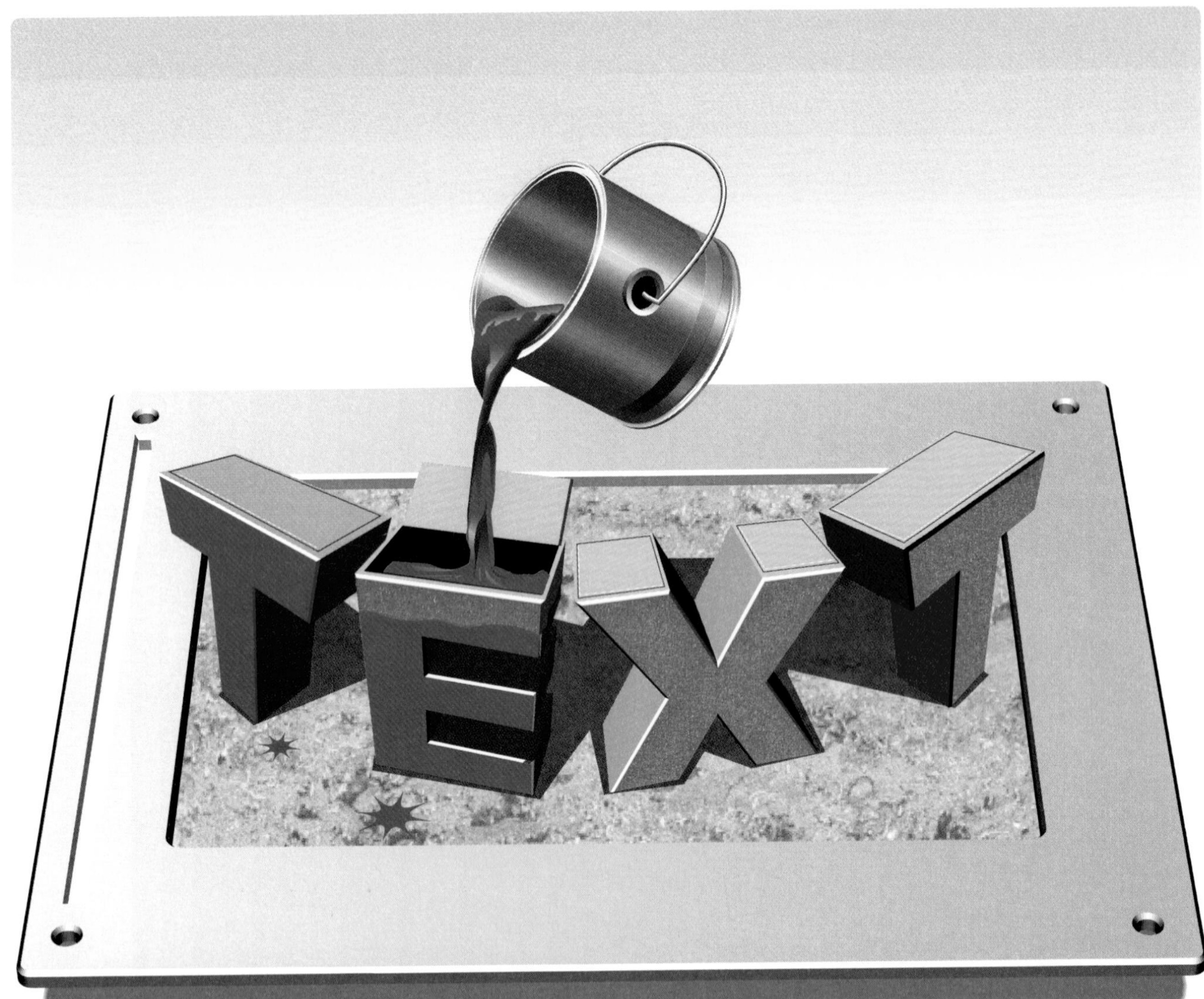
TEXT

CHAPTER 4

Format Text

Are you ready to emphasize and enhance the text in your presentation? Read this chapter to learn how.

CHANGE FONT OF TEXT

You can change the design of text on a slide to enhance the appearance of the slide.

CHANGE FONT OF TEXT

1 Select the text you want to change. To select text, see page 48.

2 Click ▼ in this area to display a list of the available fonts.

3 Click the font you want to use.

■ The text you selected changes to the new font.

■ To deselect text, click outside the selected area.

CHANGE SIZE OF TEXT

You can increase or decrease the size of text on a slide.

CHANGE SIZE OF TEXT

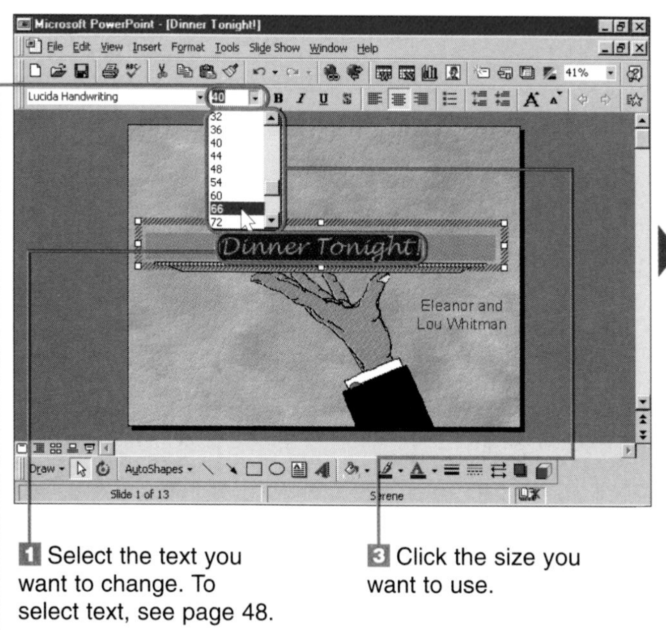

1 Select the text you want to change. To select text, see page 48.

2 Click ▾ in this area to display a list of the available sizes.

3 Click the size you want to use.

■ The text you selected changes to the new size.

■ To deselect text, click outside the selected area.

CHANGE SIZE USING BUTTONS

1 Select the text you want to change. To select text, see page 48.

2 Click an option to increase (A) or decrease (A) the size of the text. Repeat this step until the text is the size you want.

CHANGE STYLE OF TEXT

PowerPoint offers several styles that you can use to emphasize information on a slide.

CHANGE STYLE OF TEXT

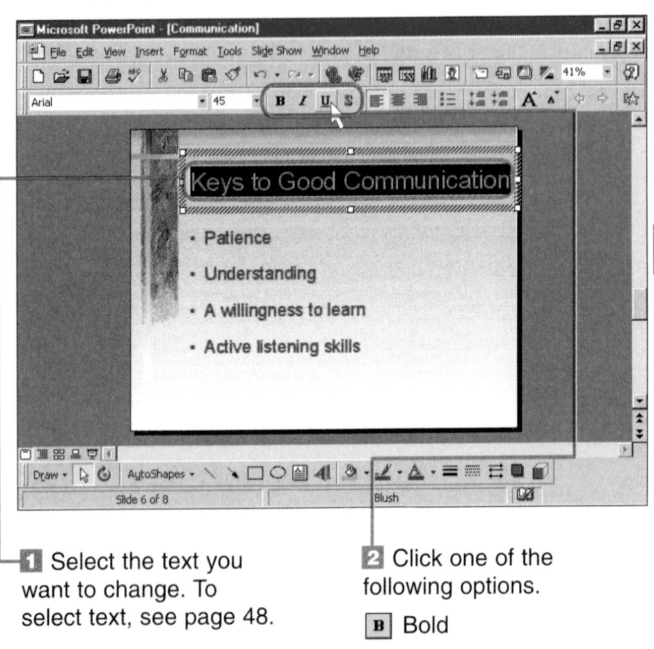

1 Select the text you want to change. To select text, see page 48.

2 Click one of the following options.

B Bold

I Italic

U Underline

S Shadow

■ The text you selected appears in the new style.

■ To deselect text, click outside the selected area.

■ To remove a style, repeat steps **1** and **2**.

CHANGE COLOR OF TEXT

You can change the color of text on a slide.

CHANGE COLOR OF TEXT

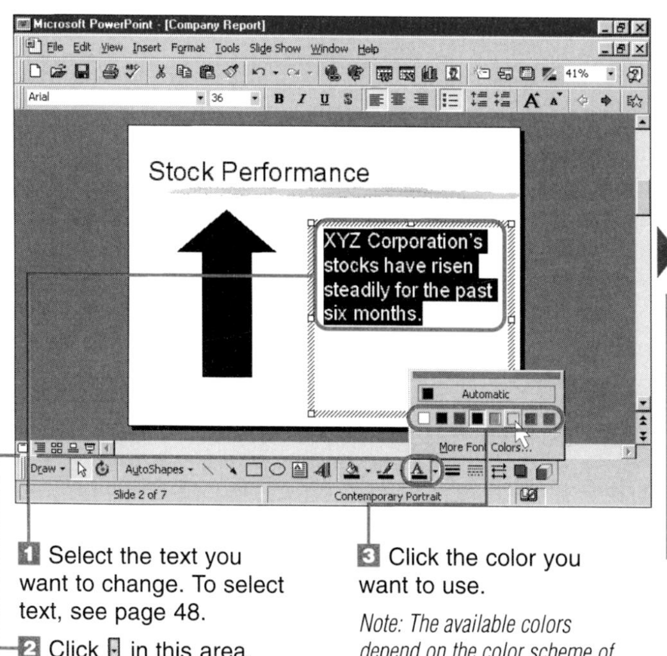

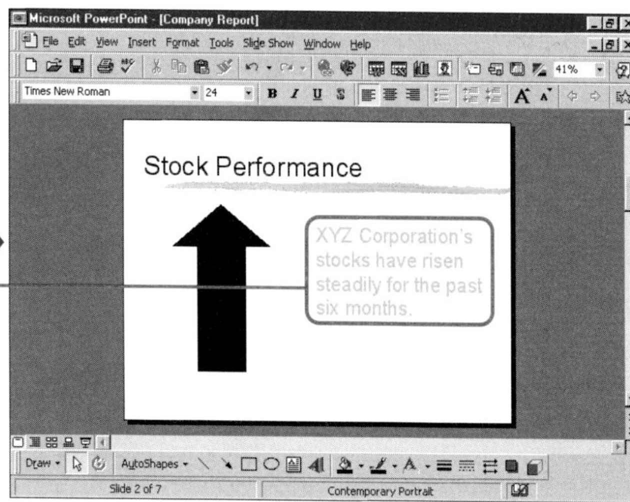

1 Select the text you want to change. To select text, see page 48.

2 Click ▾ in this area.

3 Click the color you want to use.

Note: The available colors depend on the color scheme of the slide. For information on color schemes, see page 102.

■ The text you selected appears in the new color.

■ To deselect text, click outside the selected area.

CHANGE APPEARANCE OF TEXT

You can use various fonts, styles, sizes, effects and colors to enhance the appearance of text in your presentation.

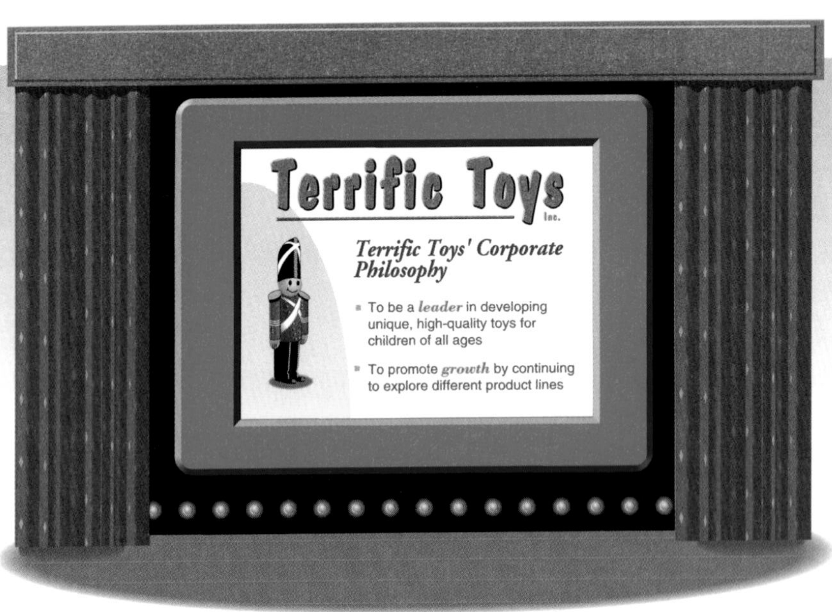

CHANGE APPEARANCE OF TEXT

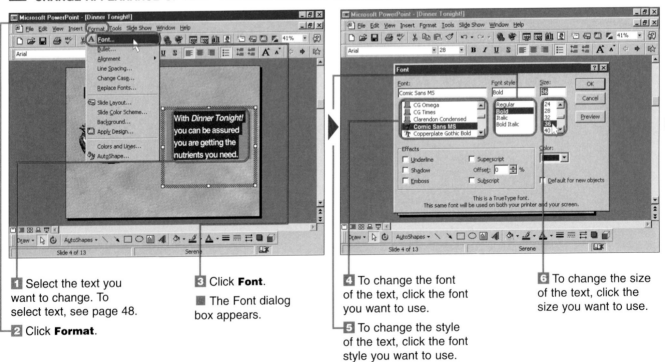

1 Select the text you want to change. To select text, see page 48.

2 Click **Format**.

3 Click **Font**.

■ The Font dialog box appears.

4 To change the font of the text, click the font you want to use.

5 To change the style of the text, click the font style you want to use.

6 To change the size of the text, click the size you want to use.

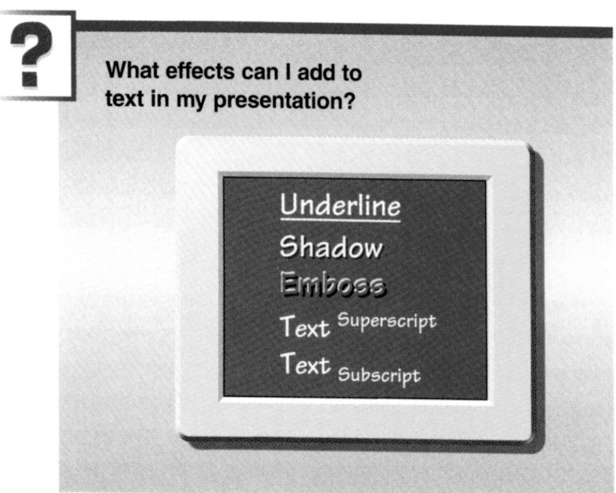

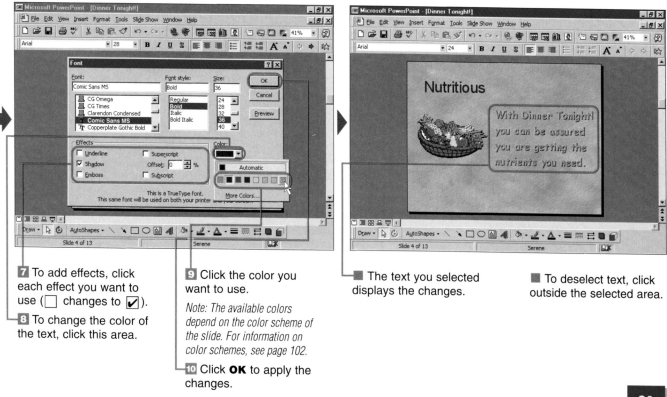

7 To add effects, click each effect you want to use (☐ changes to ☑).

8 To change the color of the text, click this area.

9 Click the color you want to use.

Note: The available colors depend on the color scheme of the slide. For information on color schemes, see page 102.

10 Click **OK** to apply the changes.

■ The text you selected displays the changes.

■ To deselect text, click outside the selected area.

COPY FORMATTING

You can make one area of text in your presentation look exactly like another.

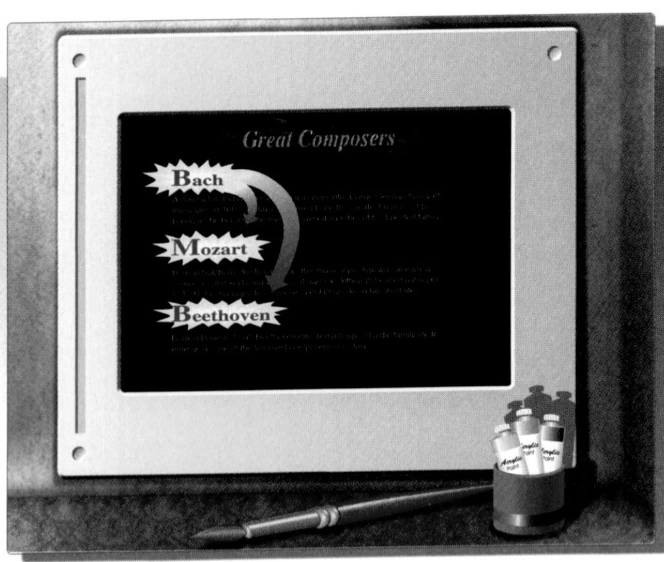

You may want to copy the formatting of text to give all the headings or important words in your presentation a consistent appearance.

COPY FORMATTING

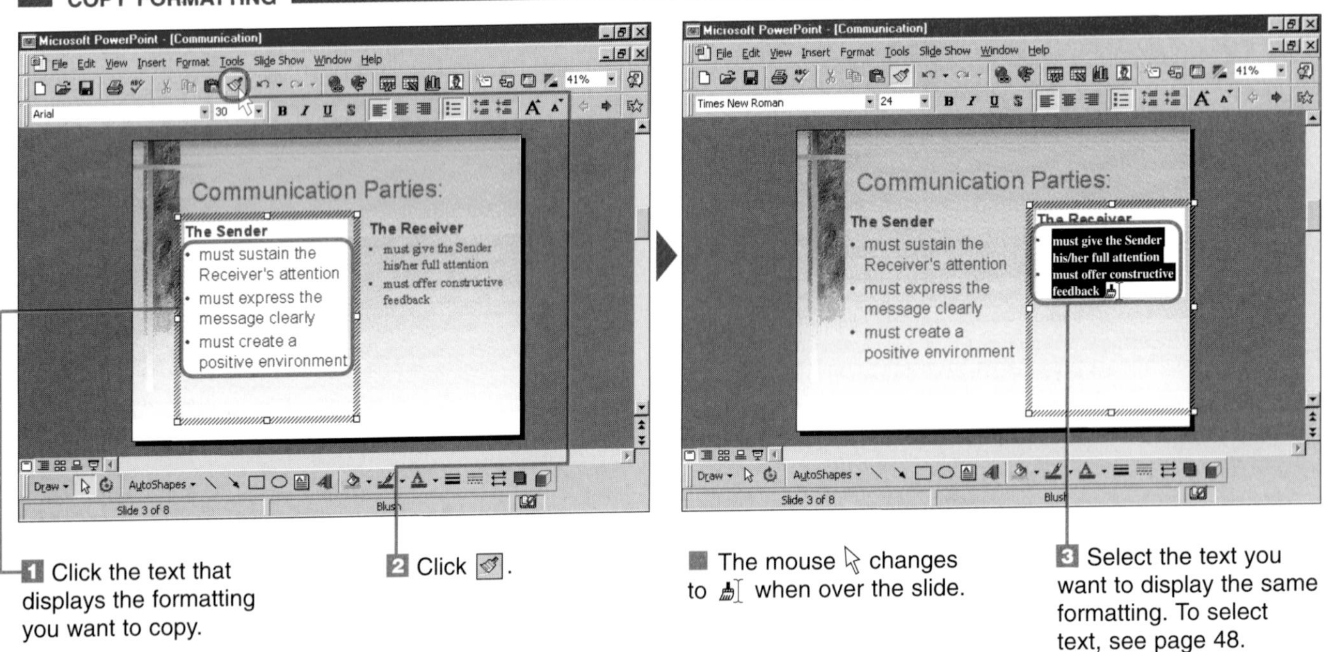

1 Click the text that displays the formatting you want to copy.

2 Click the Format Painter button.

■ The mouse changes to the paintbrush I-beam when over the slide.

3 Select the text you want to display the same formatting. To select text, see page 48.

How do I copy formatting between slides in my presentation?

To copy formatting between slides, perform steps 1 and 2 on page 82. Then display the slide containing the text you want to display the same formatting and select the text.

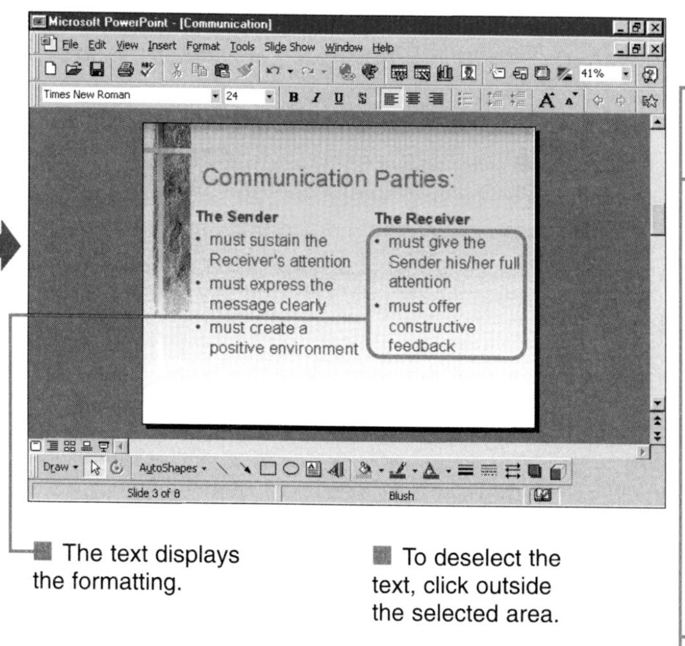

■ The text displays the formatting.

■ To deselect the text, click outside the selected area.

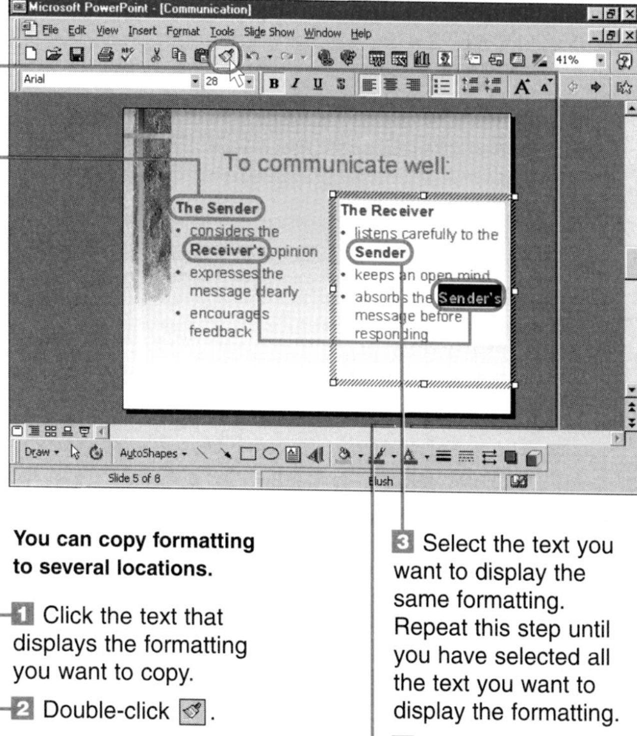

You can copy formatting to several locations.

1 Click the text that displays the formatting you want to copy.

2 Double-click 🖌.

3 Select the text you want to display the same formatting. Repeat this step until you have selected all the text you want to display the formatting.

4 Click 🖌.

REPLACE A FONT

If you do not like a font used throughout your presentation, you can replace all occurrences of the font with a font you prefer.

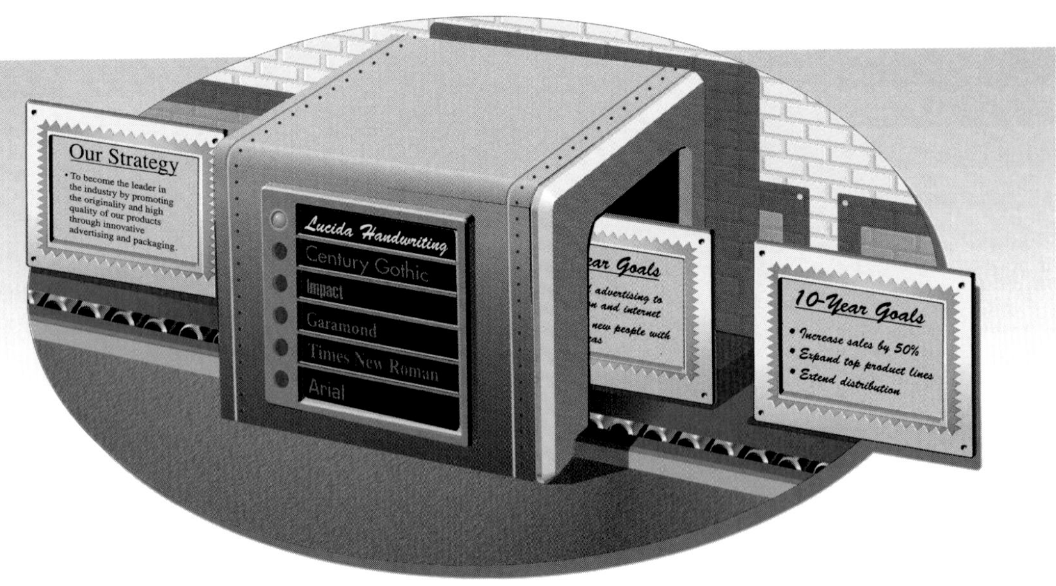

REPLACE A FONT

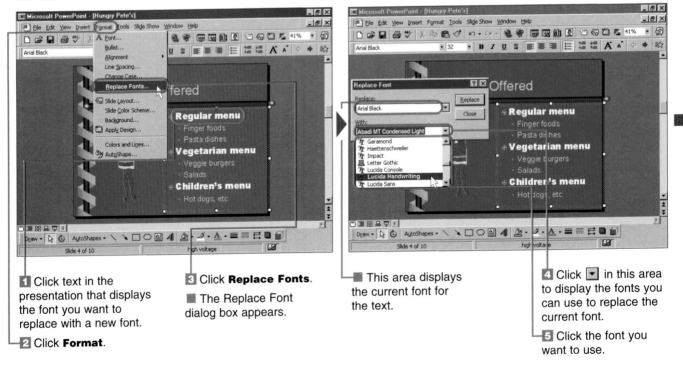

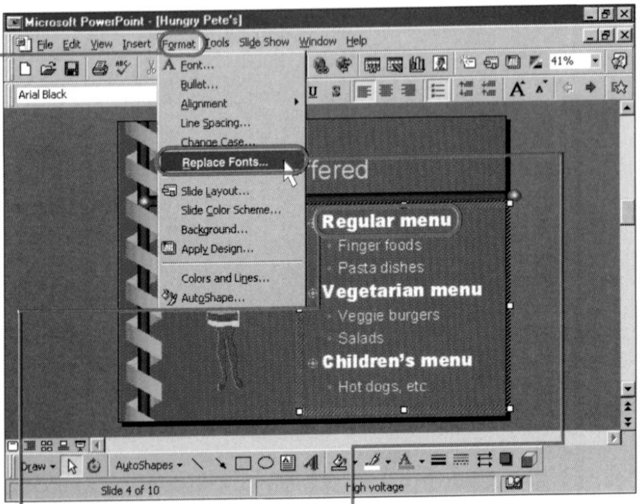

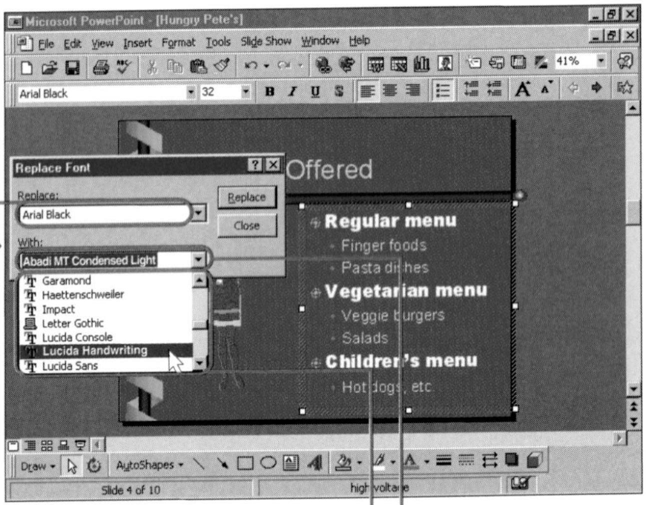

1 Click text in the presentation that displays the font you want to replace with a new font.

2 Click **Format**.

3 Click **Replace Fonts**.

■ The Replace Font dialog box appears.

■ This area displays the current font for the text.

4 Click ▼ in this area to display the fonts you can use to replace the current font.

5 Click the font you want to use.

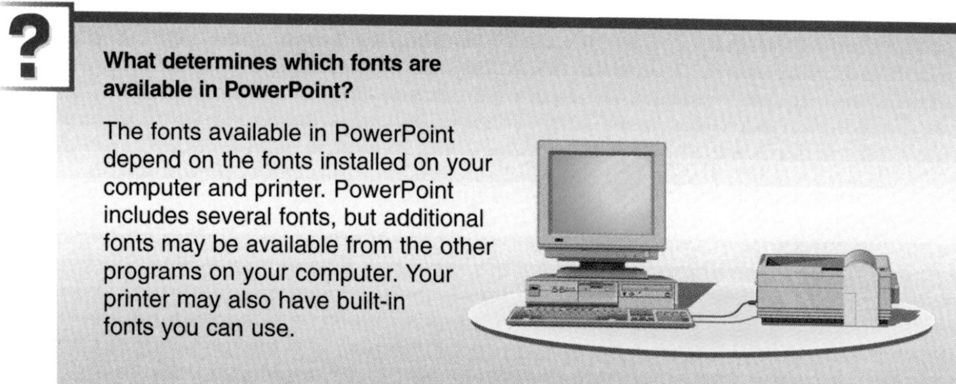

What determines which fonts are available in PowerPoint?

The fonts available in PowerPoint depend on the fonts installed on your computer and printer. PowerPoint includes several fonts, but additional fonts may be available from the other programs on your computer. Your printer may also have built-in fonts you can use.

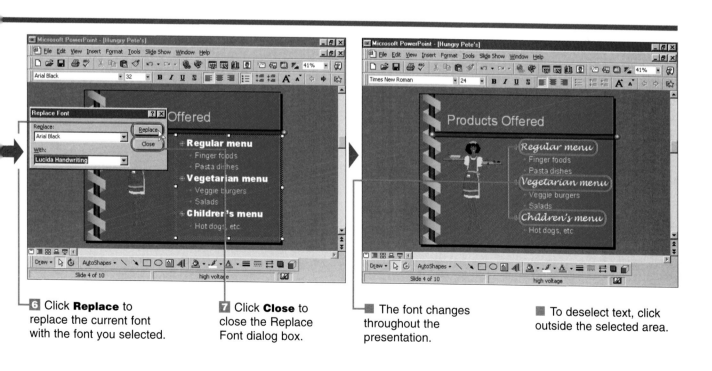

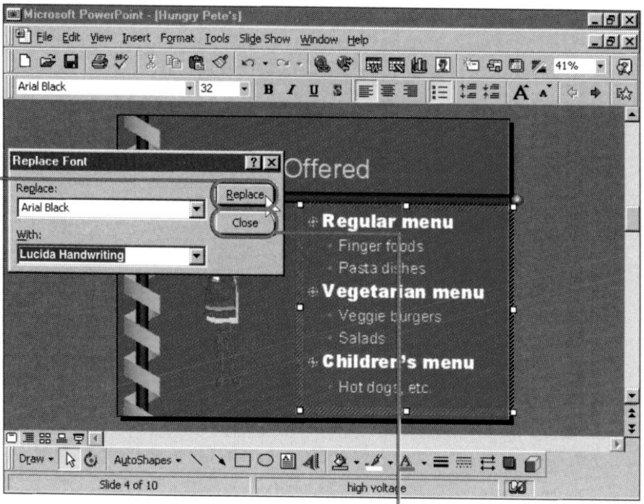

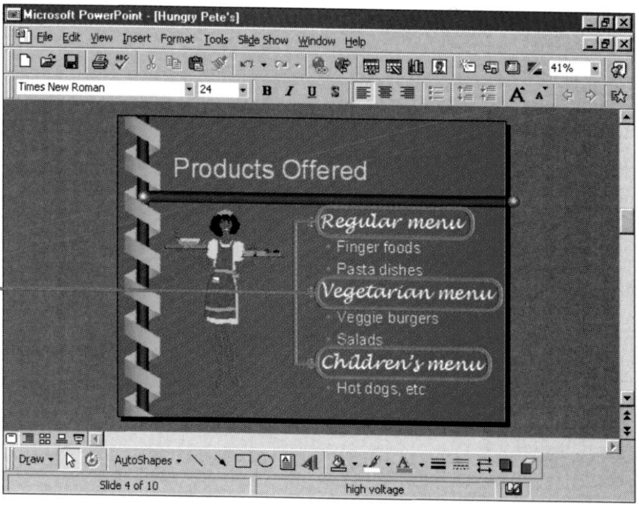

6 Click **Replace** to replace the current font with the font you selected.

7 Click **Close** to close the Replace Font dialog box.

■ The font changes throughout the presentation.

■ To deselect text, click outside the selected area.

CHANGE ALIGNMENT OF TEXT

You can enhance the appearance of a slide by aligning text in different ways.

CHANGE ALIGNMENT OF TEXT

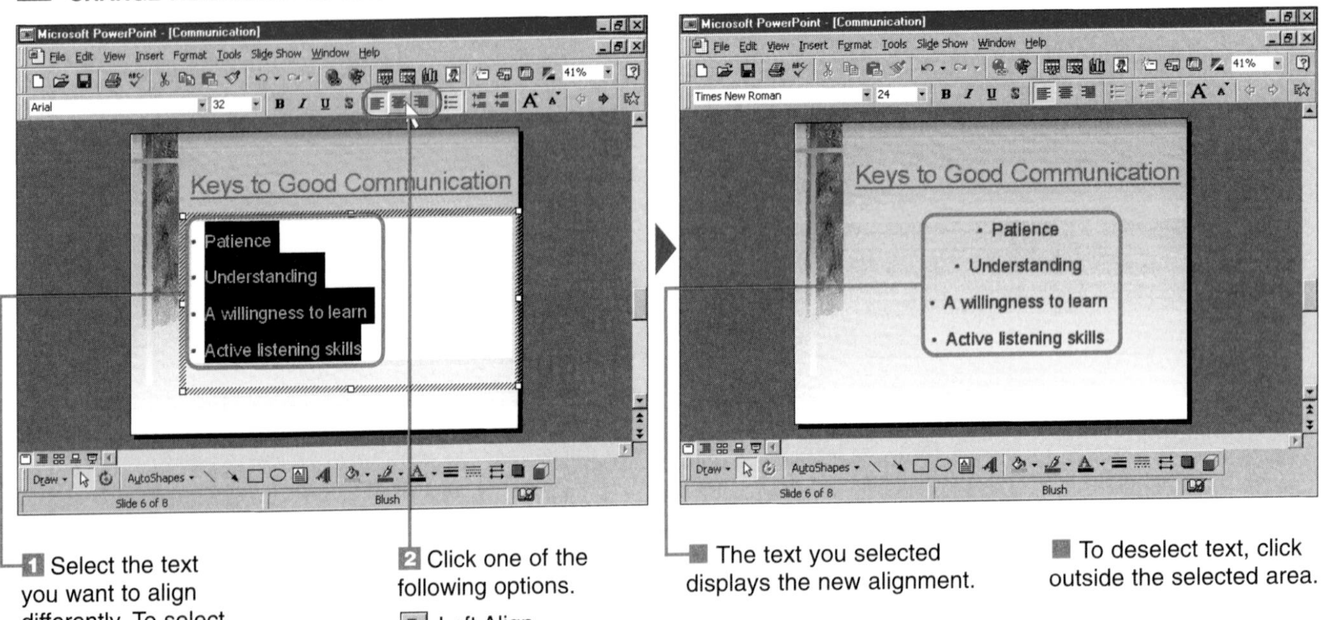

1. Select the text you want to align differently. To select text, see page 48.

2. Click one of the following options.

   Left Align

   Center

   Right Align

■ The text you selected displays the new alignment.

■ To deselect text, click outside the selected area.

CHANGE CASE OF TEXT

You can change the case of text in your presentation without having to retype the text.

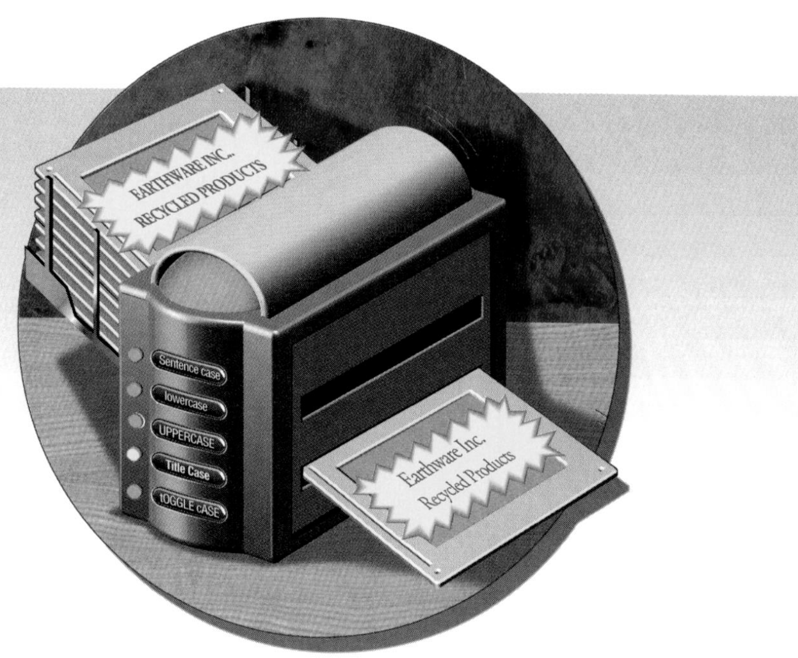

CHANGE CASE OF TEXT

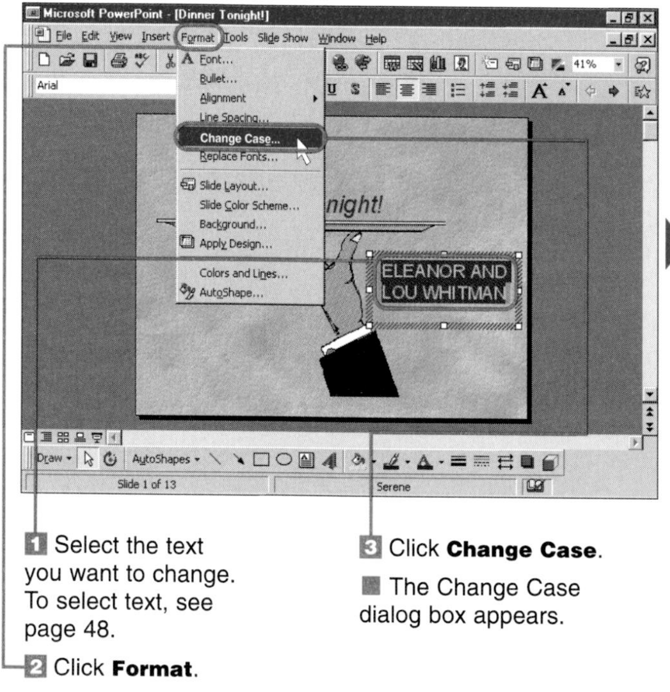

1. Select the text you want to change. To select text, see page 48.
2. Click **Format**.
3. Click **Change Case**.

■ The Change Case dialog box appears.

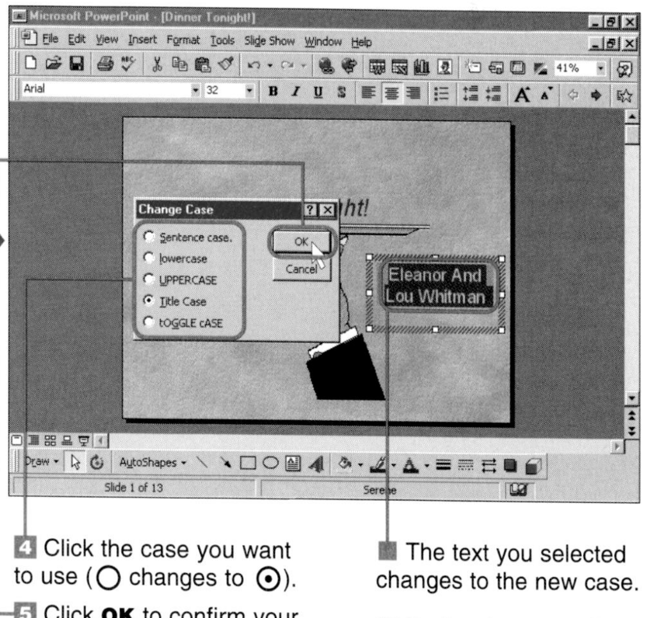

4. Click the case you want to use (○ changes to ⊙).
5. Click **OK** to confirm your change.

■ The text you selected changes to the new case.

■ To deselect text, click outside the selected area.

CHANGE BULLET CHARACTER

You can change the appearance of the bullets on a slide.

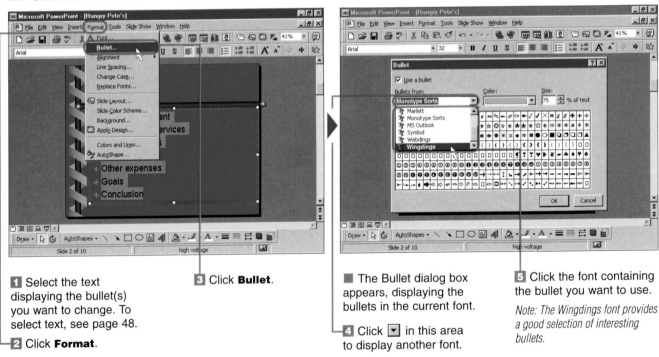

CHANGE BULLET CHARACTER

1 Select the text displaying the bullet(s) you want to change. To select text, see page 48.

2 Click **Format**.

3 Click **Bullet**.

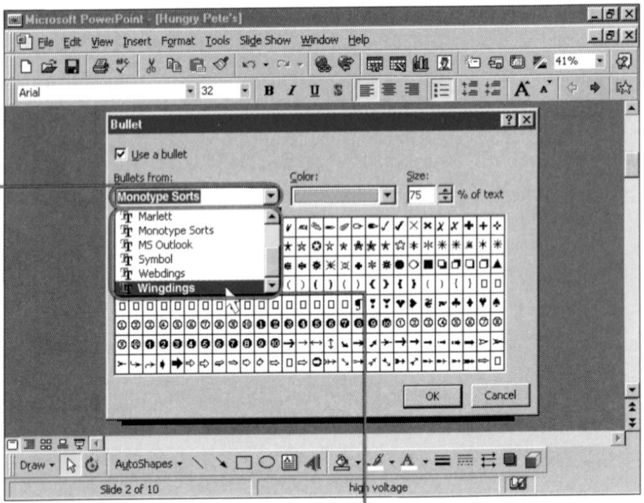

■ The Bullet dialog box appears, displaying the bullets in the current font.

4 Click ▼ in this area to display another font.

5 Click the font containing the bullet you want to use.

Note: The Wingdings font provides a good selection of interesting bullets.

?

How can I change the appearance of the bullets on all my slides at once?

You can change the appearance of the bullets on the Slide Master to change the bullets on all of your slides at once. For information on the Slide Master, see page 110.

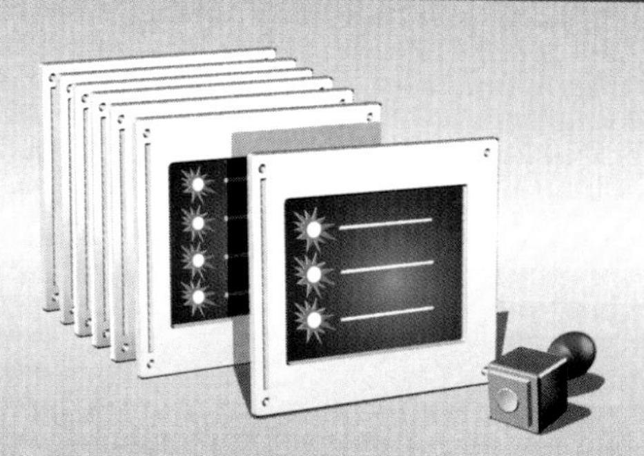

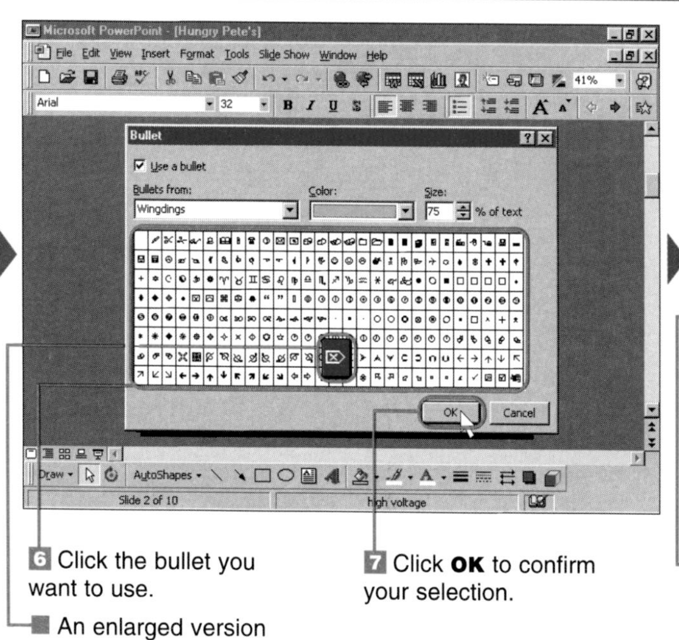

6 Click the bullet you want to use.

■ An enlarged version of the bullet appears.

7 Click **OK** to confirm your selection.

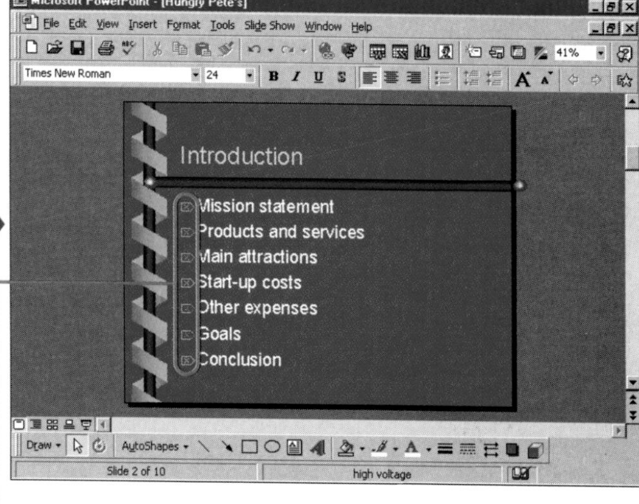

■ The text you selected displays the new bullet(s).

■ To deselect text, click outside the selected area.

REMOVE BULLETS

You can remove the bullets from text on a slide. Removing bullets is useful when a slide contains text you do not want to appear in a bulleted list, such as a quotation or a single point.

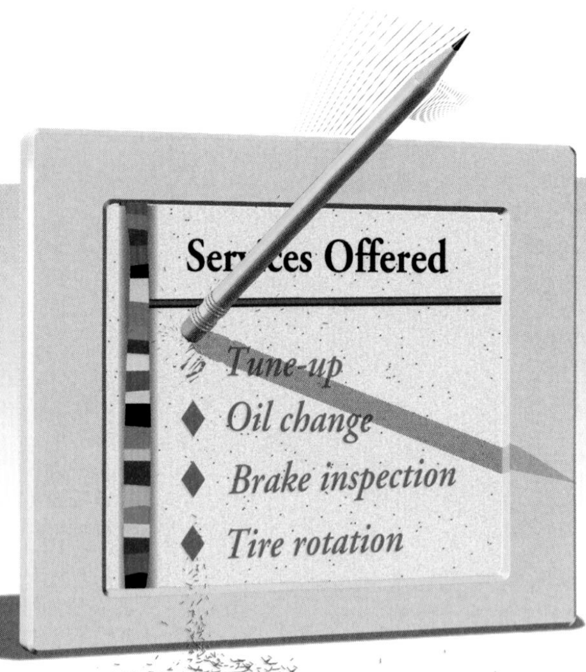

REMOVE BULLETS

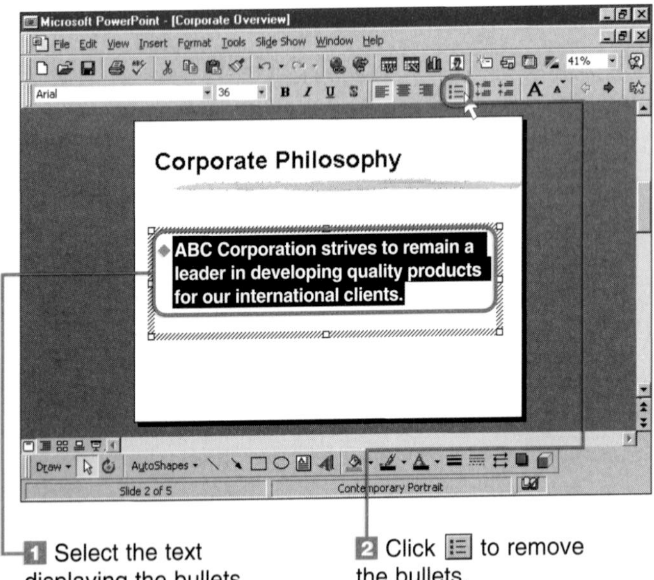

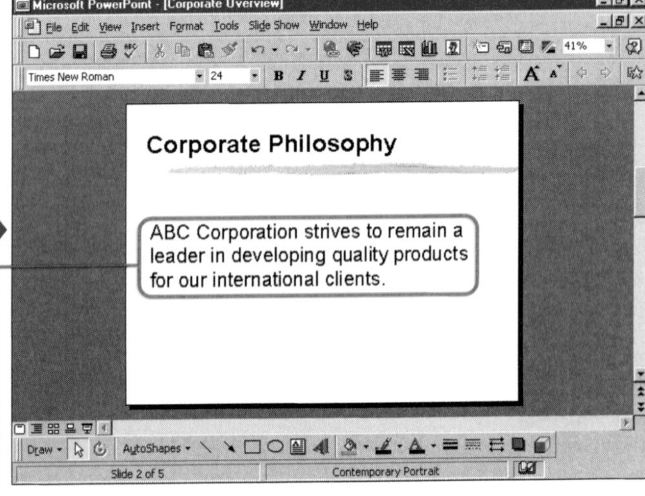

1 Select the text displaying the bullets you want to remove. To select text, see page 48.

2 Click ☰ to remove the bullets.

■ The bullets disappear.

■ To deselect text, click outside the selected area.

■ After removing the bullets, you may want to change the indentation of the text. For information on indenting text, see page 92.

■ To once again display bullets, repeat steps 1 and 2.

CHANGE LINE SPACING

You can change the amount of space between the lines of text on a slide. Changing the line spacing can help make a slide easier to read.

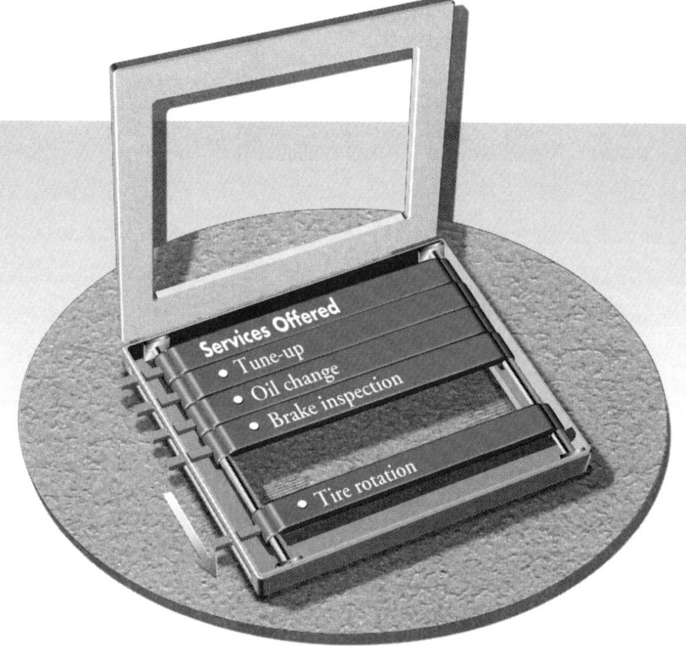

CHANGE LINE SPACING

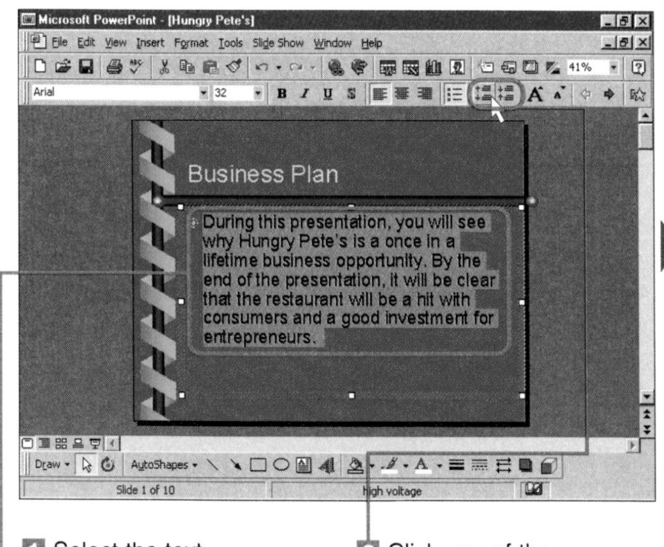

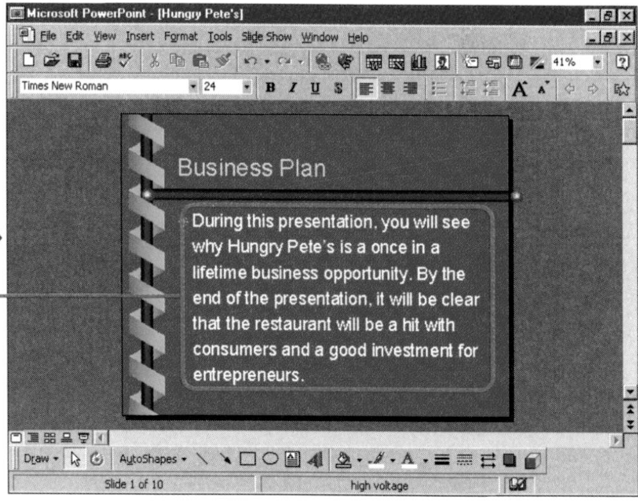

1 Select the text you want to change. To select text, see page 48.

2 Click one of the following options.

- Increase line spacing
- Decrease line spacing

Note: You can repeat step 2 until the text appears the way you want.

■ The line spacing of the text you selected changes.

■ To deselect text, click outside the selected area.

CHANGE INDENTATION OF TEXT

You can change the indentation of text to emphasize the start of a new paragraph.

Our Strategy

To become the leader in the industry by promoting the originality and high quality of our products through innovative advertising and packaging.

Indent first line

Our Strategy

To become the leader in the industry by promoting the originality and high quality of our products through innovative advertising and packaging.

Indent all but first line

CHANGE INDENTATION OF TEXT

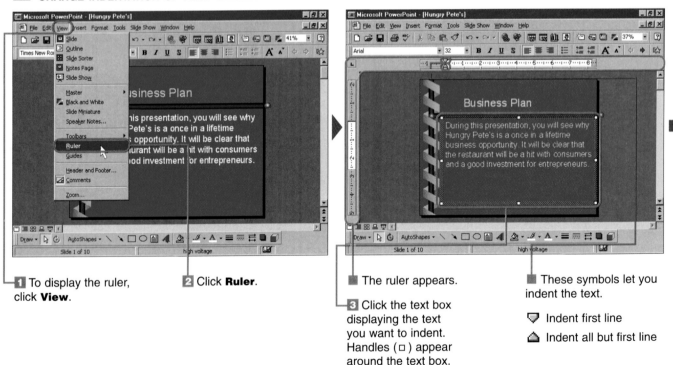

1 To display the ruler, click **View**.

2 Click **Ruler**.

■ The ruler appears.

3 Click the text box displaying the text you want to indent. Handles (□) appear around the text box.

■ These symbols let you indent the text.

▽ Indent first line

△ Indent all but first line

?

I tried to indent all the text except the first line, but it did not work properly. What is wrong?

If the text you are indenting displays bullets, all the text will indent to the same location. To indent all but the first line of the text, you must first remove the bullets. For information on removing bullets, see page 90.

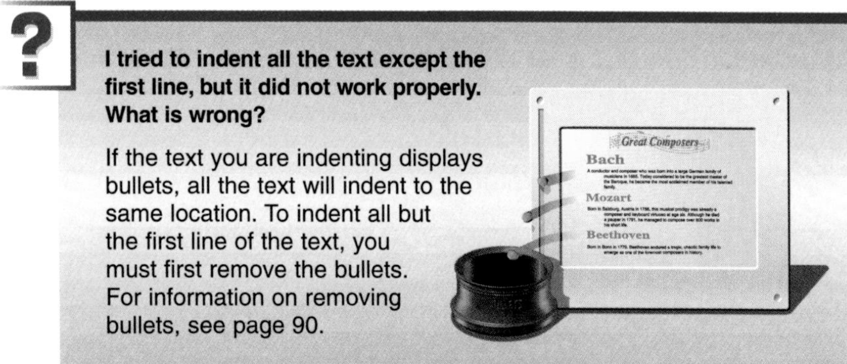

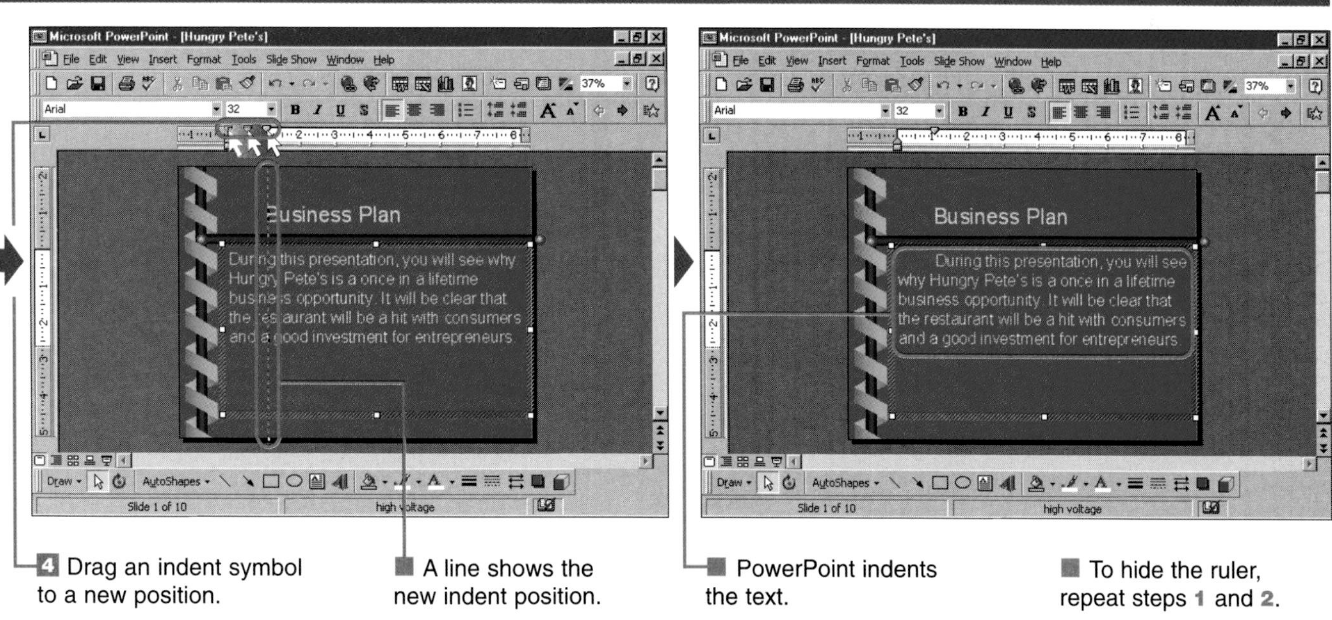

4 Drag an indent symbol to a new position.

■ A line shows the new indent position.

■ PowerPoint indents the text.

■ To hide the ruler, repeat steps 1 and 2.

ADD TABS

You can use tabs to line up columns of text on a slide. PowerPoint offers four types of tabs.

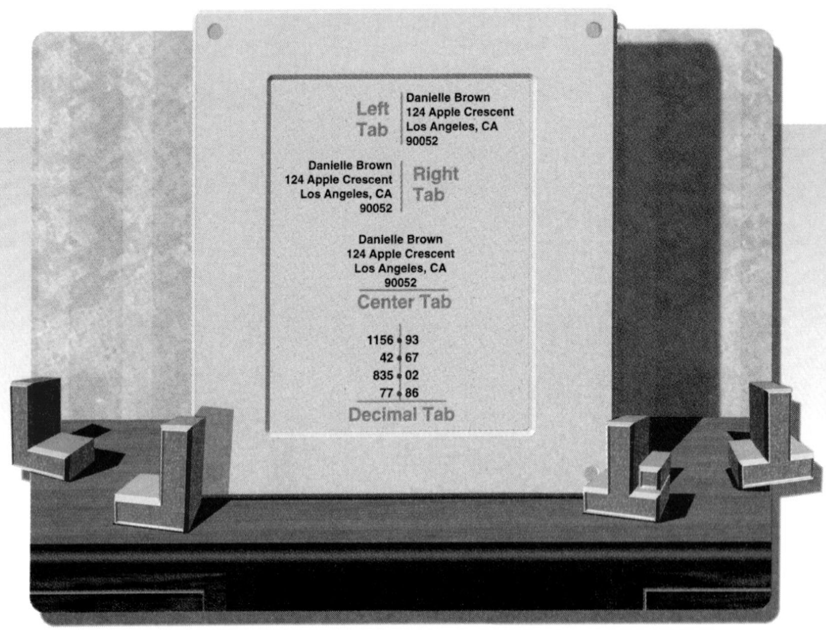

ADD TABS

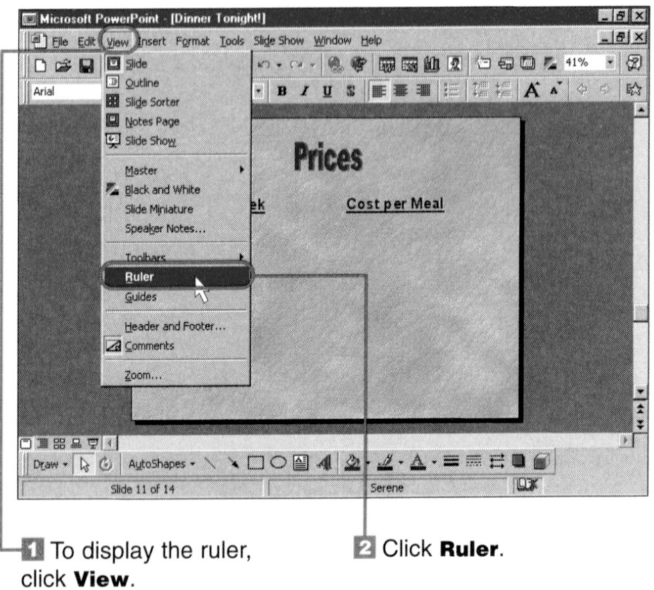

1 To display the ruler, click **View**.

2 Click **Ruler**.

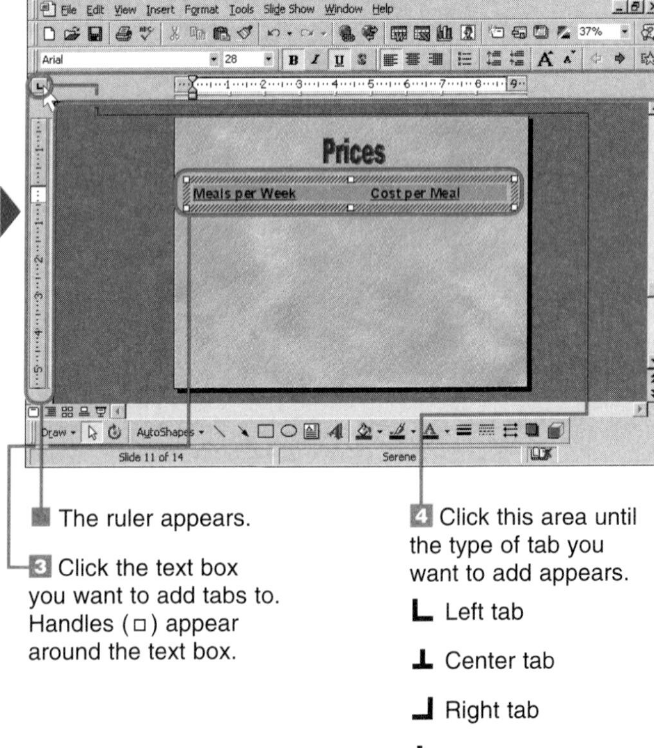

■ The ruler appears.

3 Click the text box you want to add tabs to. Handles (□) appear around the text box.

4 Click this area until the type of tab you want to add appears.

- Left tab
- Center tab
- Right tab
- Decimal tab

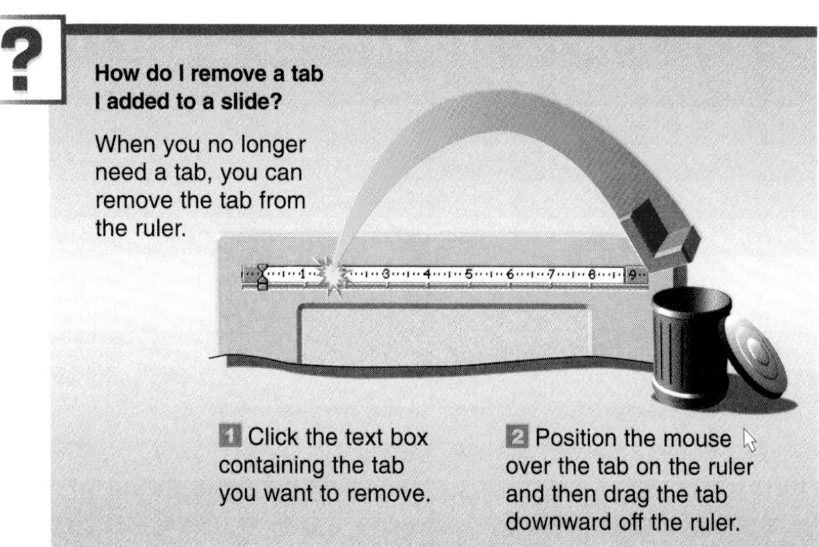

How do I remove a tab I added to a slide?

When you no longer need a tab, you can remove the tab from the ruler.

1 Click the text box containing the tab you want to remove.

2 Position the mouse over the tab on the ruler and then drag the tab downward off the ruler.

5 Click the bottom half of the ruler where you want to add the tab.

■ The tab appears on the ruler.

■ You can repeat steps 4 and 5 for each tab you want to add.

■ To hide the ruler, repeat steps 1 and 2.

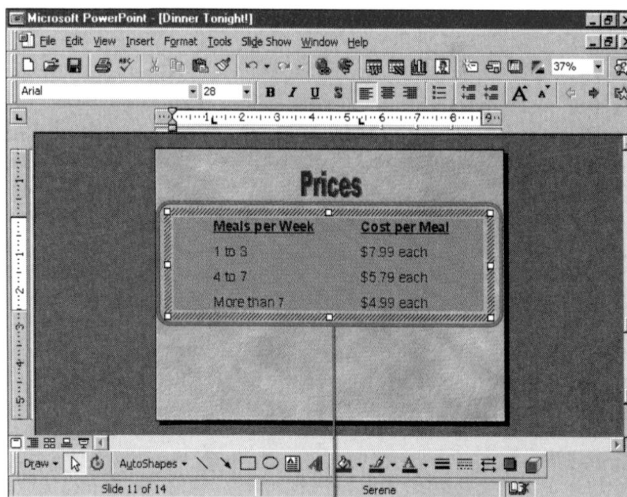

USING TABS

1 When you want to move to a tab, press the Tab key.

■ The flashing insertion point moves to the next tab.

2 Type the text you want to appear at the tab.

USING THE STYLE CHECKER

You can use the Style Checker to improve the consistency and style of your presentation.

The Style Checker also finds spelling errors in your presentation. If you want to spell check your presentation separately, see page 66.

USING THE STYLE CHECKER

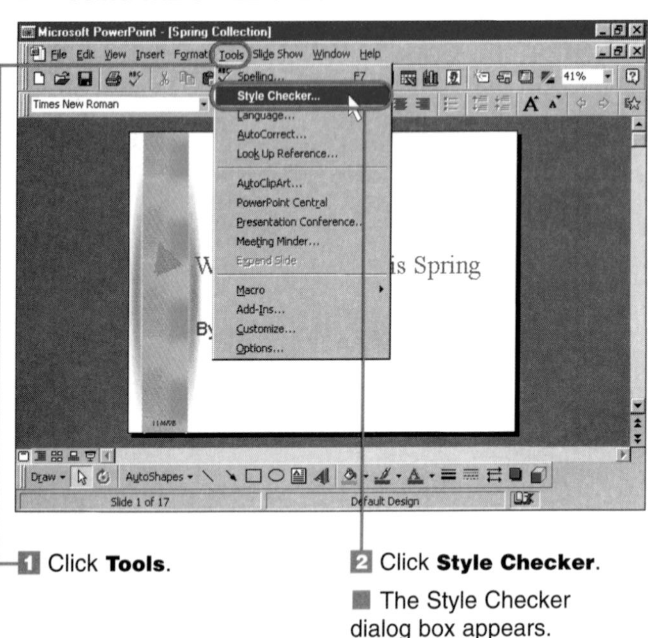

1 Click **Tools**.

2 Click **Style Checker**.

■ The Style Checker dialog box appears.

■ The Style Checker will check the spelling, visual clarity, and case and end punctuation in your presentation.

3 If you do not want the Style Checker to check an option, click the option (☑ changes to ☐).

4 Click **Start** to begin checking your presentation.

*Note: A dialog box appears if the Style Checker does not find any errors. Click **OK** to close the dialog box.*

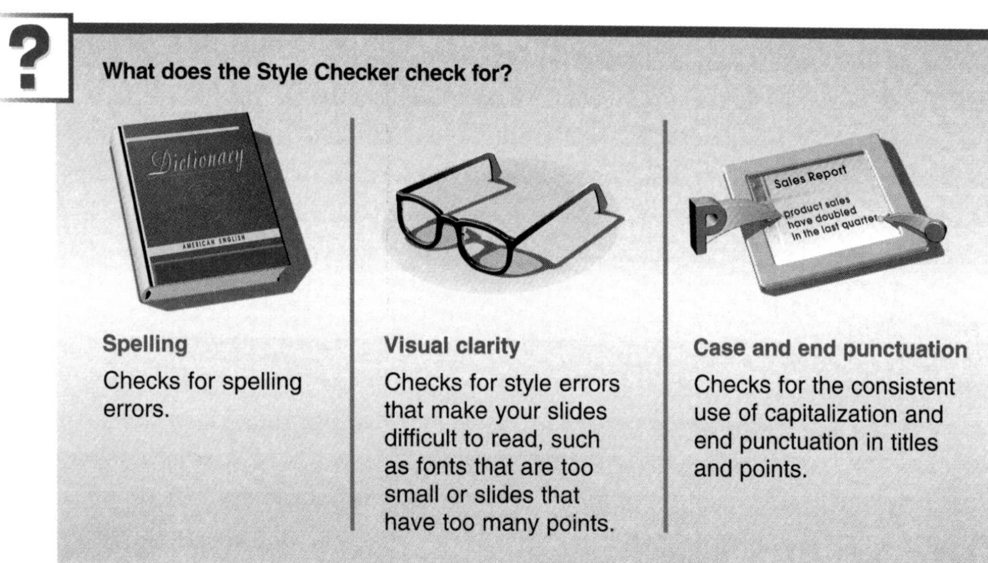

?

What does the Style Checker check for?

Spelling

Checks for spelling errors.

Visual clarity

Checks for style errors that make your slides difficult to read, such as fonts that are too small or slides that have too many points.

Case and end punctuation

Checks for the consistent use of capitalization and end punctuation in titles and points.

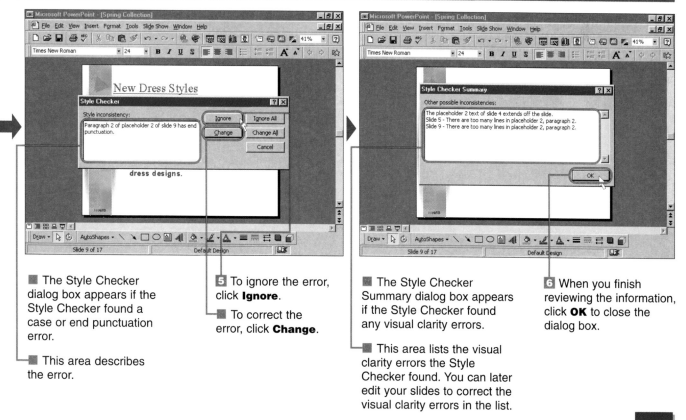

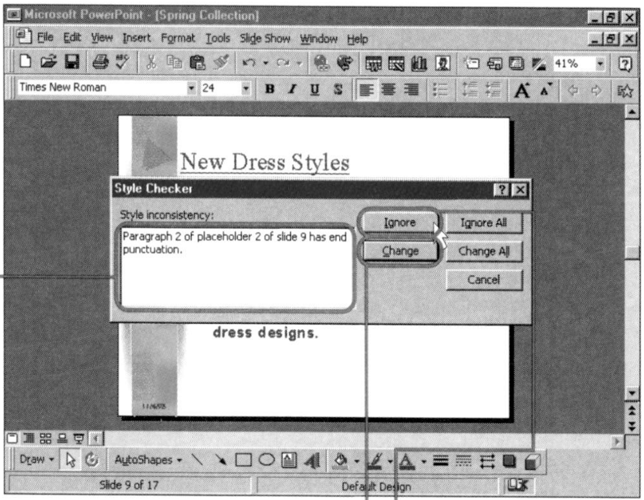

■ The Style Checker dialog box appears if the Style Checker found a case or end punctuation error.

■ This area describes the error.

5 To ignore the error, click **Ignore**.

■ To correct the error, click **Change**.

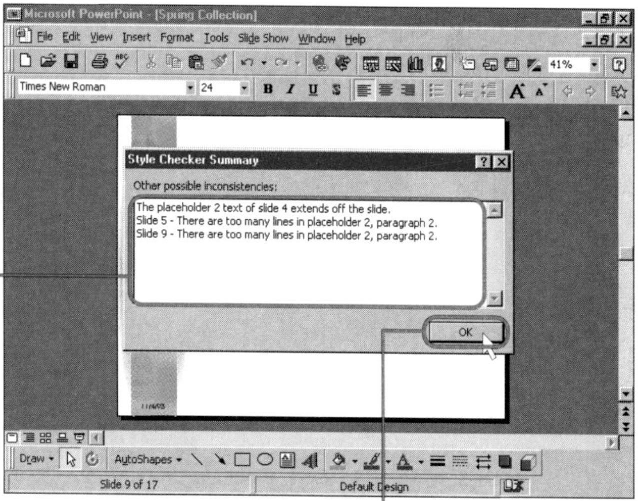

■ The Style Checker Summary dialog box appears if the Style Checker found any visual clarity errors.

■ This area lists the visual clarity errors the Style Checker found. You can later edit your slides to correct the visual clarity errors in the list.

6 When you finish reviewing the information, click **OK** to close the dialog box.

Marketing Plan
Joanne Smith
Marketing Director
Terrific Toys
Marketing Plan
Joanne Smith
Marketing Director
Terrific Toys
Marketing Plan
Joanne Smith
Marketing Director
Terrific Toys
Marketing Plan
Joanne Smith
Marketing Director
Terrific Toys
Marketing Plan
Joanne Smith
Marketing Director
Terrific Toys
Marketing Plan
Joanne Smith
Marketing Director
Terrific Toys

CHAPTER 5

Change Appearance of Slides

Are you wondering how to change the overall look of the slides in your presentation? In this chapter you will learn how to change the design, color scheme and background of your slides.

CHANGE SLIDE DESIGN

PowerPoint offers many ready-to-use designs that you can choose from to give your entire presentation a new appearance.

CHANGE SLIDE DESIGN

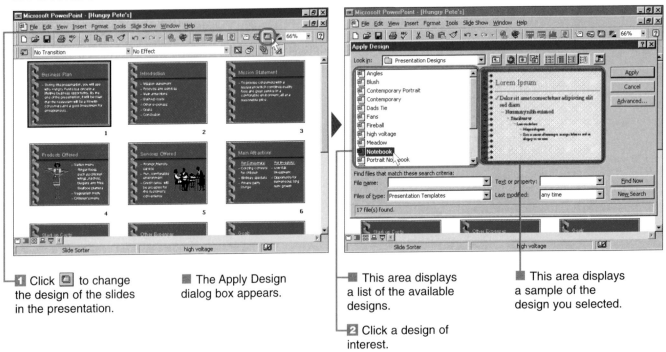

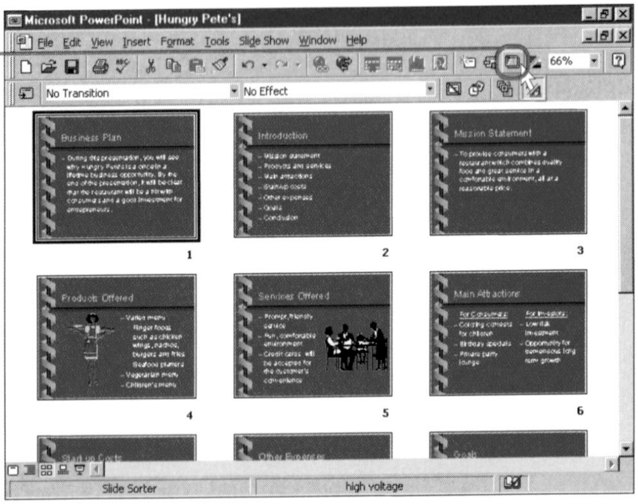

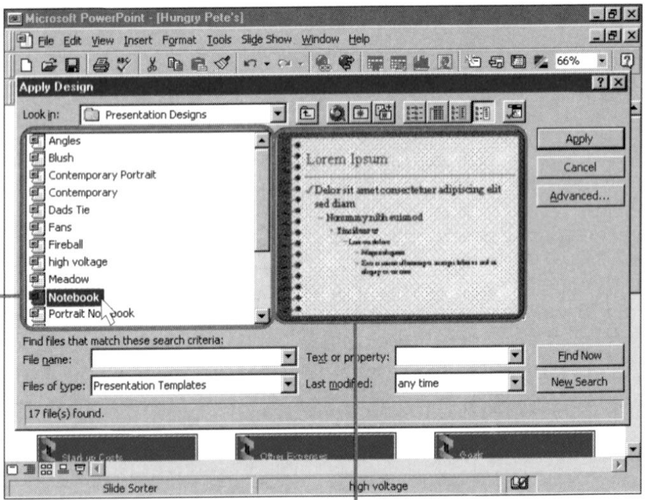

1 Click [icon] to change the design of the slides in the presentation.

■ The Apply Design dialog box appears.

■ This area displays a list of the available designs.

2 Click a design of interest.

■ This area displays a sample of the design you selected.

When I changed the slide design for my presentation, why did some parts of my slides not change?

The new slide design may not affect parts of a slide you have previously changed. For example, if you changed the color of text before changing the slide design, the text you changed will not be affected by the new slide design.

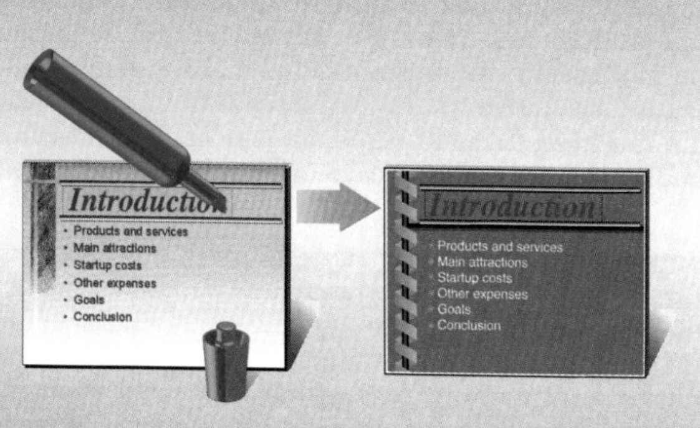

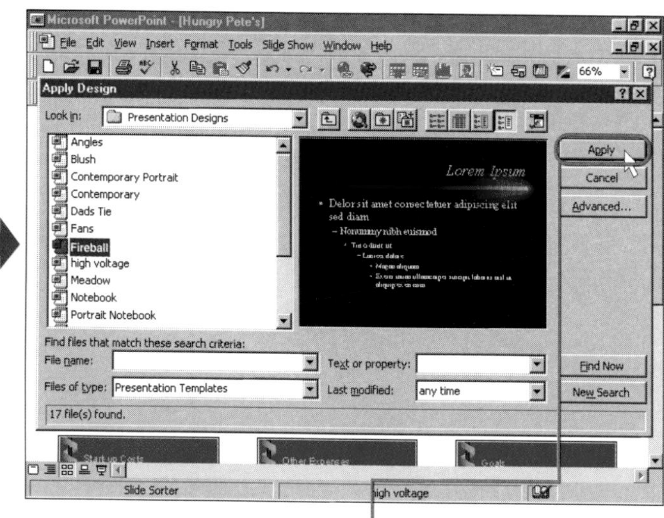

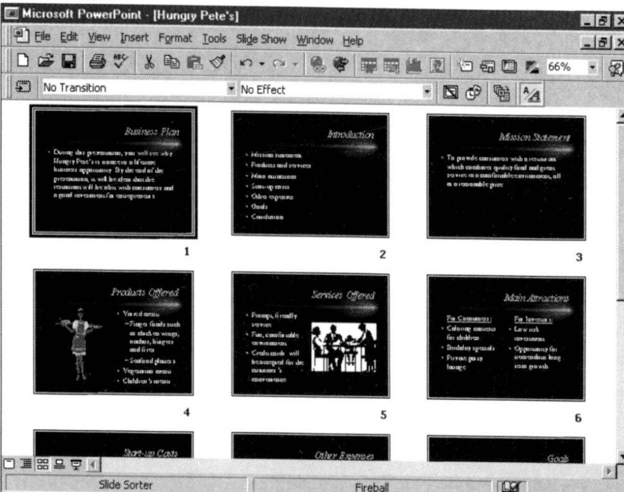

3 Repeat step 2 until the design you want to use appears.

4 Click **Apply** to apply the design to all the slides in the presentation.

■ The slides in the presentation display the new design.

CHANGE COLOR SCHEME

You can change the color scheme of your entire presentation.

If your presentation uses overheads, you should choose a color scheme with a light background for best results. If your presentation uses 35mm slides, you should choose a color scheme with a dark background.

CHANGE COLOR SCHEME

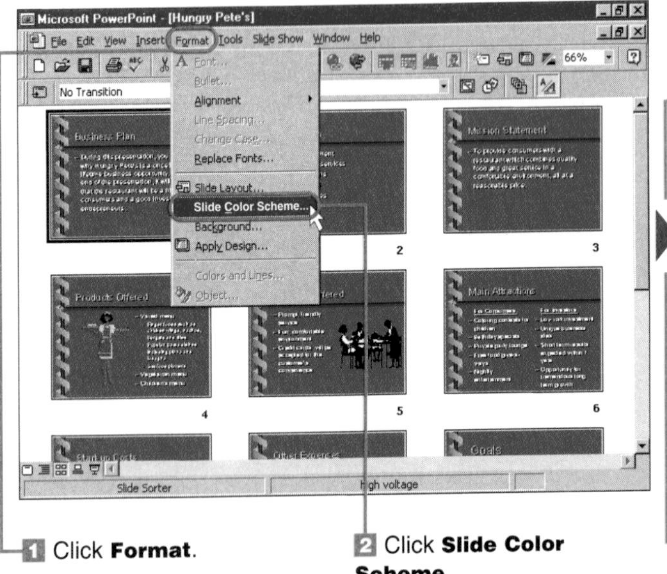

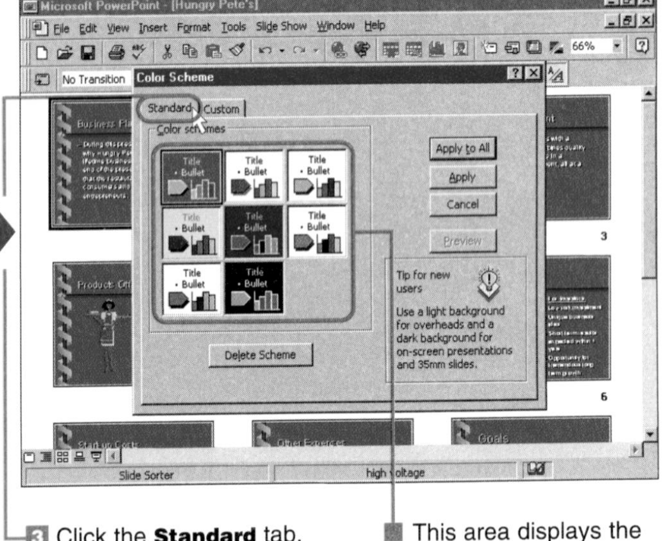

1 Click **Format**.

2 Click **Slide Color Scheme**.

■ The Color Scheme dialog box appears.

3 Click the **Standard** tab.

■ This area displays the available color schemes.

Note: The available color schemes depend on the slide design. To change the slide design, see page 100.

?

Can I use a color scheme to emphasize one slide in my presentation?

You can change the color scheme for one slide to make the slide stand out from the rest of your presentation. To change the color scheme for a single slide, display the slide you want to change in the Slide view. Then perform steps 1 to 5 below, except select **Apply** in step 5.

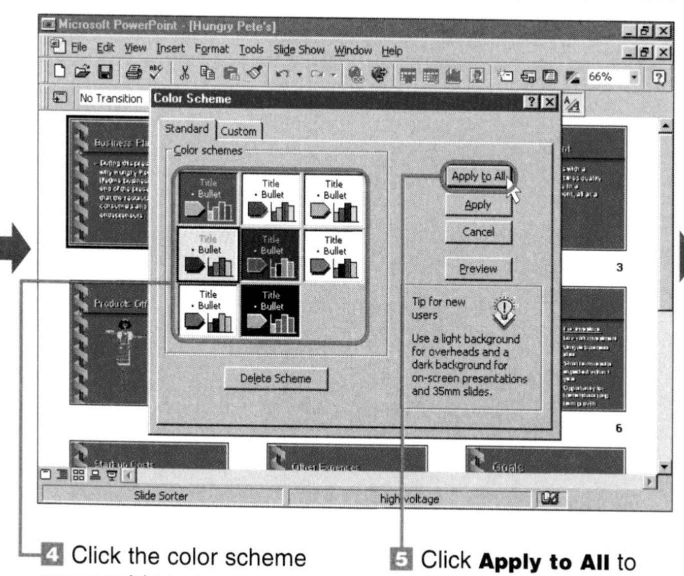

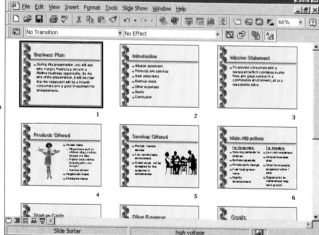

4 Click the color scheme you want to use.

5 Click **Apply to All** to apply the color scheme to all the slides in the presentation.

■ All the slides in the presentation display the new color scheme.

CHANGE SLIDE BACKGROUND

You can change the background of your slides to make your presentation more attractive.

You can select a new, solid color for the background or apply a gradient, texture or pattern to your slides.

CHANGE SLIDE BACKGROUND

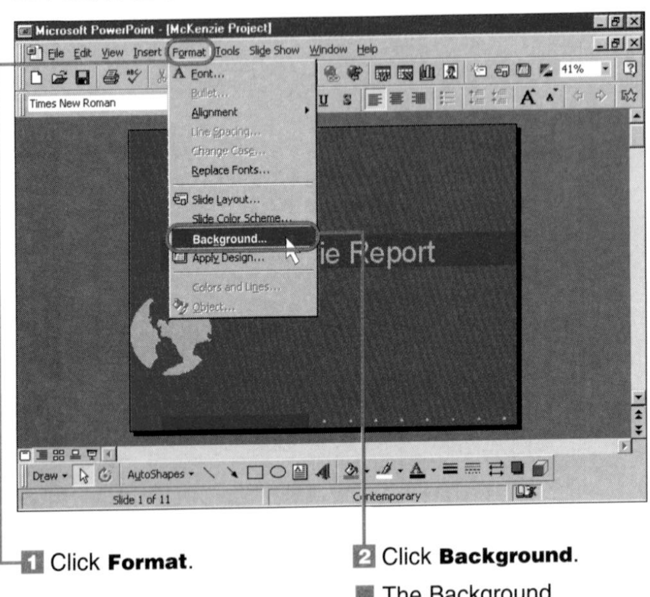

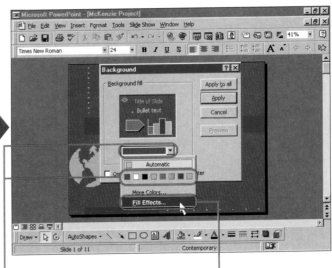

1 Click **Format**.

2 Click **Background**.

■ The Background dialog box appears.

CHANGE THE COLOR

3 Click this area to display the colors you can use for the background.

■ To select a new, solid color, click the color and then perform step 14.

4 To apply a gradient, texture or pattern to the background, click **Fill Effects**.

■ The Fill Effects dialog box appears.

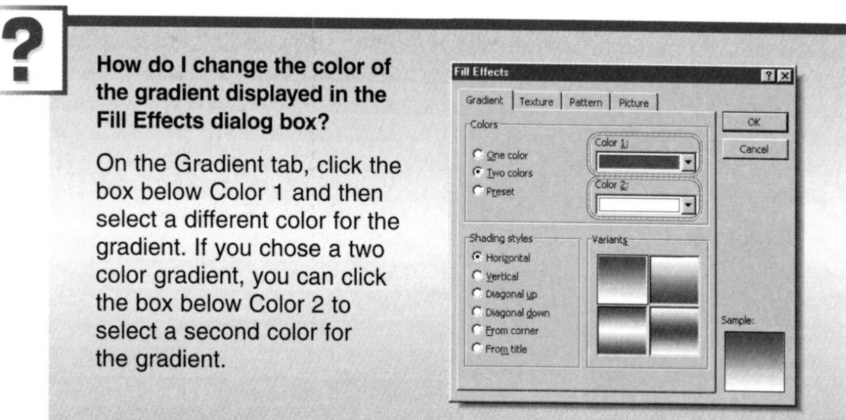

How do I change the color of the gradient displayed in the Fill Effects dialog box?

On the Gradient tab, click the box below Color 1 and then select a different color for the gradient. If you chose a two color gradient, you can click the box below Color 2 to select a second color for the gradient.

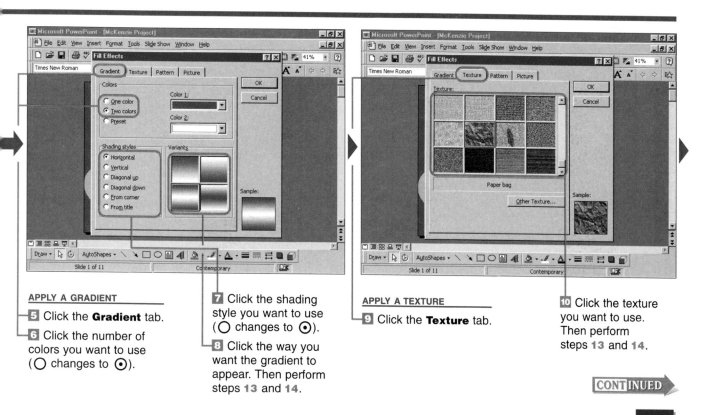

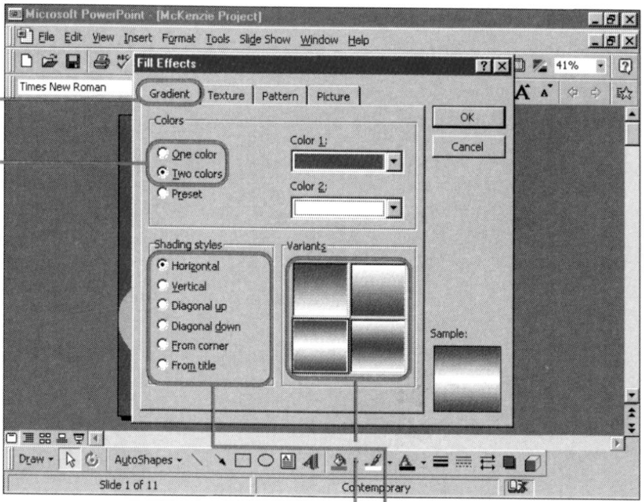

APPLY A GRADIENT

5 Click the **Gradient** tab.

6 Click the number of colors you want to use (○ changes to ⊙).

7 Click the shading style you want to use (○ changes to ⊙).

8 Click the way you want the gradient to appear. Then perform steps 13 and 14.

APPLY A TEXTURE

9 Click the **Texture** tab.

10 Click the texture you want to use. Then perform steps 13 and 14.

CONTINUED

CHANGE SLIDE BACKGROUND

After changing the slide background, you can choose to display the background on all the slides in your presentation or on a single slide.

Displaying a different background on one slide can help emphasize a slide or introduce a new part of your presentation.

CHANGE SLIDE BACKGROUND (CONTINUED)

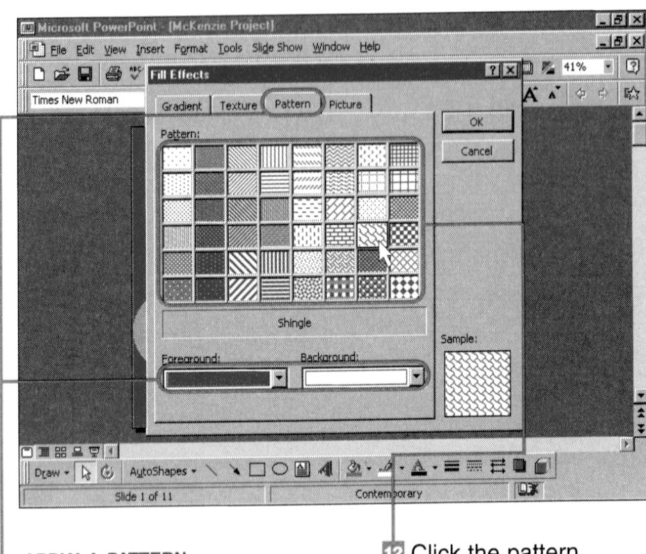

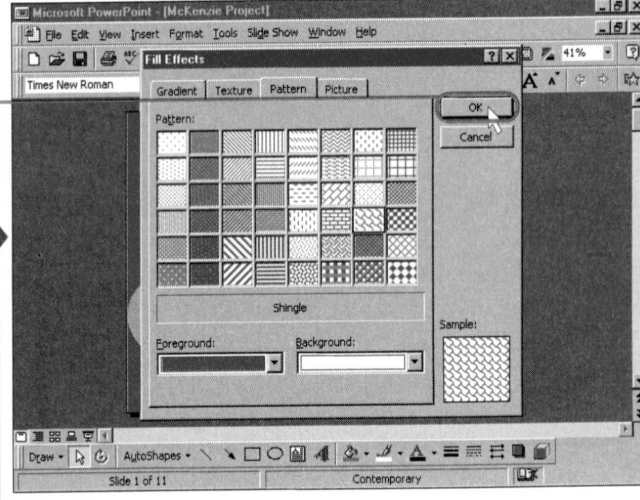

APPLY A PATTERN

11 Click the **Pattern** tab.

■ These areas display the foreground and background colors for the current patterns. You can click one of these areas to select a different color.

12 Click the pattern you want to use. Then perform steps 13 and 14.

CONFIRM CHANGES

13 Click **OK** to confirm your changes.

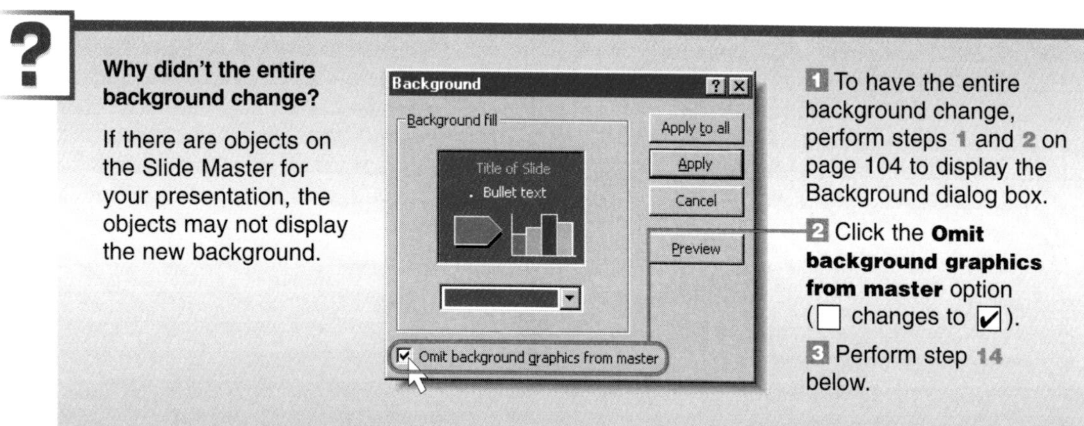

?

Why didn't the entire background change?

If there are objects on the Slide Master for your presentation, the objects may not display the new background.

1 To have the entire background change, perform steps 1 and 2 on page 104 to display the Background dialog box.

2 Click the **Omit background graphics from master** option (☐ changes to ☑).

3 Perform step 14 below.

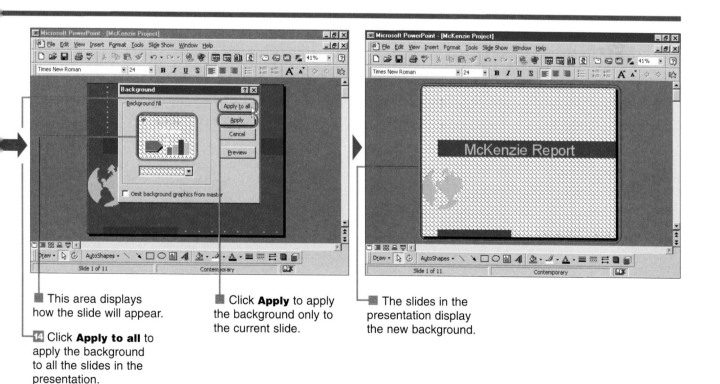

■ This area displays how the slide will appear.

14 Click **Apply to all** to apply the background to all the slides in the presentation.

■ Click **Apply** to apply the background only to the current slide.

■ The slides in the presentation display the new background.

CHANGE A HEADER OR FOOTER

You can display specific information on every slide in your presentation. This is useful when you want the audience to keep information, such as your company name, in mind as they view your presentation.

Slides can display the date and time, a slide number and footer text.

CHANGE A HEADER OR FOOTER

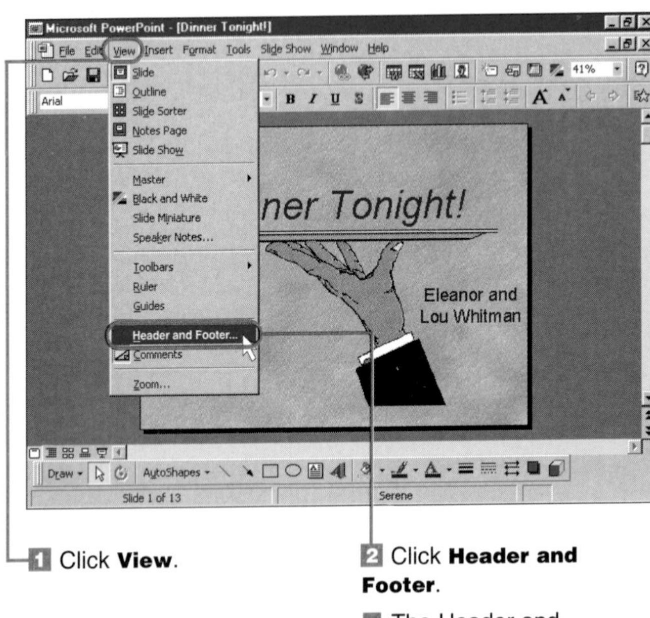

1 Click **View**.

2 Click **Header and Footer**.

■ The Header and Footer dialog box appears.

3 Click the **Slide** tab.

4 Each item that displays a check mark (✔) will appear on all the slides in the presentation. Click an item to add (☑) or remove (☐) a check mark.

5 To type the footer text you want to appear on each slide, click this area and then type the footer text.

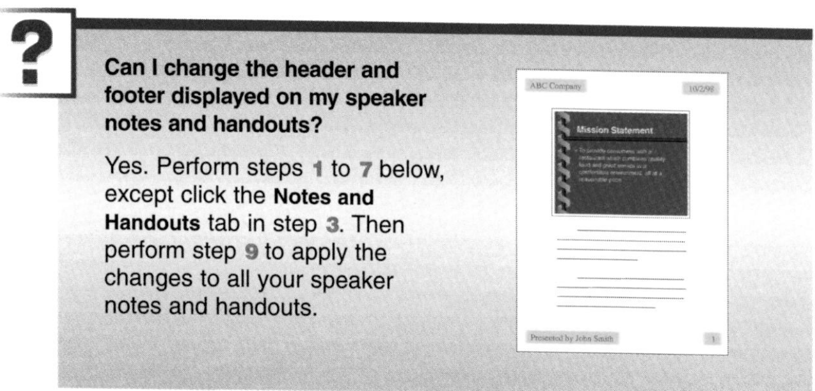

Can I change the header and footer displayed on my speaker notes and handouts?

Yes. Perform steps 1 to 7 below, except click the **Notes and Handouts** tab in step 3. Then perform step 9 to apply the changes to all your speaker notes and handouts.

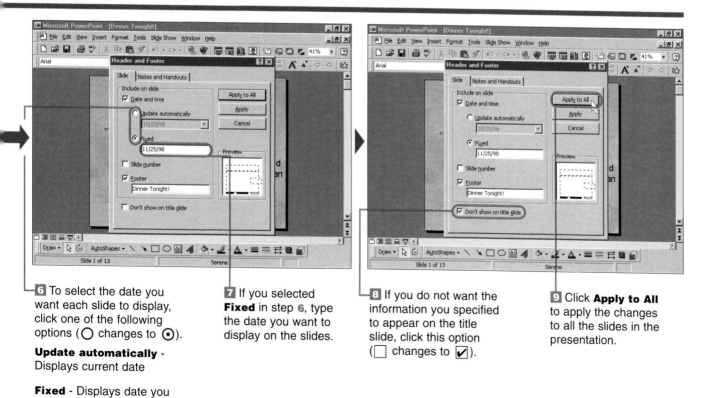

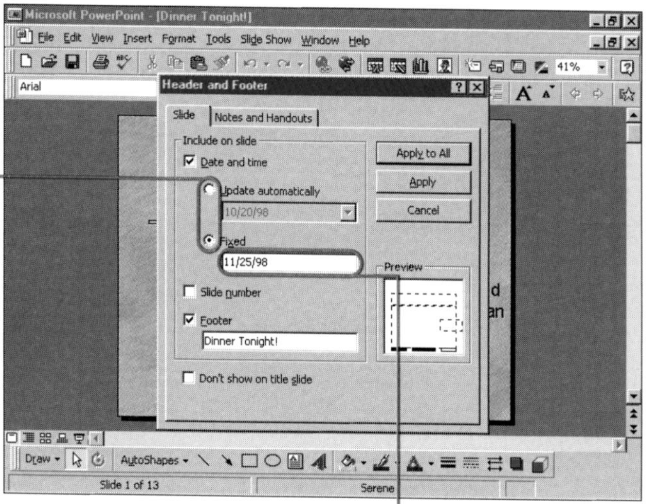

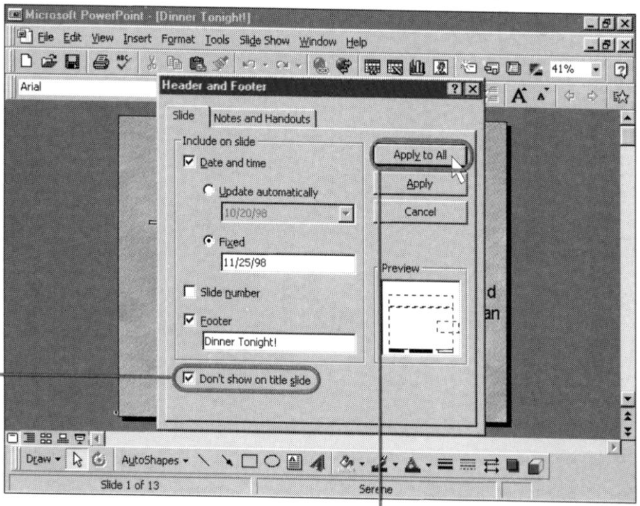

6 To select the date you want each slide to display, click one of the following options (○ changes to ⊙).

Update automatically - Displays current date

Fixed - Displays date you specify

7 If you selected **Fixed** in step 6, type the date you want to display on the slides.

8 If you do not want the information you specified to appear on the title slide, click this option (☐ changes to ☑).

9 Click **Apply to All** to apply the changes to all the slides in the presentation.

USING THE SLIDE MASTER

You can use the Slide Master to change the appearance of all the slides in your presentation at once.

USING THE SLIDE MASTER

1 Click **View**.

2 Click **Master**.

3 Click **Slide Master**.

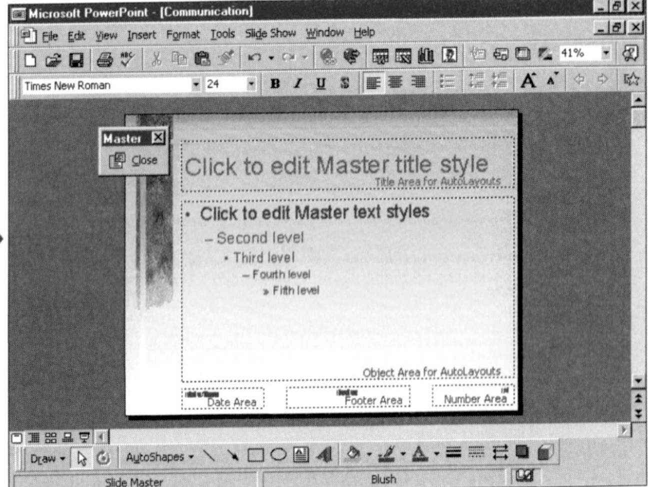

■ The Slide Master appears. Changes you make to this slide will affect all the slides in the presentation.

Note: The dotted lines that appear on the Slide Master do not appear on the slides in the presentation.

?

What changes can I make to the Slide Master?

You can change the location and size of placeholders on the Slide Master, such as the placeholder for the title. You can also change the appearance of text, such as the font and color, or add a picture, such as your company logo.

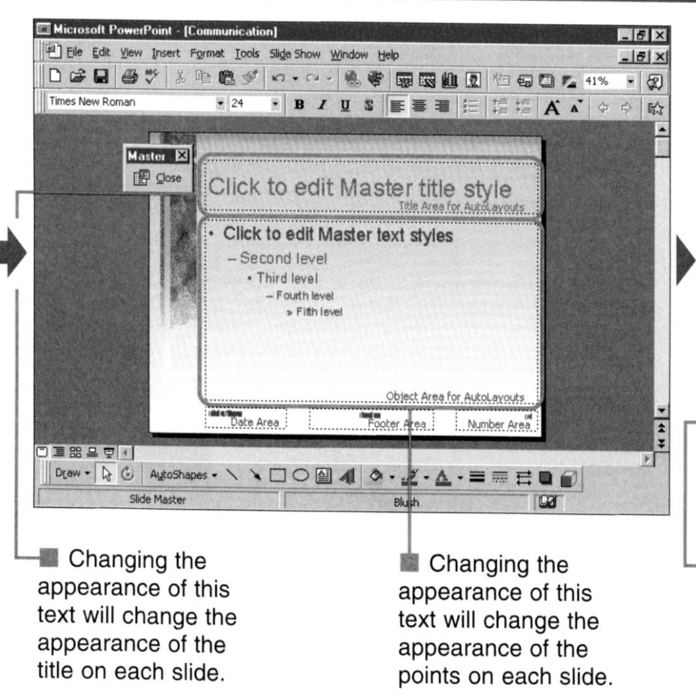

■ Changing the appearance of this text will change the appearance of the title on each slide.

■ Changing the appearance of this text will change the appearance of the points on each slide.

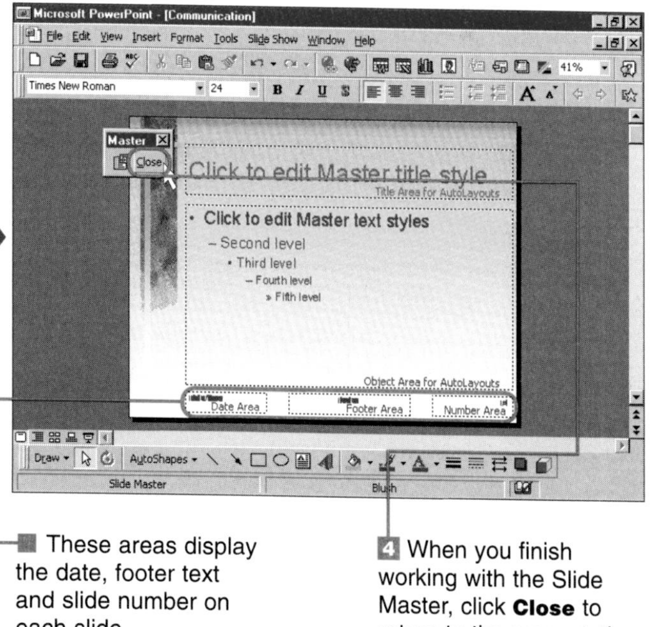

■ These areas display the date, footer text and slide number on each slide.

4 When you finish working with the Slide Master, click **Close** to return to the presentation.

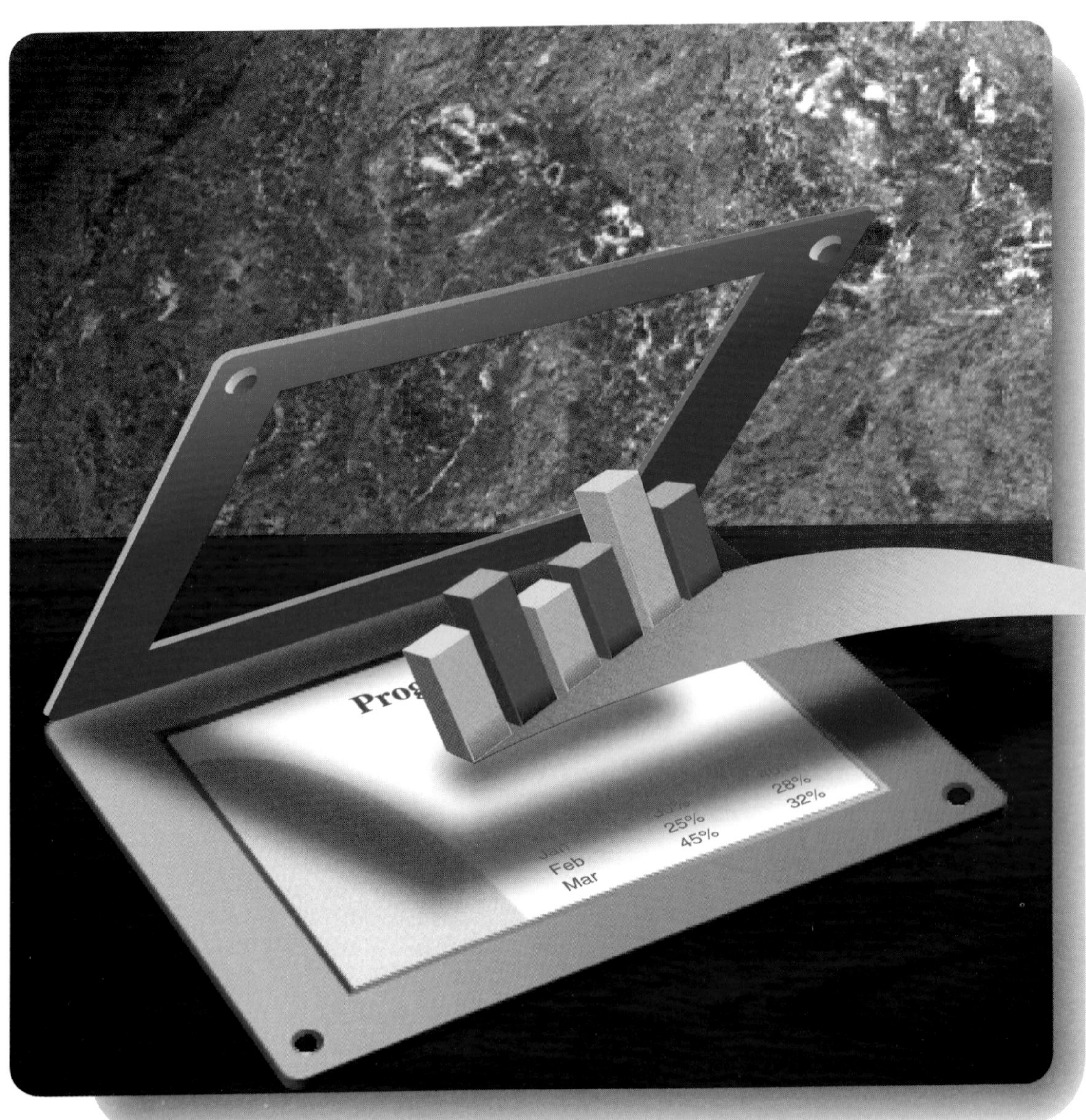
Feb
Mar
25%
45%
28%
32%

CHAPTER 6

Add Objects to Slides

Would you like to learn how to add objects to slides? This chapter shows you how to add objects such as pictures, charts and tables to your slides.

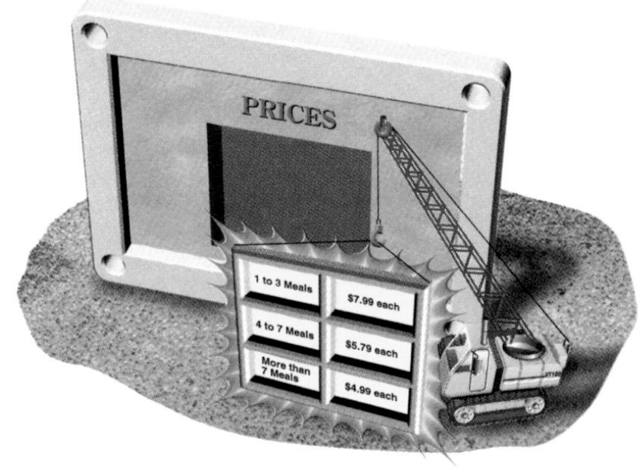

ADD AN AUTOSHAPE

You can add simple shapes such as arrows and stars to the slides in your presentation.

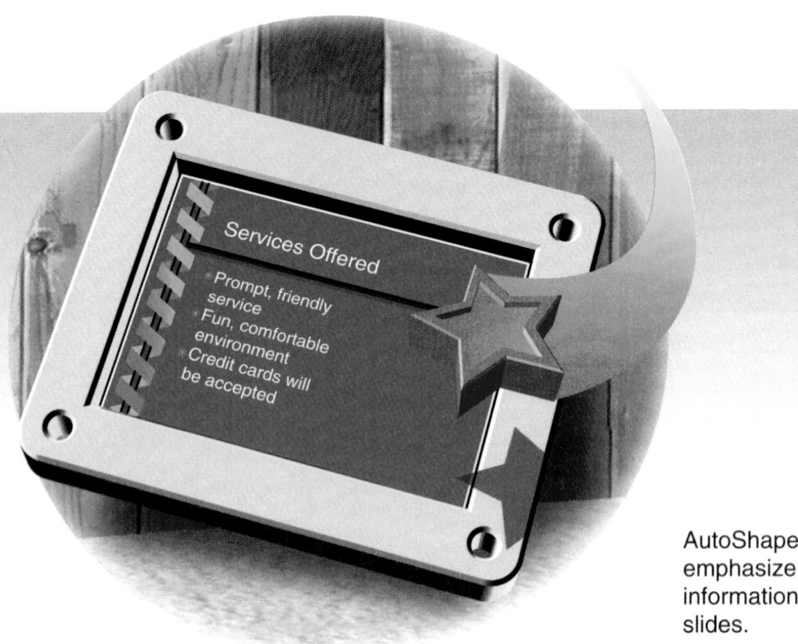

AutoShapes can help emphasize important information on your slides.

ADD AN AUTOSHAPE

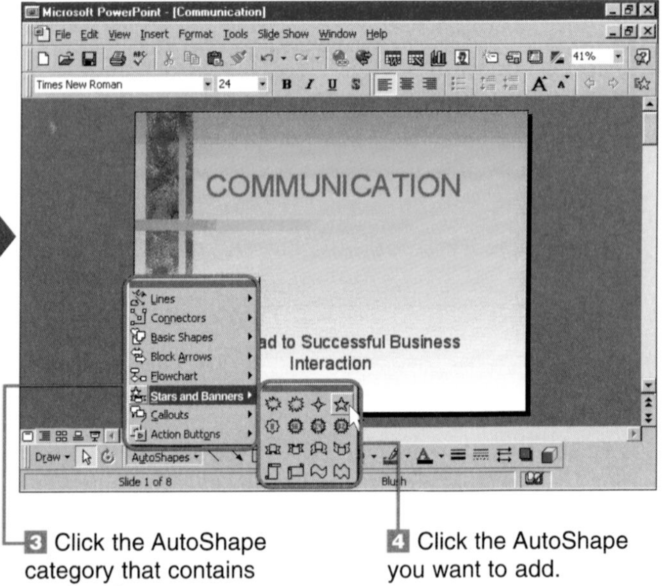

1 Display the slide you want to add an AutoShape to.

2 Click **AutoShapes**.

3 Click the AutoShape category that contains the AutoShape you want to add.

4 Click the AutoShape you want to add.

?

Can I add text to an AutoShape?

You can add text to most AutoShapes. This is particularly useful for AutoShapes such as banners. To add text to an AutoShape, click the AutoShape and then type the text you want the AutoShape to display.

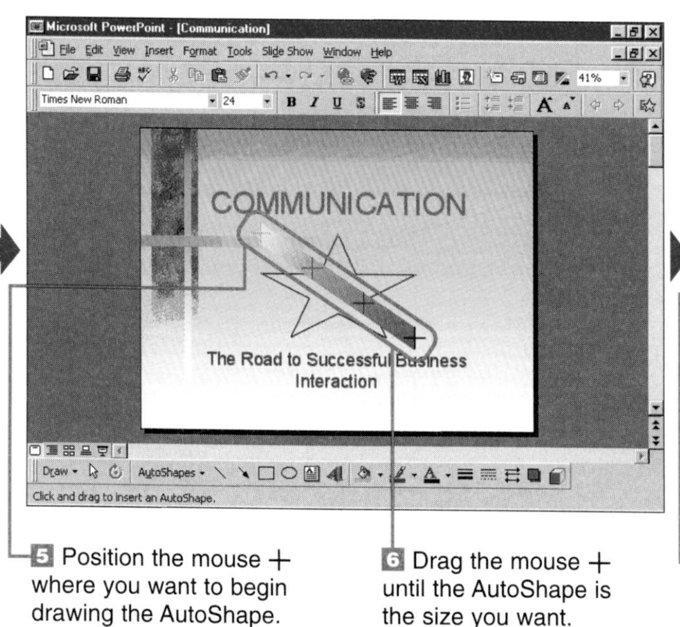

5 Position the mouse + where you want to begin drawing the AutoShape.

6 Drag the mouse + until the AutoShape is the size you want.

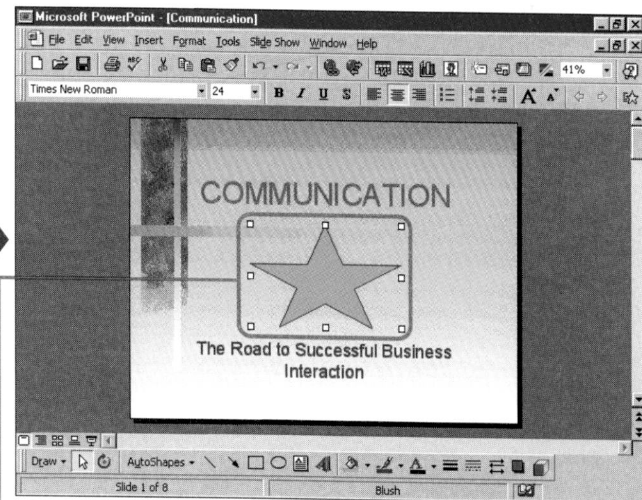

■ The AutoShape appears on the slide. The handles (□) around the AutoShape let you change the size of the shape.

7 To hide the handles, click outside the AutoShape area.

Note: To move, size or delete an AutoShape, see pages 154 to 156.

ADD A TEXT BOX

You can add a text box to a slide to include additional information in your presentation.

ADD A TEXT BOX

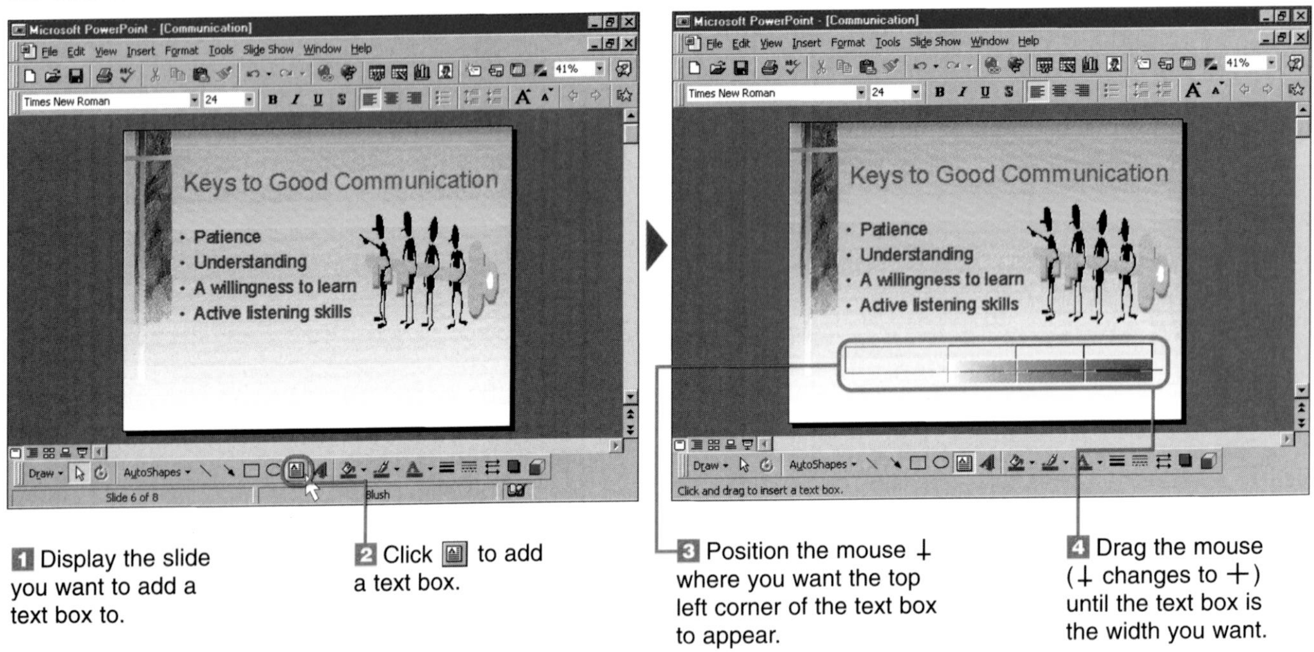

1 Display the slide you want to add a text box to.

2 Click ▤ to add a text box.

3 Position the mouse ⊥ where you want the top left corner of the text box to appear.

4 Drag the mouse (⊥ changes to +) until the text box is the width you want.

?

Why does the text in the text box I added not appear in the Outline view?

Text in a text box you added will not appear in the Outline view. To have text appear in the Outline view, you must enter the text in a text placeholder. To change the layout of a slide to one that includes a placeholder for text, see page 38.

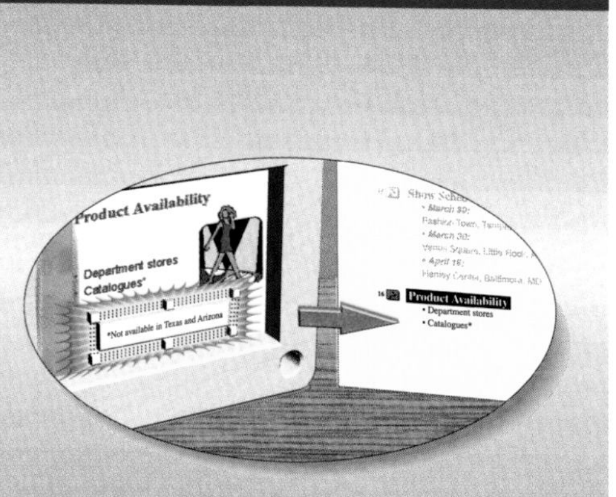

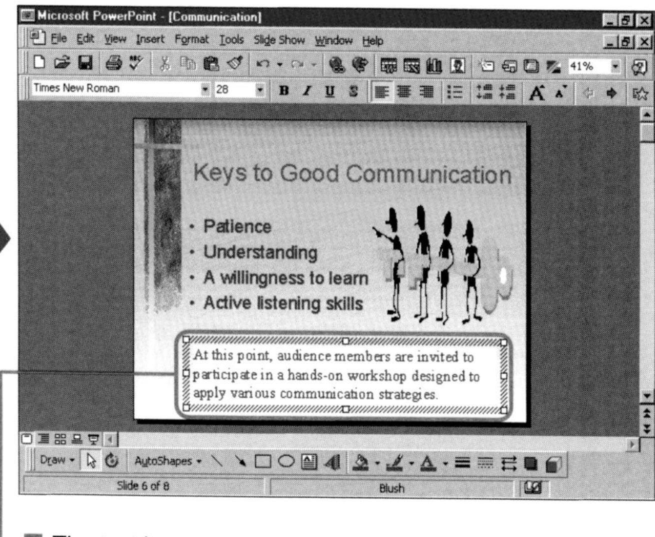

■ The text box appears on the slide.

5 Type the text you want to appear in the text box.

Note: PowerPoint automatically adjusts the height of the text box to accommodate the text you type.

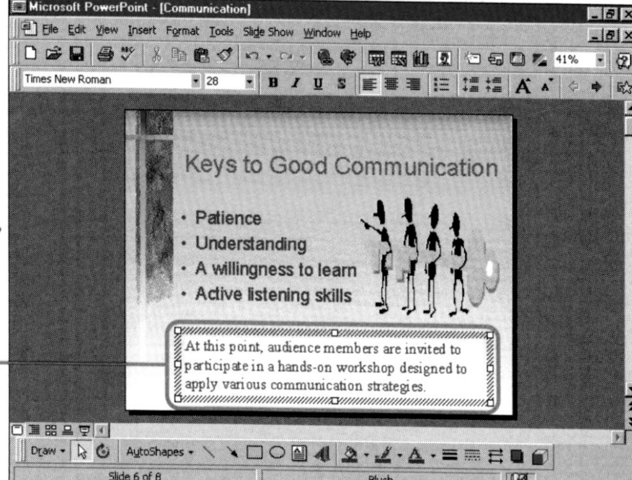

■ The handles (□) around the text box let you change the size of the text box.

6 To hide the handles, click outside the text box area.

Note: To move, size or delete a text box, see pages 154 to 156.

■ To later edit the text, click the text box and then edit the text as you would any text.

ADD A TEXT EFFECT

You can add a text effect to a slide in your presentation. Text effects can enhance the appearance of a title or draw attention to an important point.

ADD A TEXT EFFECT

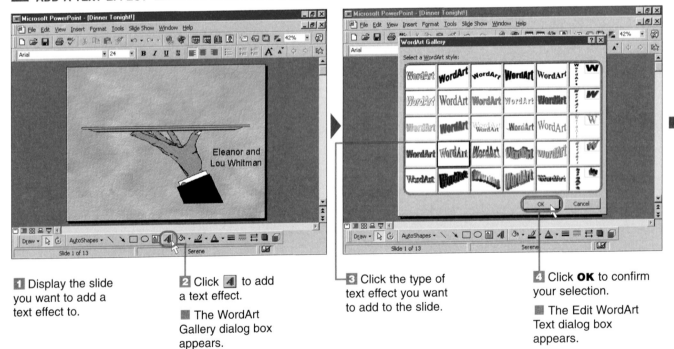

1 Display the slide you want to add a text effect to.

2 Click [WordArt button] to add a text effect.

■ The WordArt Gallery dialog box appears.

3 Click the type of text effect you want to add to the slide.

4 Click **OK** to confirm your selection.

■ The Edit WordArt Text dialog box appears.

?

How do I edit a text effect?

Double-click the text effect to display the Edit WordArt Text dialog box. Then edit the text in the dialog box. When you are finished editing the text effect, click **OK** to display the changes on the slide.

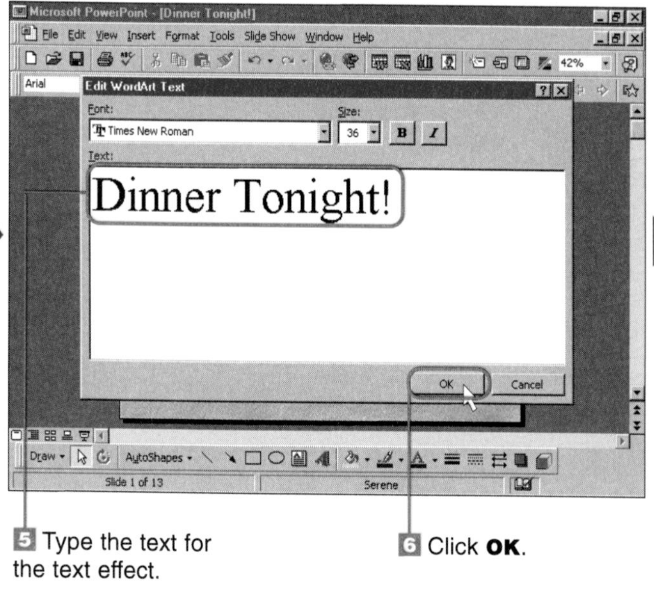

5 Type the text for the text effect.

6 Click **OK**.

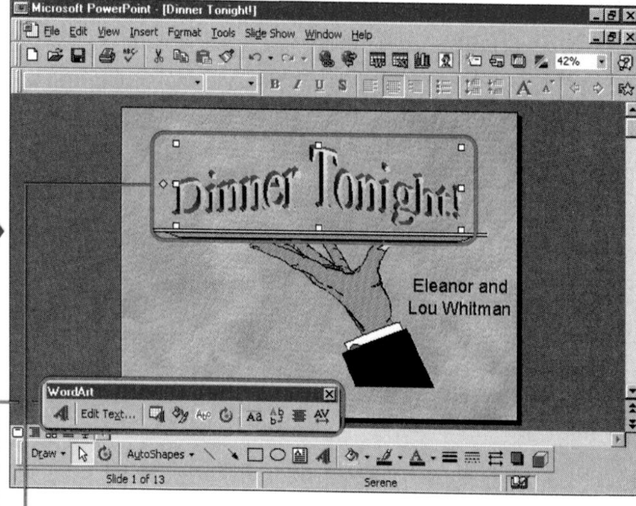

■ The text effect appears on the slide. The handles (□) around the text effect let you change the size of the text effect.

■ The WordArt toolbar also appears, providing tools to help you work with the text effect.

7 To hide the handles and the WordArt toolbar, click outside the text effect area.

Note: To move, size or delete a text effect, see pages 154 to 156.

ADD CLIP ART

You can add a clip art image to a slide to make your presentation more interesting and entertaining.

PowerPoint provides thousands of clip art images that you can choose from.

ADD CLIP ART

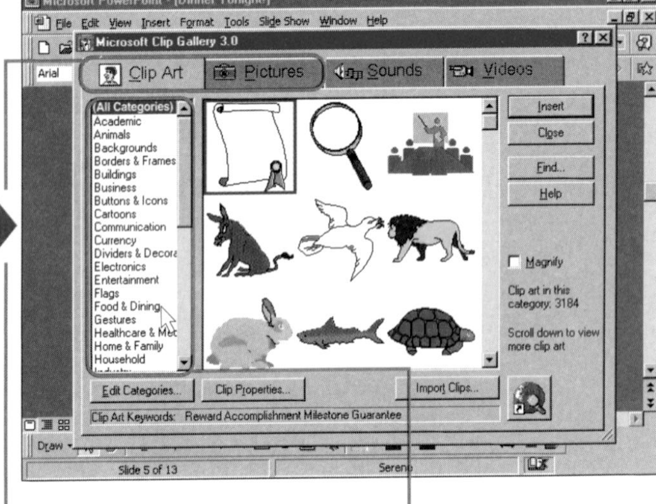

1 Insert the CD-ROM disc you used to install PowerPoint into your CD-ROM drive.

Note: If a window appears for the CD-ROM disc, click ☒ to close the window.

2 Display the slide you want to add a clip art image to.

3 Change the layout of the slide to one that includes a placeholder for a clip art image. See page 38.

4 Double-click the clip art area.

■ The Microsoft Clip Gallery dialog box appears.

5 Click the **Clip Art** or **Pictures** tab.

6 Click the category of images you want to display.

Can I add a clip art image without changing the slide layout?

Yes. Insert the CD-ROM disc you used to install PowerPoint into your CD-ROM drive. Then click [icon] and perform steps 5 to 9 below to add a clip art image.

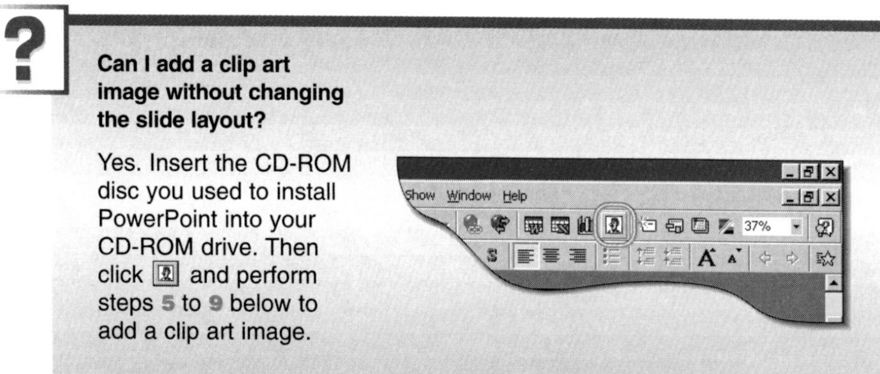

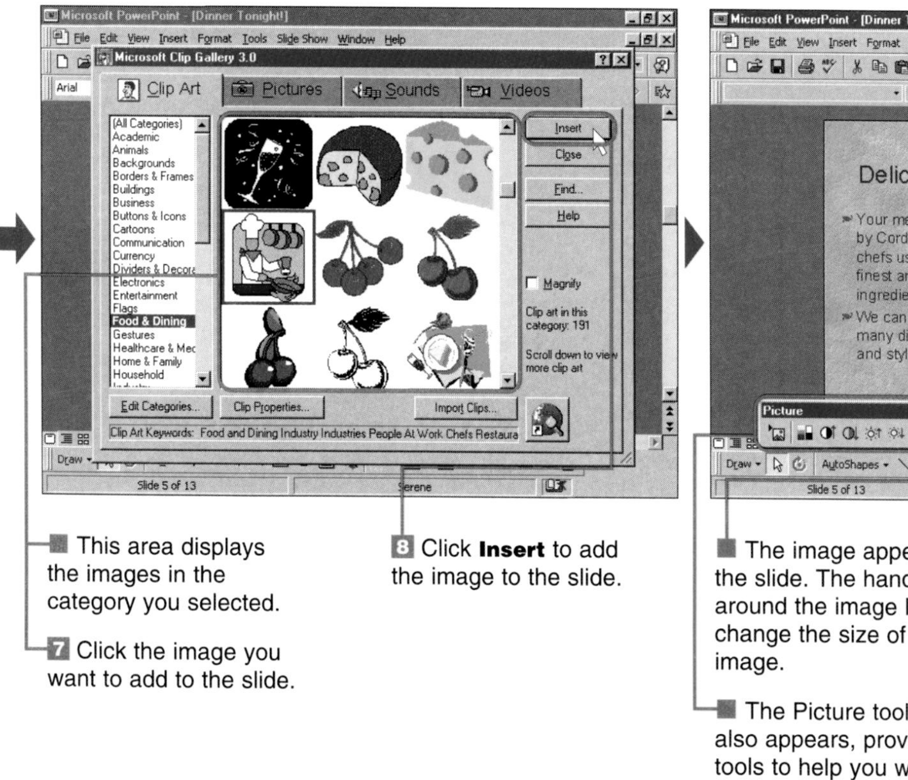

■ This area displays the images in the category you selected.

7 Click the image you want to add to the slide.

8 Click **Insert** to add the image to the slide.

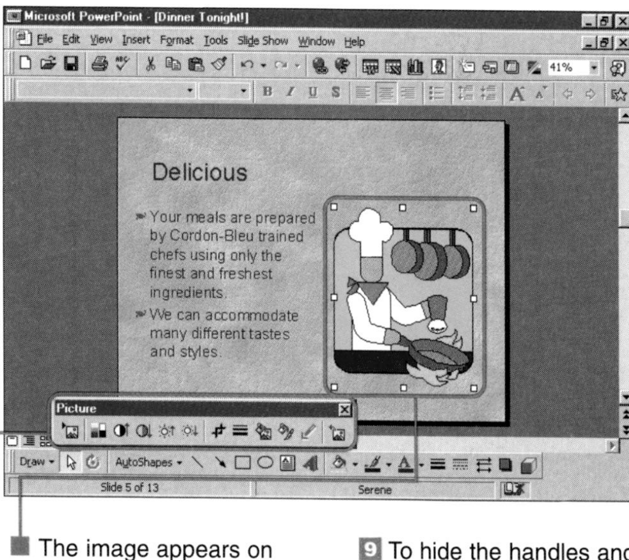

■ The image appears on the slide. The handles (□) around the image let you change the size of the image.

■ The Picture toolbar also appears, providing tools to help you work with the image.

9 To hide the handles and the Picture toolbar, click outside the image area.

Note: To move, size or delete an image, see pages 154 to 156.

USING AUTOCLIPART

You can have PowerPoint find appropriate clip art images for the slides in your presentation.

USING AUTOCLIPART

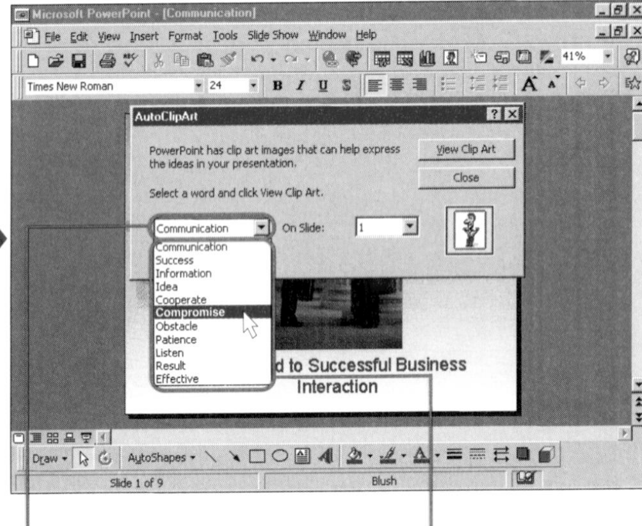

1 Insert the CD-ROM disc you used to install PowerPoint into your CD-ROM drive.

Note: If a window appears for the CD-ROM disc, click ☒ to close the window.

2 Click **Tools**.

3 Click **AutoClipArt**.

■ PowerPoint scans the presentation for keywords and then displays the AutoClipArt dialog box.

4 Click this area to display a list of keywords that PowerPoint found in the presentation.

5 Click the keyword you want to illustrate with a clip art image.

How does PowerPoint find appropriate clip art images for my slides?

PowerPoint compares keywords in your presentation to keywords associated with the clip art images in the Microsoft Clip Gallery. For example, the keywords **timeline**, **schedule** and **wait** are associated with the clock clip art image. If one of these keywords appears in your presentation, PowerPoint will suggest the clock clip art image.

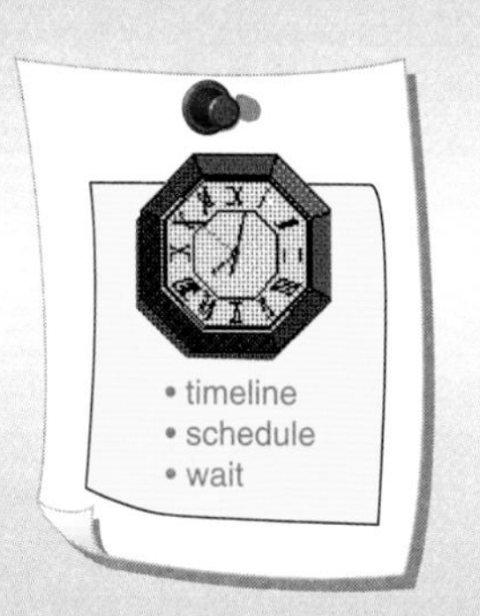

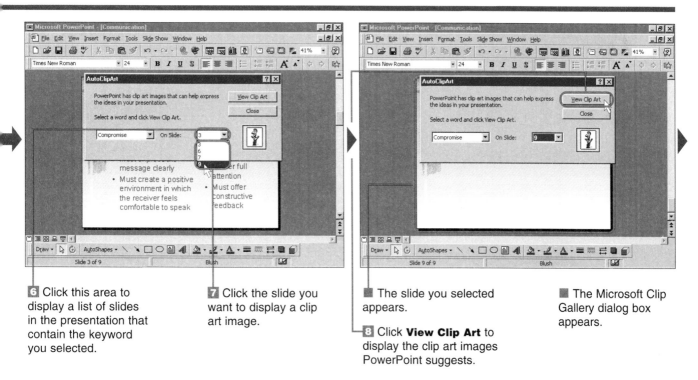

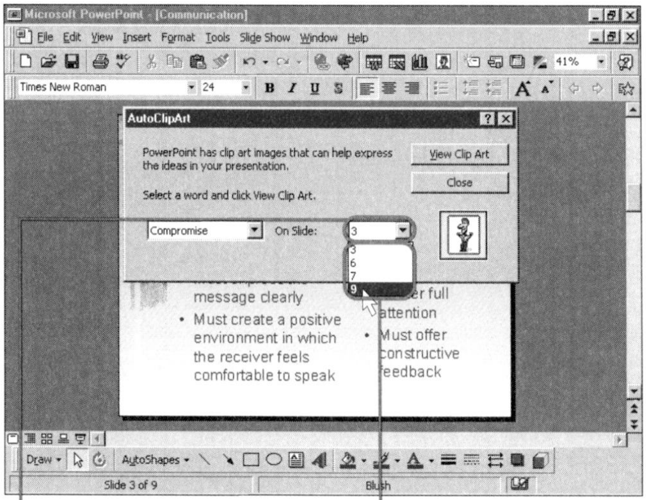

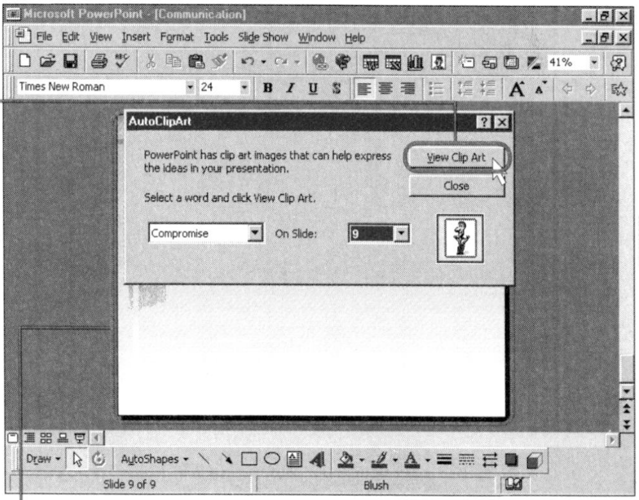

6 Click this area to display a list of slides in the presentation that contain the keyword you selected.

7 Click the slide you want to display a clip art image.

■ The slide you selected appears.

8 Click **View Clip Art** to display the clip art images PowerPoint suggests.

■ The Microsoft Clip Gallery dialog box appears.

CONTINUED

After PowerPoint finds the clip art images relating to a keyword in your presentation, you can select the clip art image you want to use.

USING AUTOCLIPART (CONTINUED)

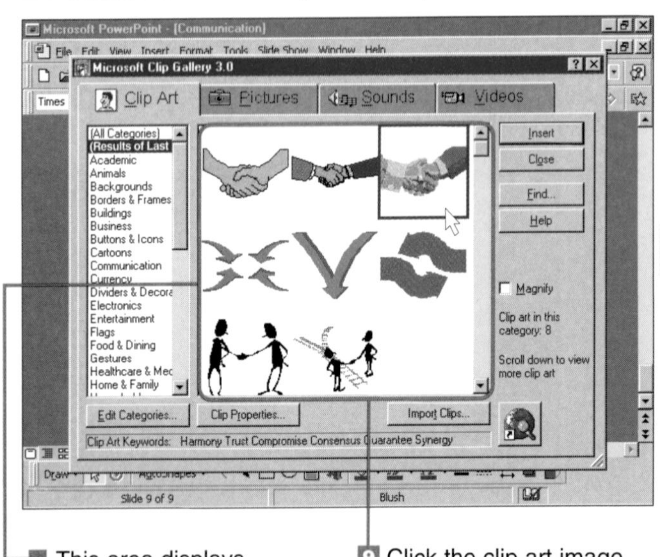

■ This area displays the clip art images relating to the keyword you selected.

9 Click the clip art image you want to use.

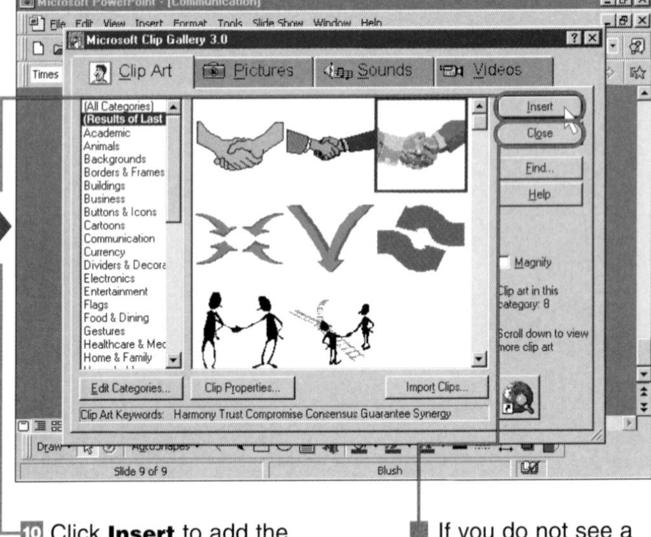

10 Click **Insert** to add the clip art image to the slide.

■ If you do not see a clip art image you want to use, click **Close** to close the dialog box.

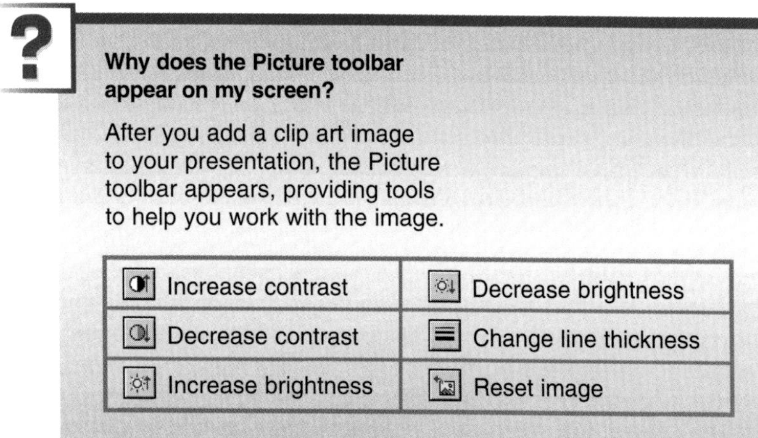

Why does the Picture toolbar appear on my screen?

After you add a clip art image to your presentation, the Picture toolbar appears, providing tools to help you work with the image.

Increase contrast	Decrease brightness
Decrease contrast	Change line thickness
Increase brightness	Reset image

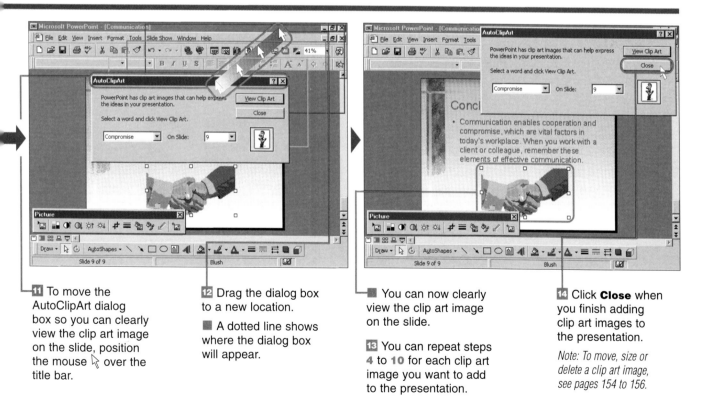

11 To move the AutoClipArt dialog box so you can clearly view the clip art image on the slide, position the mouse over the title bar.

12 Drag the dialog box to a new location.

■ A dotted line shows where the dialog box will appear.

■ You can now clearly view the clip art image on the slide.

13 You can repeat steps **4** to **10** for each clip art image you want to add to the presentation.

14 Click **Close** when you finish adding clip art images to the presentation.

Note: To move, size or delete a clip art image, see pages 154 to 156.

ADD A PICTURE

You can add a picture stored on your computer to a slide in your presentation.

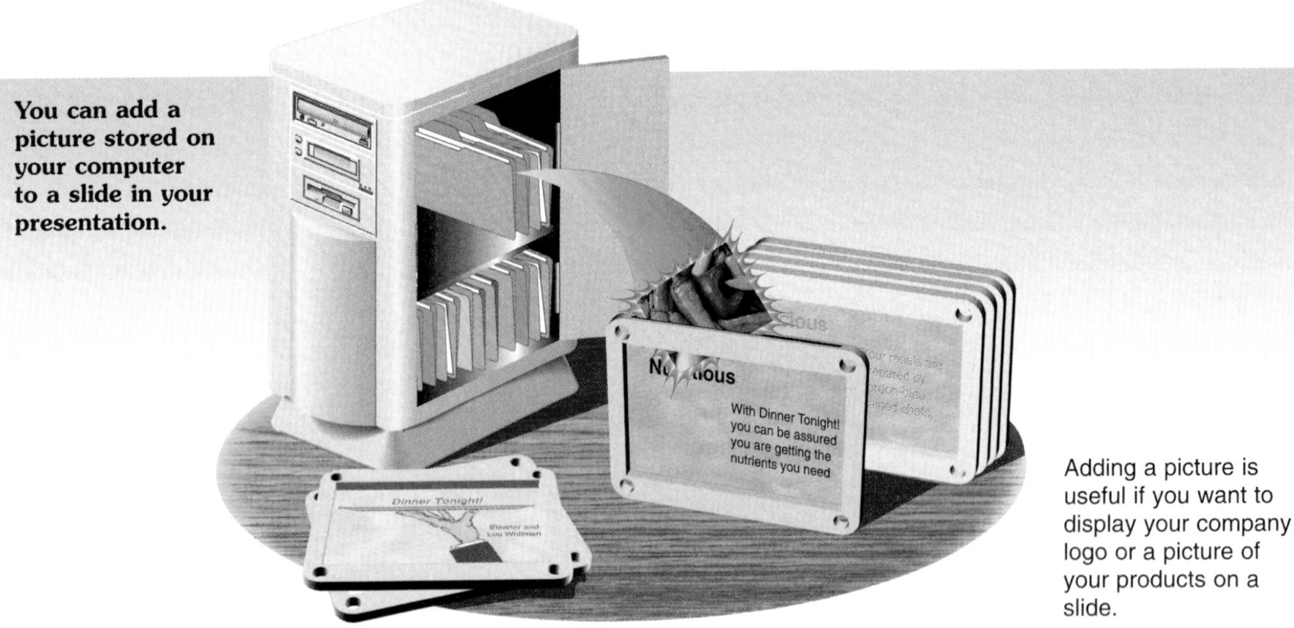

Adding a picture is useful if you want to display your company logo or a picture of your products on a slide.

ADD A PICTURE

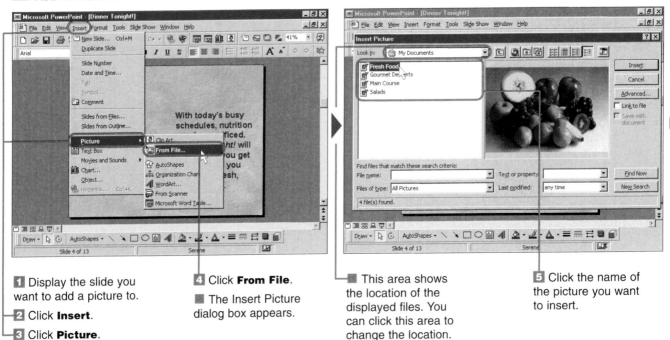

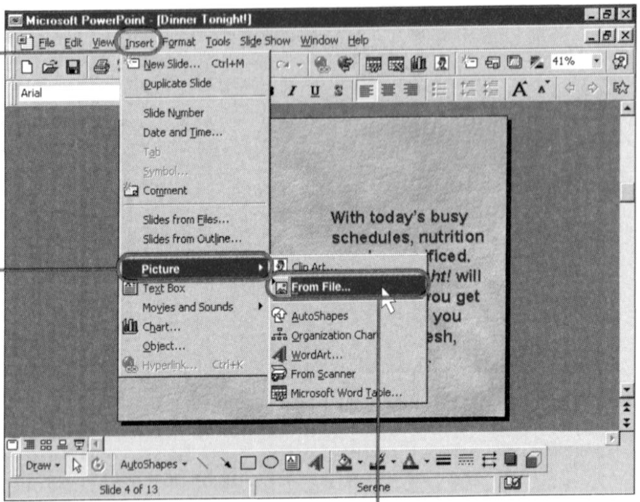

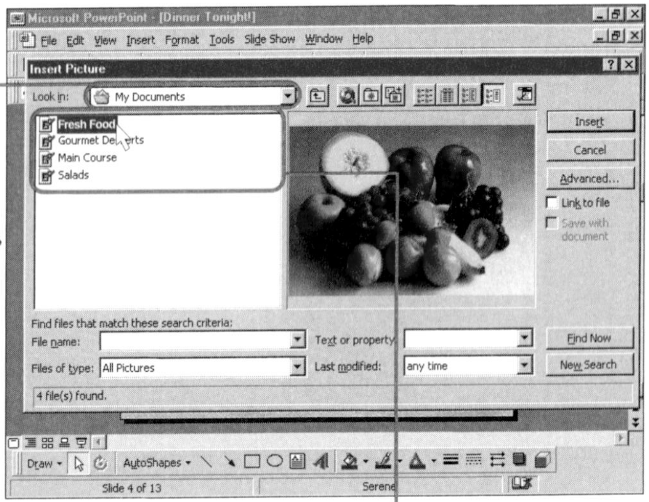

1 Display the slide you want to add a picture to.

2 Click **Insert**.

3 Click **Picture**.

4 Click **From File**.

■ The Insert Picture dialog box appears.

■ This area shows the location of the displayed files. You can click this area to change the location.

5 Click the name of the picture you want to insert.

Can I have the same picture appear on each slide in my presentation?

You can add a picture to the Slide Master to have the picture appear on each slide in your presentation. For information on the Slide Master, see page 110.

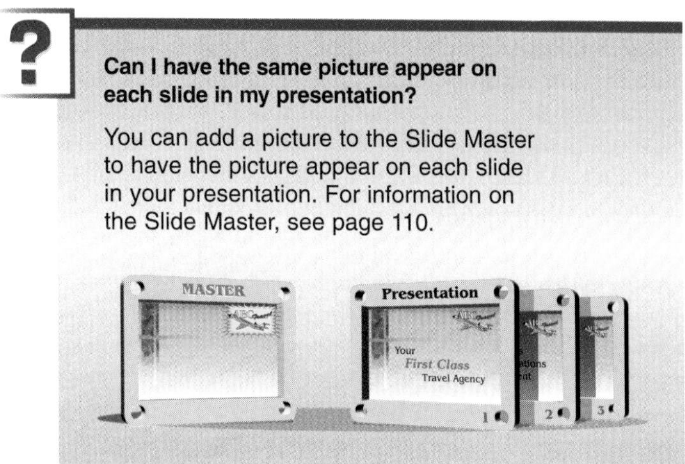

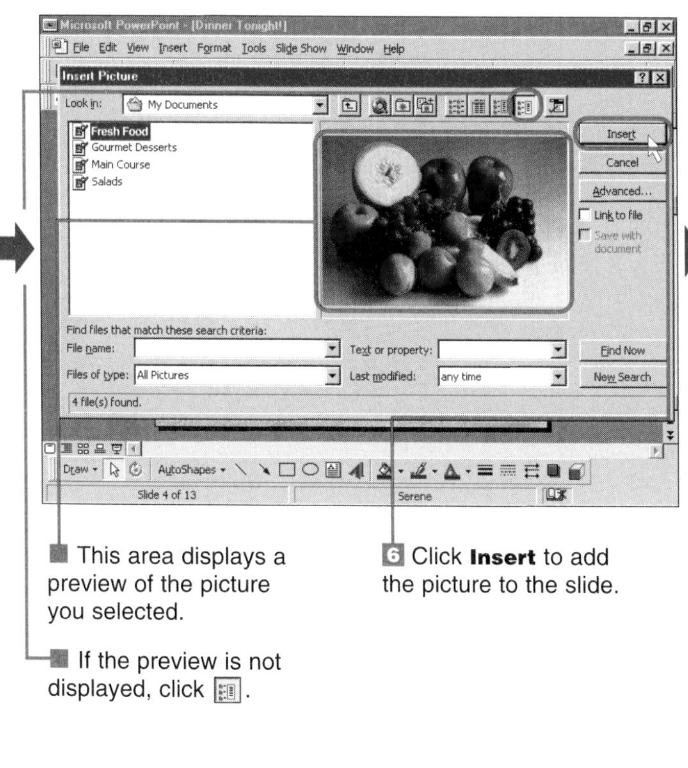

■ This area displays a preview of the picture you selected.

■ If the preview is not displayed, click ▦.

6 Click **Insert** to add the picture to the slide.

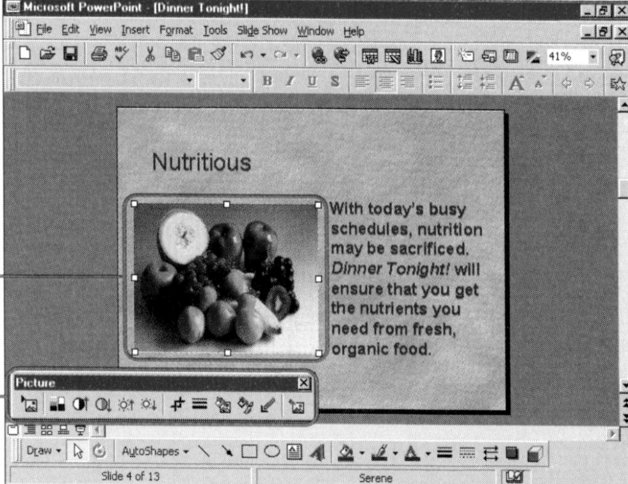

■ The picture appears on the slide. The handles (□) around the picture let you change the size of the picture.

■ The Picture toolbar also appears, providing tools to help you work with the picture.

7 To hide the handles and the Picture toolbar, click outside the picture area.

Note: To move, size or delete a picture, see pages 154 to 156.

ADD A CHART

You can add a chart to a slide to show trends and compare data.

A chart is more appealing and often easier to understand than a list of numbers.

ADD A CHART

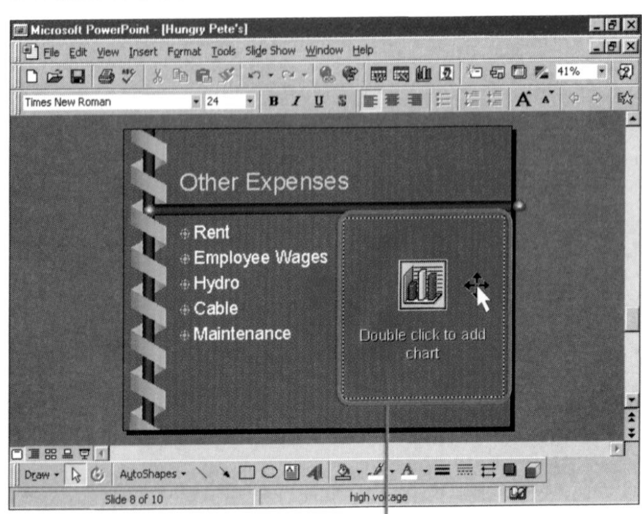

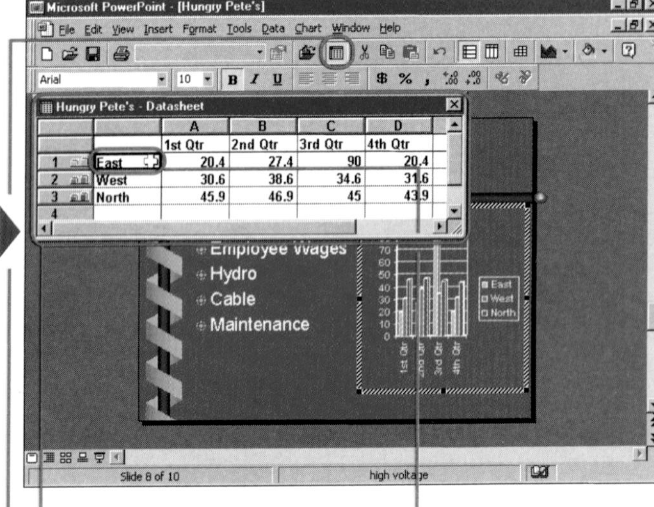

1 Display the slide you want to add a chart to.

2 Change the layout of the slide to one that includes a placeholder for a chart. To change the slide layout, see page 38.

3 Double-click the chart area to add a chart.

■ A datasheet appears, displaying sample data to show you where to enter your information.

■ If the datasheet does not appear, click ▦ to display the datasheet.

4 To replace the data in a cell, click the cell. A thick border appears around the cell.

?

Can I add a chart without changing the slide layout?

Yes. Click [chart button] and then perform steps 4 to 7 below to add a chart without changing the slide layout.

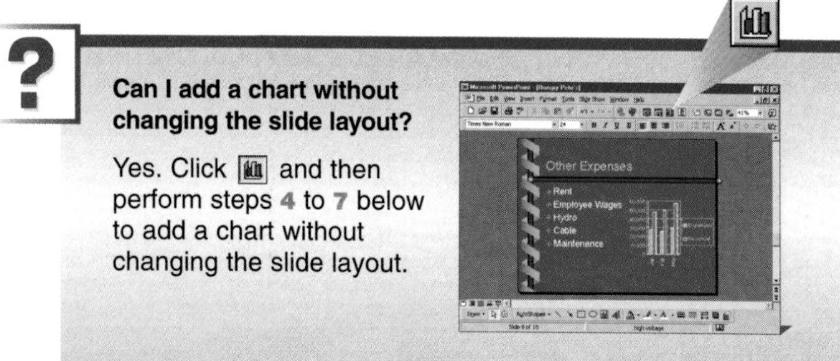

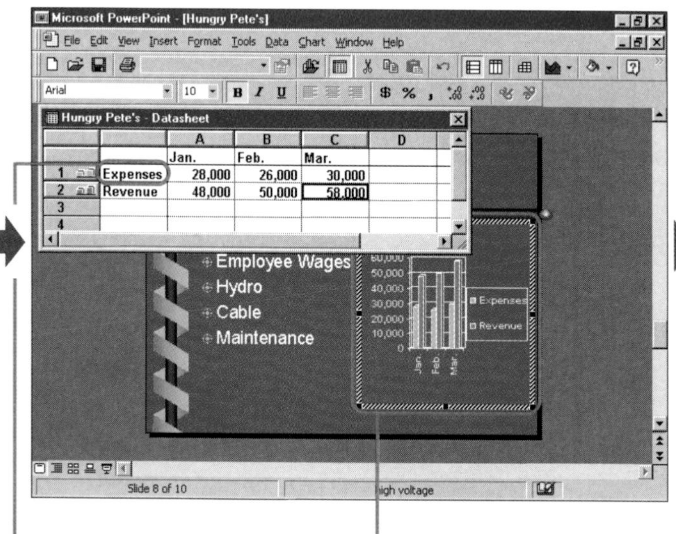

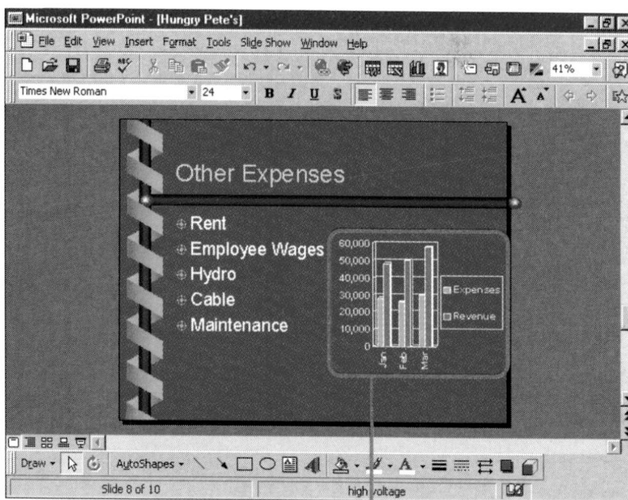

5 Type your data and then press the Enter key.

Note: To remove data from a cell and leave the cell empty, click the cell and then press the Delete key.

6 Repeat steps 4 and 5 until you finish entering all of your data.

■ As you enter data, PowerPoint updates the chart on the slide.

7 When you finish entering data for the chart, click a blank area on the slide to hide the datasheet.

■ The datasheet disappears and you can clearly view the chart on the slide.

Note: To move, size or delete a chart, see pages 154 to 156.

■ To change the data in the chart, double-click the chart and then perform steps 4 to 7.

MAKE CHANGES TO A CHART

You can change the chart type to better suit your data.

The type of chart you should use depends on your data. For example, area, column and line charts are ideal for showing changes to values over time, whereas pie charts are ideal for showing percentages.

CHANGE THE CHART TYPE

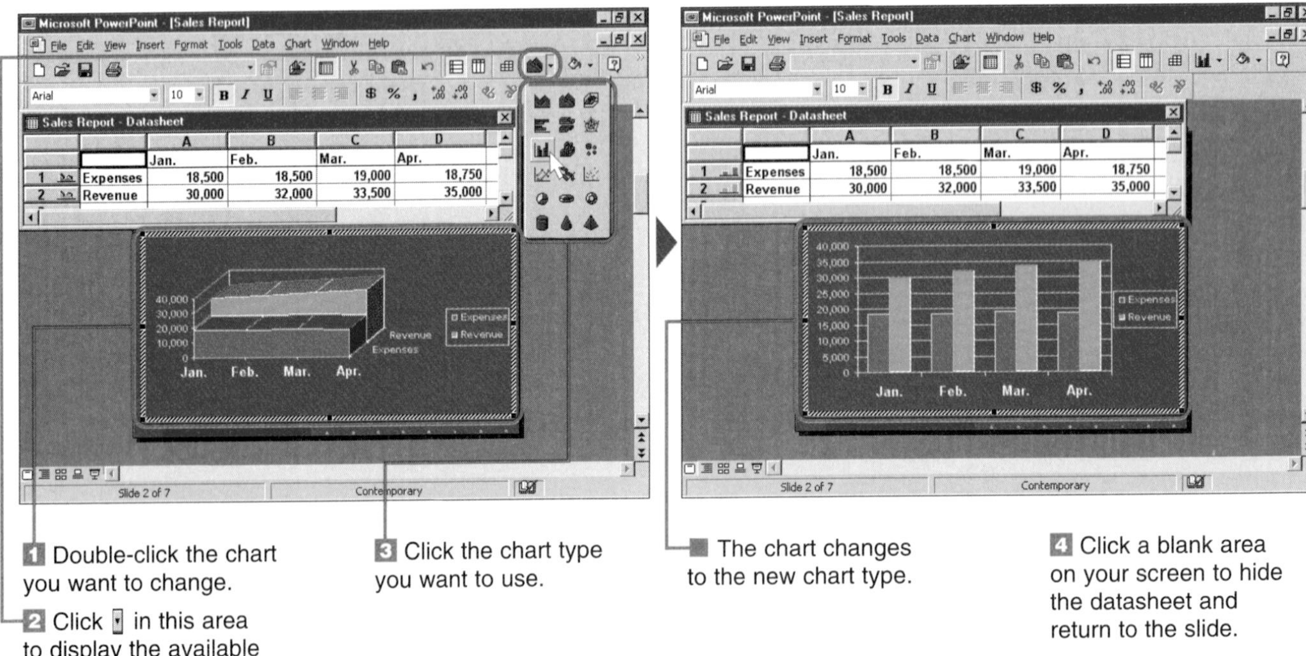

1 Double-click the chart you want to change.

2 Click ▾ in this area to display the available chart types.

3 Click the chart type you want to use.

■ The chart changes to the new chart type.

4 Click a blank area on your screen to hide the datasheet and return to the slide.

You can change the way data is plotted in your chart. This allows you to emphasize different information in the chart.

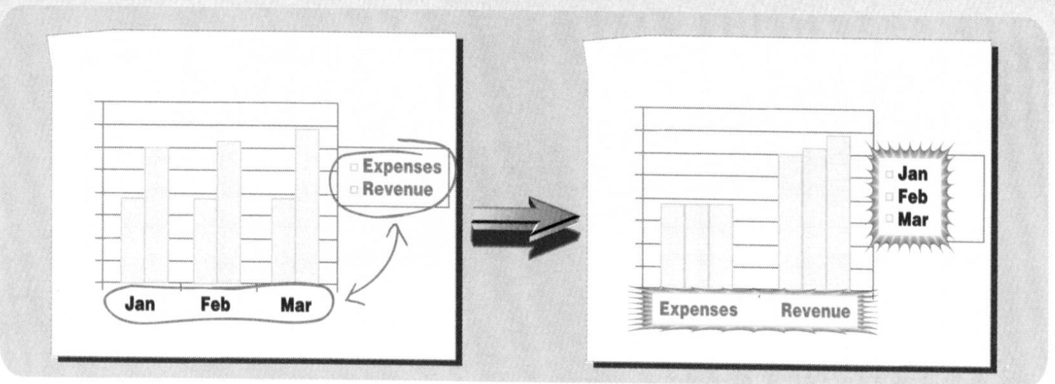

CHANGE THE WAY DATA IS PLOTTED

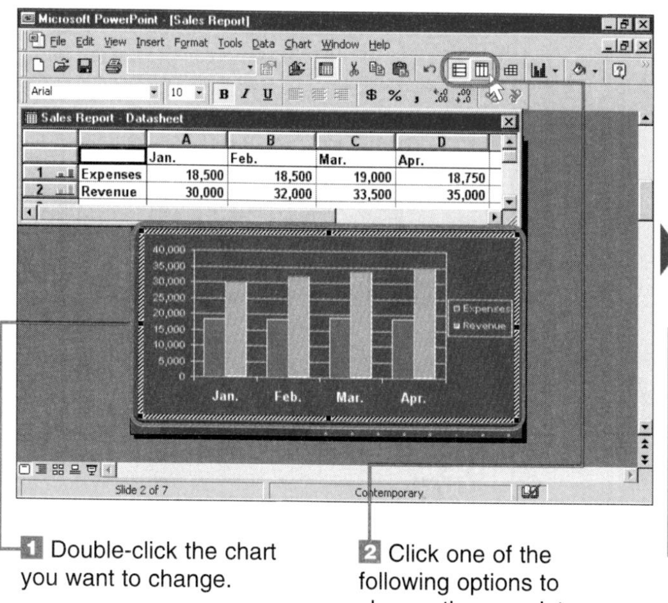

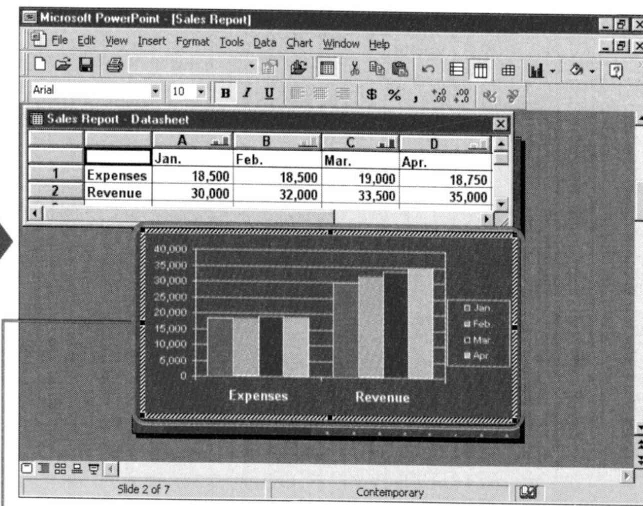

1 Double-click the chart you want to change.

2 Click one of the following options to change the way data is plotted.

- Plot data by row
- Plot data by column

■ The chart displays the change.

3 Click a blank area on your screen to hide the datasheet and return to the slide.

MAKE CHANGES TO A CHART

You can change the appearance of numbers in a chart without retyping the numbers.

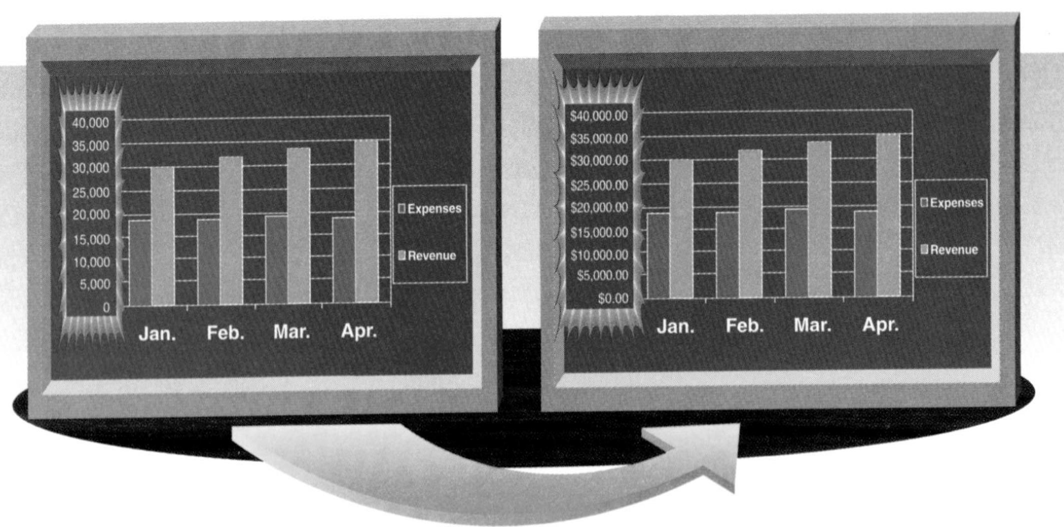

CHANGE NUMBER APPEARANCE

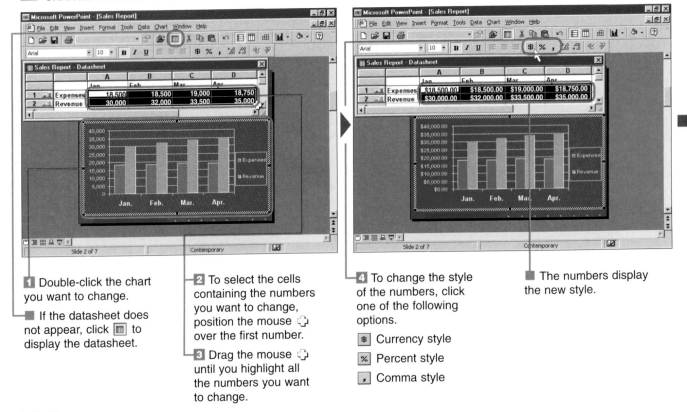

1 Double-click the chart you want to change.

■ If the datasheet does not appear, click [datasheet icon] to display the datasheet.

2 To select the cells containing the numbers you want to change, position the mouse ✥ over the first number.

3 Drag the mouse ✥ until you highlight all the numbers you want to change.

4 To change the style of the numbers, click one of the following options.

- $ Currency style
- % Percent style
- , Comma style

■ The numbers display the new style.

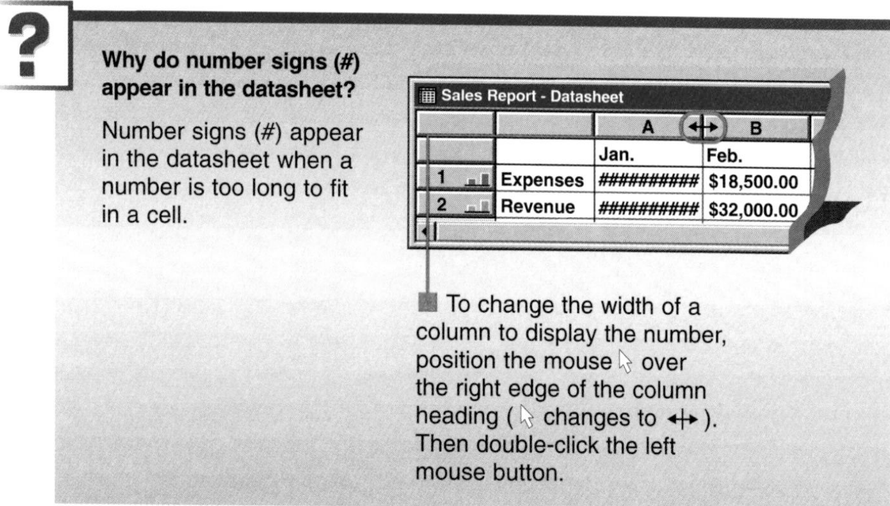

Why do number signs (#) appear in the datasheet?

Number signs (#) appear in the datasheet when a number is too long to fit in a cell.

■ To change the width of a column to display the number, position the mouse over the right edge of the column heading (changes to ↔). Then double-click the left mouse button.

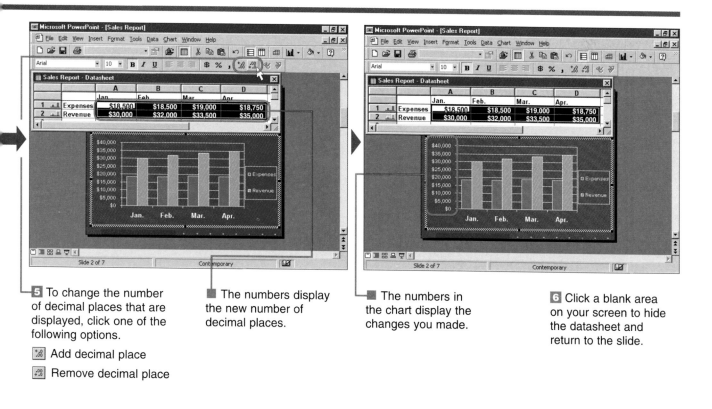

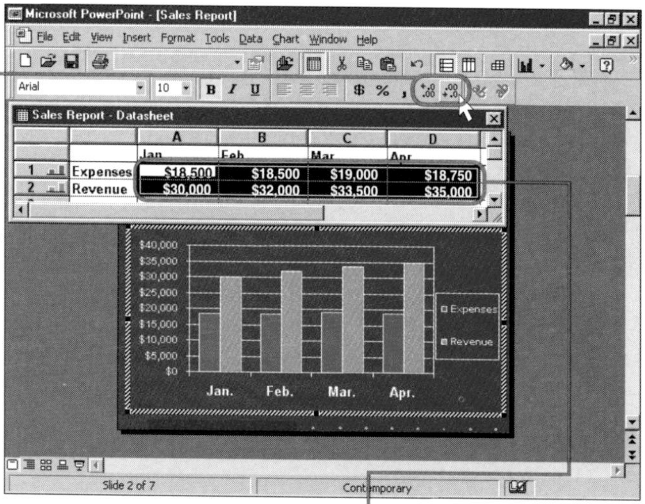

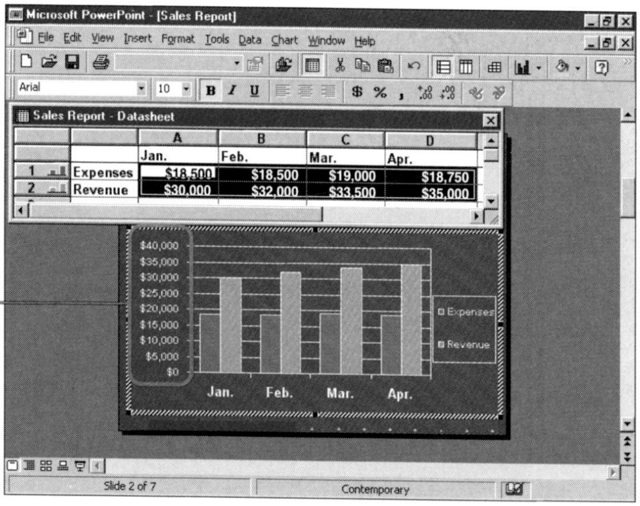

5 To change the number of decimal places that are displayed, click one of the following options.

- Add decimal place
- Remove decimal place

■ The numbers display the new number of decimal places.

■ The numbers in the chart display the changes you made.

6 Click a blank area on your screen to hide the datasheet and return to the slide.

MAKE CHANGES TO A CHART

The datasheet is not displayed during a slide show or when you print your presentation. If you want to display or print the information from the datasheet, you must add a data table to your chart.

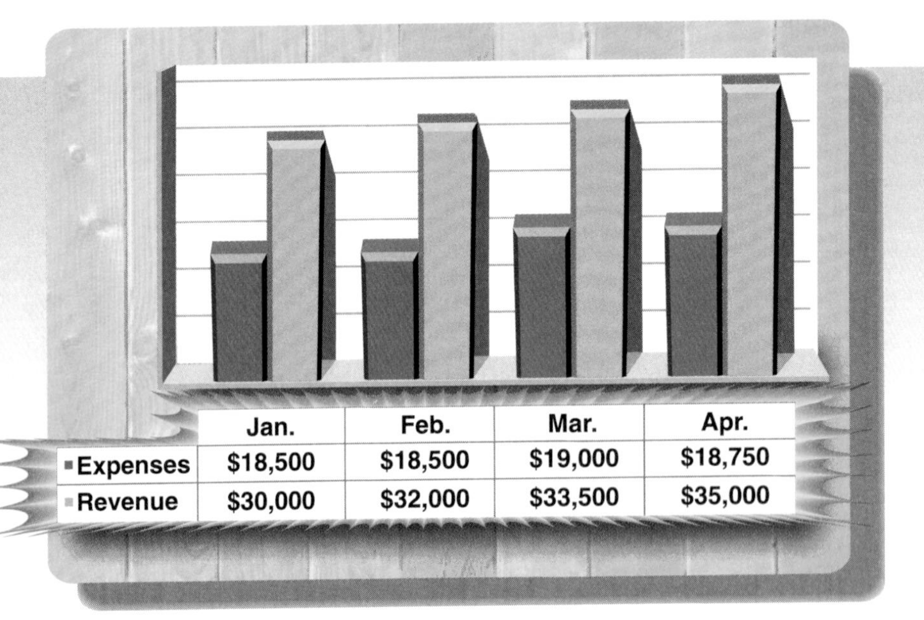

	Jan.	Feb.	Mar.	Apr.
Expenses	$18,500	$18,500	$19,000	$18,750
Revenue	$30,000	$32,000	$33,500	$35,000

ADD A DATA TABLE

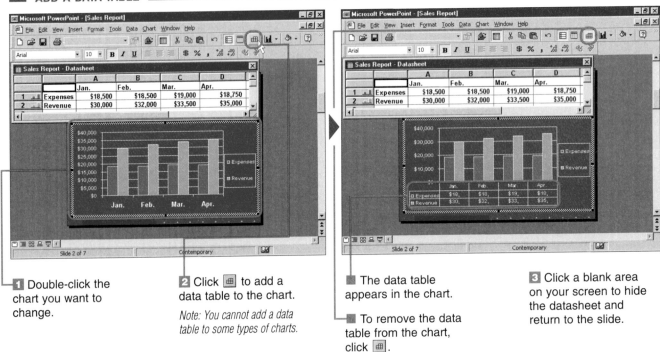

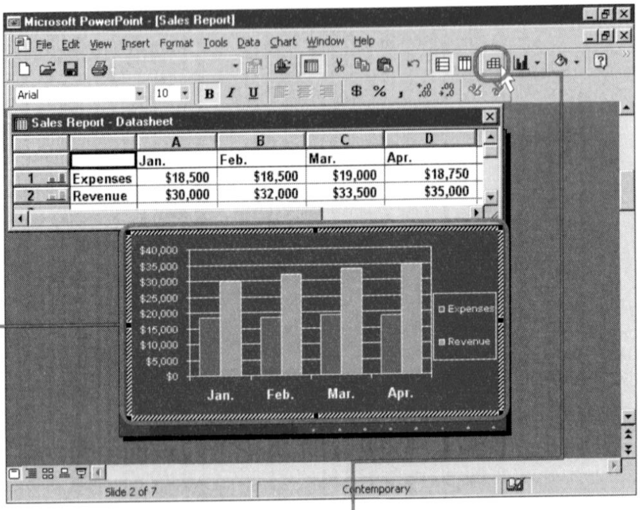

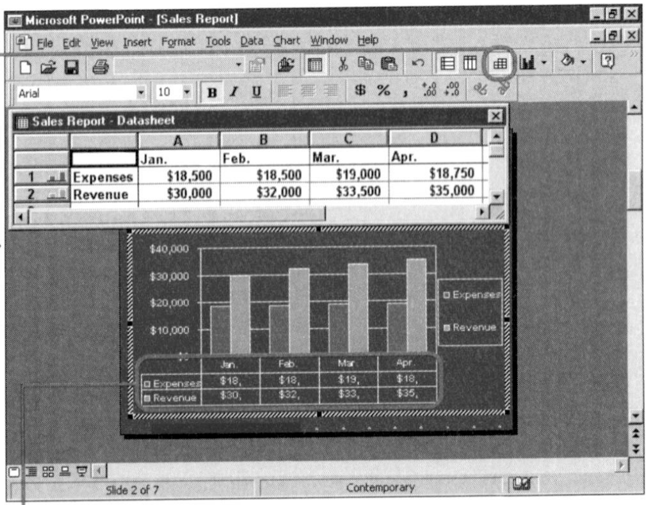

1 Double-click the chart you want to change.

2 Click ⊞ to add a data table to the chart.

Note: You cannot add a data table to some types of charts.

■ The data table appears in the chart.

■ To remove the data table from the chart, click ⊞.

3 Click a blank area on your screen to hide the datasheet and return to the slide.

You can rotate text on a chart axis to improve the appearance of the chart.

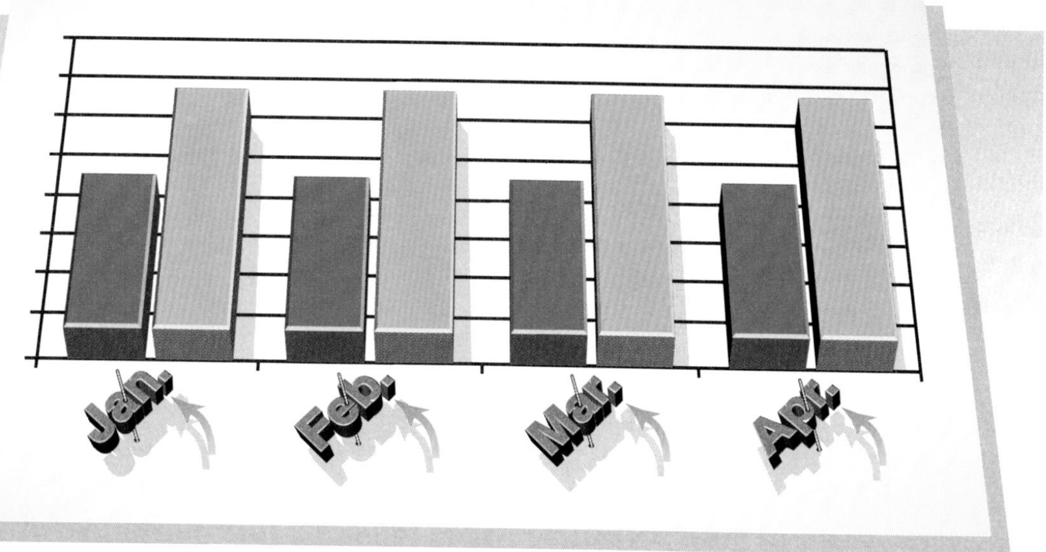

ROTATE TEXT

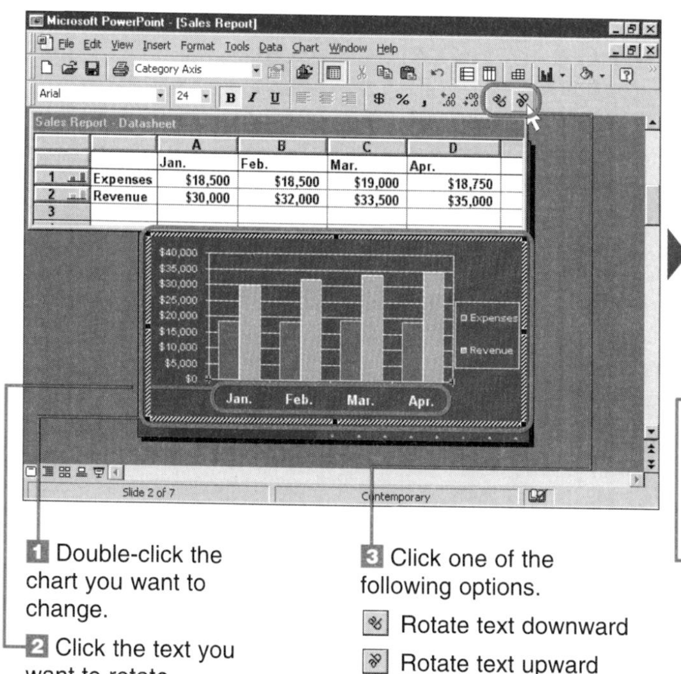

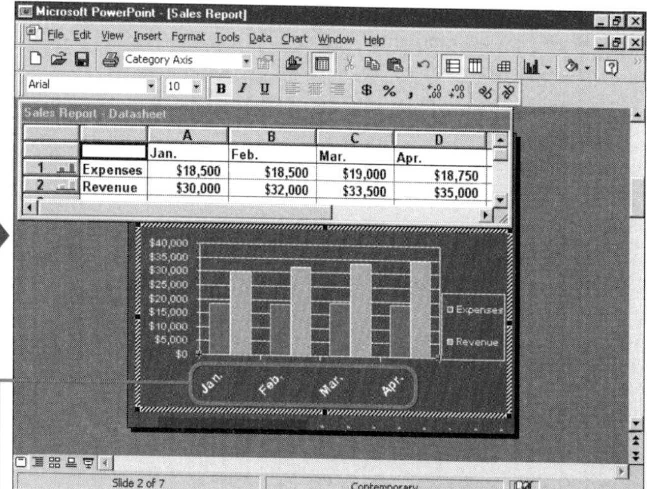

1 Double-click the chart you want to change.

2 Click the text you want to rotate.

3 Click one of the following options.

- Rotate text downward
- Rotate text upward

■ The text is rotated.

■ To return the text to its original position, repeat steps **2** and **3**.

4 Click a blank area on your screen to hide the datasheet and return to the slide.

ADD AN ORGANIZATION CHART

You can add an organization chart to a slide in your presentation. Organization charts are useful for showing information such as the structure of a company.

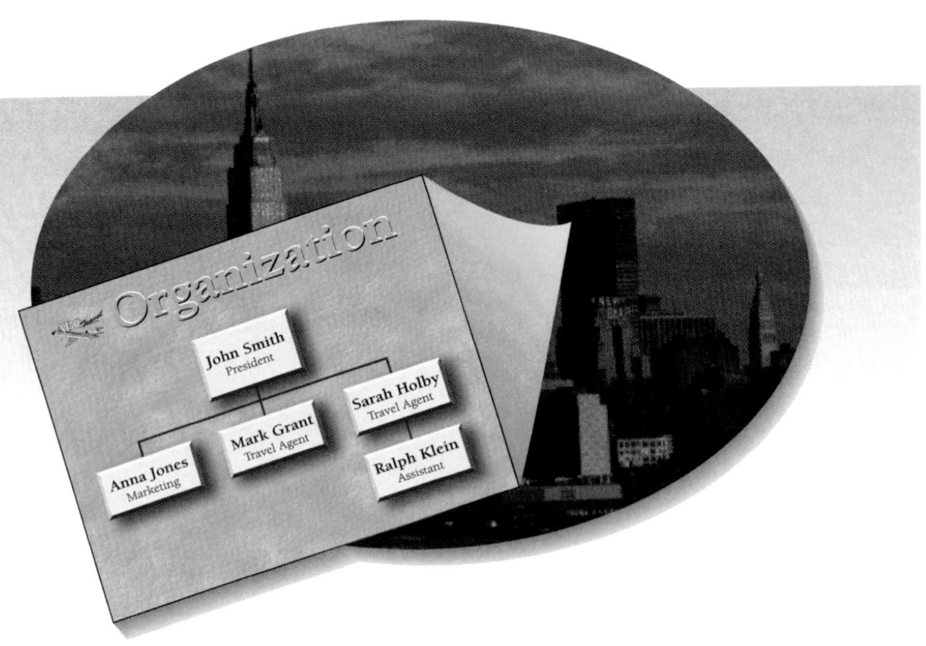

ADD AN ORGANIZATION CHART

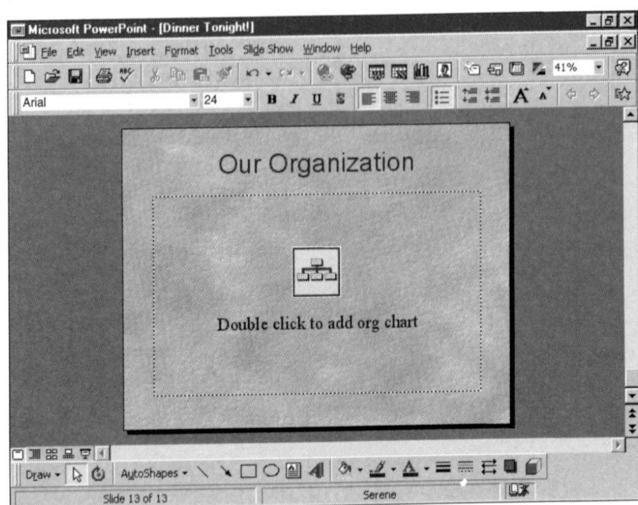

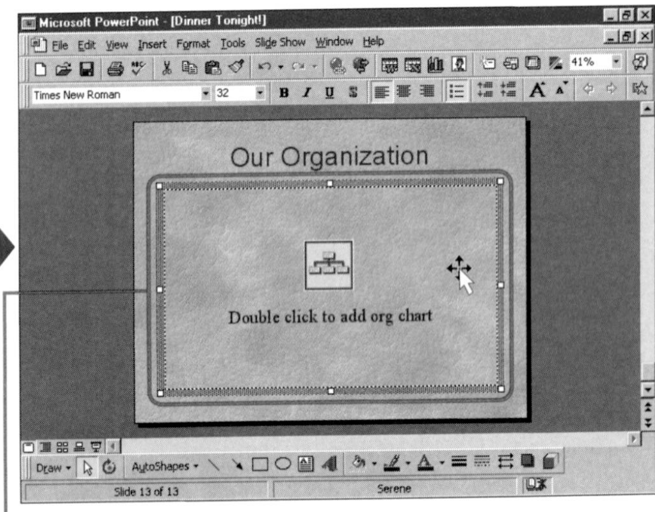

1 Display the slide you want to add an organization chart to.

2 Change the layout of the slide to one that includes a placeholder for an organization chart. To change the slide layout, see page 38.

3 Double-click the organization chart area to add an organization chart.

What other types of information can an organization chart display?

An organization chart can also be used to illustrate a process, such as how a product is manufactured, or to summarize information, such as the main ideas in a report.

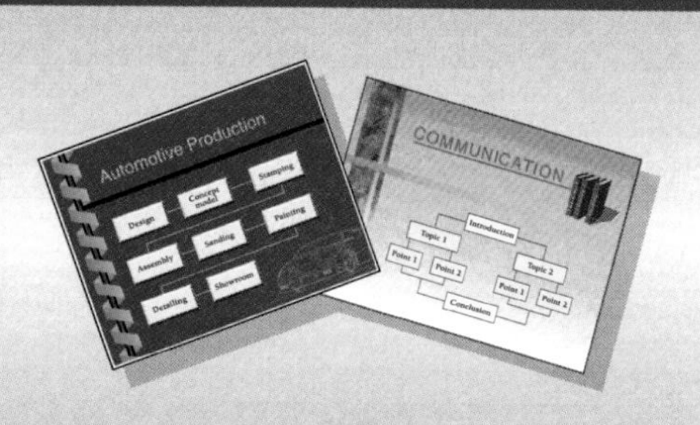

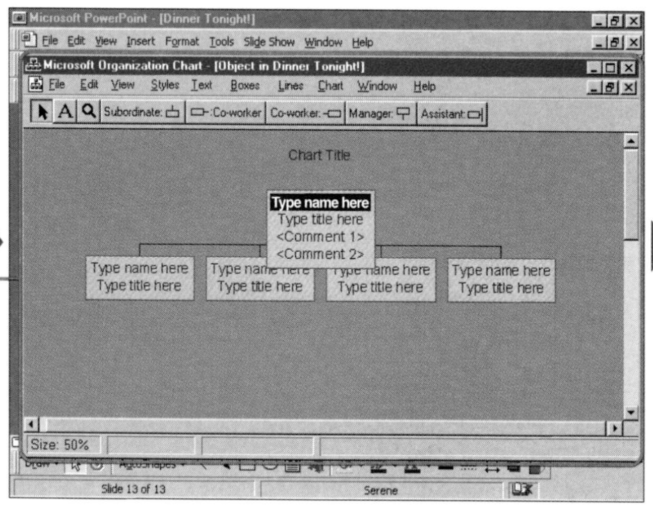

■ The Microsoft Organization Chart window appears, displaying a simple organization chart that you can customize.

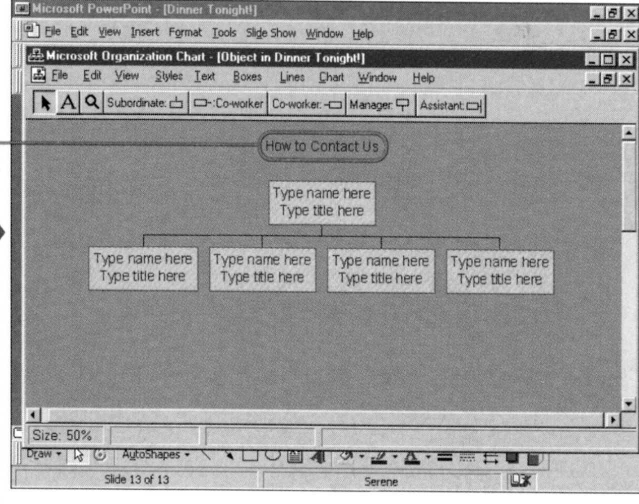

CHANGE THE TITLE

4 To change the title of the organization chart, drag the mouse I over the existing title and then type a new title.

■ If you do not want the chart to display a title, drag the mouse I over the existing title and then press the Delete key.

CONTINUED

ADD AN ORGANIZATION CHART

You can enter text into each box in an organization chart. You can also add a new box to include an additional person, such as a co-worker or manager.

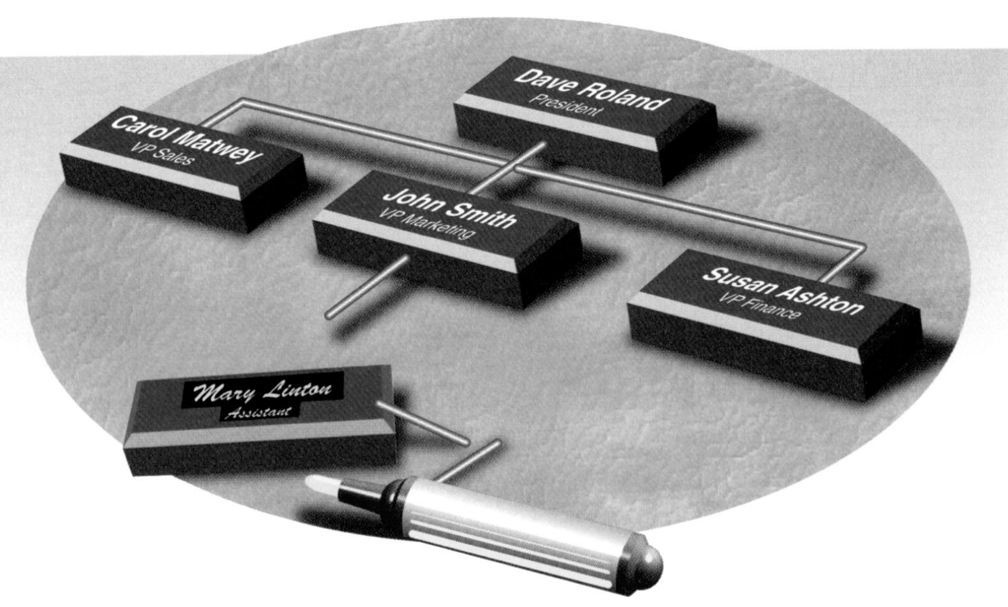

ADD AN ORGANIZATION CHART (CONTINUED)

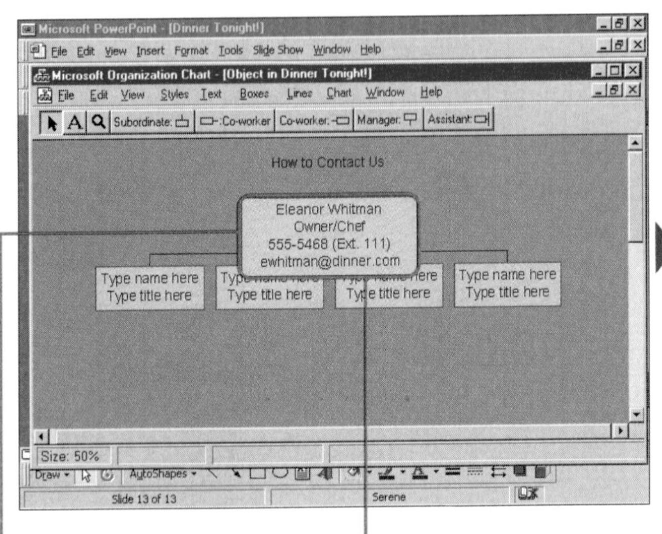

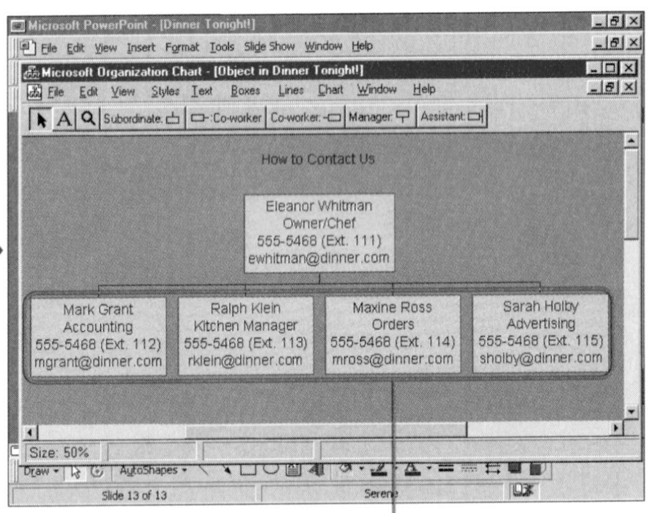

ENTER INFORMATION

5 Click a box where you want to enter information.

6 Type the information for the first line of the box and then press the Enter key. Repeat this step until you have typed all the information for the box.

Note: You can enter up to four lines of information in each box of an organization chart.

7 When you finish entering the information for the box, click outside the box.

8 Repeat steps 5 to 7 for each box you want to display information.

?

What type of information can I enter into a box?

Although each box prompts you to enter a name, title and comments, you can enter any information you want into a box. The information you enter will depend on the purpose of the organization chart and the information you want to display.

Type name here
Type title here
<Comment 1>
<Comment 2>

Step 5
Glue pieces together
Use only a small
amount of glue

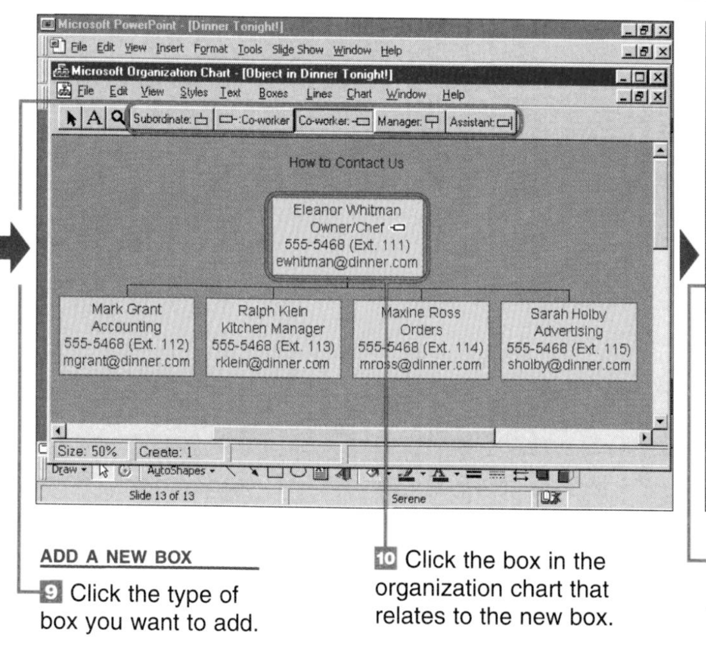

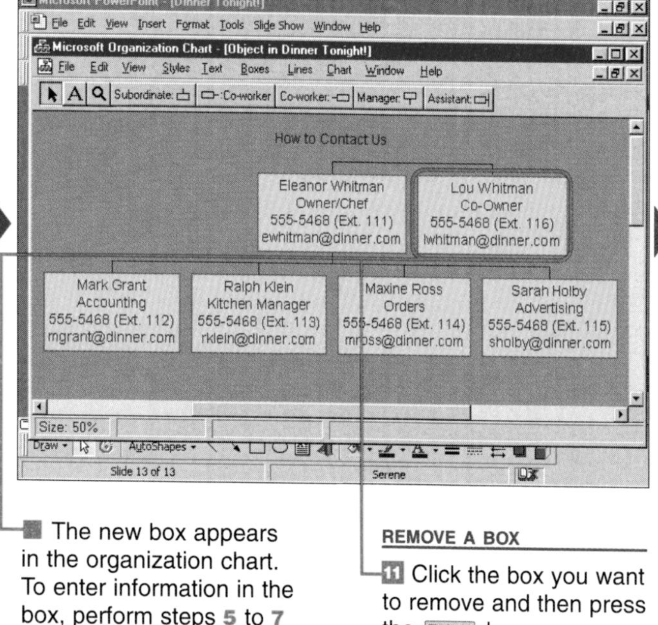

ADD A NEW BOX

9 Click the type of box you want to add.

10 Click the box in the organization chart that relates to the new box.

■ The new box appears in the organization chart. To enter information in the box, perform steps 5 to 7 on page 138.

REMOVE A BOX

11 Click the box you want to remove and then press the **Delete** key.

CONTINUED

You can move boxes in an organization chart to reflect changes in the structure of your company.

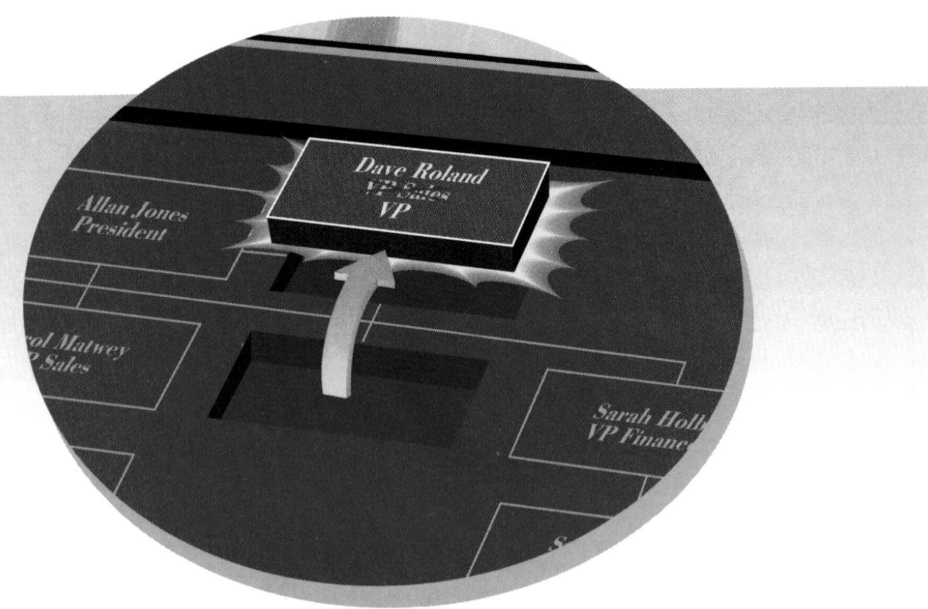

ADD AN ORGANIZATION CHART (CONTINUED)

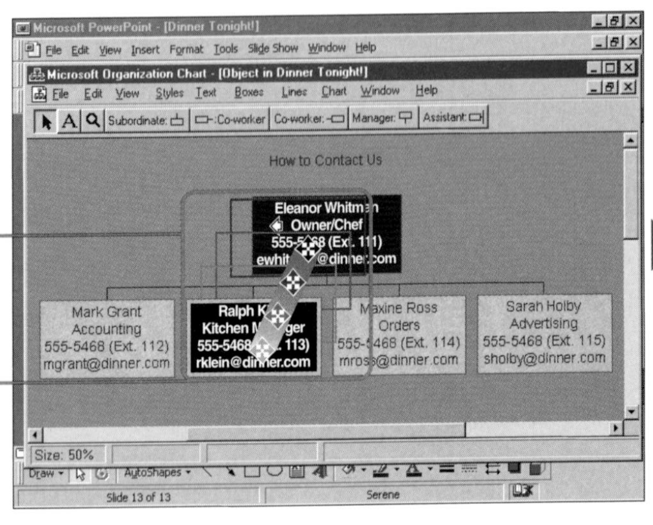

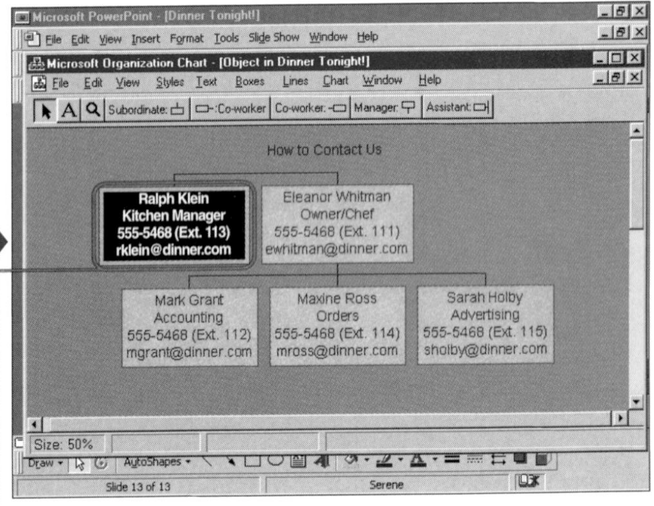

MOVE A BOX

12 Position the mouse over the box you want to move.

13 Drag the box over a new manager or co-worker.

■ A dotted outline appears when you drag the box. An arrow (⇦ or ⇨) or icon (┴) displays where the box will appear in relation to the manager or co-worker.

■ The box moves to the new location.

?

Can I make changes to an organization chart after adding it to a slide?

Yes. Double-click the organization chart on the slide to display the chart in the Microsoft Organization Chart window. You can then make changes to the organization chart.

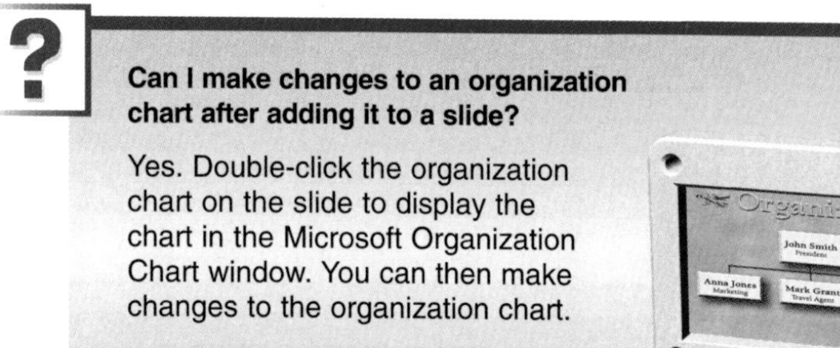

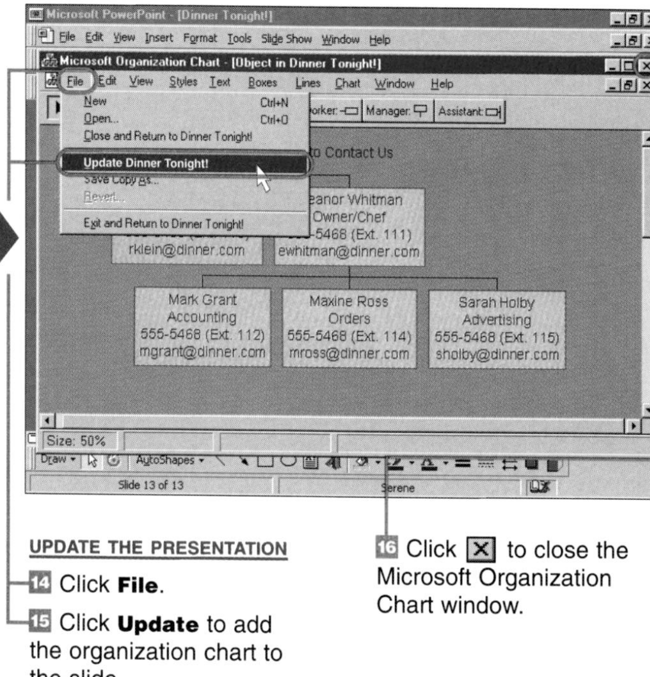

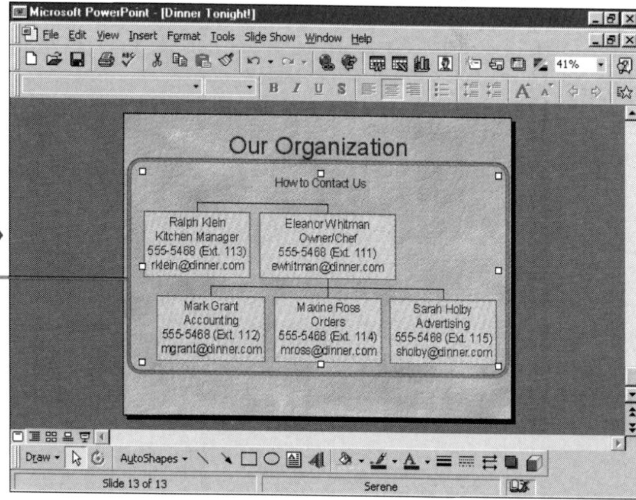

UPDATE THE PRESENTATION

14 Click **File**.

15 Click **Update** to add the organization chart to the slide.

16 Click ☒ to close the Microsoft Organization Chart window.

■ The organization chart appears on the slide. The handles (□) around the chart let you change the size of the chart.

17 To hide the handles, click outside the organization chart area.

Note: To move, size or delete an organization chart, see pages 154 to 156.

ADD A TABLE

You can add a table to a slide to present data in an easy-to-read format.

You need Microsoft Word installed on your computer to create a table.

ADD A TABLE

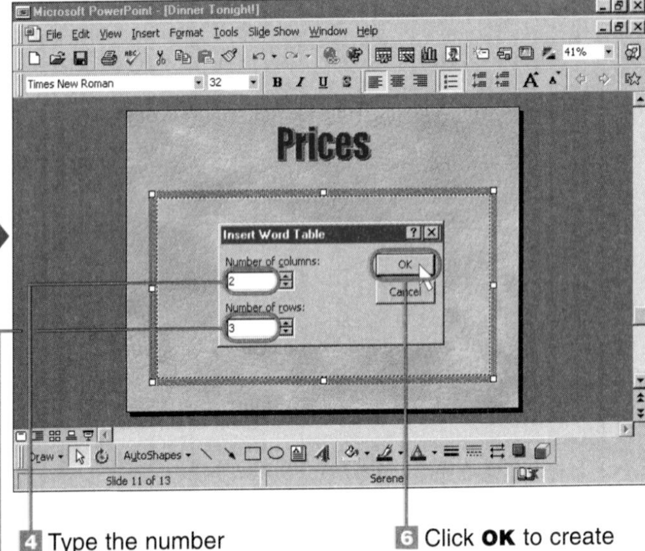

1 Display the slide you want to add a table to.

2 Change the layout of the slide to one that includes a placeholder for a table. To change the slide layout, see page 38.

3 Double-click the table area to add a table.

■ The Insert Word Table dialog box appears.

4 Type the number of columns you want to include in the table.

5 Double-click this area and then type the number of rows you want to include in the table.

6 Click **OK** to create the table.

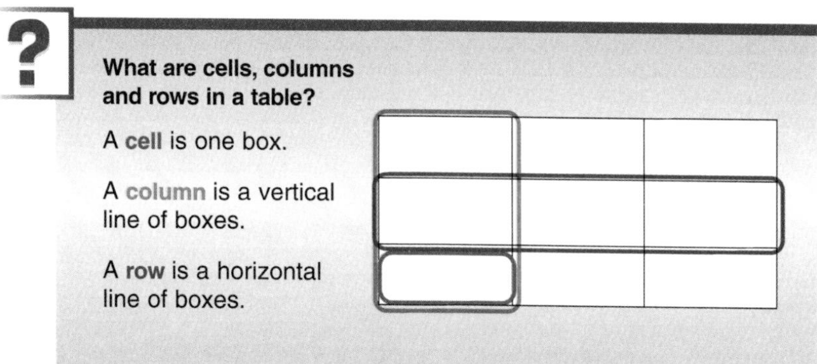

What are cells, columns and rows in a table?

A **cell** is one box.

A **column** is a vertical line of boxes.

A **row** is a horizontal line of boxes.

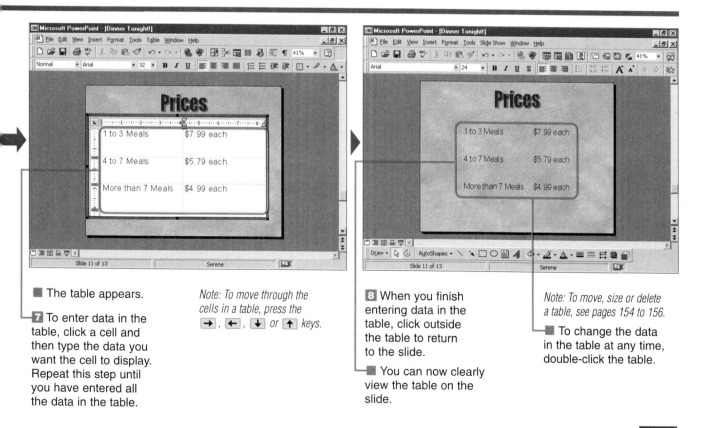

■ The table appears.

7 To enter data in the table, click a cell and then type the data you want the cell to display. Repeat this step until you have entered all the data in the table.

Note: To move through the cells in a table, press the →, ←, ↓ or ↑ keys.

8 When you finish entering data in the table, click outside the table to return to the slide.

■ You can now clearly view the table on the slide.

Note: To move, size or delete a table, see pages 154 to 156.

■ To change the data in the table at any time, double-click the table.

MAKE CHANGES TO A TABLE

You can change the width of columns and the height of rows in a table.

CHANGE COLUMN WIDTH OR ROW HEIGHT

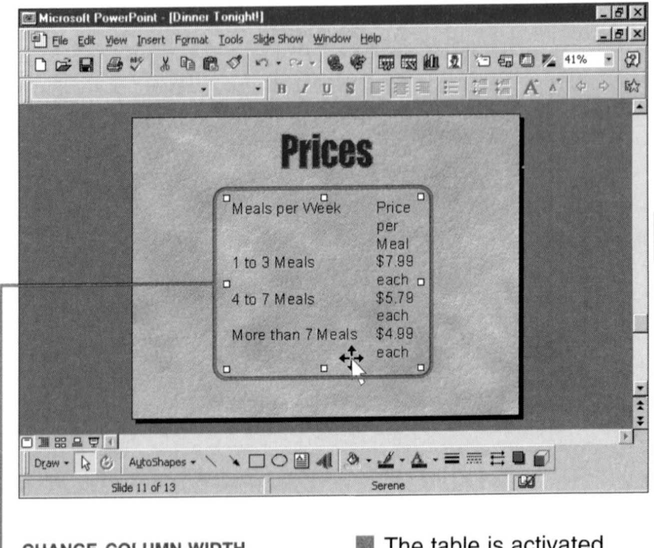

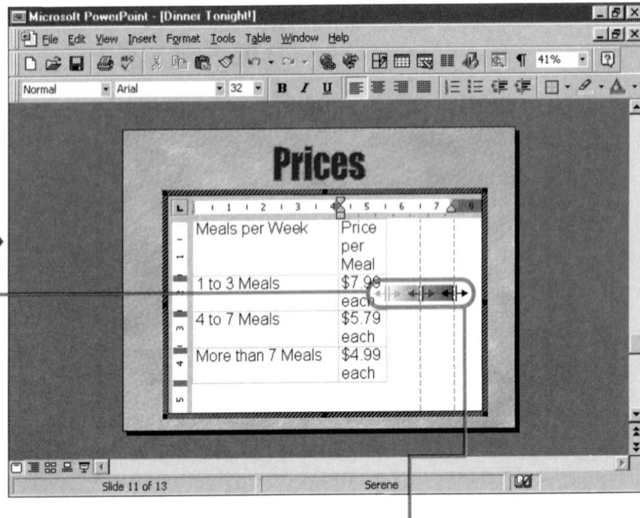

CHANGE COLUMN WIDTH

1 Double-click the table you want to change.

■ The table is activated and displays a thick border.

2 Position the mouse I over the right edge of the column you want to change (I changes to ↔).

3 Drag the column edge to a new position. A dotted line shows the new position.

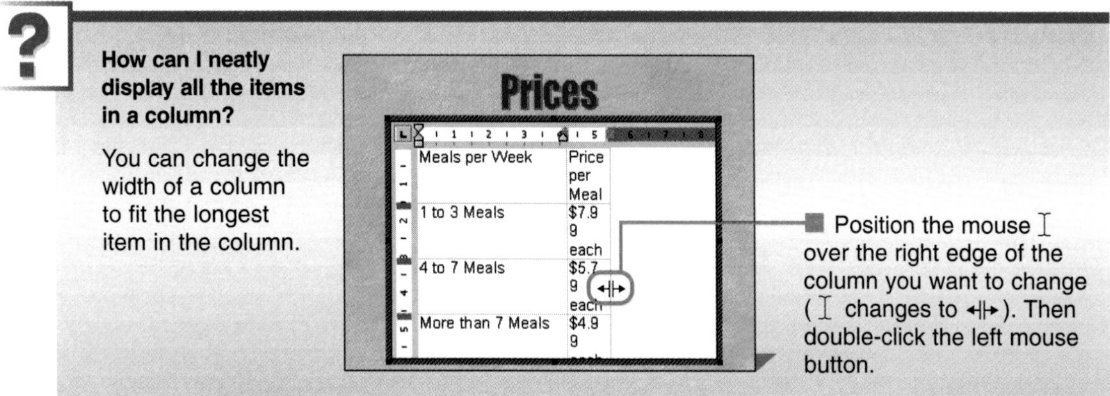

How can I neatly display all the items in a column?

You can change the width of a column to fit the longest item in the column.

■ Position the mouse I over the right edge of the column you want to change (I changes to ↔). Then double-click the left mouse button.

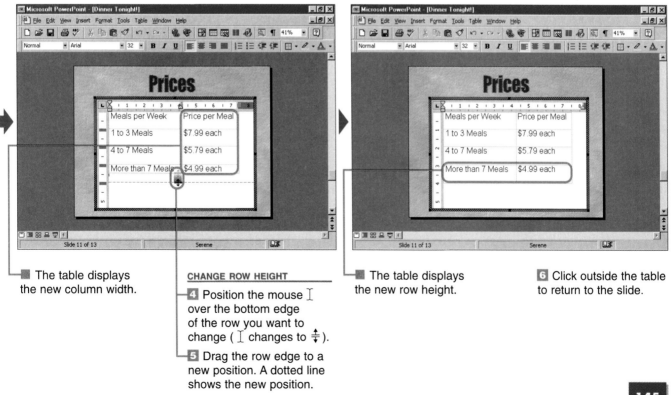

■ The table displays the new column width.

CHANGE ROW HEIGHT

4 Position the mouse I over the bottom edge of the row you want to change (I changes to ‡).

5 Drag the row edge to a new position. A dotted line shows the new position.

■ The table displays the new row height.

6 Click outside the table to return to the slide.

MAKE CHANGES TO A TABLE

You can add a column to a table to insert additional data. You can also delete a column from a table to remove data you no longer need.

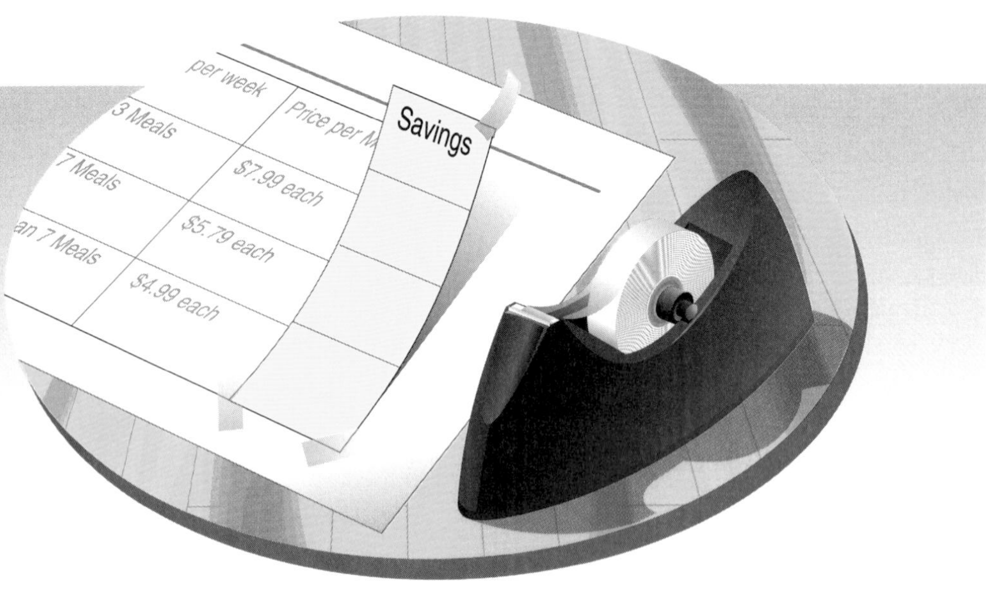

ADD OR DELETE A COLUMN

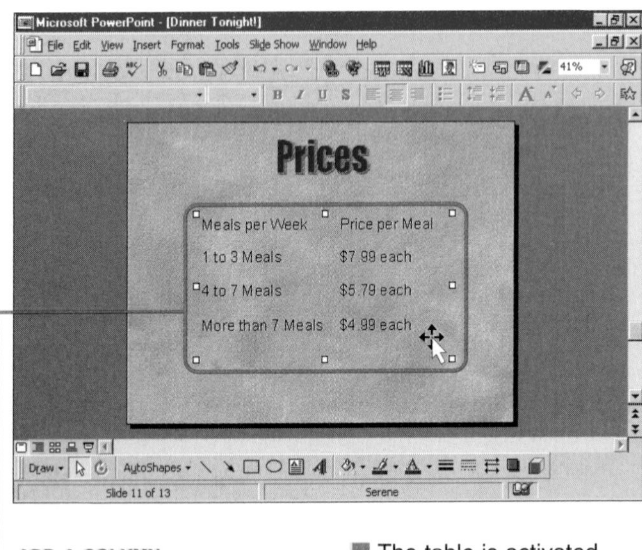

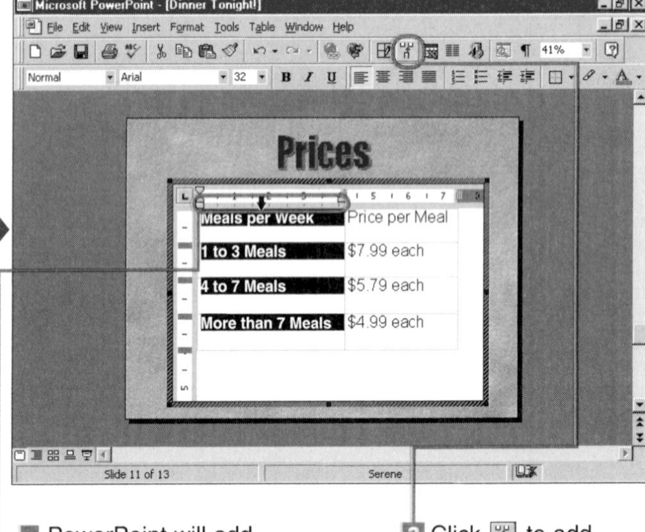

ADD A COLUMN

1 Double-click the table you want to change.

■ The table is activated and displays a thick border.

2 To select a column, position the mouse over the top of the column (changes to ⬇). Then click the left mouse button.

■ PowerPoint will add a column to the left of the column you select.

3 Click to add a column.

?

How do I add a column to the end of my table?

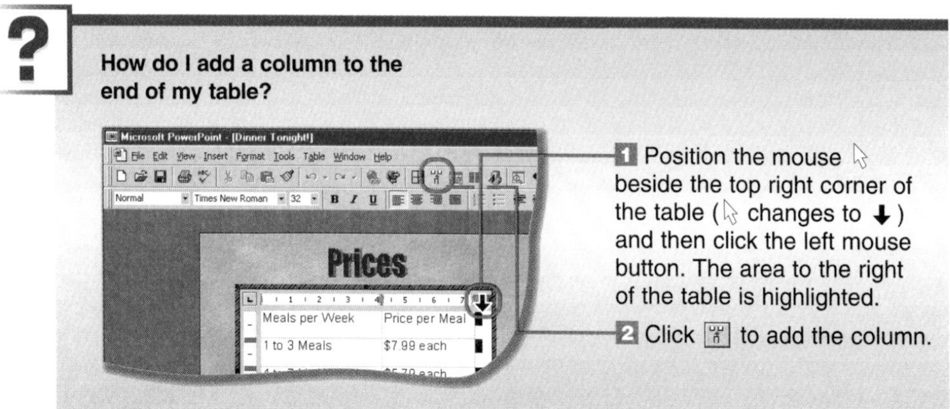

1 Position the mouse beside the top right corner of the table (changes to ⬇) and then click the left mouse button. The area to the right of the table is highlighted.

2 Click to add the column.

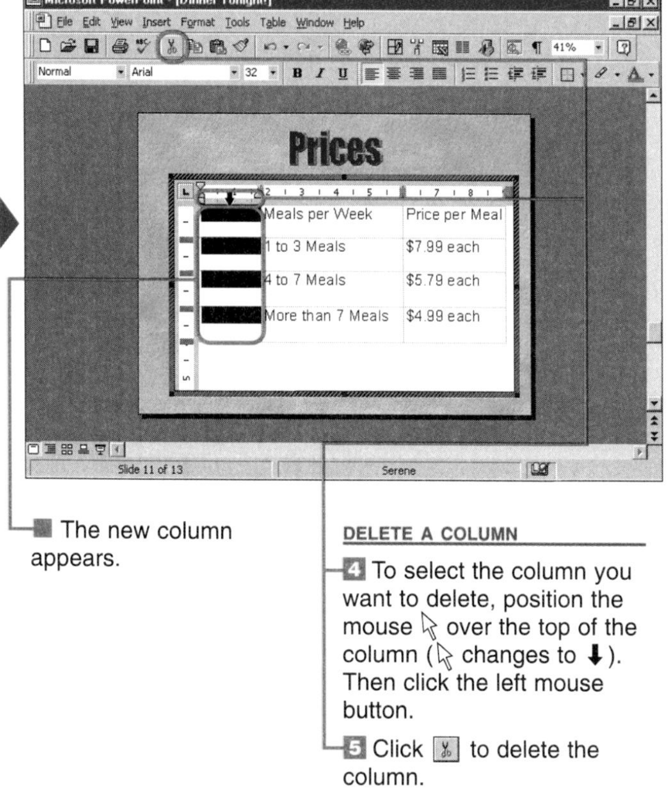

■ The new column appears.

DELETE A COLUMN

4 To select the column you want to delete, position the mouse over the top of the column (changes to ⬇). Then click the left mouse button.

5 Click to delete the column.

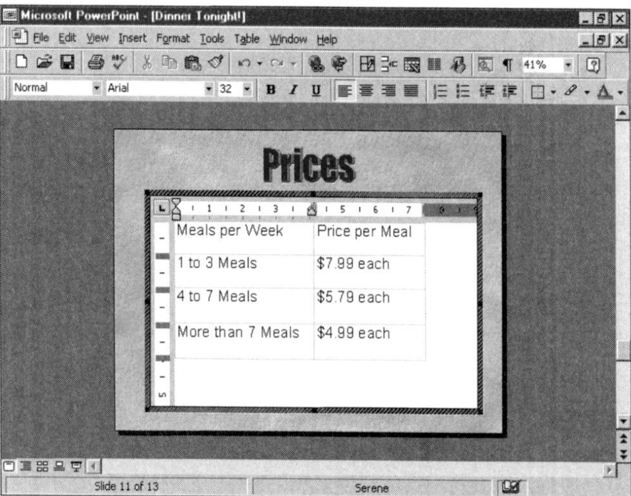

■ The column disappears from the table.

6 Click outside the table to return to the slide.

MAKE CHANGES TO A TABLE

You can add or delete a row in a table.

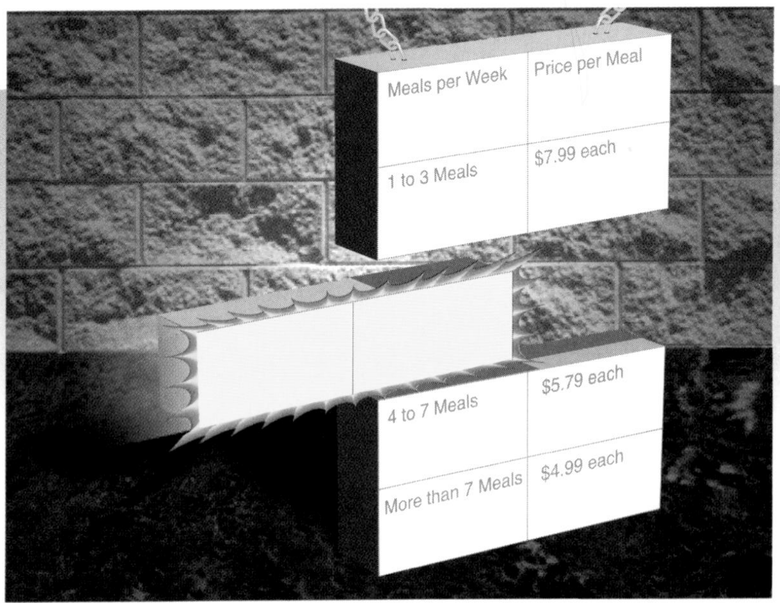

When you delete a row in a table, the remaining rows shift to fill the empty space.

ADD OR DELETE A ROW

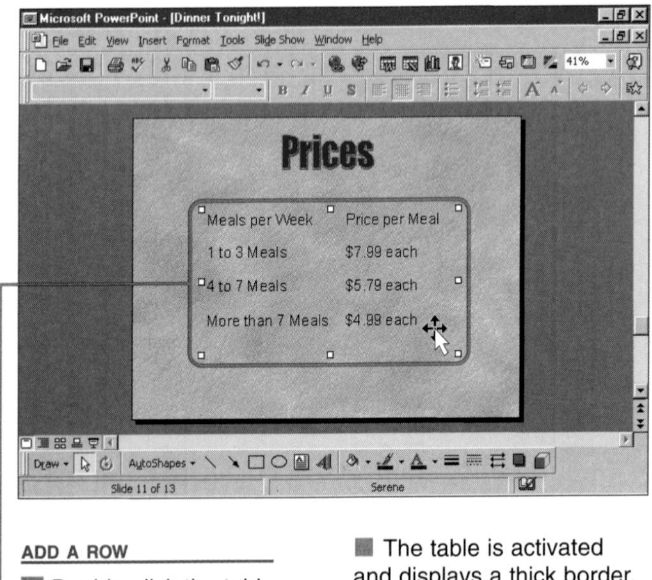

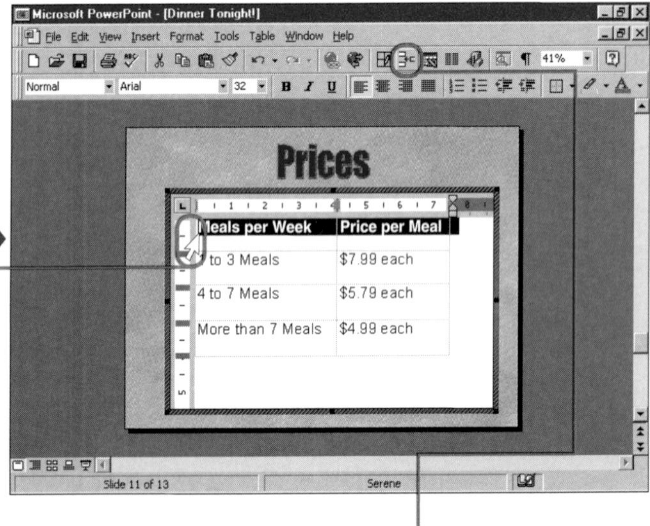

ADD A ROW

1 Double-click the table you want to change.

■ The table is activated and displays a thick border.

■ PowerPoint will add a row above the row you select.

2 To select a row, position the mouse over the left edge of the first cell in the row (changes to). Then double-click the left mouse button.

3 Click to add a row.

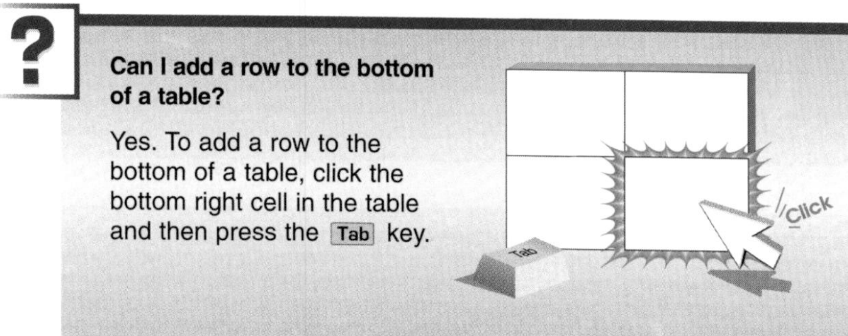

Can I add a row to the bottom of a table?

Yes. To add a row to the bottom of a table, click the bottom right cell in the table and then press the Tab key.

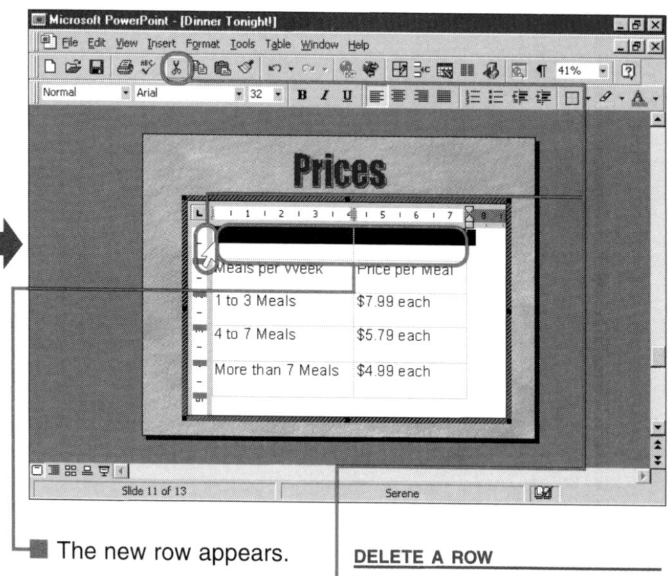

- The new row appears.

DELETE A ROW

4 To select the row you want to delete, position the mouse over the left edge of the first cell in the row (changes to). Then double-click the left mouse button.

5 Click to delete the row.

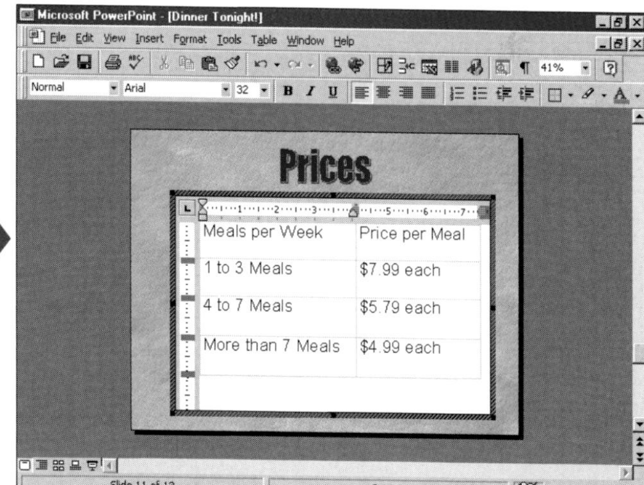

- The row disappears from the table.

6 Click outside the table to return to the slide.

MAKE CHANGES TO A TABLE

PowerPoint offers many ready-to-use formats that you can choose from to give your table a new appearance.

FORMAT A TABLE

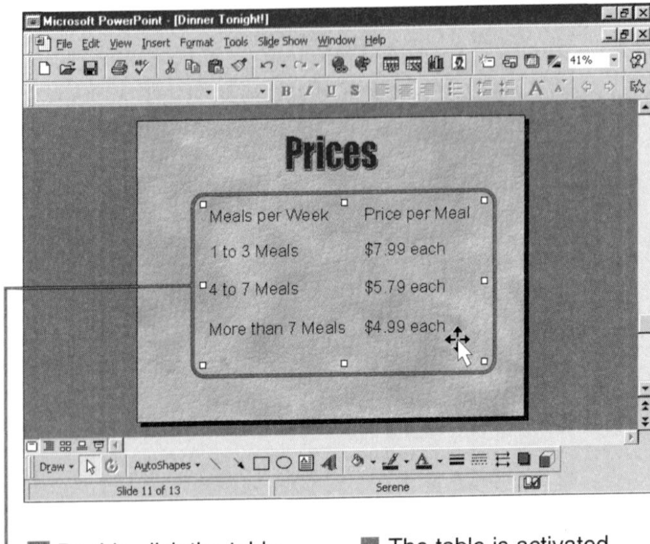

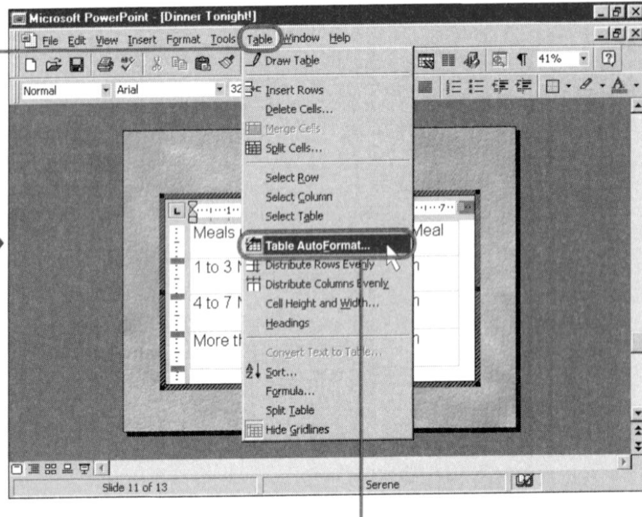

1 Double-click the table you want to change.

■ The table is activated and displays a thick border.

2 Click **Table**.

3 Click **Table AutoFormat**.

■ The Table AutoFormat dialog box appears.

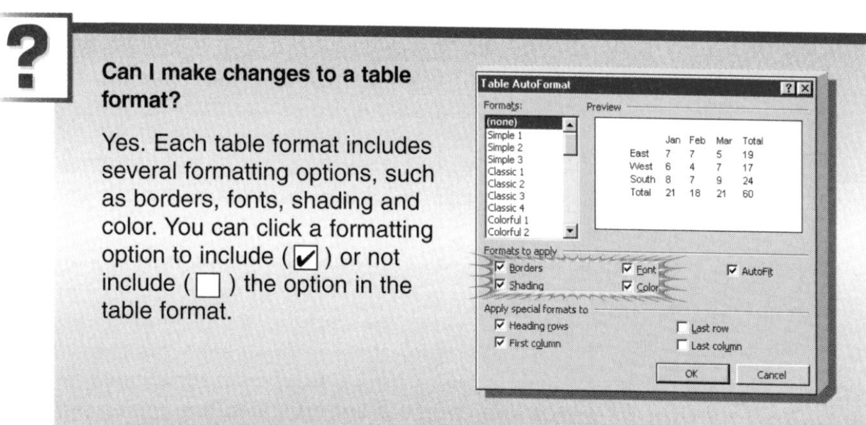

?

Can I make changes to a table format?

Yes. Each table format includes several formatting options, such as borders, fonts, shading and color. You can click a formatting option to include (✔) or not include (☐) the option in the table format.

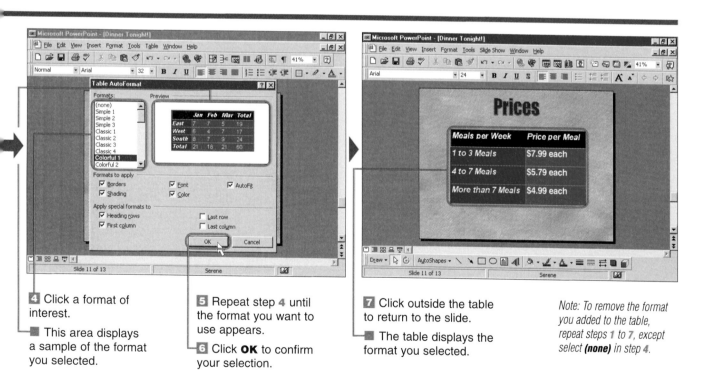

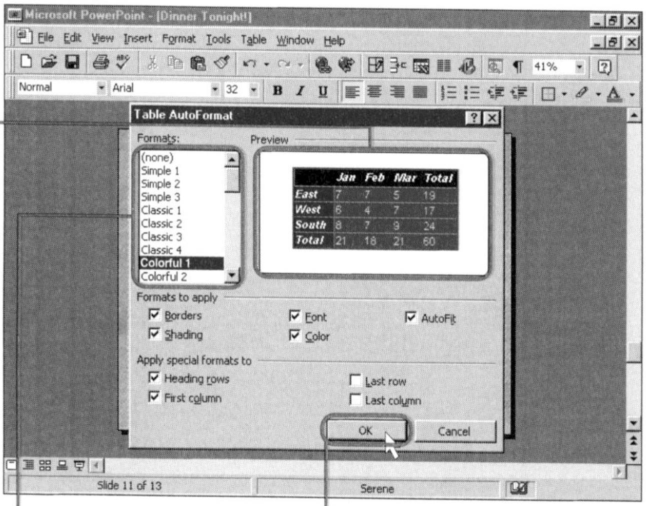

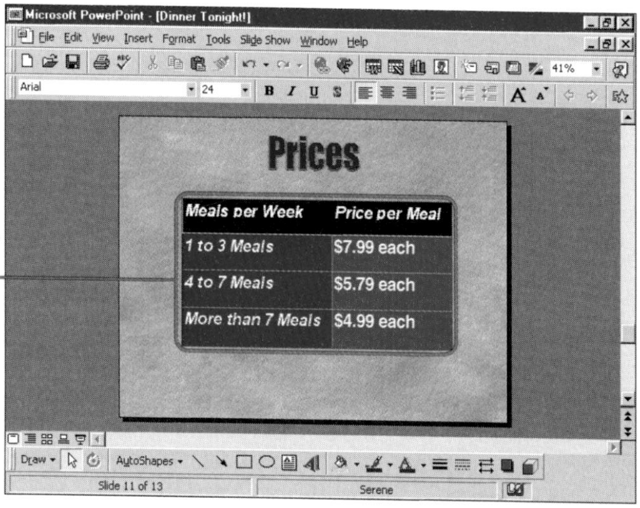

4 Click a format of interest.

■ This area displays a sample of the format you selected.

5 Repeat step **4** until the format you want to use appears.

6 Click **OK** to confirm your selection.

7 Click outside the table to return to the slide.

■ The table displays the format you selected.

*Note: To remove the format you added to the table, repeat steps 1 to 7, except select **(none)** in step 4.*

Terrific Toys Corporate Philosophy
To be a leader in developing unique, high-quality toys for children of all ages
Acrylic
Paint
Acrylic
Paint
Acrylic
Paint

CHAPTER 7

Work With Objects on Slides

Do you want to customize the objects on your slides? Read this chapter to learn how to change the size or color of an object and how to make an object 3-D.

MOVE OR SIZE AN OBJECT

You can change the location or size of an object on a slide.

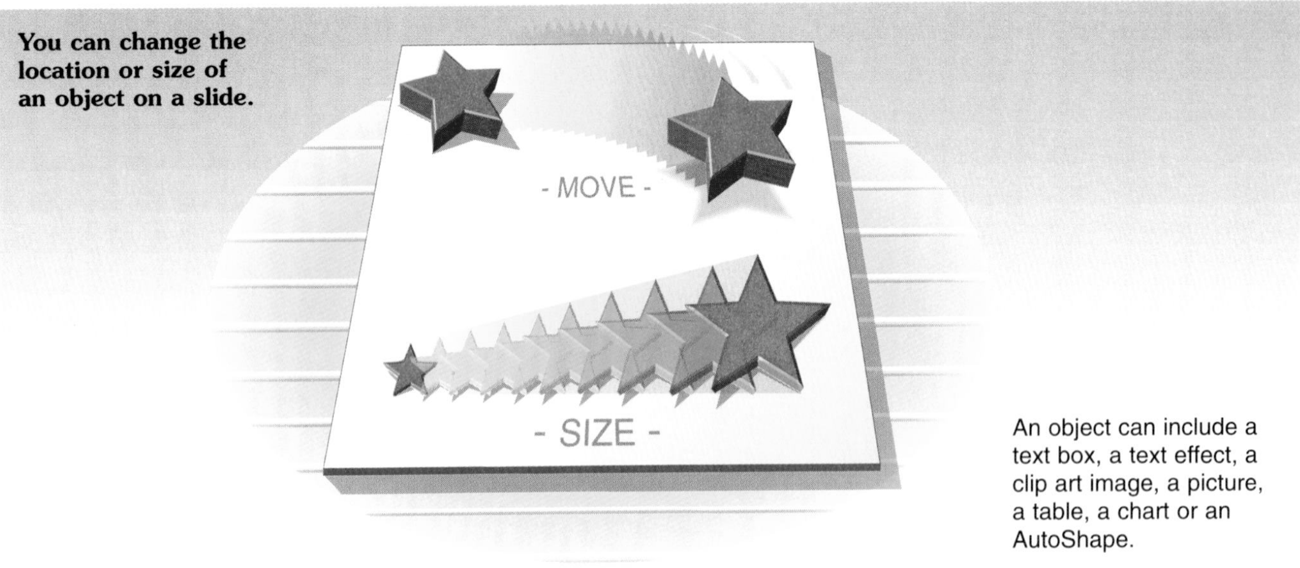

An object can include a text box, a text effect, a clip art image, a picture, a table, a chart or an AutoShape.

MOVE AN OBJECT

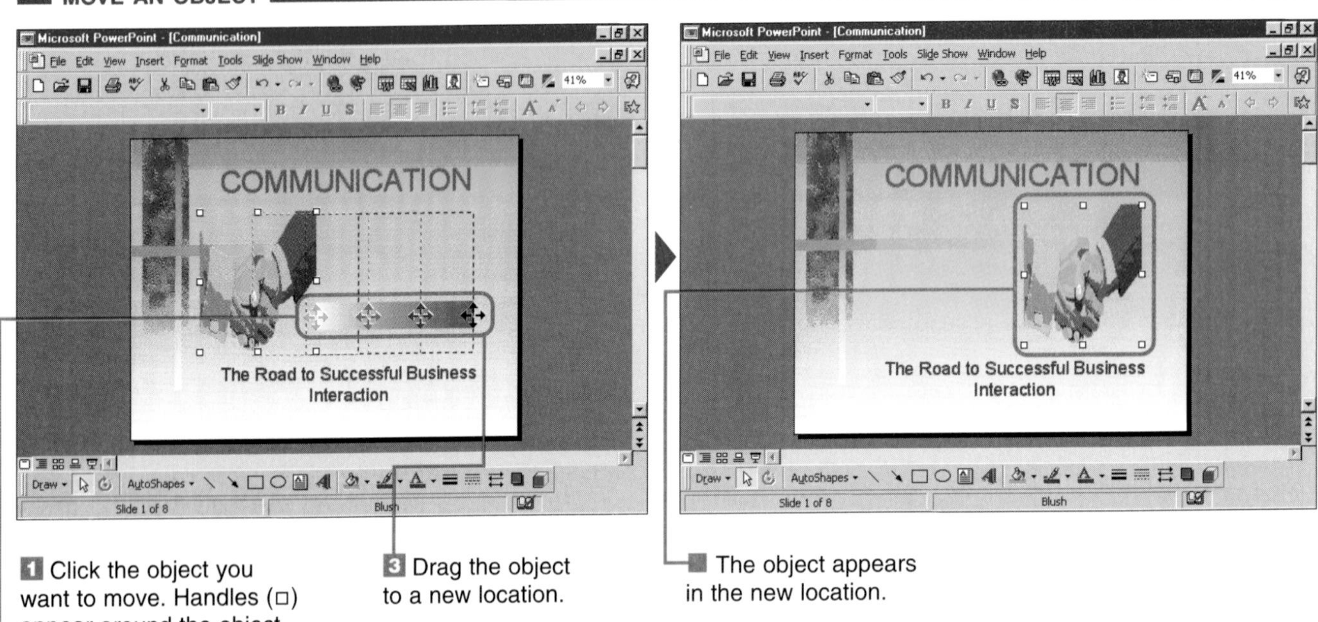

1 Click the object you want to move. Handles (□) appear around the object.

2 Position the mouse over an edge of the object (changes to ✥).

3 Drag the object to a new location.

■ The object appears in the new location.

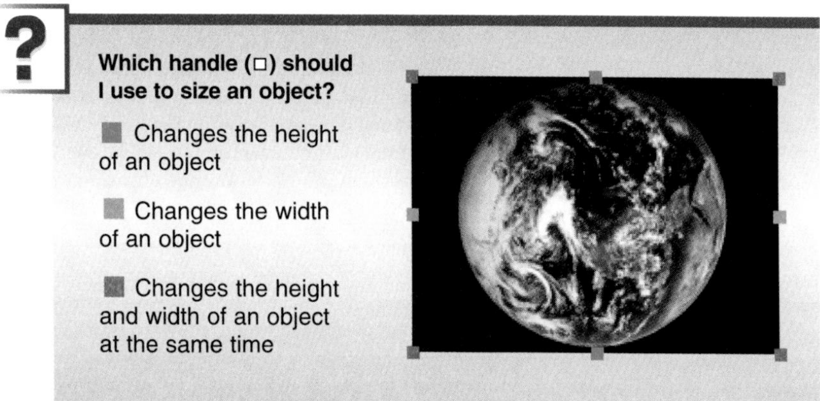

Which handle (□) should I use to size an object?

■ Changes the height of an object

■ Changes the width of an object

■ Changes the height and width of an object at the same time

SIZE AN OBJECT

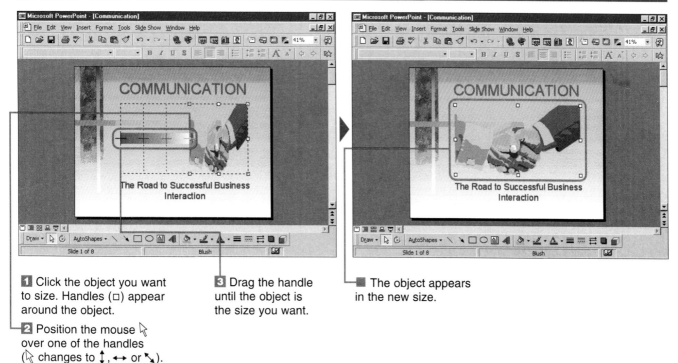

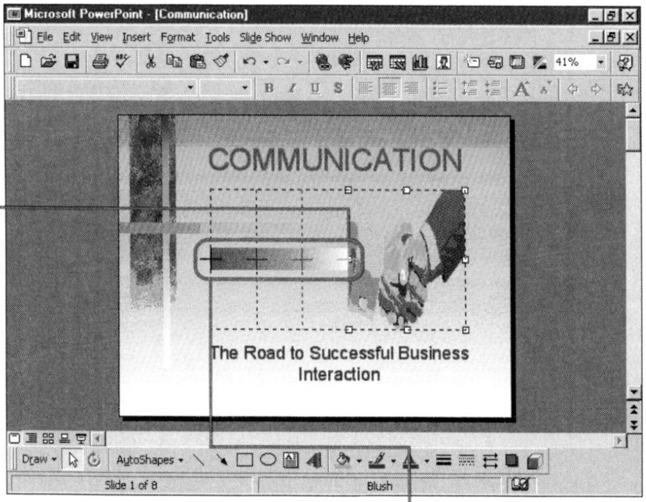

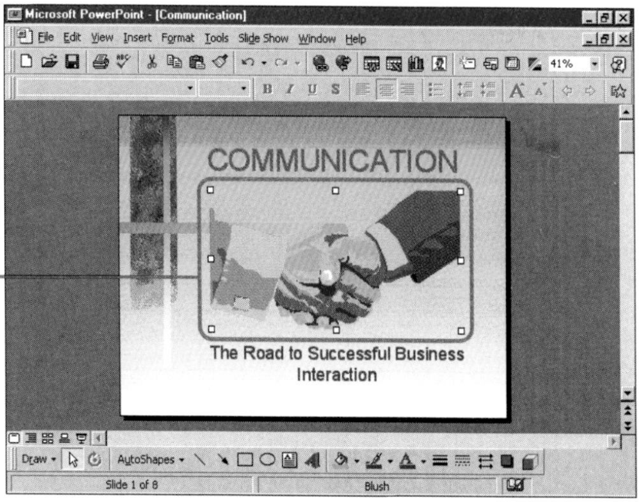

1 Click the object you want to size. Handles (□) appear around the object.

2 Position the mouse over one of the handles (changes to ↕, ↔ or ⤡).

3 Drag the handle until the object is the size you want.

■ The object appears in the new size.

DELETE AN OBJECT

You can delete an object, such as an AutoShape or text box, you no longer want to appear on a slide.

DELETE AN OBJECT

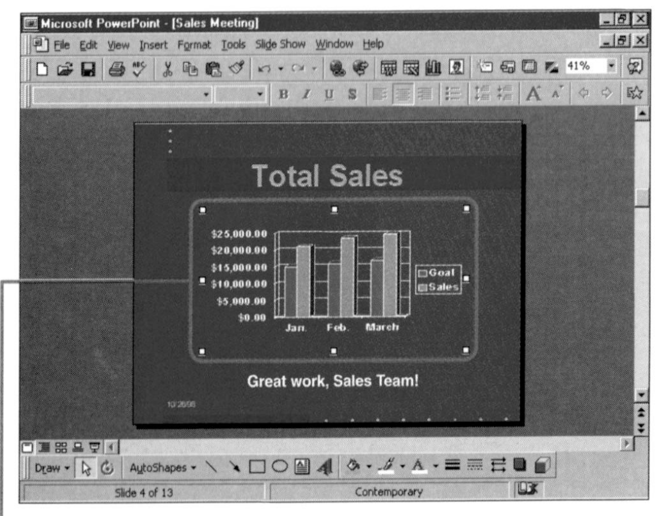

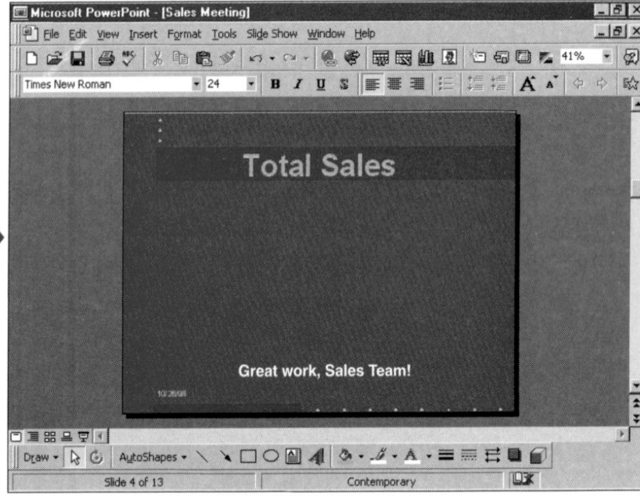

1 Click the object you want to delete. Handles (□) appear around the object.

2 Press the Delete key.

■ The object disappears.

?

What types of text boxes can I remove from a slide?

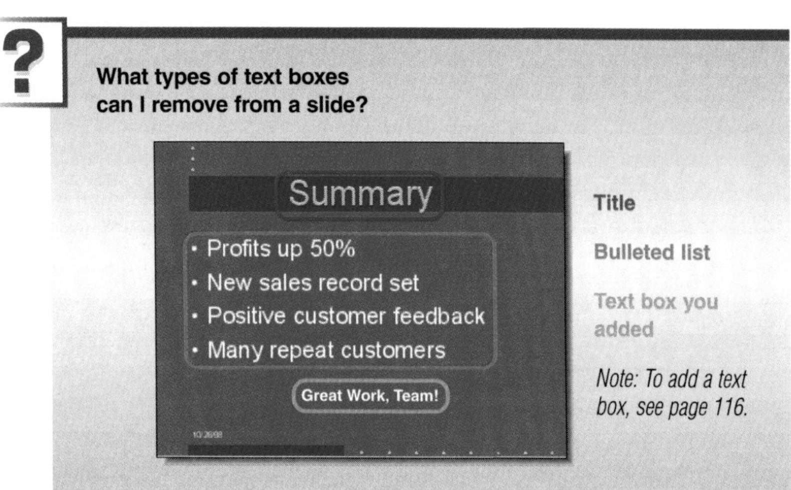

Title

Bulleted list

Text box you added

Note: To add a text box, see page 116.

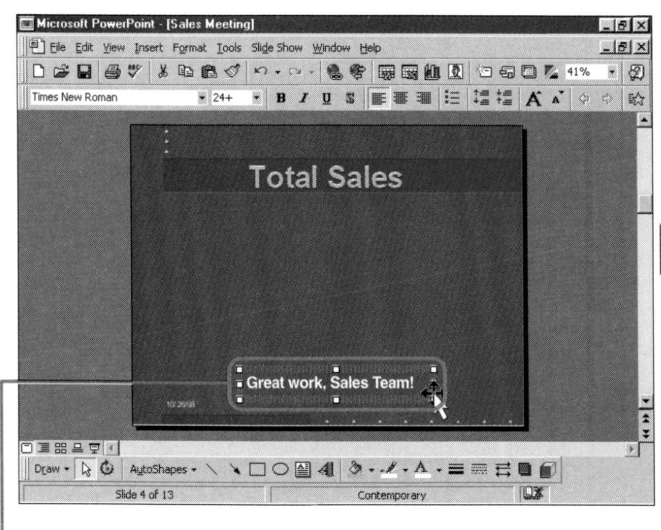

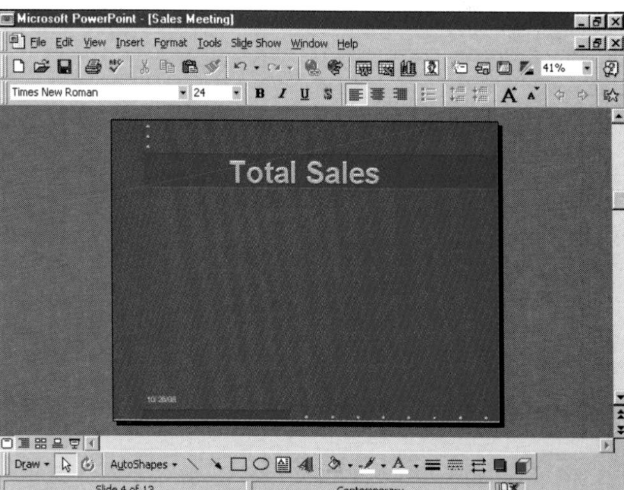

DELETE A TEXT BOX

1 Click the text box you want to delete. Handles (□) appear around the text box.

2 Click an edge of the text box to select the text box.

3 Press the Delete key.

4 If necessary, press the Delete key again to remove the text box.

■ The text box disappears.

CHANGE OBJECT COLOR

You can change the color of an object on a slide.

CHANGE OBJECT COLOR

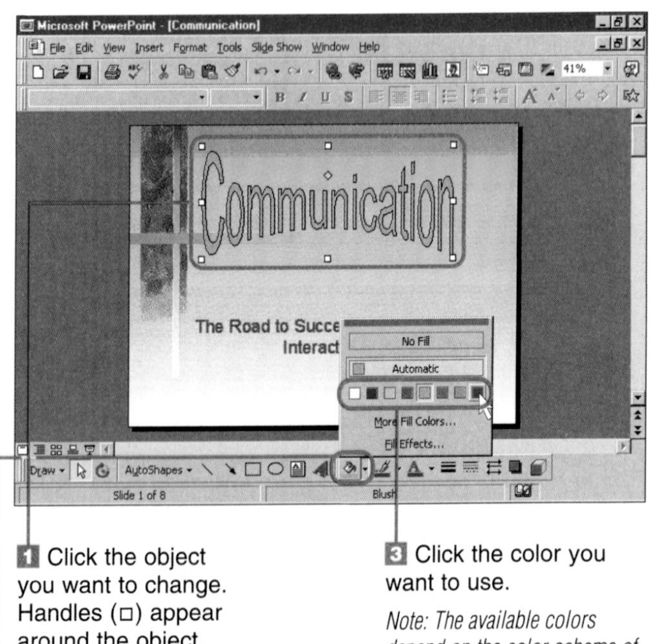

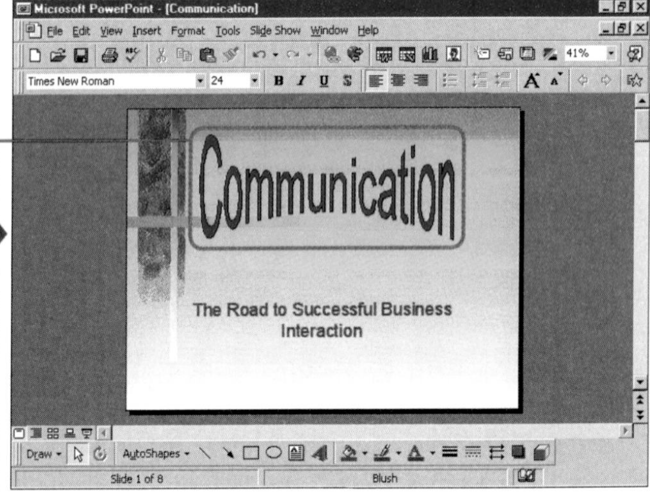

1 Click the object you want to change. Handles (□) appear around the object.

2 Click ▾ in this area.

3 Click the color you want to use.

Note: The available colors depend on the color scheme of the slide. For information on color schemes, see page 102.

■ The object you selected appears in the new color.

■ To deselect the object, click outside the object area.

CHANGE LINE COLOR

You can change the color of the line surrounding an object on a slide.

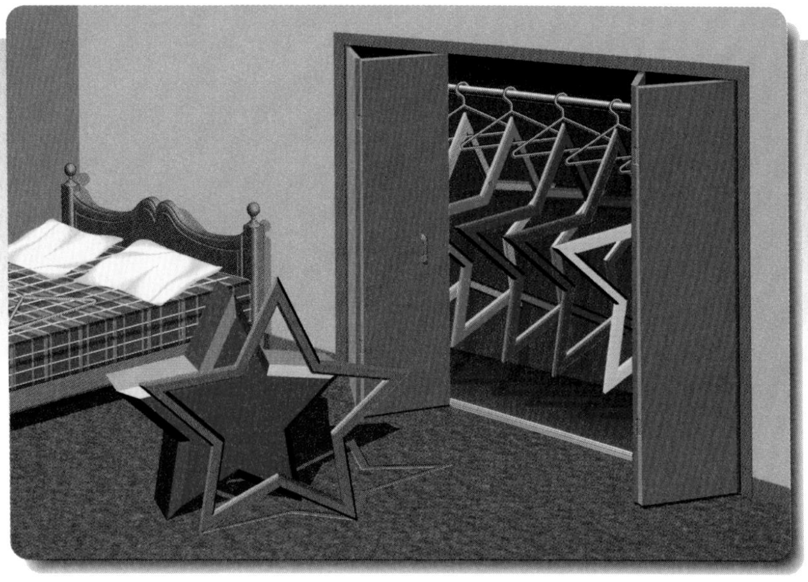

You can change the line color for objects such as text boxes, pictures, charts, tables and AutoShapes.

CHANGE LINE COLOR

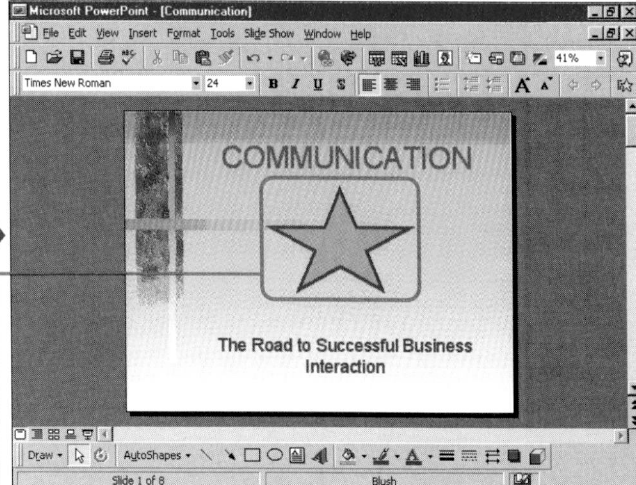

1 Click the object you want to change. Handles (□) appear around the object.

2 Click ▾ in this area to display the available line colors.

3 Click the color you want to use.

Note: The available colors depend on the color scheme of the slide. For information on color schemes, see page 102.

■ The line surrounding the object displays the new color.

■ To deselect the object, click outside the object area.

REMOVE THE LINE

■ To remove the line surrounding an object, repeat steps 1 to 3, except select **No Line** in step 3.

CHANGE LINE THICKNESS

You can emphasize an object by changing the thickness of the line surrounding the object.

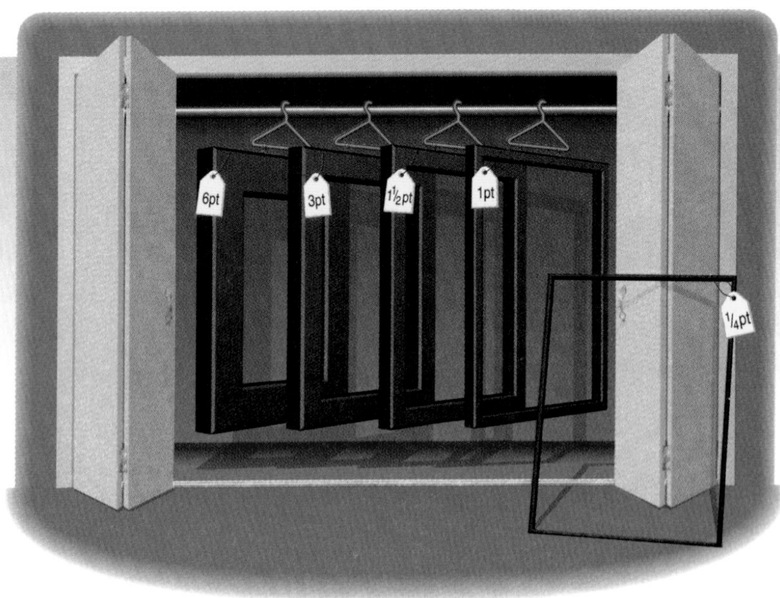

You can change the line thickness for objects such as text boxes, pictures, charts, tables and AutoShapes.

CHANGE LINE THICKNESS

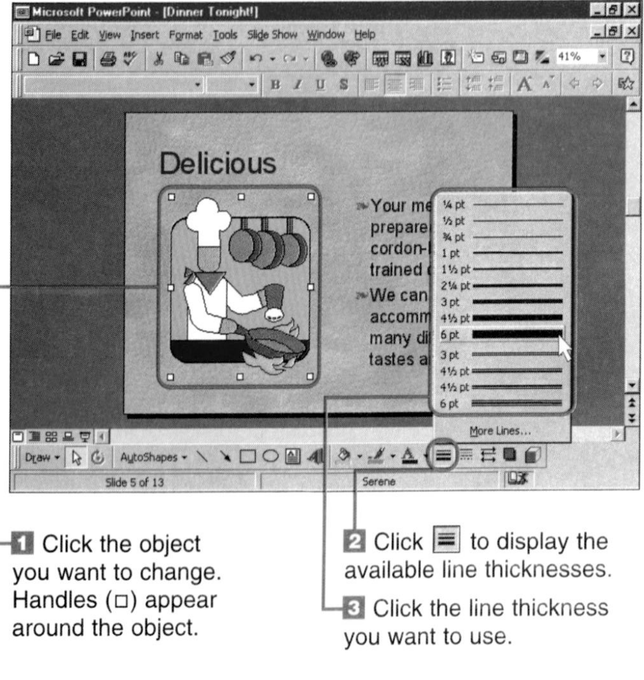

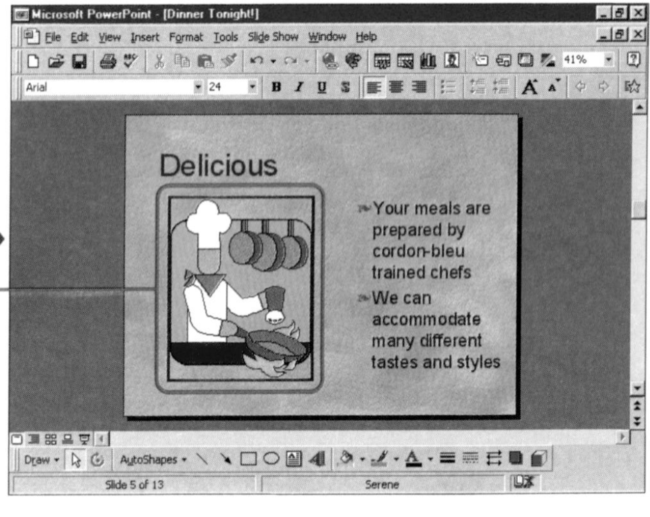

1 Click the object you want to change. Handles (□) appear around the object.

2 Click ▤ to display the available line thicknesses.

3 Click the line thickness you want to use.

■ The line surrounding the object displays the new thickness.

■ To deselect the object, click outside the object area.

Note: To remove the line surrounding an object, see page 159.

CHANGE DASH STYLE

You can change the line surrounding an object to a dashed or dotted line.

CHANGE DASH STYLE

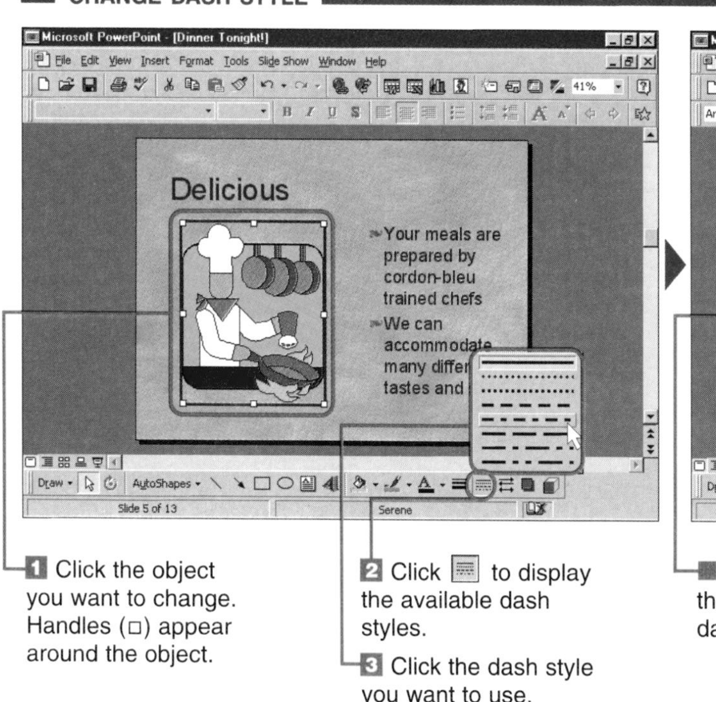

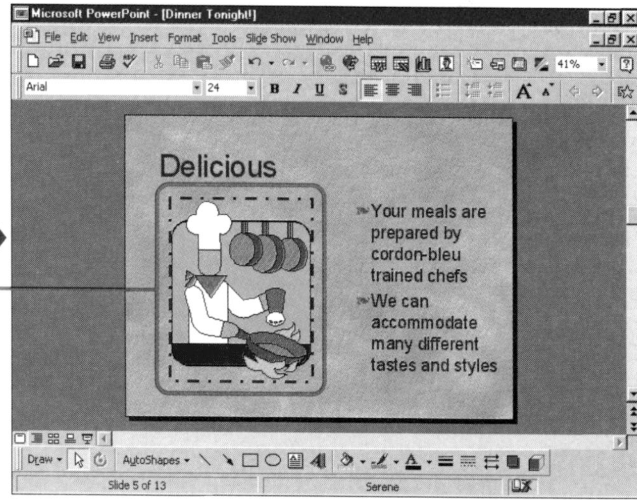

1 Click the object you want to change. Handles (□) appear around the object.

2 Click ▤ to display the available dash styles.

3 Click the dash style you want to use.

■ The line surrounding the object displays the dash style.

■ To deselect the object, click outside the object area.

Note: To remove the line surrounding an object, see page 159.

ADD A TEXTURE OR PATTERN

You can enhance the appearance of an object on a slide by adding a texture or pattern to the object.

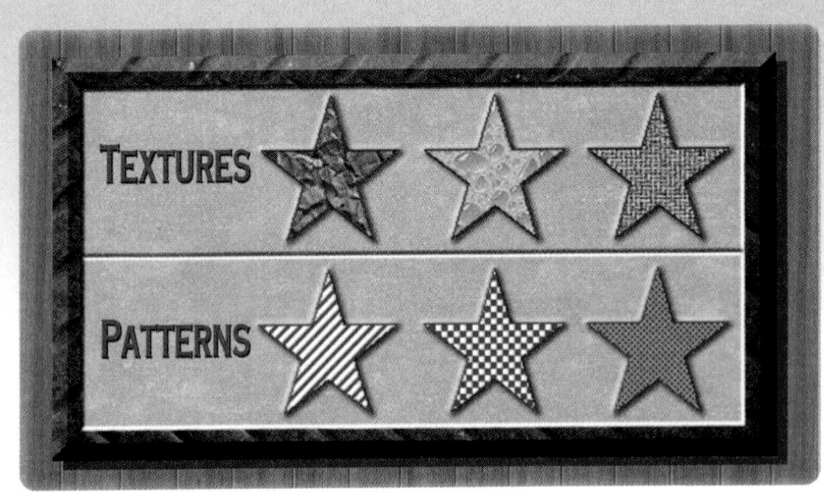

You can add a texture or pattern to several types of objects, including AutoShapes, text effects, tables and text boxes.

ADD A TEXTURE OR PATTERN

1 Click the object you want to add a texture or pattern to.

2 Click ▾ in this area.

3 Click **Fill Effects**.

■ The Fill Effects dialog box appears.

ADD A TEXTURE

4 To add a texture, click the **Texture** tab.

5 Click the texture you want to add. Then skip to step **8**.

?

How can I change the color of the patterns displayed in the Fill Effects dialog box?

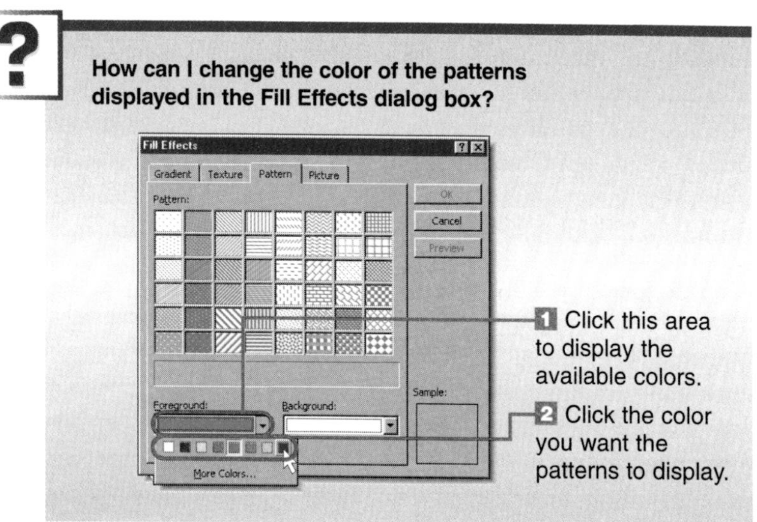

1 Click this area to display the available colors.

2 Click the color you want the patterns to display.

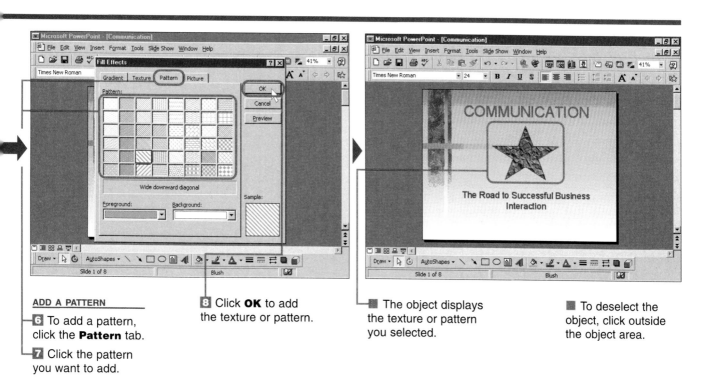

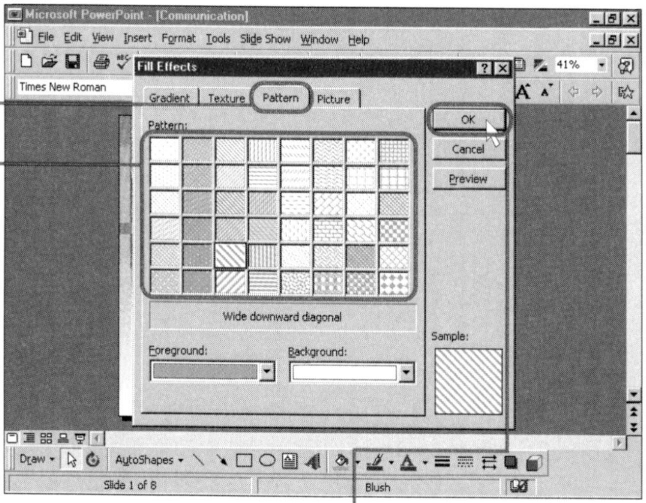

ADD A PATTERN

6 To add a pattern, click the **Pattern** tab.

7 Click the pattern you want to add.

8 Click **OK** to add the texture or pattern.

■ The object displays the texture or pattern you selected.

■ To deselect the object, click outside the object area.

ROTATE AN OBJECT

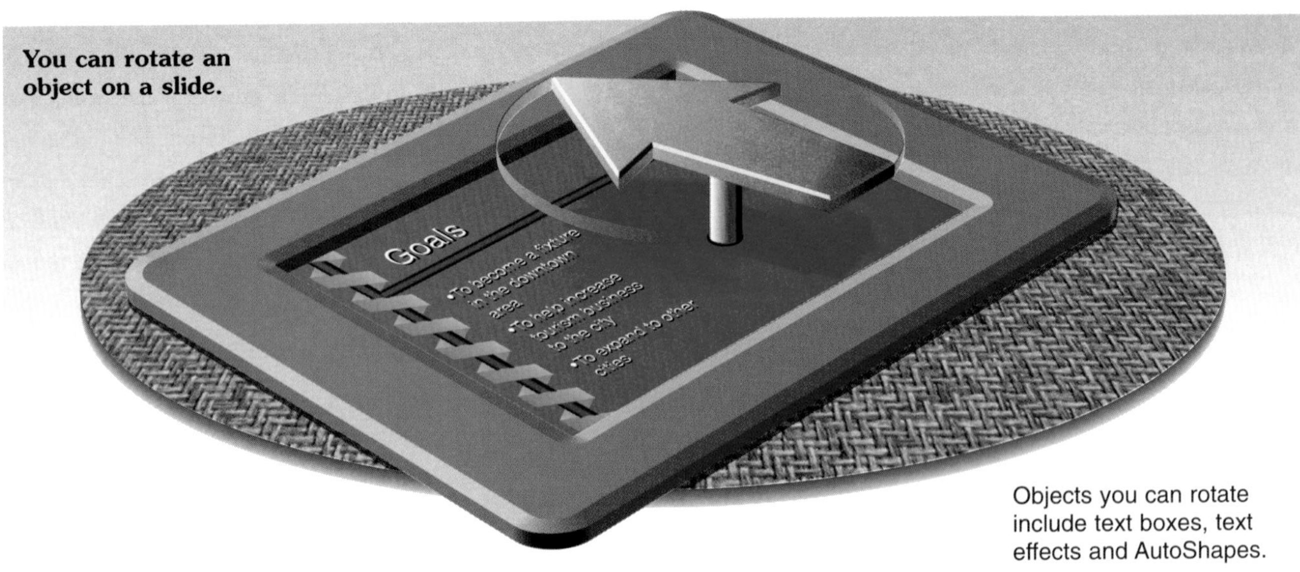

You can rotate an object on a slide.

Objects you can rotate include text boxes, text effects and AutoShapes.

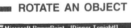

ROTATE AN OBJECT

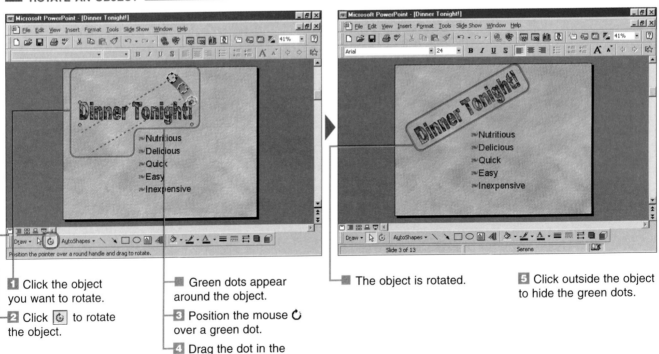

1 Click the object you want to rotate.

2 Click [rotate icon] to rotate the object.

- Green dots appear around the object.

3 Position the mouse over a green dot.

4 Drag the dot in the direction you want to rotate the object.

- The object is rotated.

5 Click outside the object to hide the green dots.

MAKE AN OBJECT 3-D

You can make an object on a slide appear three-dimensional.

MAKE AN OBJECT 3-D

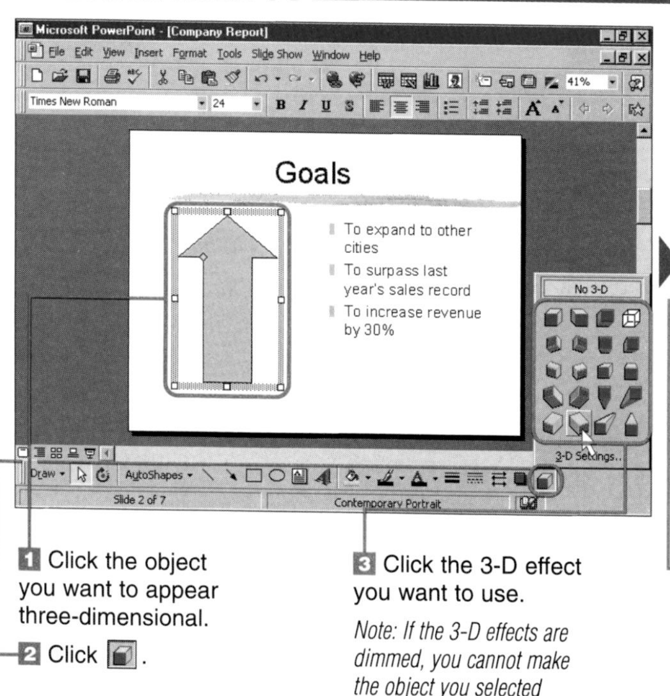

1 Click the object you want to appear three-dimensional.

2 Click .

3 Click the 3-D effect you want to use.

Note: If the 3-D effects are dimmed, you cannot make the object you selected three-dimensional.

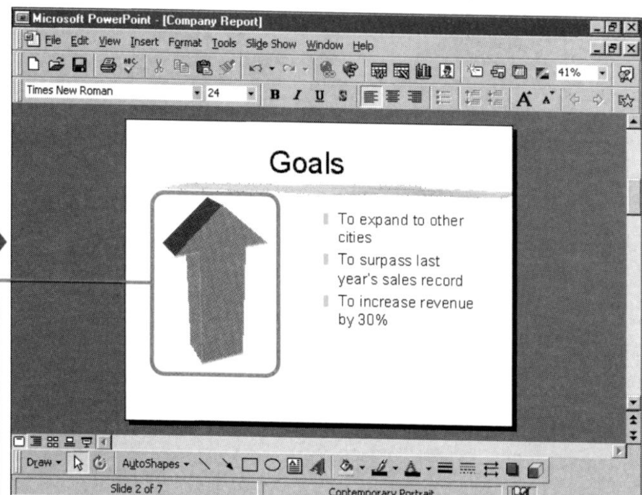

■ The object displays the 3-D effect.

■ To deselect the object, click outside the object area.

*Note: To remove a 3-D effect from an object, repeat steps **1** to **3**, selecting **No 3-D** in step **3**.*

56

CHAPTER 8

Add Multimedia to Slides

Would you like to learn how to add multimedia, such as movies and sounds, to your slides? This chapter shows you how.

ADD A SOUND

You can add a sound to a slide. This is useful for drawing the attention of the audience to an important slide in your presentation.

The Microsoft Clip Gallery provides many sounds that you can choose from.

ADD A SOUND FROM THE GALLERY

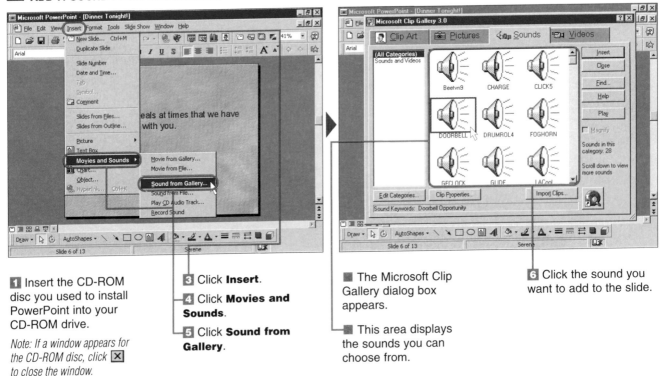

1 Insert the CD-ROM disc you used to install PowerPoint into your CD-ROM drive.

Note: If a window appears for the CD-ROM disc, click ☒ to close the window.

2 Display the slide you want to add a sound to.

3 Click **Insert**.

4 Click **Movies and Sounds**.

5 Click **Sound from Gallery**.

■ The Microsoft Clip Gallery dialog box appears.

■ This area displays the sounds you can choose from.

6 Click the sound you want to add to the slide.

?

How do I remove a sound I added to a slide in my presentation?

To remove a sound from a slide, you must delete the speaker icon (🔈) from the slide. Display the slide in the Slide view and then click the speaker icon. Then press the Delete key to remove the sound.

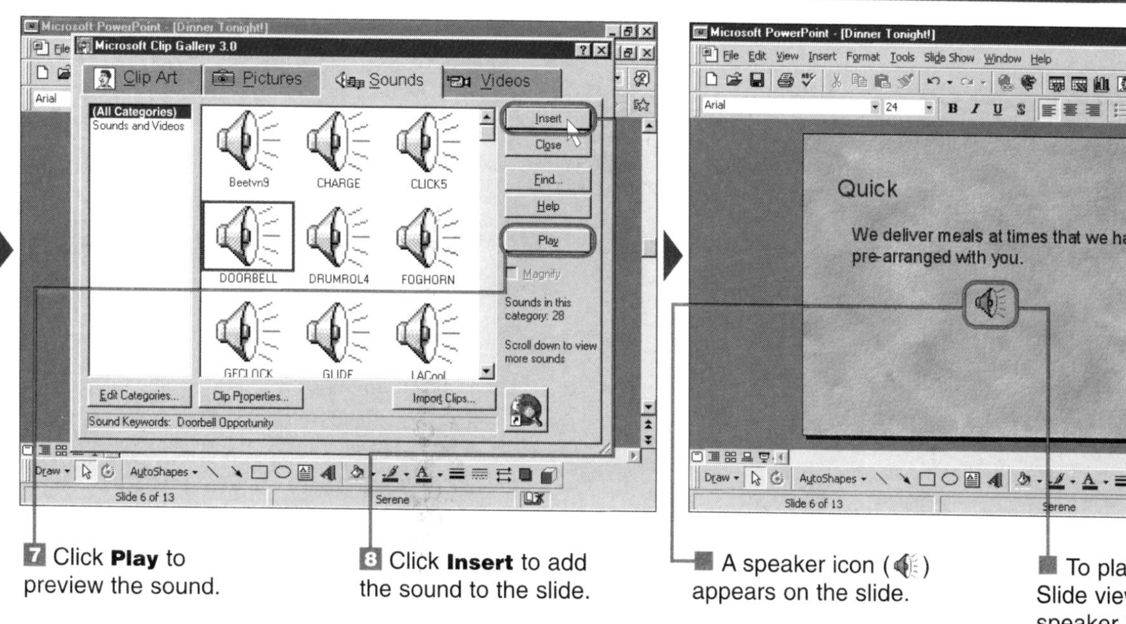

7 Click **Play** to preview the sound.

8 Click **Insert** to add the sound to the slide.

■ A speaker icon (🔈) appears on the slide.

Note: To move or size the speaker icon, see page 154.

■ To play the sound in the Slide view, double-click the speaker icon (🔈).

Note: To play the sound during the slide show, click the speaker icon (🔈) on the slide. To view a slide show, see page 238.

ADD A SOUND

You can add a sound stored on your computer to a slide. For example, you can add sounds such as theme songs, advertising jingles or clips from famous speeches.

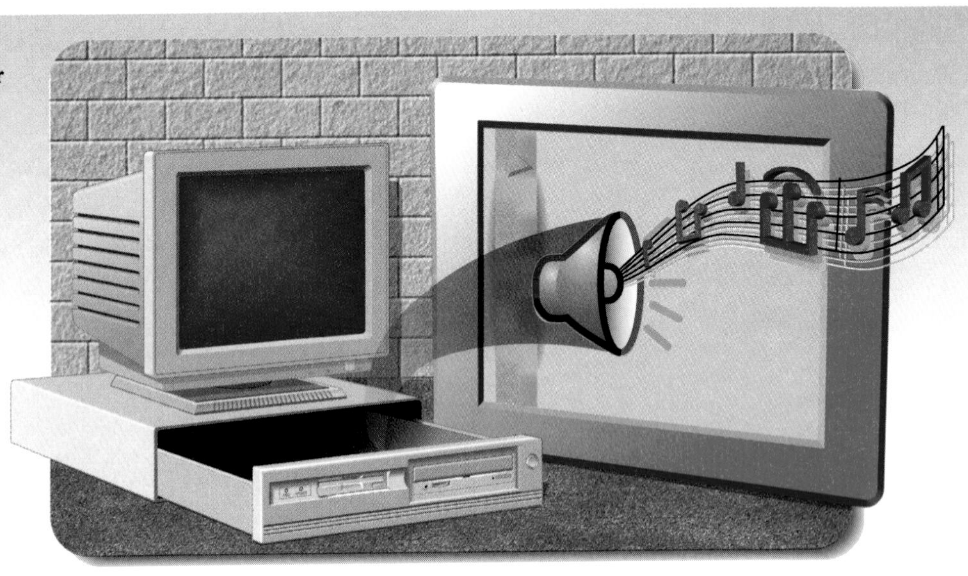

ADD A SOUND FROM A FILE

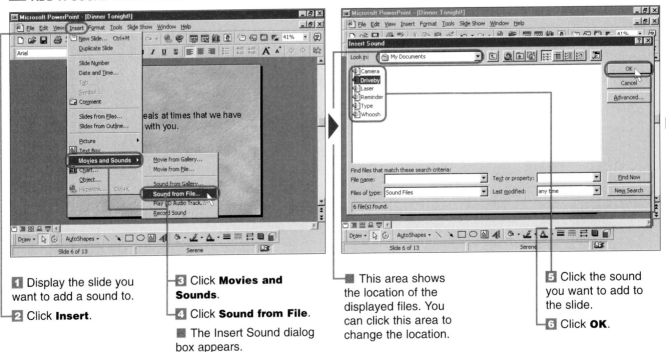

1. Display the slide you want to add a sound to.
2. Click **Insert**.
3. Click **Movies and Sounds**.
4. Click **Sound from File**.

■ The Insert Sound dialog box appears.

■ This area shows the location of the displayed files. You can click this area to change the location.

5. Click the sound you want to add to the slide.
6. Click **OK**.

?

Where can I get sounds that I can use in my presentation?

Many computer stores sell CD-ROM discs that contain collections of sounds. There are also Web sites on the Internet that offer free sounds. You can find sounds at the following Web sites:

www.dailywav.com

www.soundamerica.com

www.wavcentral.com

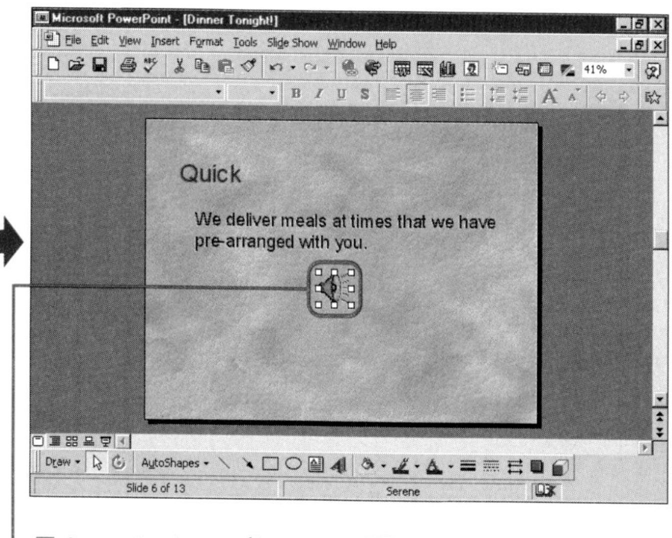

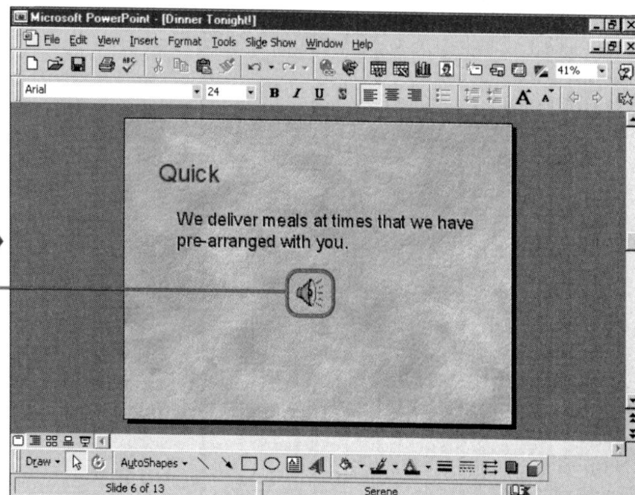

■ A speaker icon (🔈) appears on the slide. The handles (□) around the speaker icon let you change the size of the icon.

7 To hide the handles, click outside the icon area.

Note: To move or size the speaker icon, see page 154.

■ To play the sound in the Slide view, double-click the speaker icon (🔈).

Note: To play the sound during the slide show, click the speaker icon (🔈) on the slide. To view a slide show, see page 238.

■ To remove the sound from the slide, see the top of page 169.

ADD A MOVIE

You can add a movie to a slide to add interest to your presentation.

The Microsoft Clip Gallery provides many movies that you can choose from.

ADD A MOVIE FROM THE GALLERY

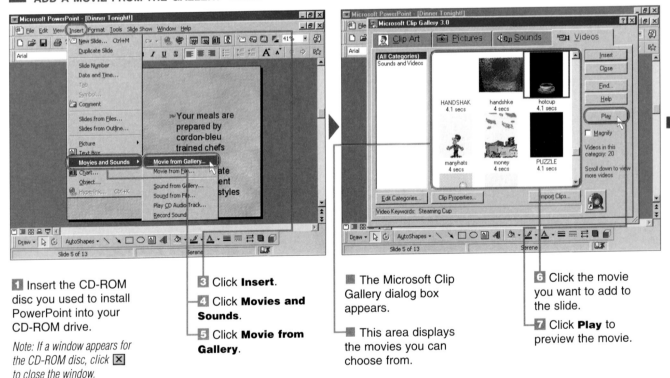

1 Insert the CD-ROM disc you used to install PowerPoint into your CD-ROM drive.

Note: If a window appears for the CD-ROM disc, click ☒ to close the window.

2 Display the slide you want to add a movie to.

3 Click **Insert**.

4 Click **Movies and Sounds**.

5 Click **Movie from Gallery**.

■ The Microsoft Clip Gallery dialog box appears.

■ This area displays the movies you can choose from.

6 Click the movie you want to add to the slide.

7 Click **Play** to preview the movie.

?

Should I change the size of the movie on my slide?

In most cases, you should not change the size of a movie. A movie is designed to play best at its original size. If you enlarge a movie, the movie may become jerky, appear grainy or display other visual distortions.

■ A window appears and the movie plays.

8 Click **Insert** to add the movie to the slide.

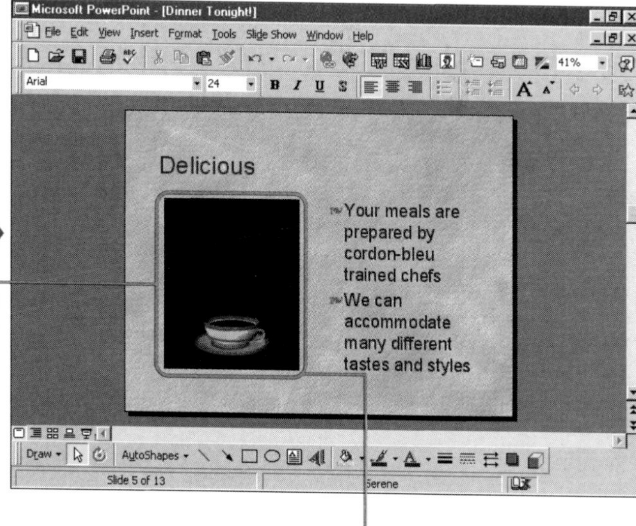

■ The first frame of the movie appears on the slide.

Note: To move, size or delete a movie, see pages 154 to 156.

■ To play the movie in the Slide view, double-click the movie.

Note: To play the movie during the slide show, click the movie on the slide. To view a slide show, see page 238.

ADD A MOVIE

You can add a movie stored on your computer to a slide. For example, you can add movie clips from television commercials, news events, sporting events or films.

ADD A MOVIE FROM A FILE

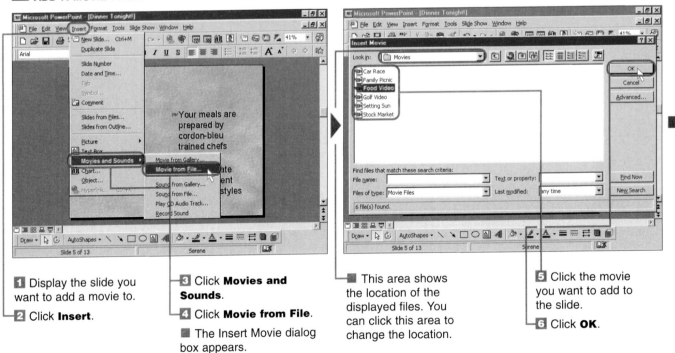

1 Display the slide you want to add a movie to.

2 Click **Insert**.

3 Click **Movies and Sounds**.

4 Click **Movie from File**.

■ The Insert Movie dialog box appears.

■ This area shows the location of the displayed files. You can click this area to change the location.

5 Click the movie you want to add to the slide.

6 Click **OK**.

?

Where can I get movies that I can use in my presentation?

You can check recent computer publications to find companies that sell CD-ROM discs containing collections of movies. There are also Web sites on the Internet that offer free movies. You can find movies at the following Web sites:

www.cnn.com/video_vault

www.cnnsi.com/almanac/video

www.pathfinder.com/people/video

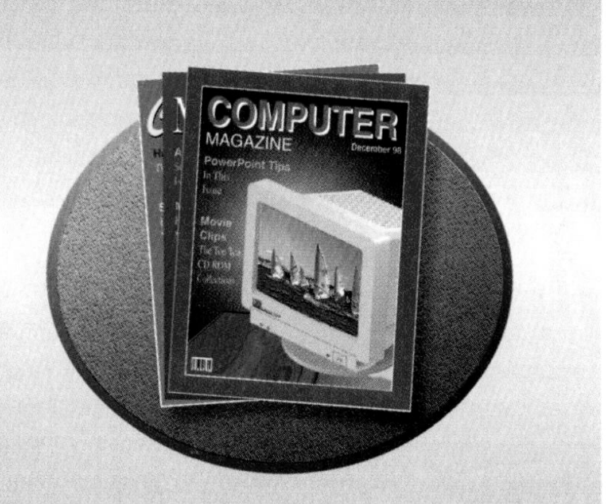

■ The first frame of the movie appears on the slide. The handles (□) around the movie let you change the size of the movie.

7 To hide the handles, click outside the movie area.

Note: To move, size or delete a movie, see pages 154 to 156.

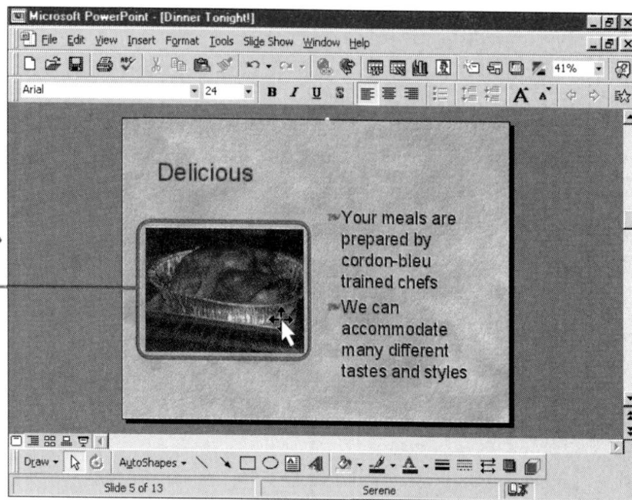

8 To play the movie in the Slide view, double-click the movie.

Note: To play the movie during the slide show, click the movie. To view a slide show, see page 238.

PLAY A MUSIC CD DURING A SLIDE SHOW

You can play tracks from a music CD during a slide show to add background music to your slides.

PLAY A MUSIC CD FOR ONE SLIDE

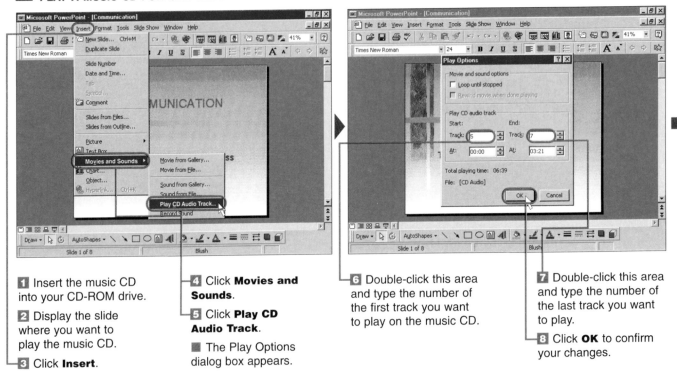

1 Insert the music CD into your CD-ROM drive.

2 Display the slide where you want to play the music CD.

3 Click **Insert**.

4 Click **Movies and Sounds**.

5 Click **Play CD Audio Track**.

■ The Play Options dialog box appears.

6 Double-click this area and type the number of the first track you want to play on the music CD.

7 Double-click this area and type the number of the last track you want to play.

8 Click **OK** to confirm your changes.

?

How do I stop my music CD from playing automatically when I insert it into the CD-ROM drive?

When you insert a music CD into a CD-ROM drive, the CD may automatically begin playing. This can be distracting when viewing a slide show. To stop the CD from playing automatically, press and hold down the Shift key as you insert the CD into the drive.

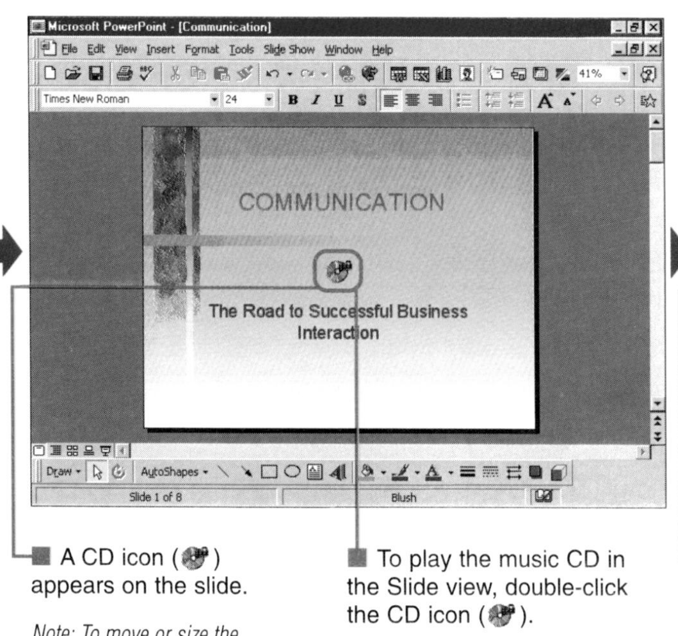

■ A CD icon ( ) appears on the slide.

Note: To move or size the CD icon, see page 154.

■ To play the music CD in the Slide view, double-click the CD icon ( ).

■ To play the music CD during the slide show, click the CD icon ( ) on the slide. To view a slide show, see page 238.

■ If you no longer want to play a music CD for a slide, display the slide in the Slide view. Then click the CD icon ( ) and press the Delete key.

PLAY A MUSIC CD DURING A SLIDE SHOW

By default, the music CD tracks you add to a slide will stop playing when you display the next slide in the slide show. If you prefer, you can have the music CD play for multiple slides.

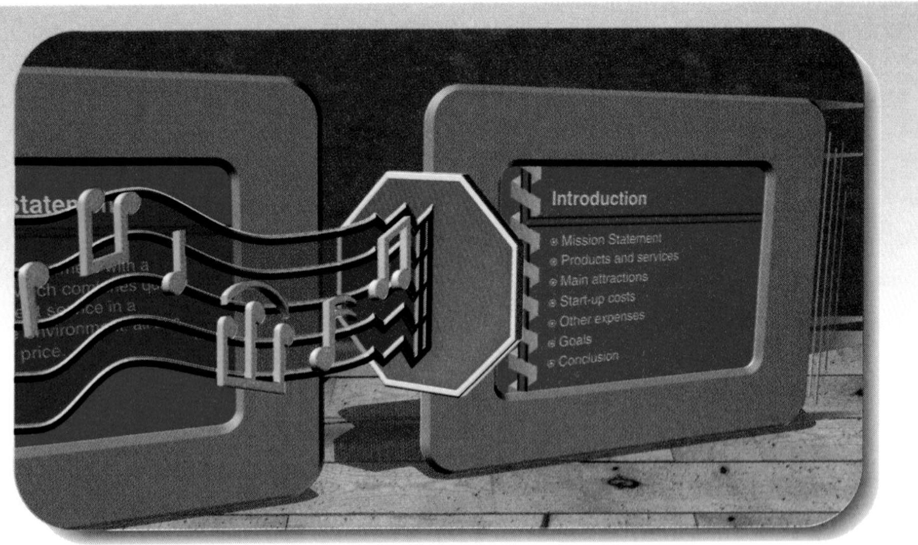

PLAY A MUSIC CD FOR MULTIPLE SLIDES

1 Click the CD icon ( ) for the music CD you want to play for multiple slides. Handles (□) appear around the icon.

Note: To set up a music CD to play during a slide show, perform steps 1 to 8 on page 176.

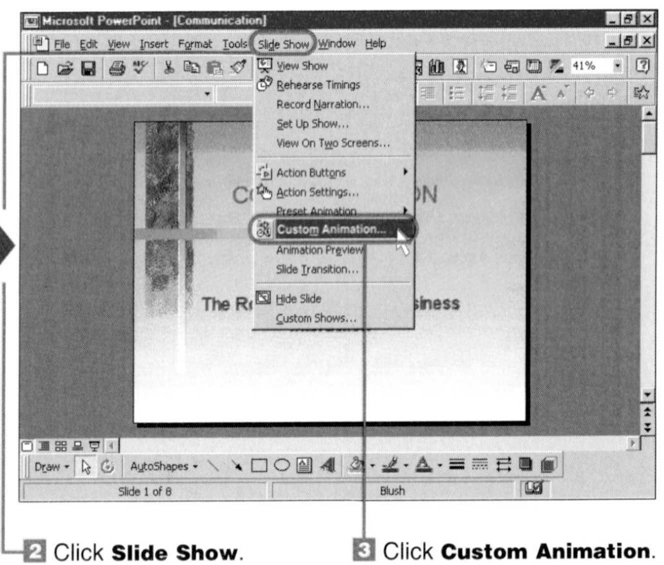

2 Click **Slide Show**.

3 Click **Custom Animation**.

■ The Custom Animation dialog box appears.

?

Why doesn't the music CD I set to play for multiple slides begin playing as soon as I click a blank area on the slide?

To play as soon as you click a blank area on the slide, the music CD must be set as the first animation. To change the animation order of objects on a slide, see page 202.

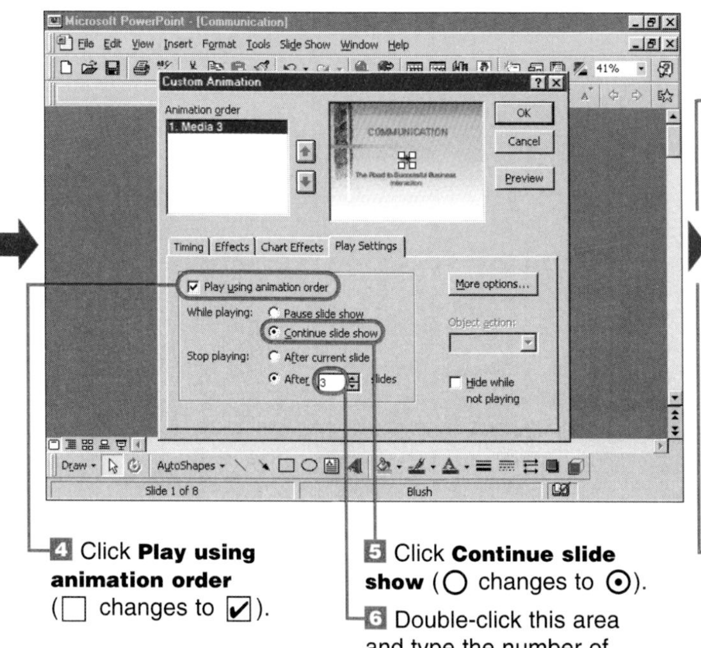

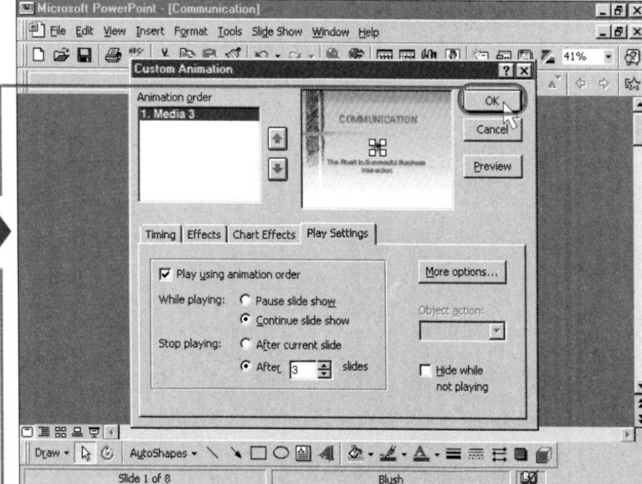

4 Click **Play using animation order** (☐ changes to ☑).

5 Click **Continue slide show** (○ changes to ⊙).

6 Double-click this area and type the number of slides you want the music CD to play for.

7 Click **OK** to confirm your changes.

■ To play the music CD for multiple slides during the slide show, make sure you click a blank area on the slide rather than the CD icon ( ) on the slide. To view a slide show, see page 238.

ADD A RECORDED SOUND

You can record your own sound and then add it to a slide. This is useful if you need to include a statement from a colleague who is unable to attend your presentation.

ADD A RECORDED SOUND

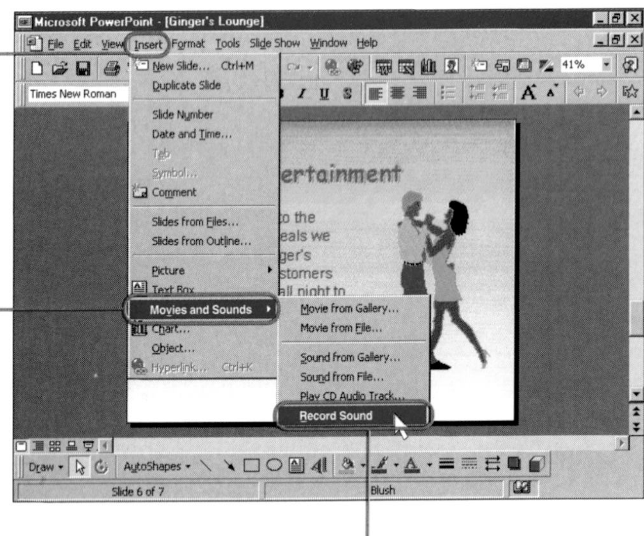

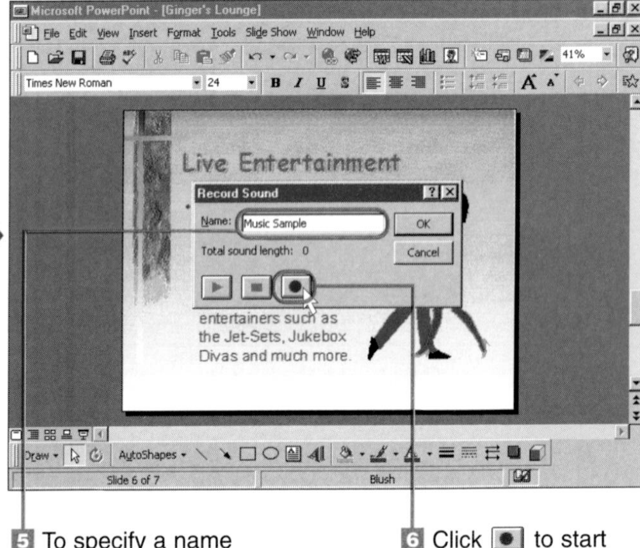

1 Display the slide you want to add a sound to.

2 Click **Insert**.

3 Click **Movies and Sounds**.

4 Click **Record Sound**.

■ The Record Sound dialog box appears.

5 To specify a name for the sound, drag the mouse I over the existing text until the text is highlighted and then type a new name.

6 Click ● to start recording.

7 Speak into your microphone or start your sound device.

What devices can I record sounds from?

You can record sounds from any sound device you can connect to your computer, such as a microphone, CD player, stereo or VCR.

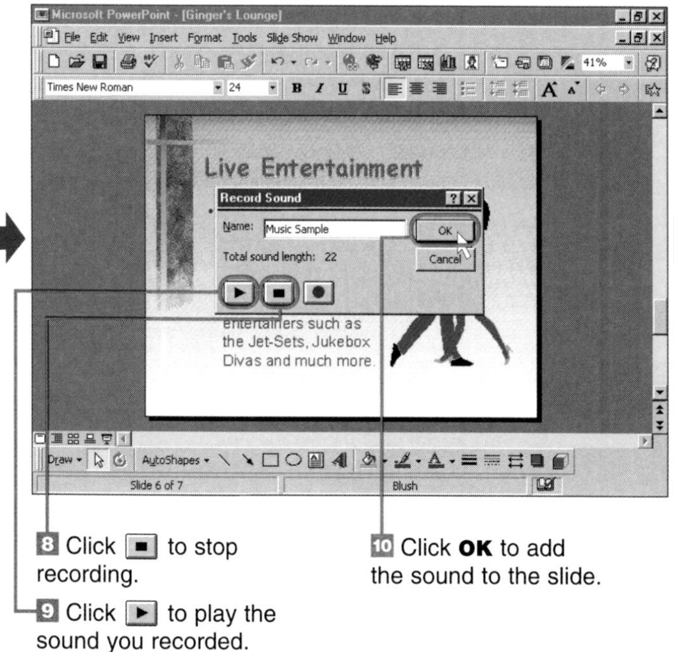

8 Click ■ to stop recording.

9 Click ▶ to play the sound you recorded.

10 Click **OK** to add the sound to the slide.

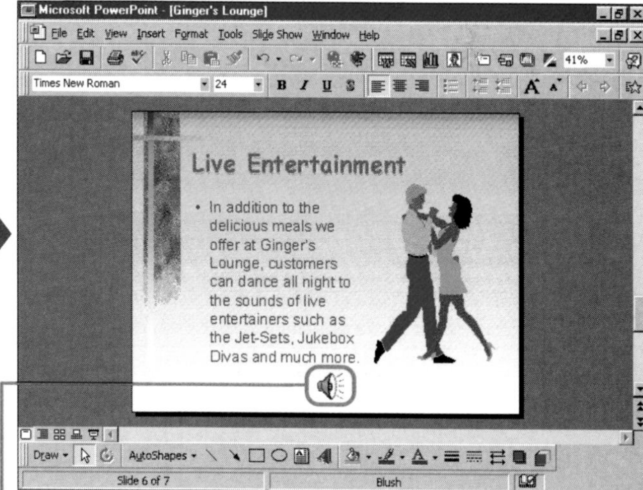

■ A speaker icon ( ) appears. To move or size the speaker icon, see page 154.

■ To play the sound in the Slide view, double-click the speaker icon.

Note: To play the sound during the slide show, click the speaker icon on the slide. To view a slide show, see page 238.

■ To remove the sound from the slide, see the top of page 169.

ADD NARRATION TO A SLIDE SHOW

You can record voice narration and add it to a slide show. This is ideal for a self-running slide show at a kiosk. Kiosks are often found at trade shows and shopping malls.

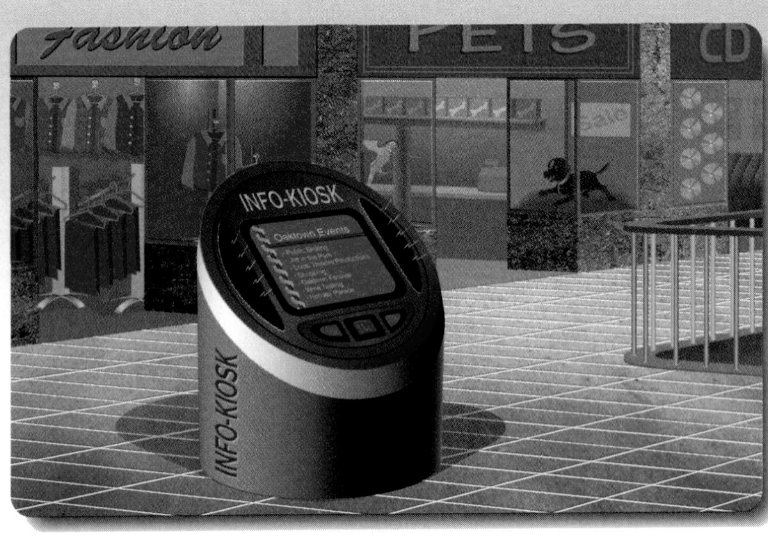

You need a sound card, microphone and speakers to record narration.

ADD NARRATION TO A SLIDE SHOW

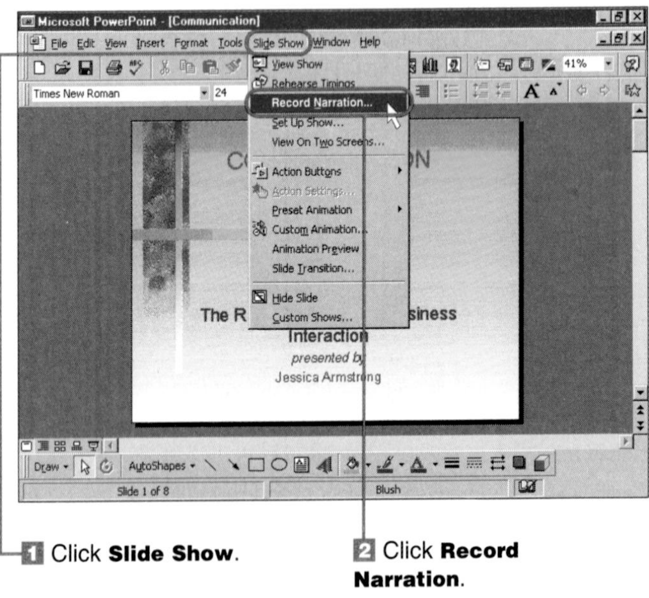

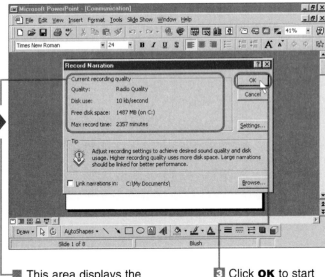

1 Click **Slide Show**.

2 Click **Record Narration**.

■ The Record Narration dialog box appears.

■ This area displays the recording quality, amount of hard disk space required for each second of narration, amount of free space on your hard disk and amount of recording time available.

3 Click **OK** to start recording.

?

What should I do to prepare for recording narration?

You should prepare and rehearse a script that includes the information you want to record for each slide in your slide show. This can help you avoid awkward pauses and long-winded sentences that may distract the audience.

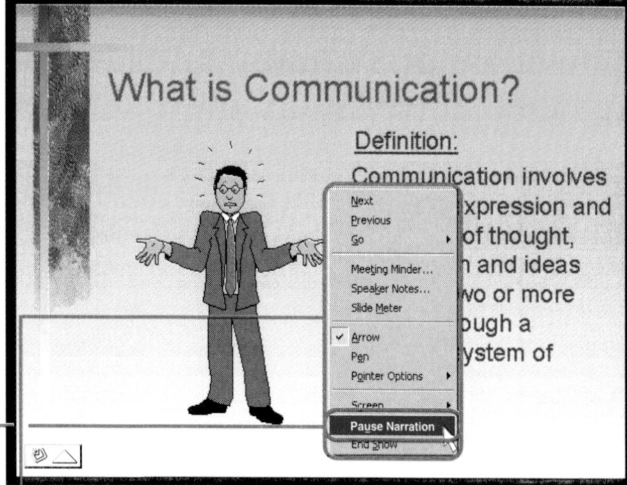

■ The first slide in the slide show appears.

4 Speak into your microphone to record narration for the slide.

5 To display the next slide, click the current slide or press the **Spacebar**.

6 To pause the recording at any time, right-click the current slide. A menu appears.

7 Click **Pause Narration**.

8 To resume recording, repeat steps 6 and 7, except select **Resume Narration** in step 7.

CONTINUED

ADD NARRATION TO A SLIDE SHOW

You can have PowerPoint save the amount of time you spent narrating each slide. PowerPoint will use these timings to advance the slides automatically during a slide show.

ADD NARRATION TO A SLIDE SHOW (CONTINUED)

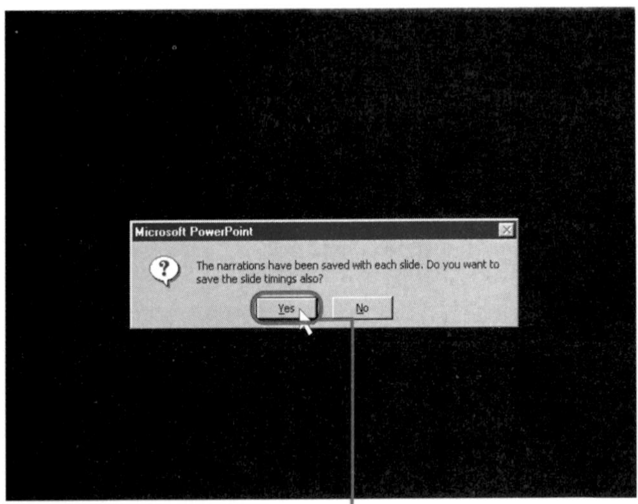

■ A dialog box appears when you complete the slide show, stating that the narrations have been saved with each slide.

9 To save the amount of time you spent narrating each slide and use the timings when you view the slide show, click **Yes**.

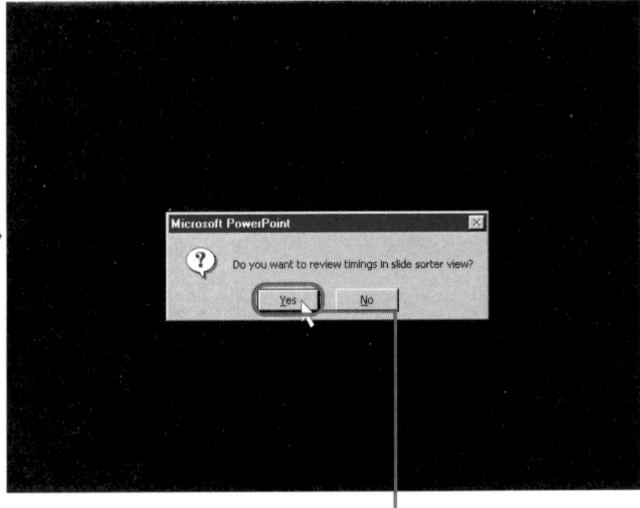

■ A dialog box appears, asking if you want to review the timings in the Slide Sorter view.

10 Click **Yes** to review the timings.

? Can I turn off the narration for a slide show?

Yes. You can temporarily turn off the narration for a slide show without deleting the narration you recorded for the slides. To temporarily turn off the narration, see page 230.

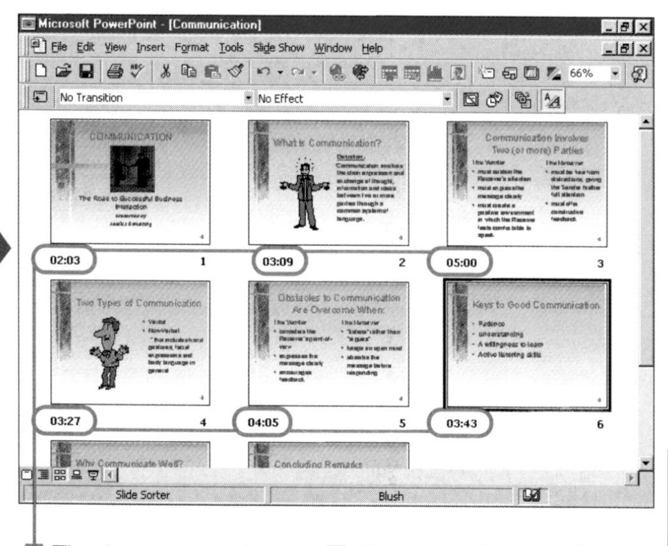

■ The time you spent narrating each slide appears below the slides.

■ When you view the slide show, you will hear the narration you recorded. To view a slide show, see page 238.

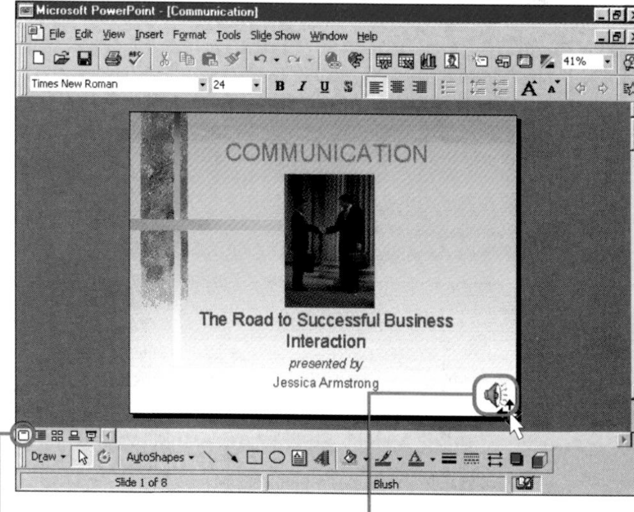

DELETE NARRATION FROM A SLIDE

1 Click (□) to change to the Slide view.

2 Display the slide you no longer want to play a narration.

3 To delete the narration, click the speaker icon (🔈) at the bottom right corner of the slide and then press the Delete key.

PLAY A SOUND OR MOVIE AUTOMATICALLY

By default, you must click a sound or movie during a slide show to play the sound or movie. If you prefer, you can have the sound or movie play automatically when you display the slide.

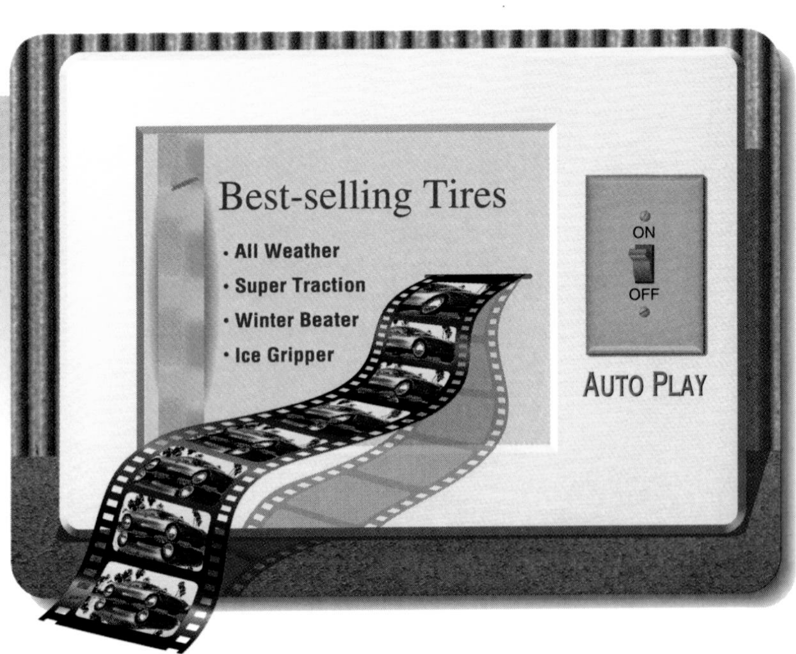

PLAY A SOUND OR MOVIE AUTOMATICALLY

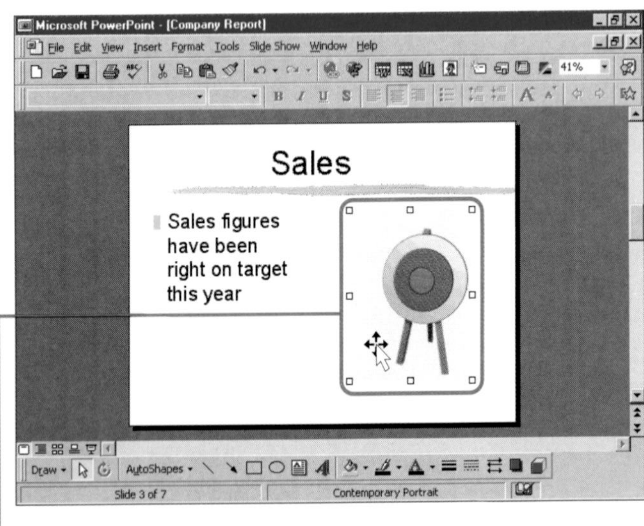

1 Click the object you want to play automatically during the slide show.

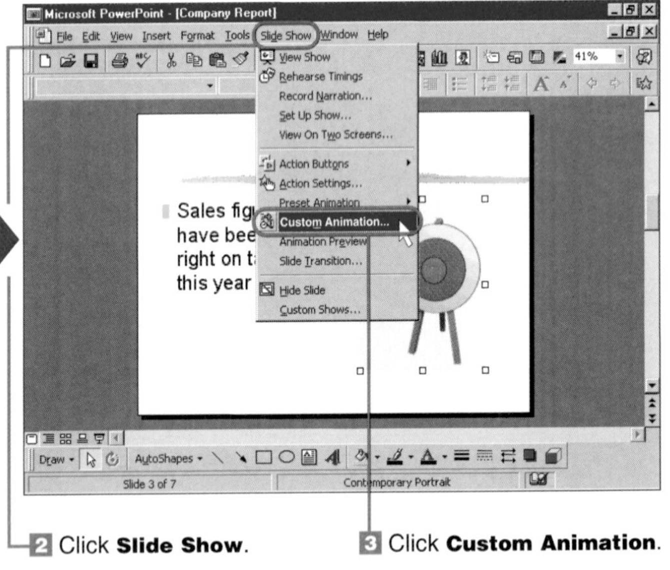

2 Click **Slide Show**.

3 Click **Custom Animation**.

■ The Custom Animation dialog box appears.

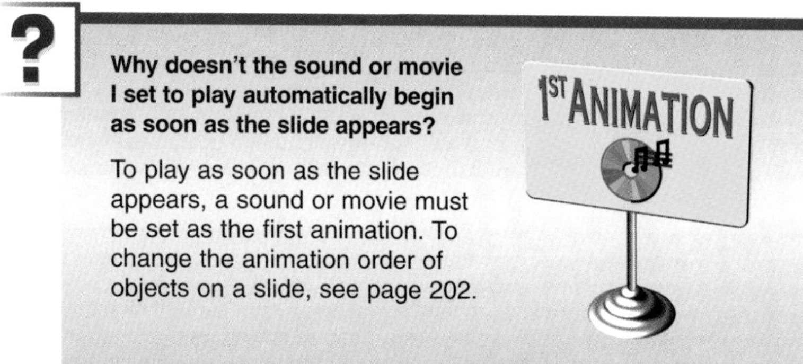

Why doesn't the sound or movie I set to play automatically begin as soon as the slide appears?

To play as soon as the slide appears, a sound or movie must be set as the first animation. To change the animation order of objects on a slide, see page 202.

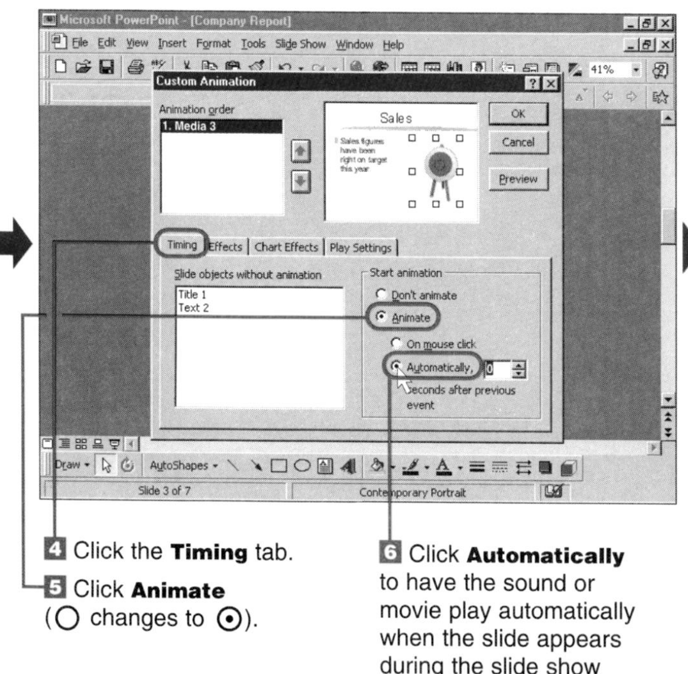

4 Click the **Timing** tab.

5 Click **Animate** (○ changes to ⊙).

6 Click **Automatically** to have the sound or movie play automatically when the slide appears during the slide show (○ changes to ⊙).

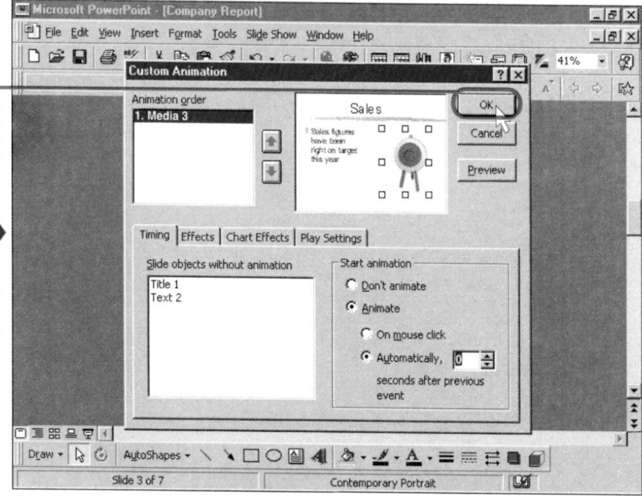

7 Click **OK** to confirm your change.

■ During the slide show, the sound or movie will play automatically when the slide appears. To view a slide show, see page 238.

■ To no longer have a sound or movie play automatically, repeat steps **1** to **7**, except select **On mouse click** in step **6**.

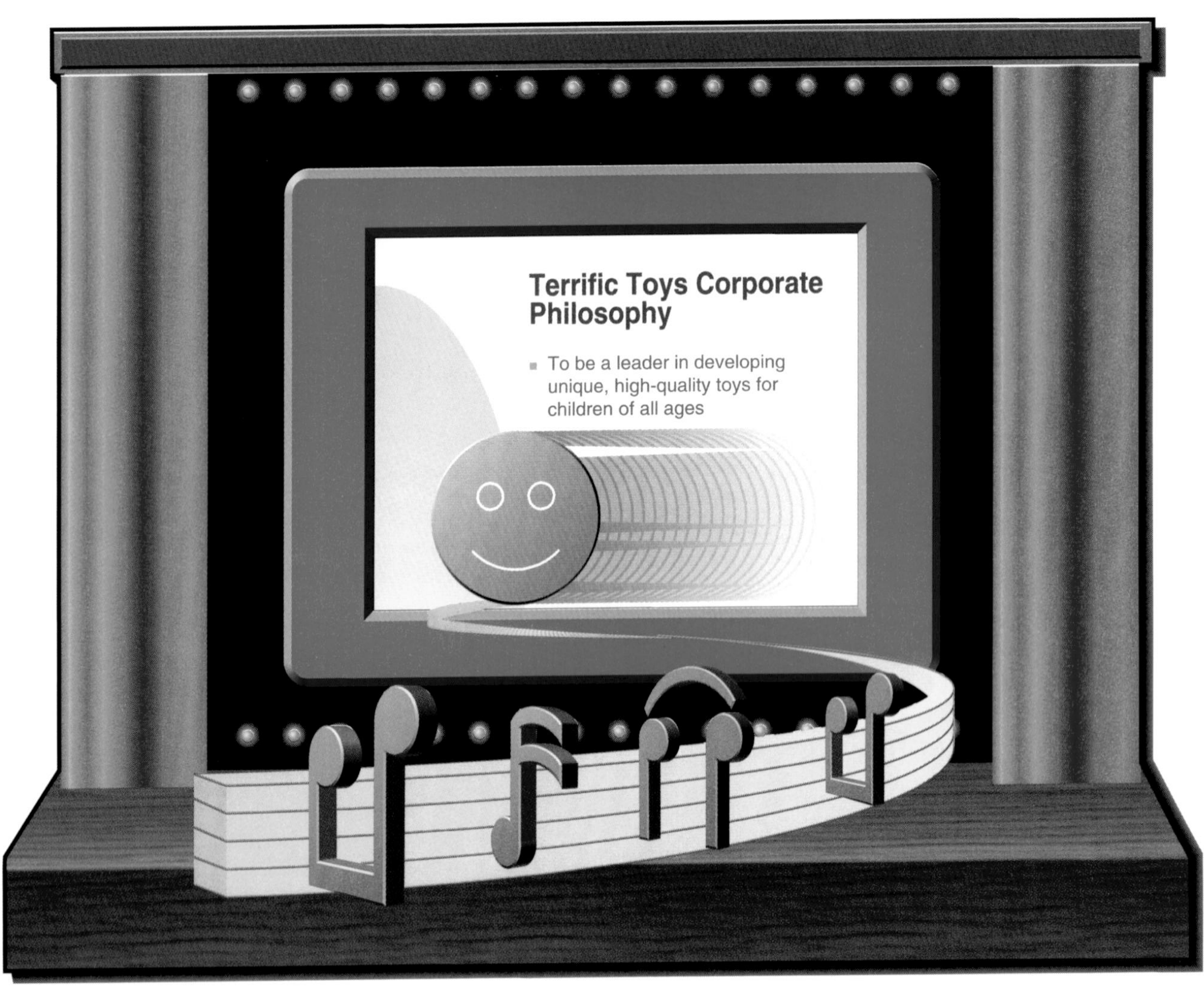
Terrific Toys Corporate Philosophy
To be a leader in developing unique, high-quality toys for children of all ages

CHAPTER 9

Add Special Effects to Slides

Are you interested in adding special effects to your presentation? This chapter teaches you how to animate objects, use interesting transitions to introduce slides and more.

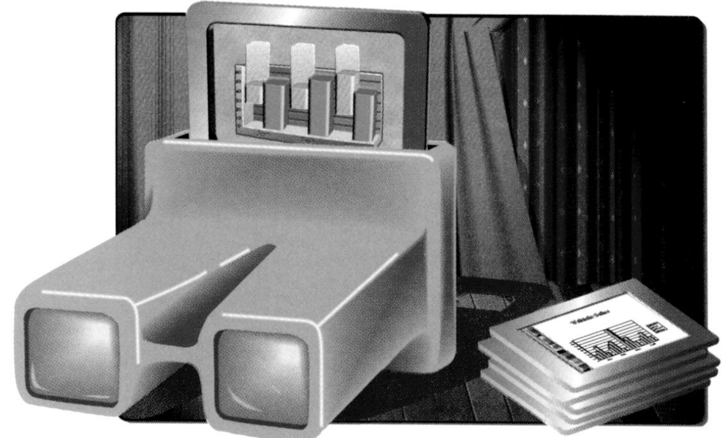

ADD SLIDE TRANSITIONS

You can use effects called transitions to help you move from one slide to the next and introduce each slide during an on-screen slide show.

PowerPoint automatically adds transitions to slides in some types of presentations.

ADD SLIDE TRANSITIONS

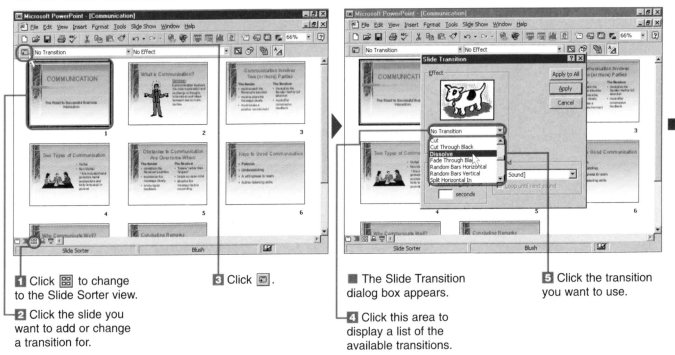

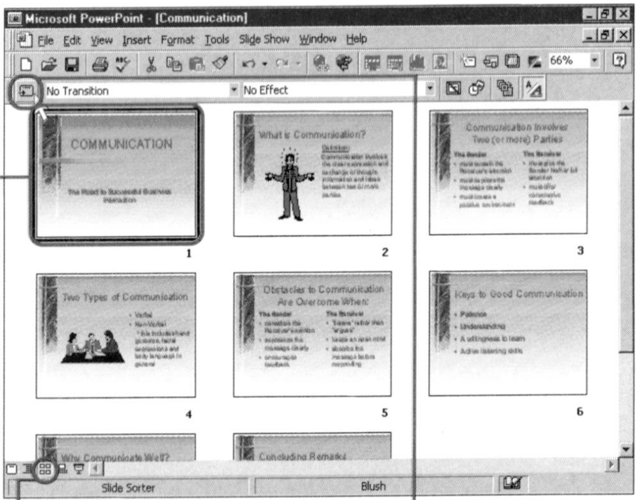

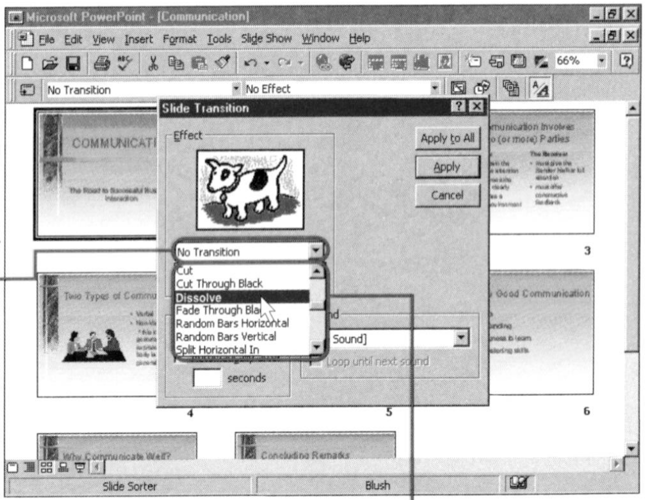

1 Click ▦ to change to the Slide Sorter view.

2 Click the slide you want to add or change a transition for.

3 Click ▣.

■ The Slide Transition dialog box appears.

4 Click this area to display a list of the available transitions.

5 Click the transition you want to use.

?

Can I add a different transition to each slide in my presentation?

Although PowerPoint allows you to add a different transition to each slide in your presentation, using too many different transitions may distract the audience. The audience may focus on how each slide is introduced, rather than the information you are presenting.

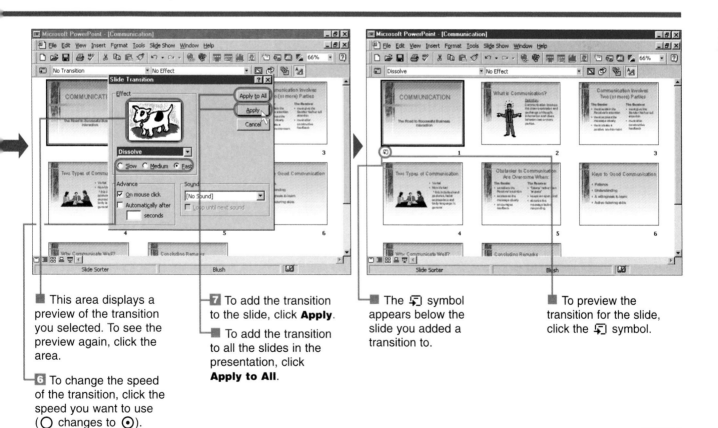

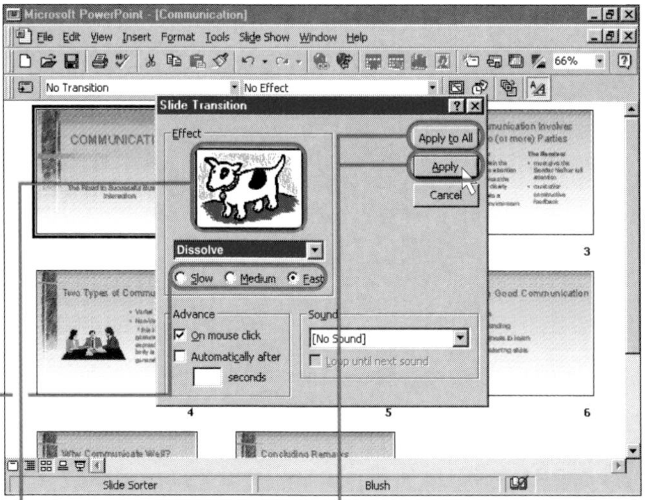

■ This area displays a preview of the transition you selected. To see the preview again, click the area.

6 To change the speed of the transition, click the speed you want to use (○ changes to ⊙).

7 To add the transition to the slide, click **Apply**.

■ To add the transition to all the slides in the presentation, click **Apply to All**.

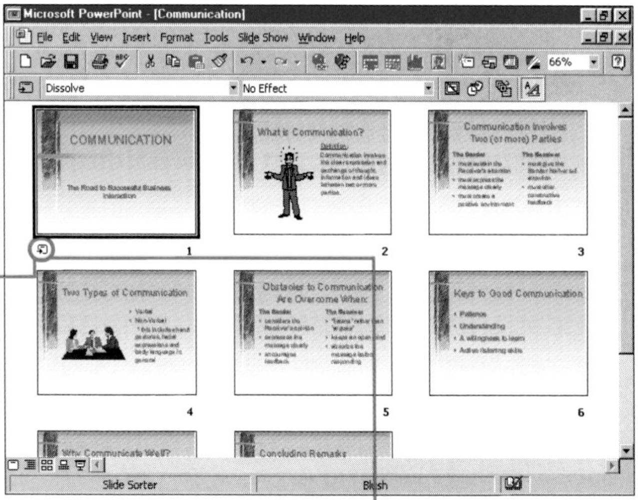

■ The symbol appears below the slide you added a transition to.

■ To preview the transition for the slide, click the symbol.

ADD SIMPLE ANIMATIONS

You can add movement and sound effects to objects on your slides. This can help keep your audience's attention throughout a presentation.

You can add simple animations to objects such as clip art images, AutoShapes and bulleted lists.

ADD SIMPLE ANIMATIONS

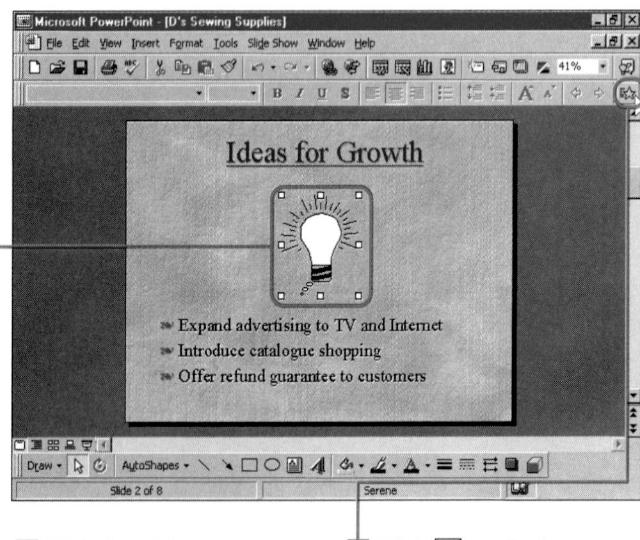

1 Click the object you want to animate. Handles (□) appear around the object.

2 Click [icon] to display the Animation Effects toolbar.

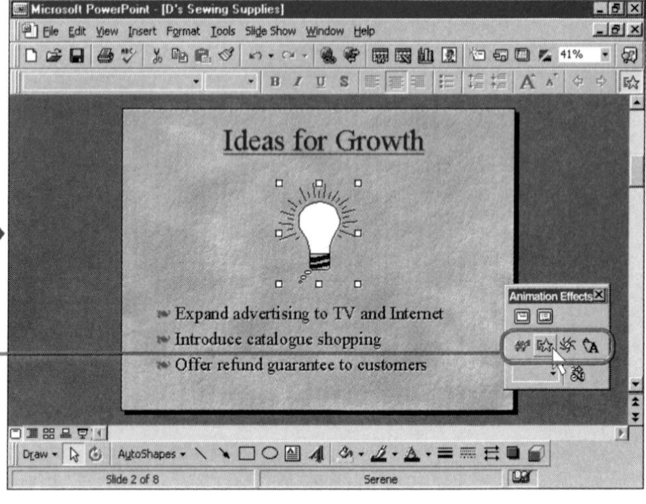

■ The Animation Effects toolbar appears.

3 Click the animation you want to use.

Note: The available animations depend on the type of object you selected in step 1.

How do I display the animated objects in my slide show?

When viewing your slide show, you must click the slide to display each animated object on the slide. For example, if you added an animation to a list of points, you must click the slide each time you want a point to appear.

If you want to have an animated object appear automatically, display the slide in the Slide view and then click the object. Then perform steps 2 to 7 on page 186.

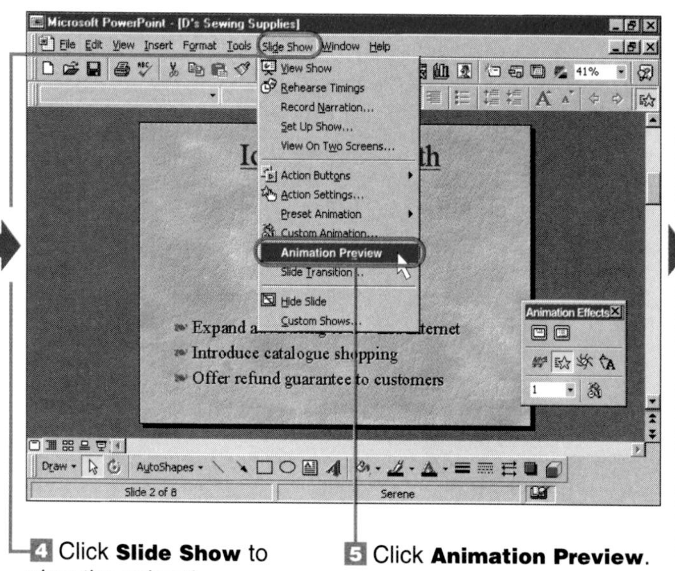

4 Click **Slide Show** to view the animation you added to the object.

5 Click **Animation Preview**.

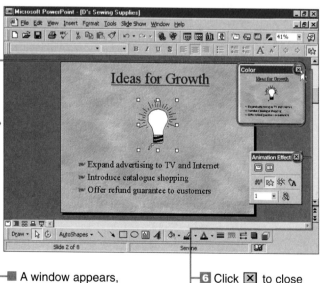

■ A window appears, displaying how the animated object will appear during the slide show. You can click the window to view the animation again.

6 Click ☒ to close the window.

7 Click ☒ to close the Animation Effects toolbar.

ADD CUSTOM ANIMATIONS

You can add a custom animation to an object such as a clip art image, an AutoShape or a bulleted list.

Adding a custom animation allows you to specify which movement and sound effect you want to use, as well as the action you want to occur after the animation.

ADD CUSTOM ANIMATIONS

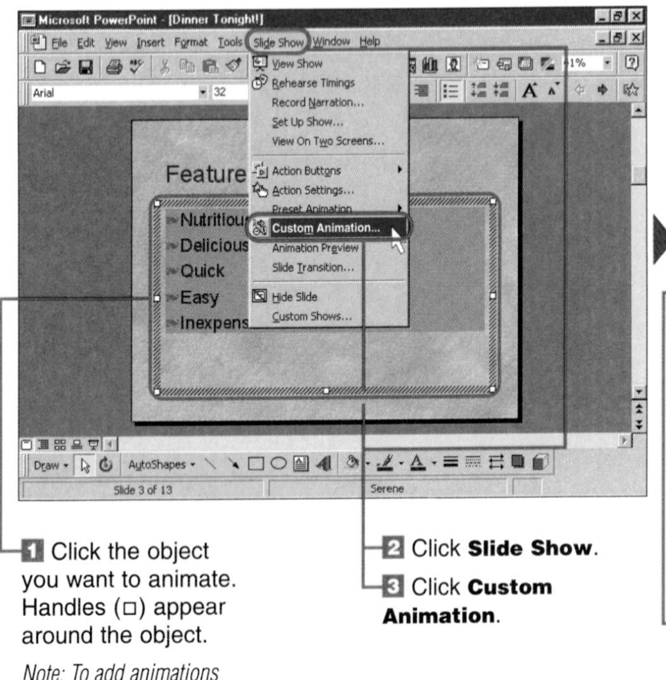

1 Click the object you want to animate. Handles (□) appear around the object.

Note: To add animations to a chart, see page 198.

2 Click **Slide Show**.

3 Click **Custom Animation**.

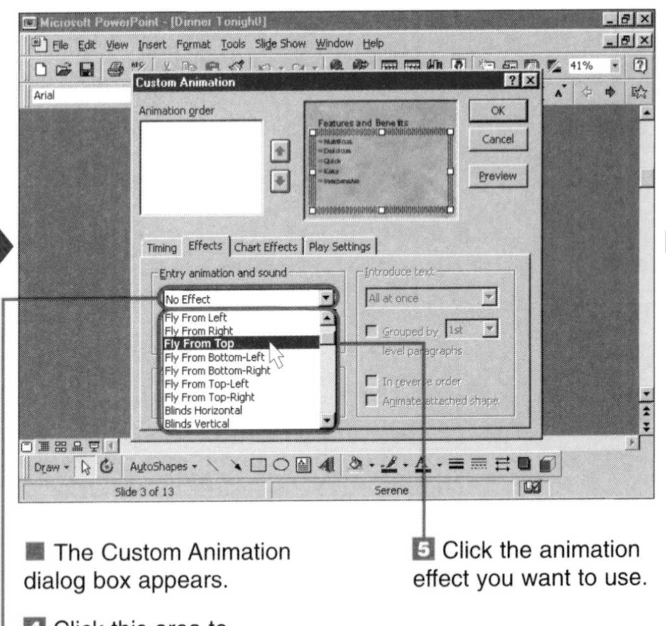

■ The Custom Animation dialog box appears.

4 Click this area to display a list of available animation effects.

5 Click the animation effect you want to use.

What actions can occur after an animation?

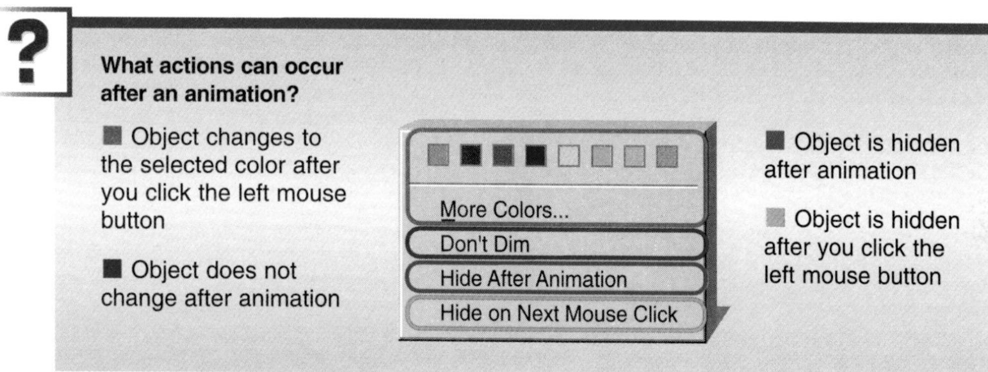

■ Object changes to the selected color after you click the left mouse button

■ Object does not change after animation

■ Object is hidden after animation

■ Object is hidden after you click the left mouse button

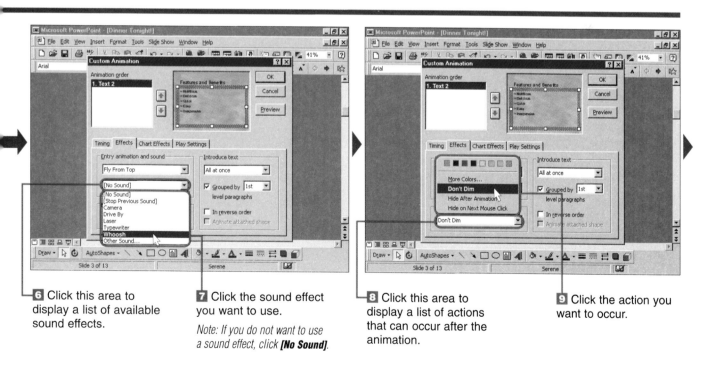

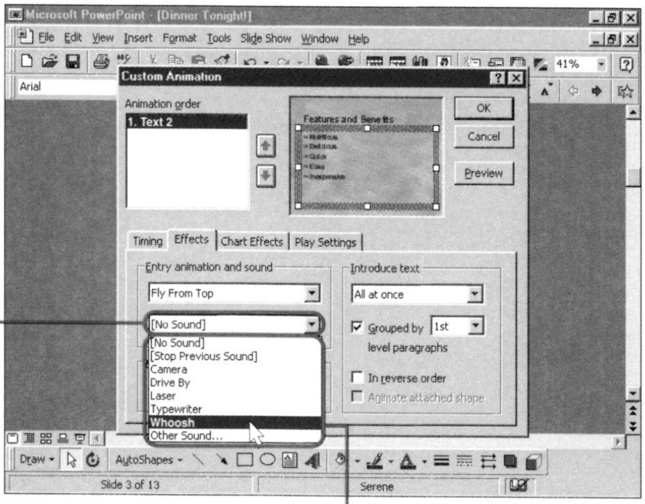

6 Click this area to display a list of available sound effects.

7 Click the sound effect you want to use.

*Note: If you do not want to use a sound effect, click **[No Sound]**.*

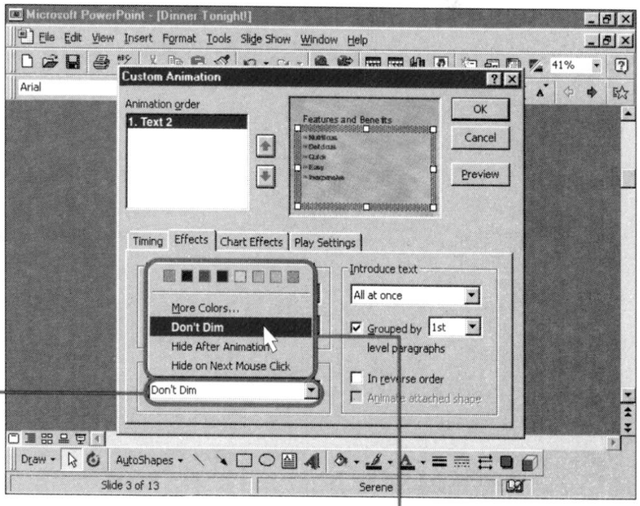

8 Click this area to display a list of actions that can occur after the animation.

9 Click the action you want to occur.

CONTINUED

ADD CUSTOM ANIMATIONS

If you are adding a custom animation to text, you can have PowerPoint display the text all at once, word by word or letter by letter.

ADD CUSTOM ANIMATIONS (CONTINUED)

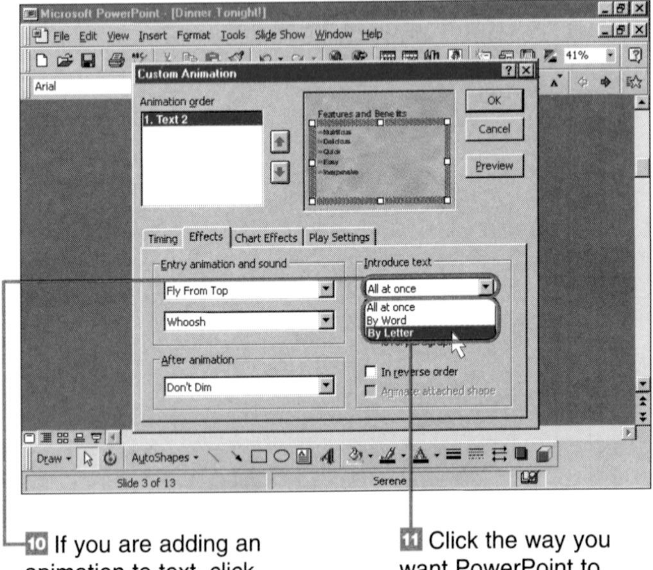

10 If you are adding an animation to text, click this area to display a list of ways PowerPoint can display the text on the slide.

11 Click the way you want PowerPoint to display the text.

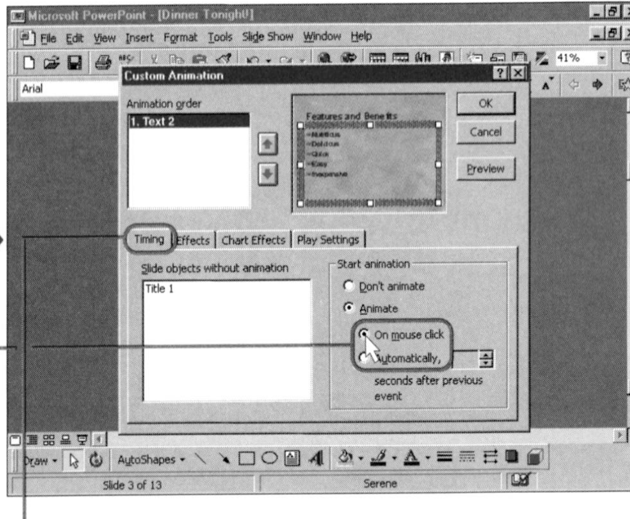

12 Click the **Timing** tab.

13 Click an option to specify when you want the animation to play during a slide show (○ changes to ⊙).

On mouse click - Plays animation after you click the left mouse button

Automatically - Plays animation automatically

? How do I remove the animation from an object?

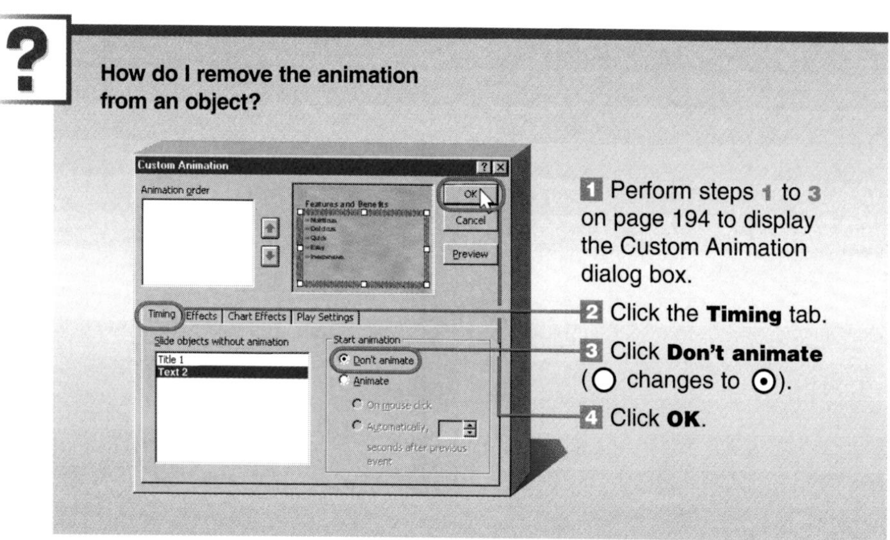

1 Perform steps 1 to 3 on page 194 to display the Custom Animation dialog box.

2 Click the **Timing** tab.

3 Click **Don't animate** (○ changes to ⊙).

4 Click **OK**.

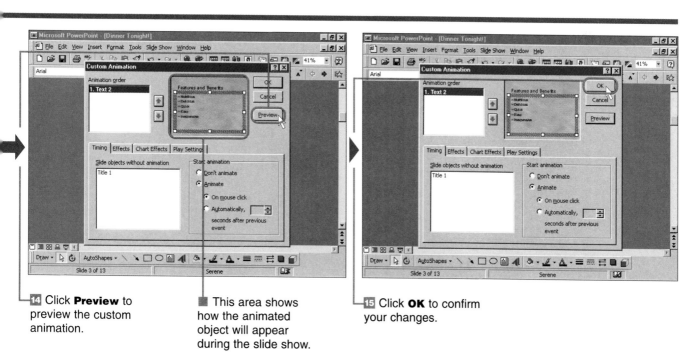

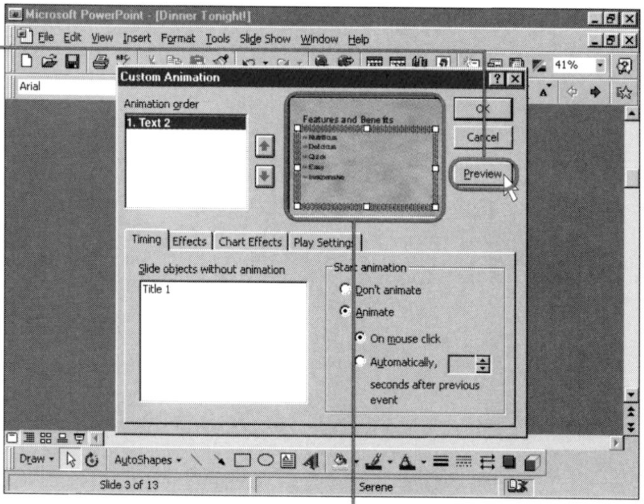

14 Click **Preview** to preview the custom animation.

■ This area shows how the animated object will appear during the slide show.

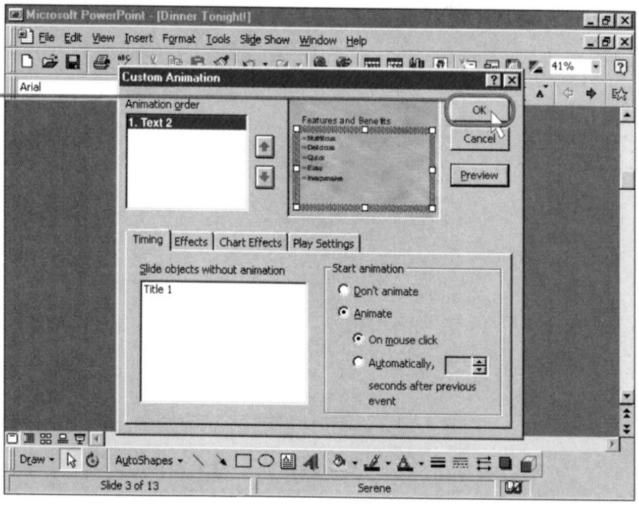

15 Click **OK** to confirm your changes.

ADD ANIMATIONS TO CHARTS

You can add an animation to a chart on a slide. This allows you to introduce the chart in a dramatic way during a slide show.

ADD ANIMATIONS TO CHARTS

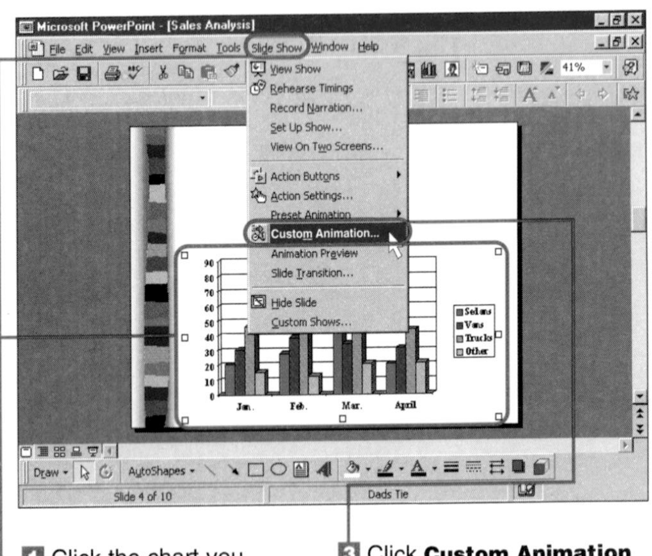

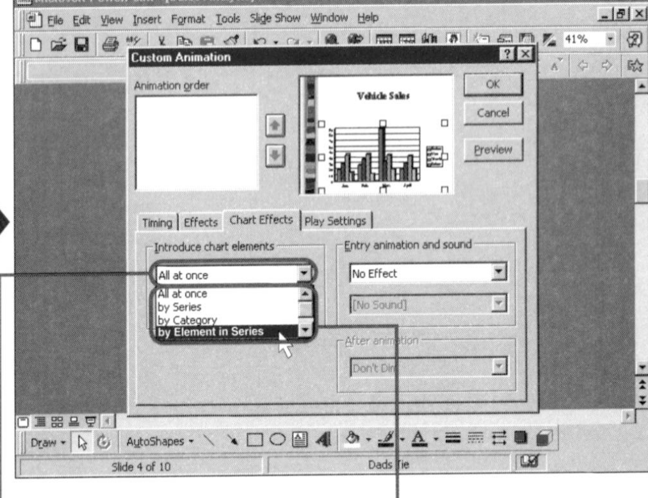

1. Click the chart you want to animate. Handles (□) appear around the chart.
2. Click **Slide Show**.
3. Click **Custom Animation**.

■ The Custom Animation dialog box appears.

4. Click this area to display a list of ways you can display the parts of the chart.
5. Click the way you want to display the parts of the chart.

?

How can I display the parts of a chart during a slide show?

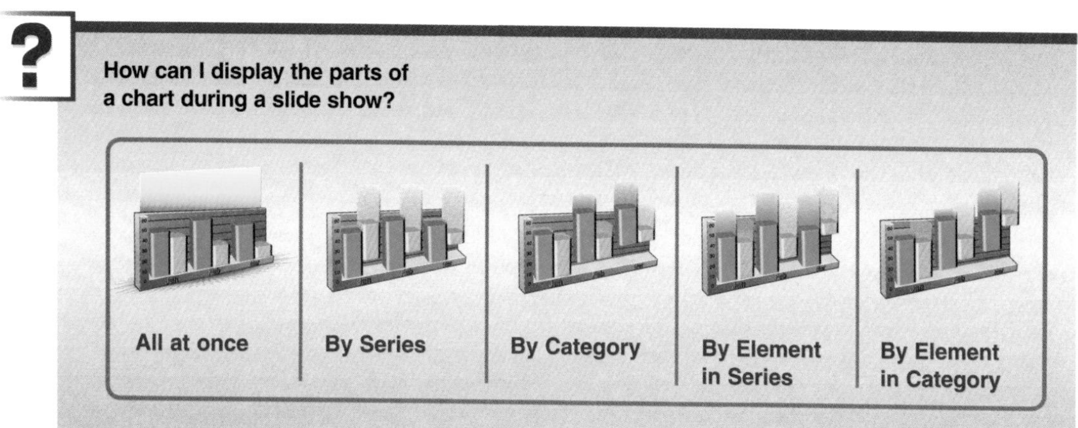

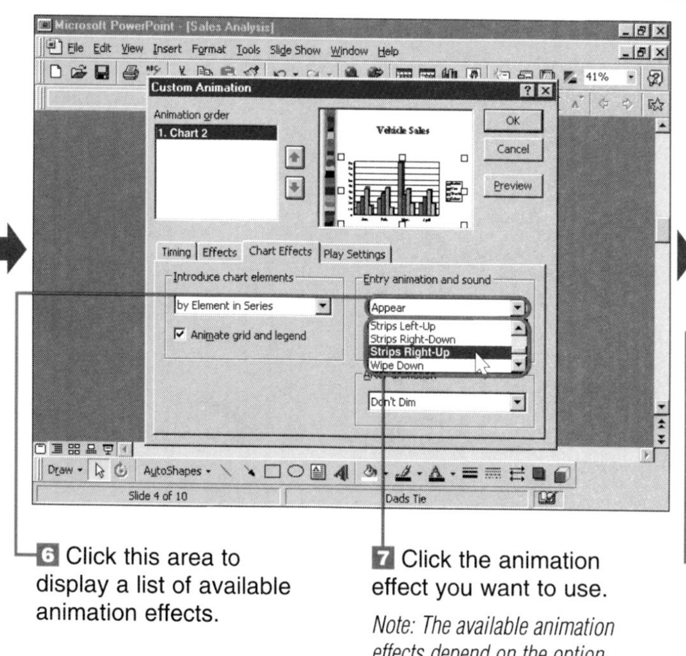

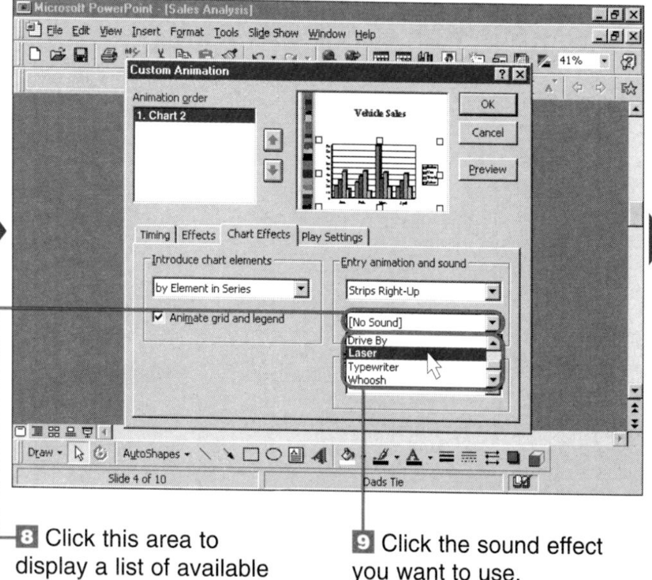

6 Click this area to display a list of available animation effects.

7 Click the animation effect you want to use.

*Note: The available animation effects depend on the option you selected in step **5**.*

8 Click this area to display a list of available sound effects.

9 Click the sound effect you want to use.

*Note: If you do not want to use a sound effect, click **[No Sound]**.*

CONTINUED

You can preview how a chart animation will appear during your slide show.

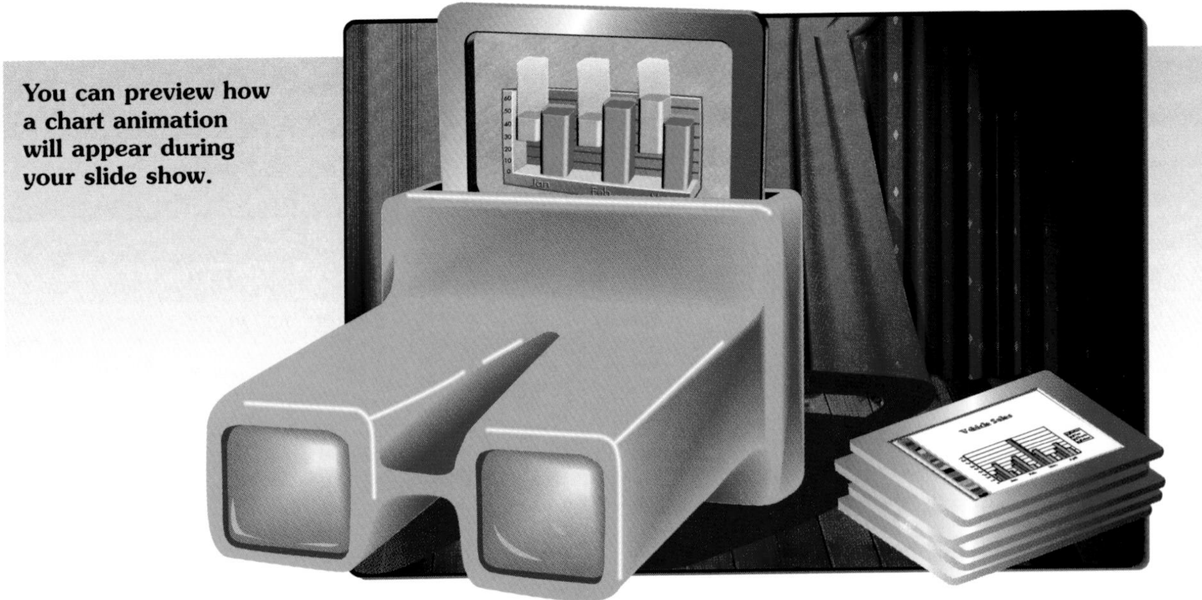

ADD ANIMATIONS TO CHARTS (CONTINUED)

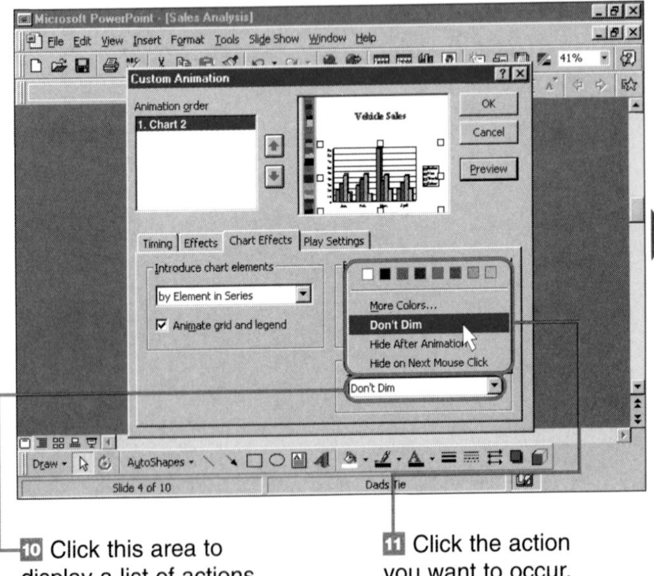

10 Click this area to display a list of actions that can occur after the chart animation.

11 Click the action you want to occur.

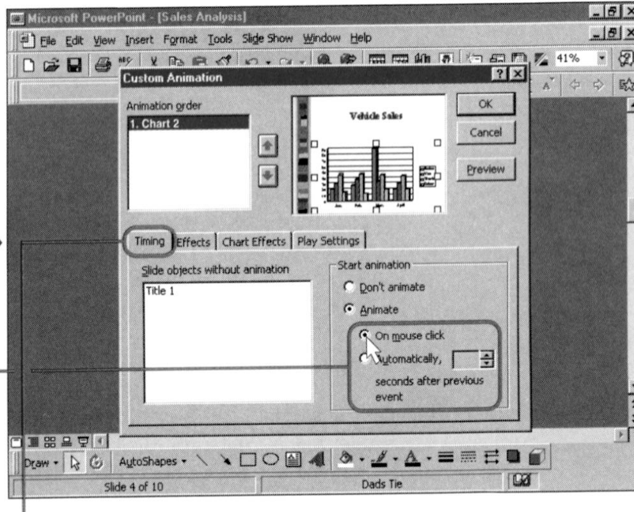

12 Click the **Timing** tab.

13 Click an option to specify when you want the chart animation to play during a slide show (○ changes to ⊙).

On mouse click - Plays chart animation when you click the left mouse button

Automatically - Plays chart animation automatically

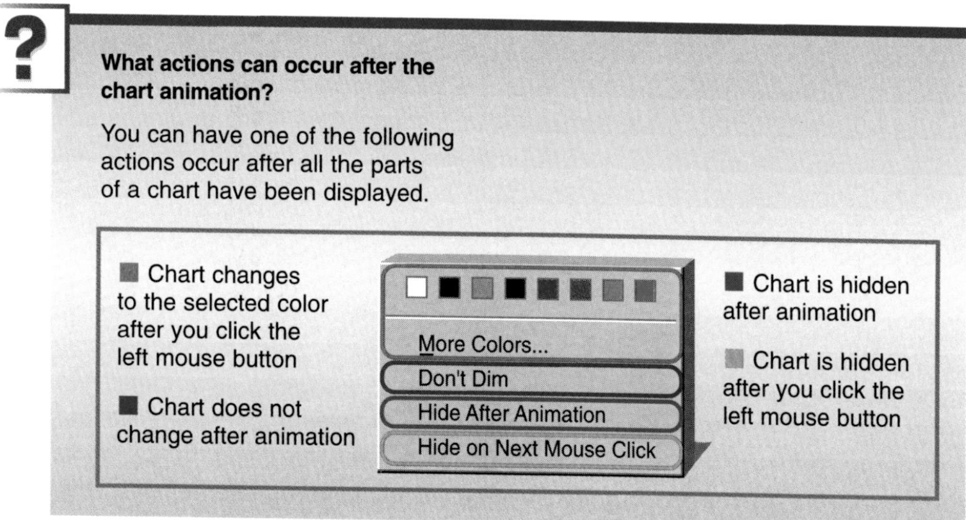

What actions can occur after the chart animation?

You can have one of the following actions occur after all the parts of a chart have been displayed.

- Chart changes to the selected color after you click the left mouse button
- Chart does not change after animation
- Chart is hidden after animation
- Chart is hidden after you click the left mouse button

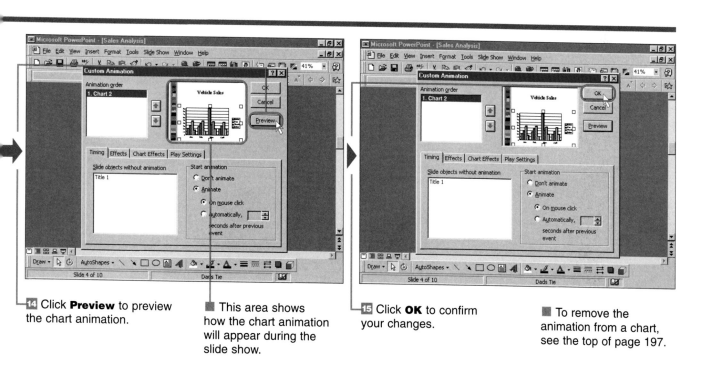

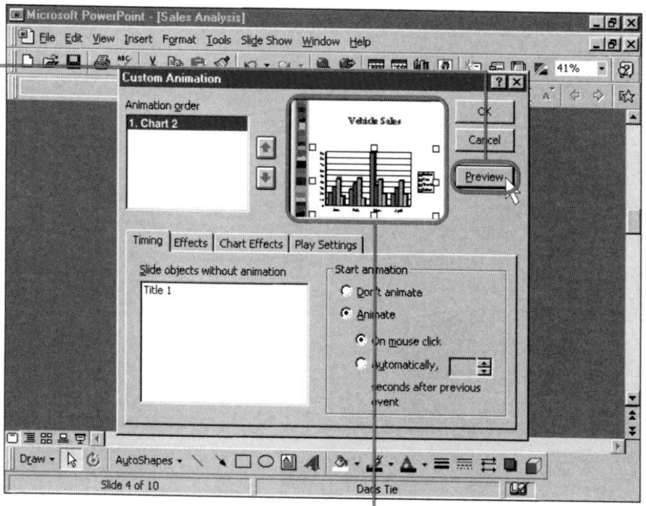

14 Click **Preview** to preview the chart animation.

- This area shows how the chart animation will appear during the slide show.

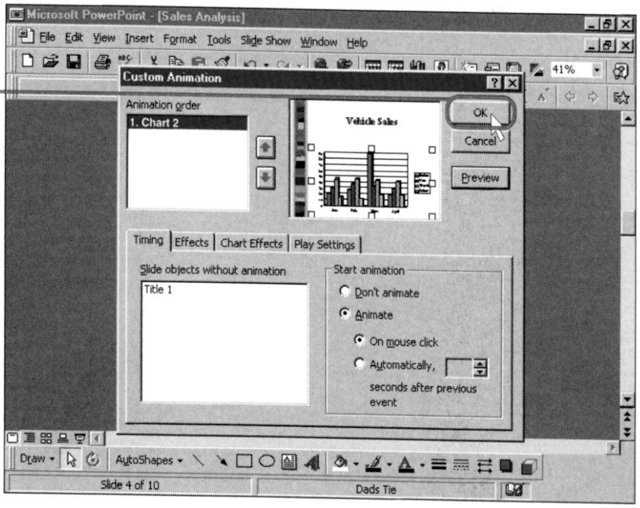

15 Click **OK** to confirm your changes.

- To remove the animation from a chart, see the top of page 197.

CHANGE ANIMATION ORDER

If you added animations to several objects on a slide, you can change the order that the animated objects will appear during a slide show.

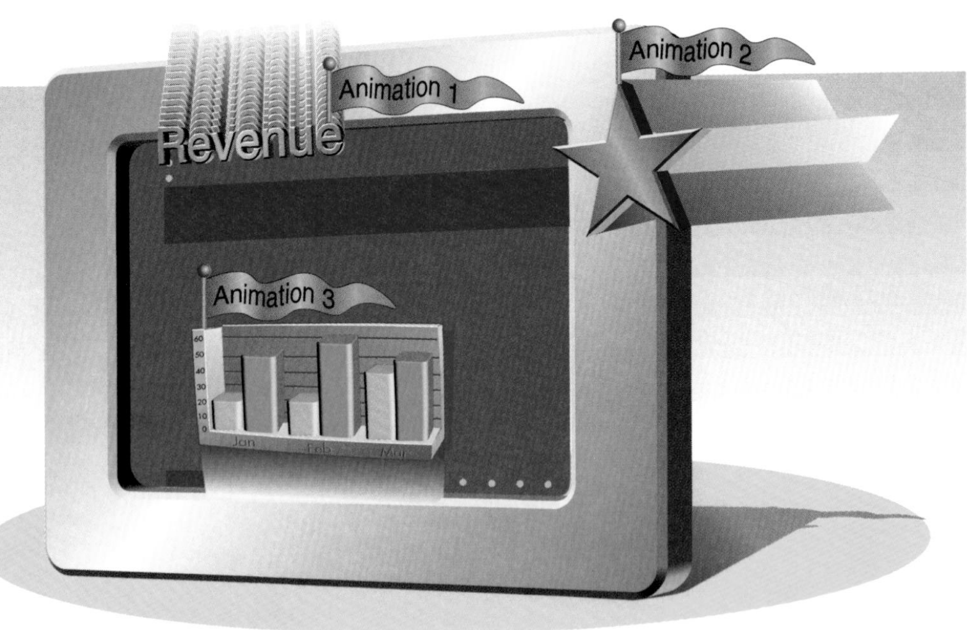

CHANGE ANIMATION ORDER

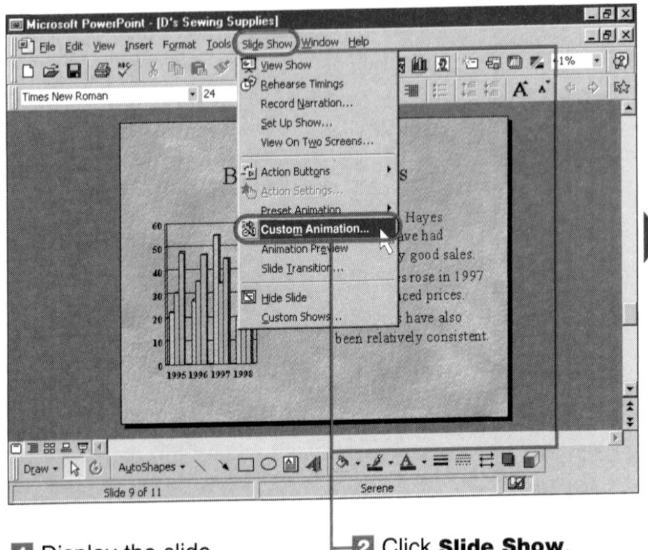

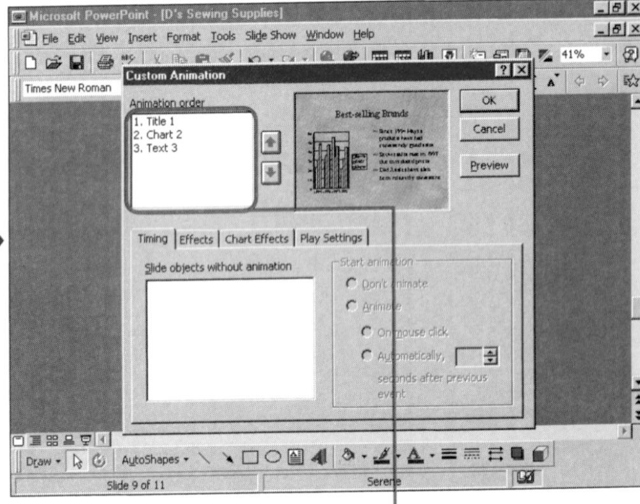

1 Display the slide containing the animated objects you want to appear in a different order.

2 Click **Slide Show**.

3 Click **Custom Animation**.

■ The Custom Animation dialog box appears.

■ This area lists the animated objects on the slide. The objects are listed in the order they will appear during the slide show.

?

Why would I change the order of the animated objects on a slide?

You may want to change the animation order to keep the audience's attention during your presentation. For example, displaying a chart before introducing text on a slide can help keep the audience focused on the information in the chart.

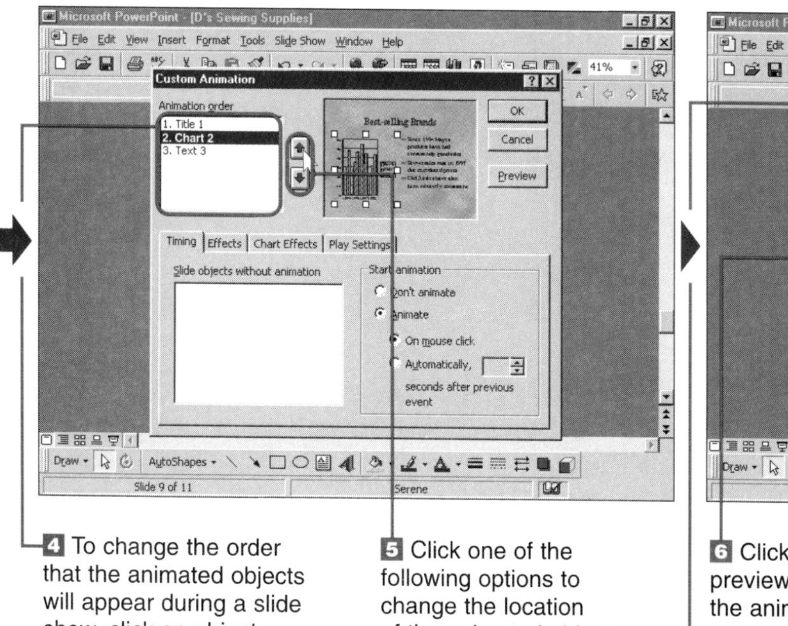

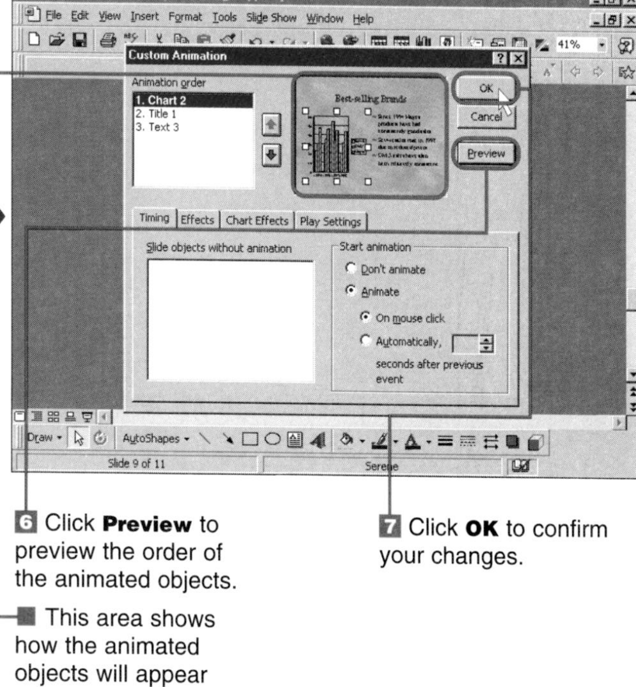

4 To change the order that the animated objects will appear during a slide show, click an object.

5 Click one of the following options to change the location of the animated object in the list.

- Move object up
- Move object down

6 Click **Preview** to preview the order of the animated objects.

■ This area shows how the animated objects will appear during the slide show.

7 Click **OK** to confirm your changes.

ADD AN ACTION BUTTON

An action button allows you to jump to another slide in your presentation. This can help make your presentation easier to browse through.

Adding action buttons to slides is useful if your presentation will be viewed by people at a kiosk or if you plan to publish your presentation on the Web.

ADD AN ACTION BUTTON

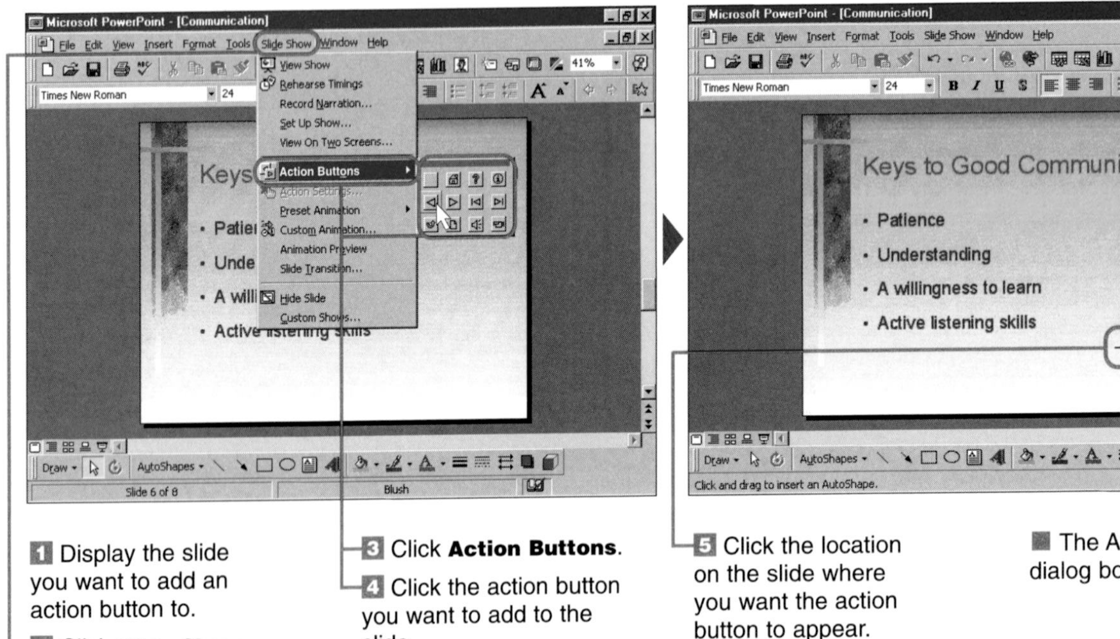

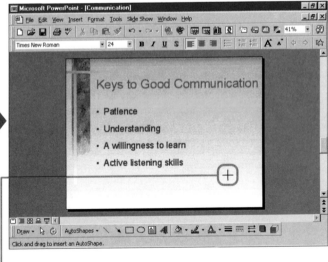

1 Display the slide you want to add an action button to.

2 Click **Slide Show**.

3 Click **Action Buttons**.

4 Click the action button you want to add to the slide.

5 Click the location on the slide where you want the action button to appear.

■ The Action Settings dialog box appears.

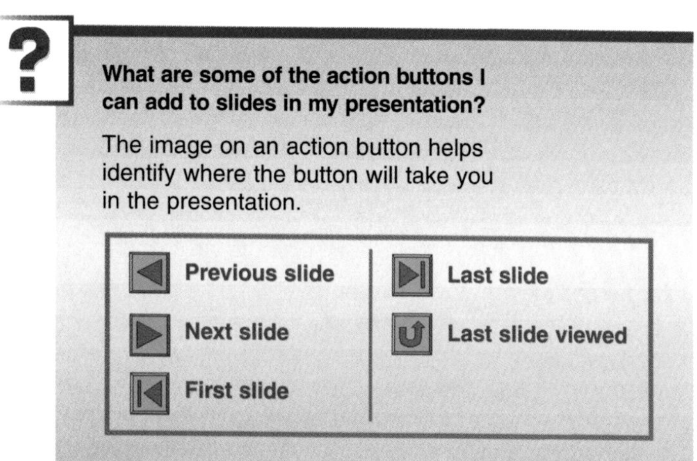

What are some of the action buttons I can add to slides in my presentation?

The image on an action button helps identify where the button will take you in the presentation.

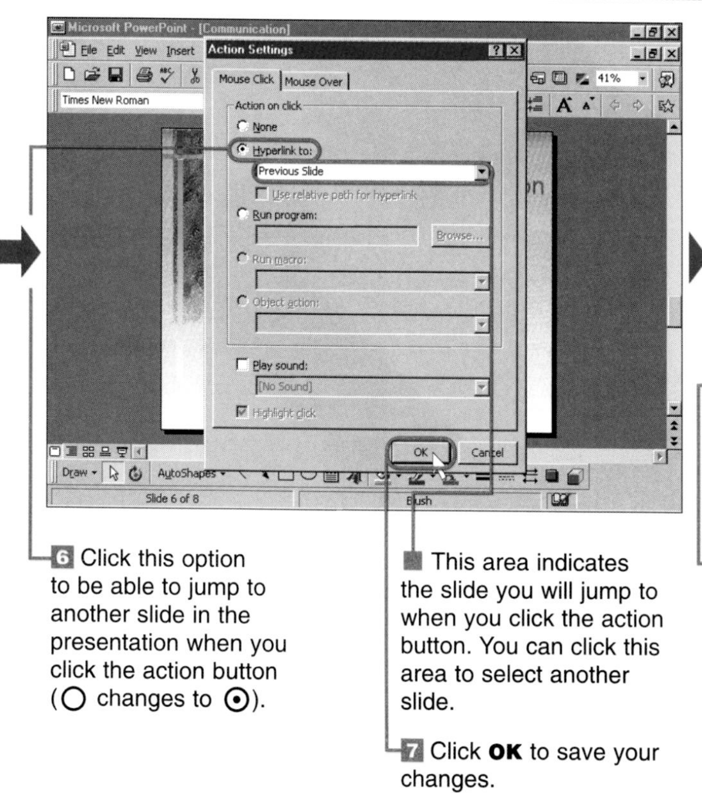

6 Click this option to be able to jump to another slide in the presentation when you click the action button (○ changes to ⊙).

■ This area indicates the slide you will jump to when you click the action button. You can click this area to select another slide.

7 Click **OK** to save your changes.

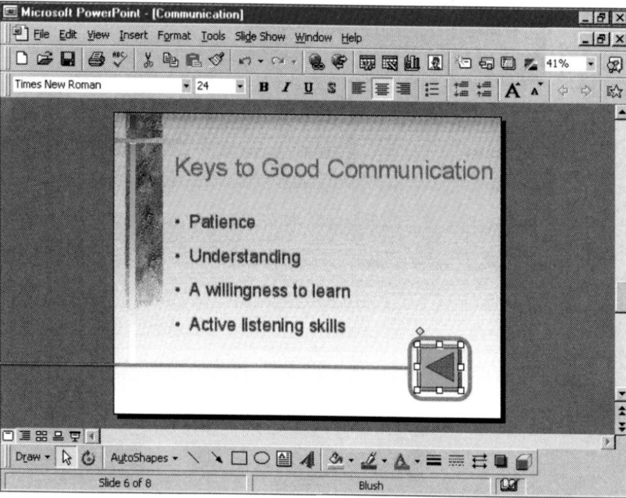

■ The action button appears on the slide. When you view the slide show, you can click the button to jump to the slide you specified. To view a slide show, see page 238.

Note: To move, size or delete an action button, see pages 154 to 156.

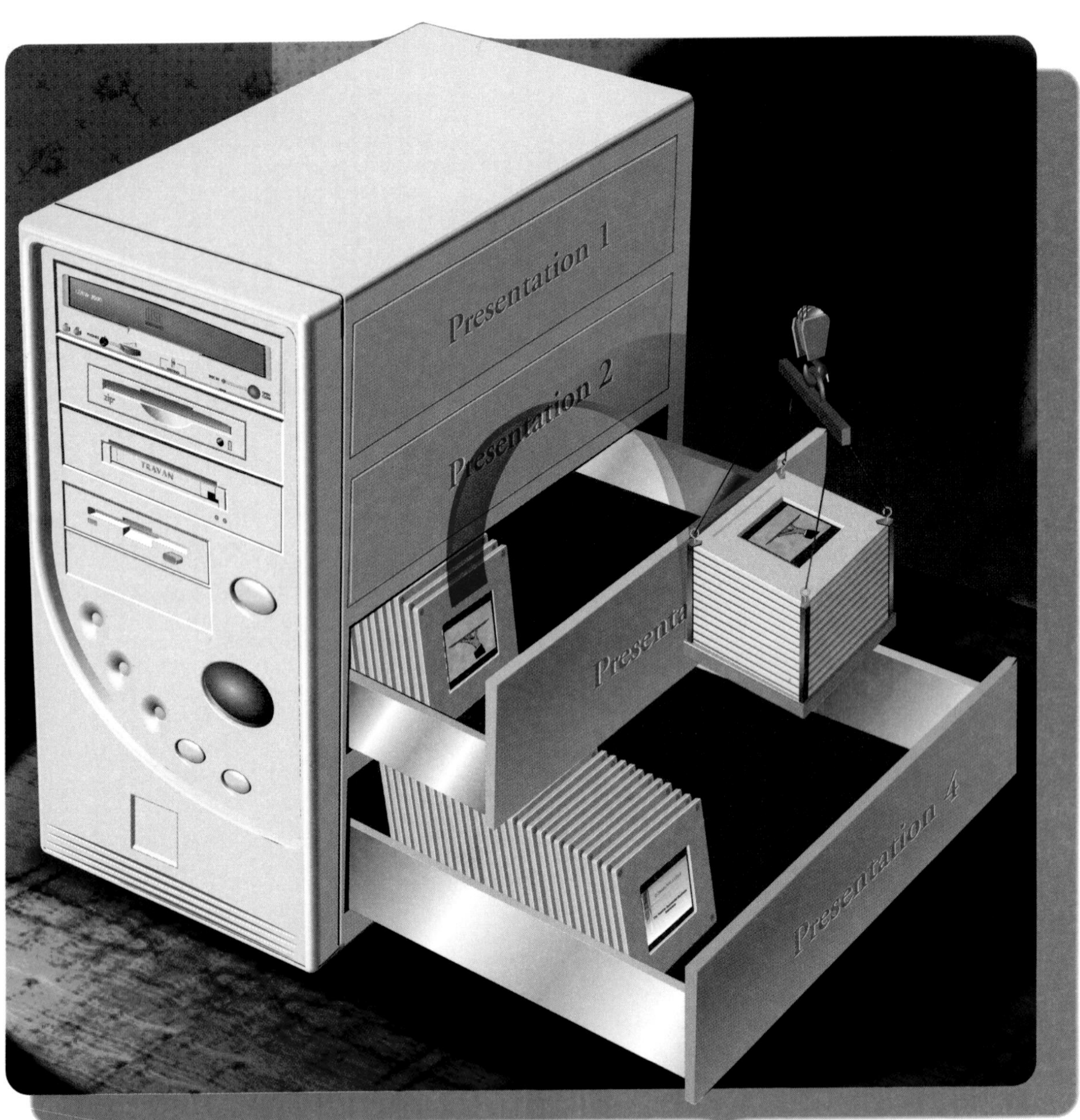
Presentation 1
Presentation 2
TRAVAN
Presentation 4

CHAPTER 10

Fine-Tune a Presentation

Are you ready to put the finishing touches on your presentation? This chapter shows you how to reorder slides, create speaker notes, print your presentation and much more.

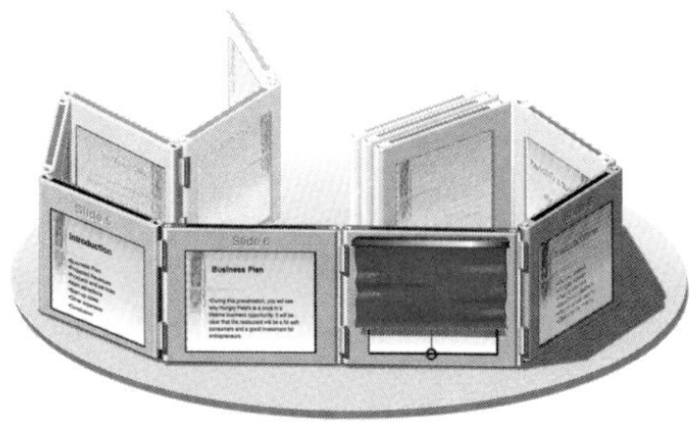

REORDER SLIDES

You can change the order of the slides in your presentation.

REORDER SLIDES

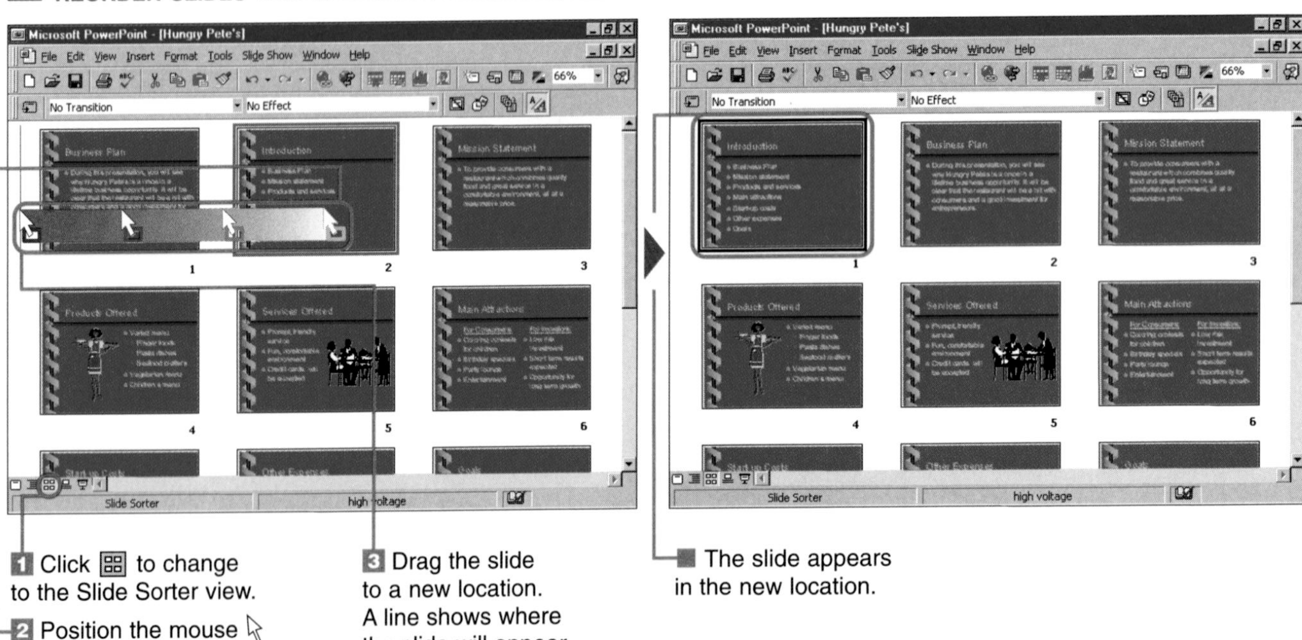

1 Click ⊞ to change to the Slide Sorter view.

2 Position the mouse ↖ over the slide you want to move.

3 Drag the slide to a new location. A line shows where the slide will appear.

■ The slide appears in the new location.

DELETE A SLIDE

You can remove a slide you no longer need in your presentation.

DELETE A SLIDE

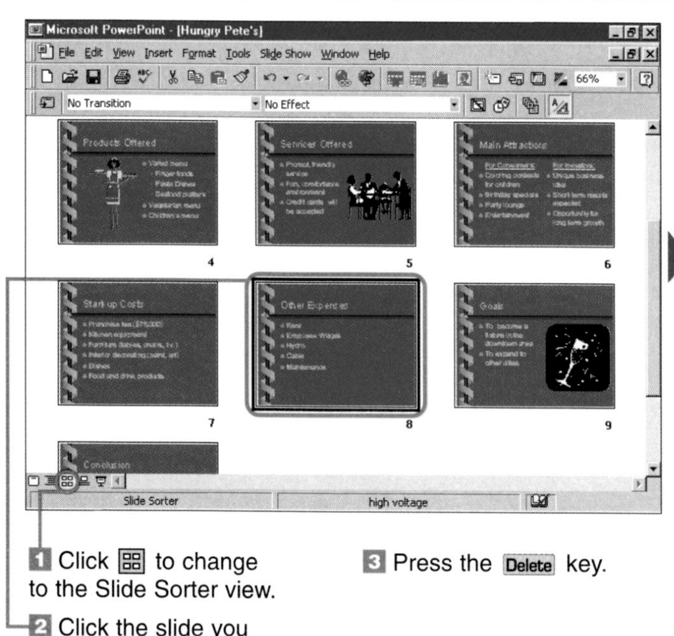

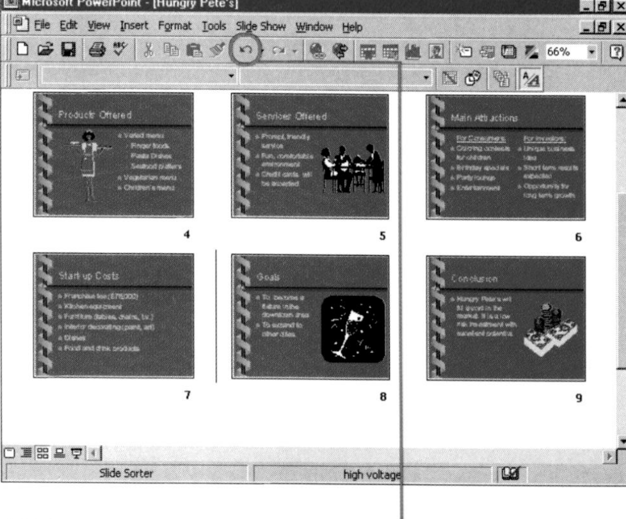

1 Click ▦ to change to the Slide Sorter view.

2 Click the slide you want to delete.

3 Press the Delete key.

■ The slide disappears.

■ To immediately return the slide to the presentation, click ↶.

HIDE A SLIDE

You can hide a slide in your presentation. This allows you to include supporting information in your slide show, but not display the information unless the audience requires clarification.

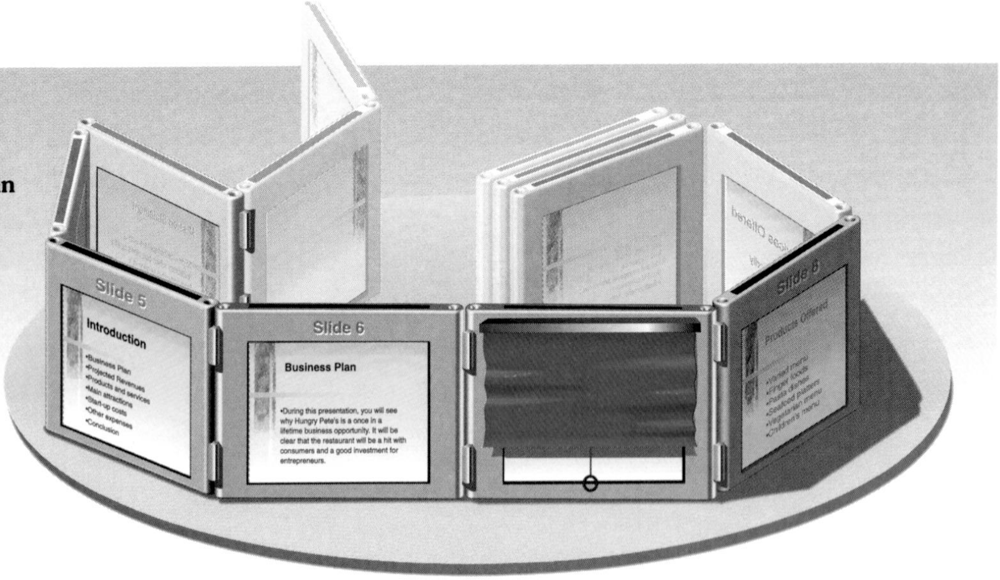

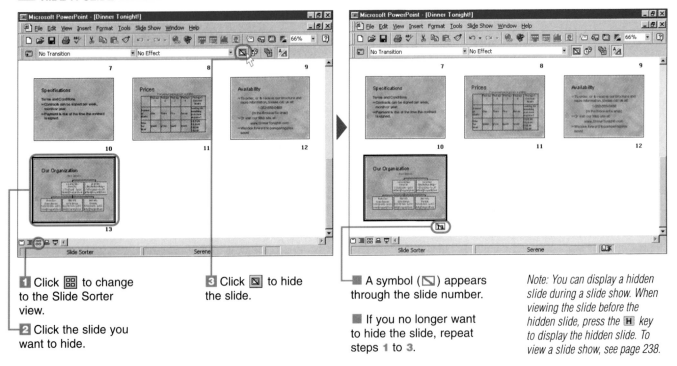

HIDE A SLIDE

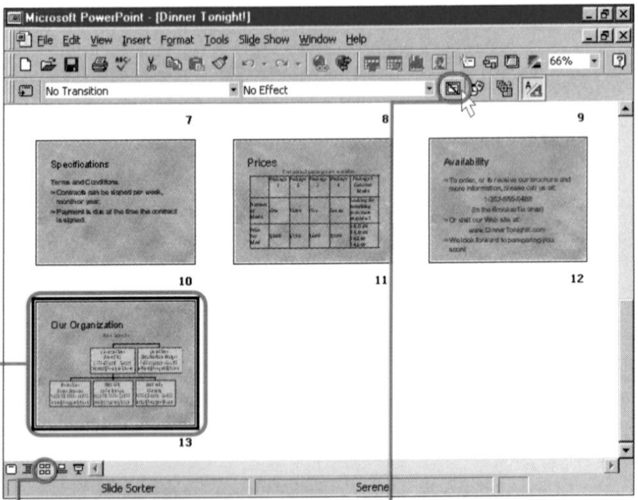

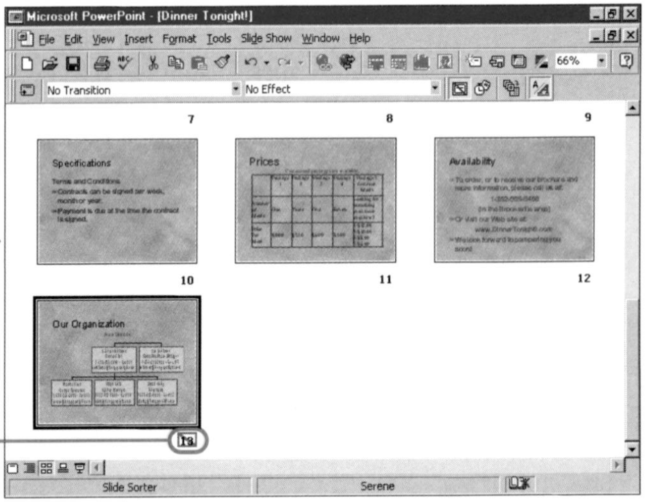

1 Click to change to the Slide Sorter view.

2 Click the slide you want to hide.

3 Click to hide the slide.

■ A symbol ( ) appears through the slide number.

■ If you no longer want to hide the slide, repeat steps 1 to 3.

Note: You can display a hidden slide during a slide show. When viewing the slide before the hidden slide, press the key to display the hidden slide. To view a slide show, see page 238.

VIEW SLIDES IN BLACK AND WHITE

You can preview how your slides will look when printed in black and white.

The Slide and Notes Page views allow you to view a single slide in black and white. The Slide Sorter view displays the entire presentation in black and white. You cannot view slides in black and white in the Outline view.

VIEW SLIDES IN BLACK AND WHITE

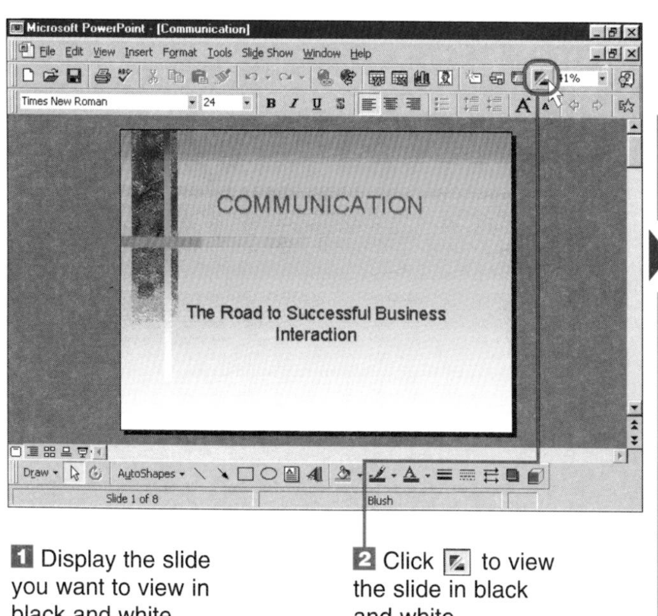

1 Display the slide you want to view in black and white.

2 Click to view the slide in black and white.

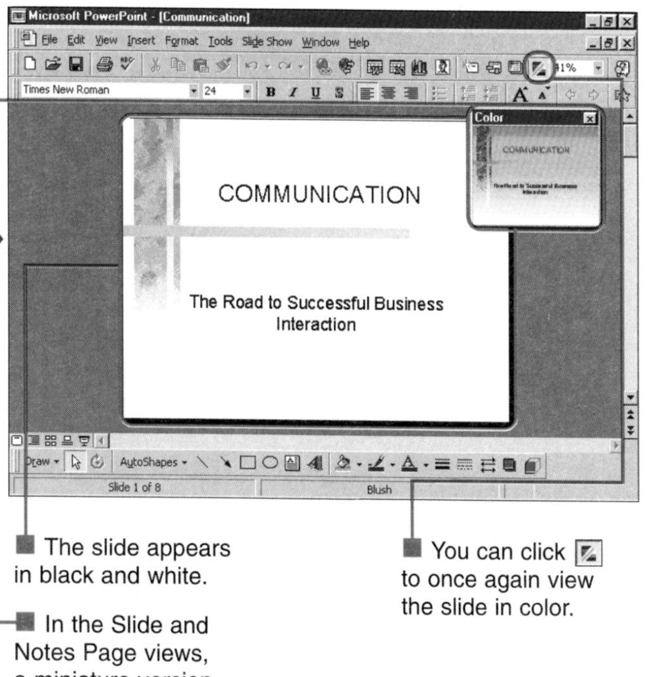

■ The slide appears in black and white.

■ In the Slide and Notes Page views, a miniature version of the color slide also appears.

■ You can click to once again view the slide in color.

CREATE A SUMMARY SLIDE

You can create a summary slide that lists the titles of all the slides in your presentation. A summary slide is useful for introducing the contents of your presentation to the audience.

CREATE A SUMMARY SLIDE

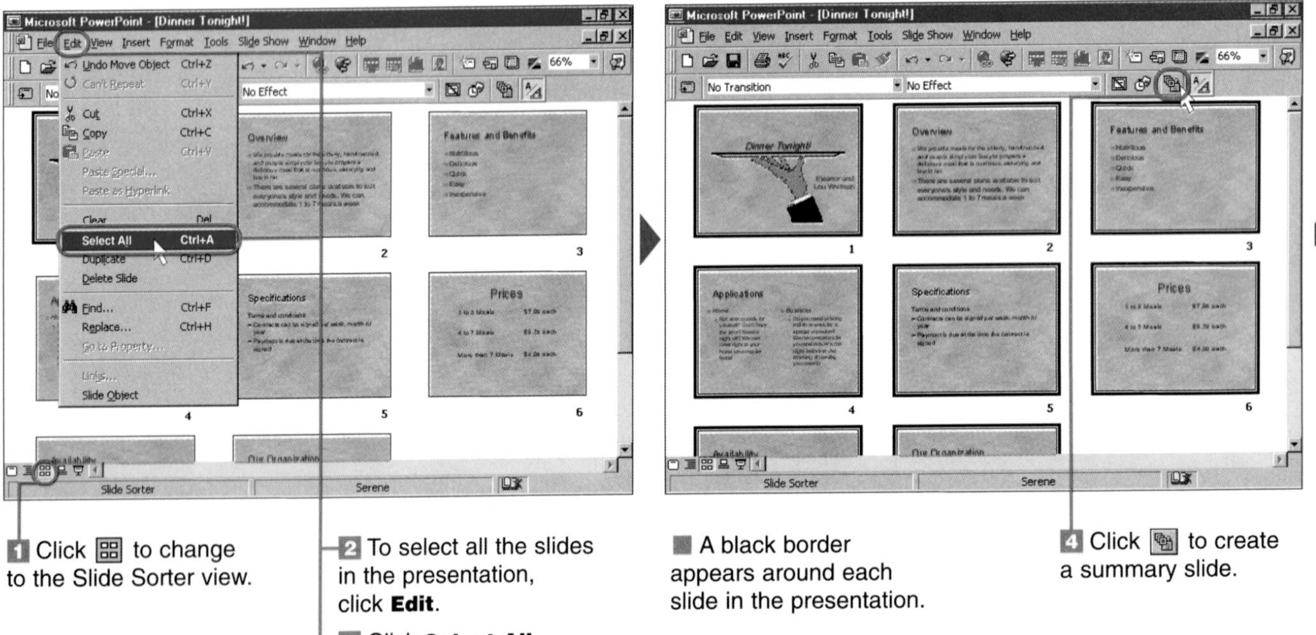

1 Click ▦ to change to the Slide Sorter view.

2 To select all the slides in the presentation, click **Edit**.

3 Click **Select All**.

■ A black border appears around each slide in the presentation.

4 Click ▦ to create a summary slide.

Why did two summary slides appear at the beginning of my presentation?

PowerPoint can only fit a certain amount of information on a slide. If your presentation contains many slides, PowerPoint may need to create two or more summary slides to list all the titles in the presentation.

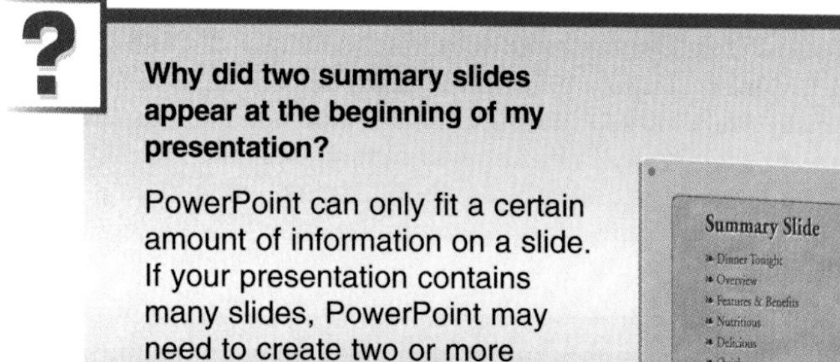

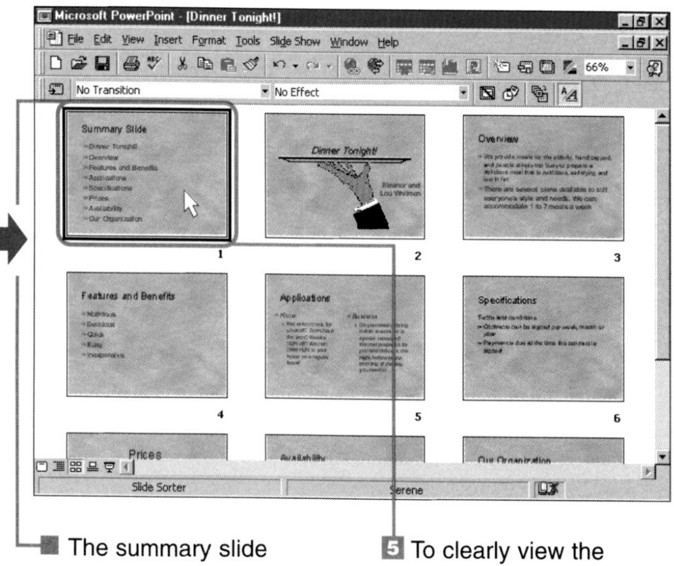

■ The summary slide appears at the beginning of the presentation, listing the title of each slide.

Note: To move the summary slide to a different location in the presentation, see page 208.

5 To clearly view the contents of the summary slide, double-click the slide.

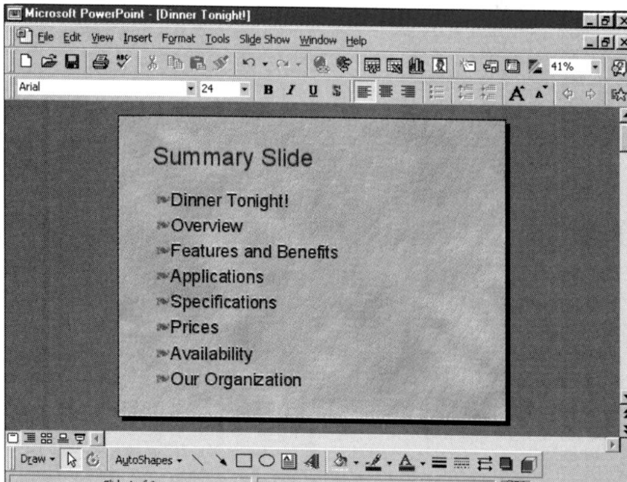

■ The summary slide appears in the Slide view. You can edit the summary slide as you would edit any slide.

ADD SLIDES FROM ANOTHER PRESENTATION

You can add slides to your current presentation from a presentation you previously created.

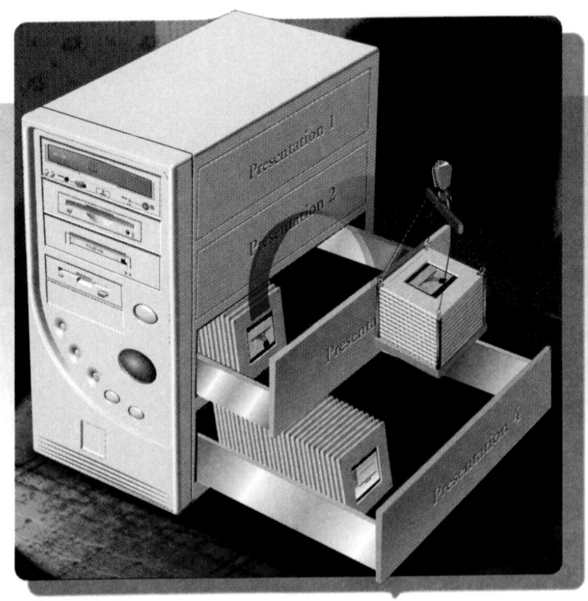

ADD SLIDES FROM ANOTHER PRESENTATION

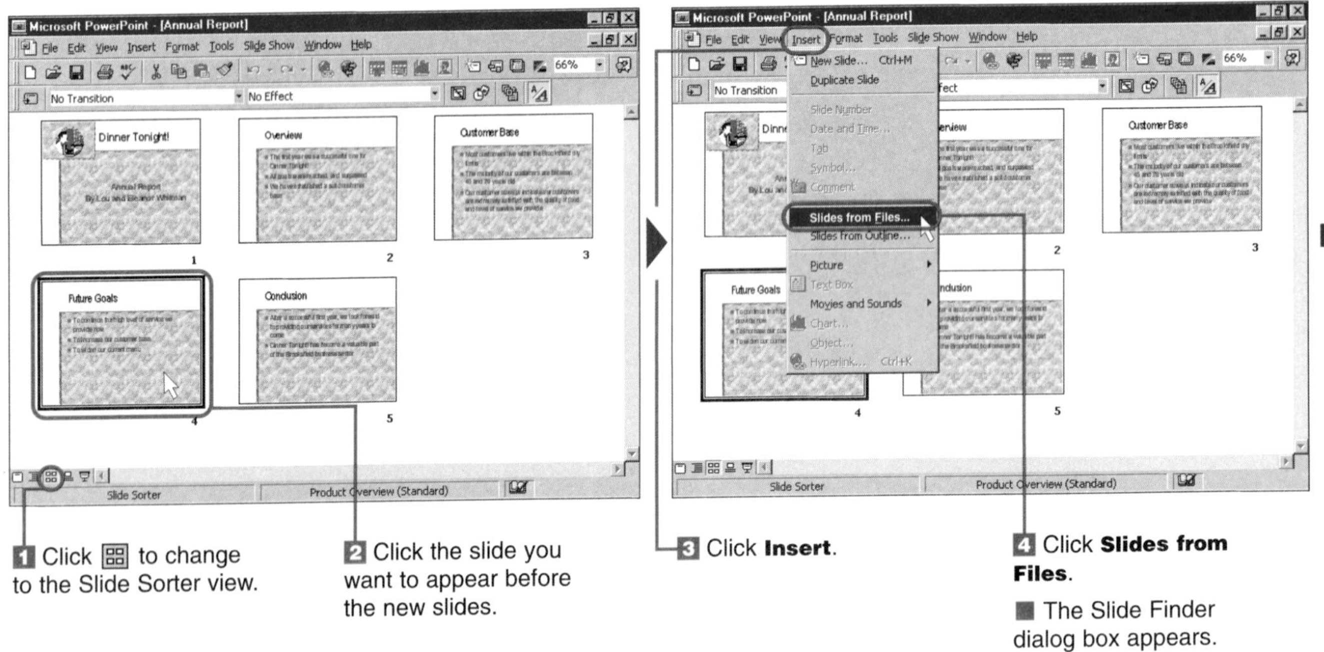

1 Click ▦ to change to the Slide Sorter view.

2 Click the slide you want to appear before the new slides.

3 Click **Insert**.

4 Click **Slides from Files**.

■ The Slide Finder dialog box appears.

When I add slides from another presentation, does PowerPoint remove the slides from the other presentation?

No. PowerPoint makes a copy of the slides in the original presentation and places the copy in your current presentation. The slides in the original presentation do not change.

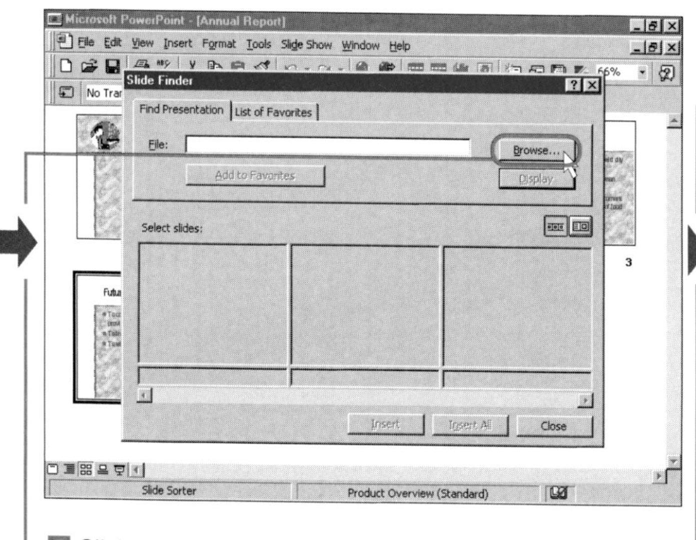

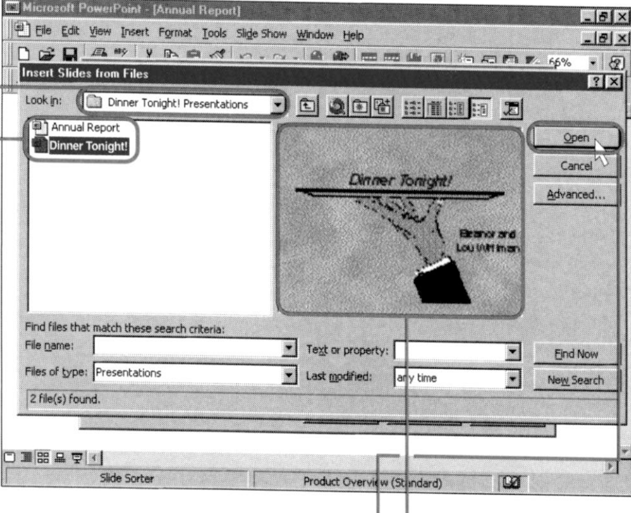

5 Click **Browse** to locate the presentation that contains the slides you want to use.

■ The Insert Slides from Files dialog box appears.

■ This area shows the location of the displayed presentations. You can click this area to change the location.

6 Click the presentation that contains the slides you want to add to the current presentation.

■ This area displays the first slide in the presentation you selected.

7 Click **Open**.

CONTINUED

ADD SLIDES FROM ANOTHER PRESENTATION

When you add slides from another presentation, PowerPoint automatically changes the design of the slides to match the design of the current presentation.

ADD SLIDES FROM ANOTHER PRESENTATION (CONTINUED)

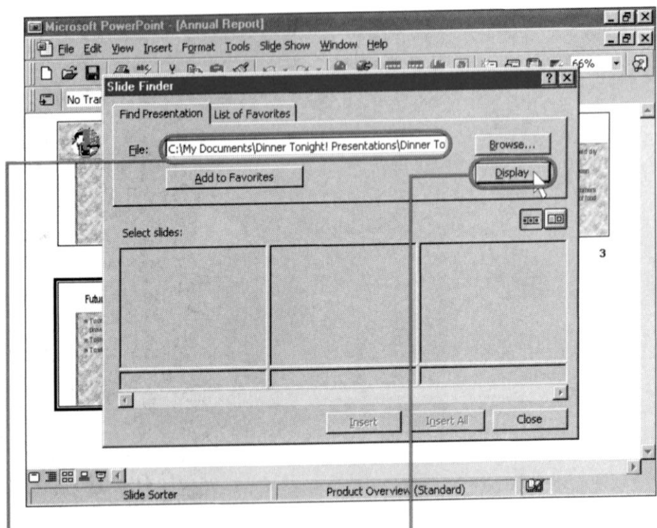

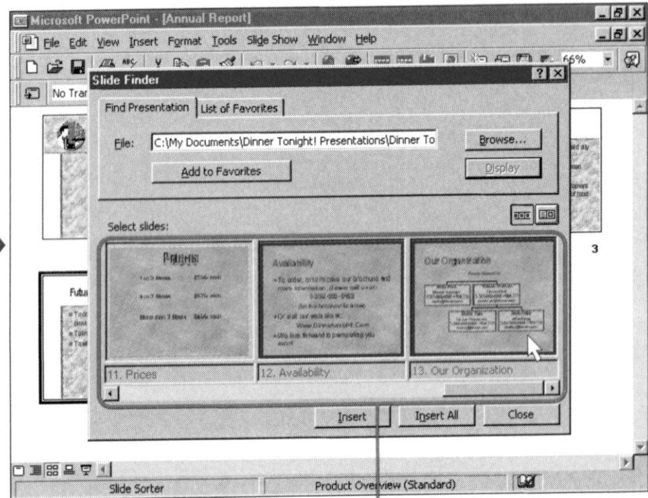

■ This area shows the location of the presentation you selected.

8 Click **Display** to view the slides in the presentation.

■ The slides in the presentation appear. PowerPoint displays the slide titles below each slide. You can use the scroll bar to browse through the slides.

9 Click each slide you want to add to the current presentation. A blue border appears around each slide you select.

Note: If you accidentally selected a slide, click the slide again to deselect the slide.

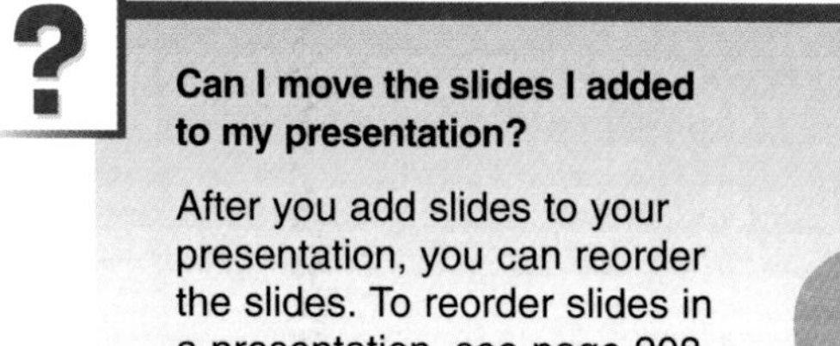

Can I move the slides I added to my presentation?

After you add slides to your presentation, you can reorder the slides. To reorder slides in a presentation, see page 208.

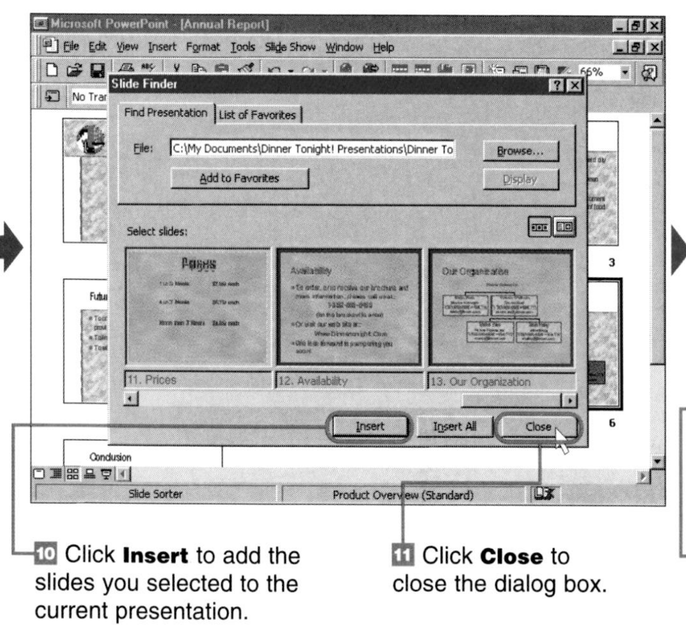

10 Click **Insert** to add the slides you selected to the current presentation.

11 Click **Close** to close the dialog box.

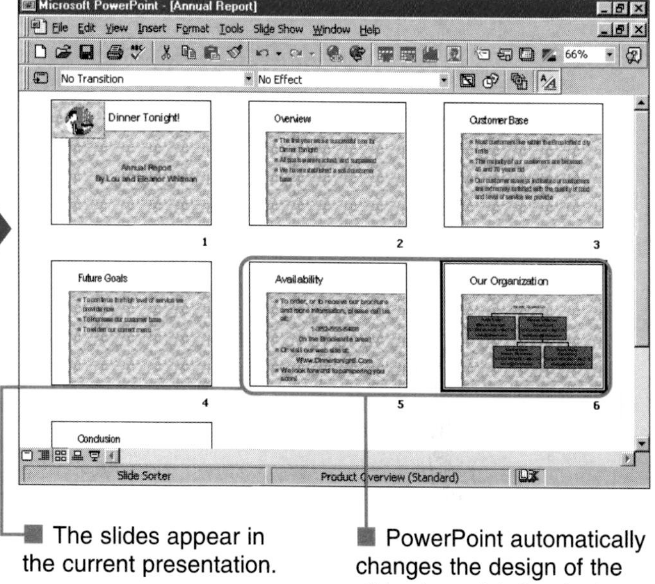

■ The slides appear in the current presentation.

■ PowerPoint automatically changes the design of the slides to match the design of the current presentation.

ADD A COMMENT

You can add a comment to your presentation to remind yourself of a task you still need to complete or a change you want to make later.

ADD A COMMENT

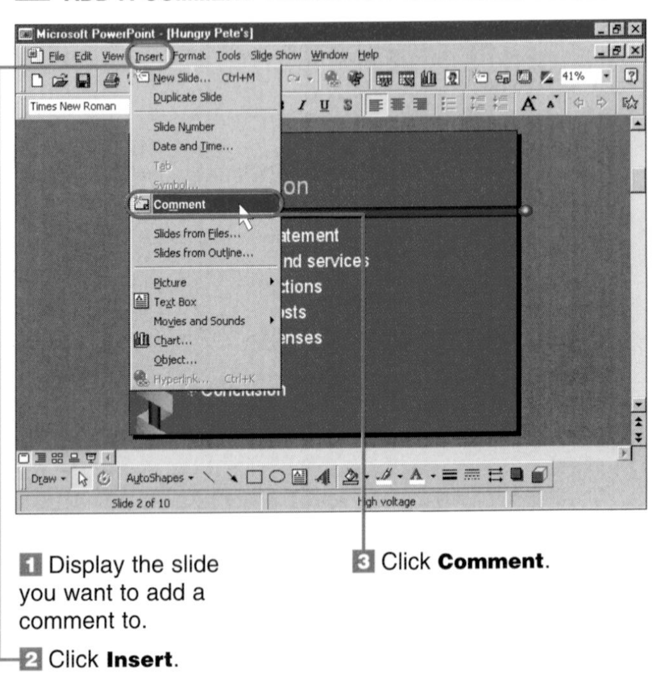

1 Display the slide you want to add a comment to.

2 Click **Insert**.

3 Click **Comment**.

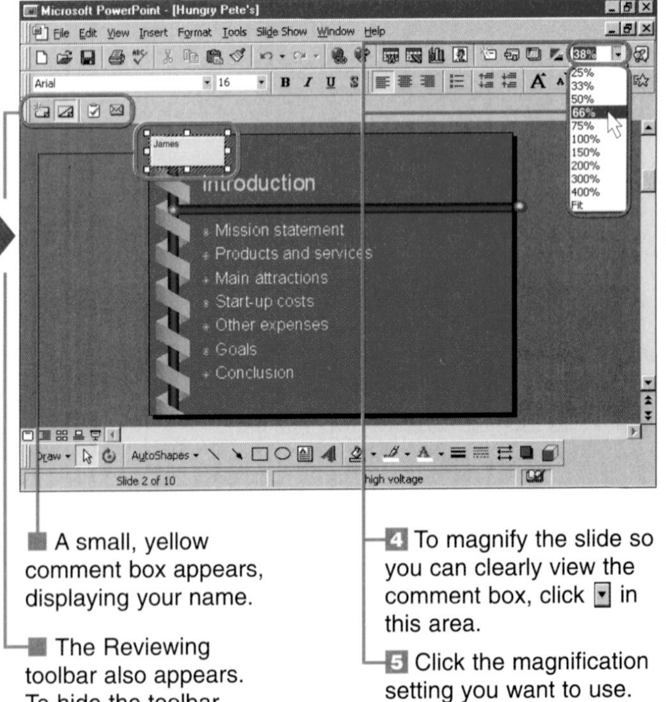

■ A small, yellow comment box appears, displaying your name.

■ The Reviewing toolbar also appears. To hide the toolbar, see page 34.

4 To magnify the slide so you can clearly view the comment box, click ▾ in this area.

5 Click the magnification setting you want to use.

Why would I hide the comments in my presentation?

You may want to hide the comments in your presentation to make the slides easier to read and work with. You may also want to hide comments to ensure the comments will not be displayed during a slide show.

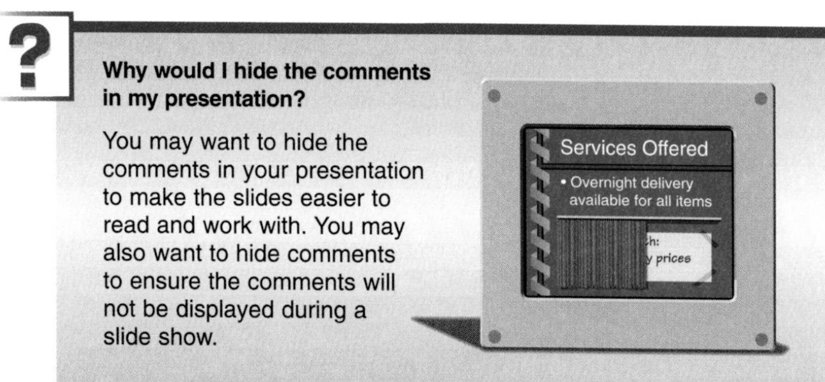

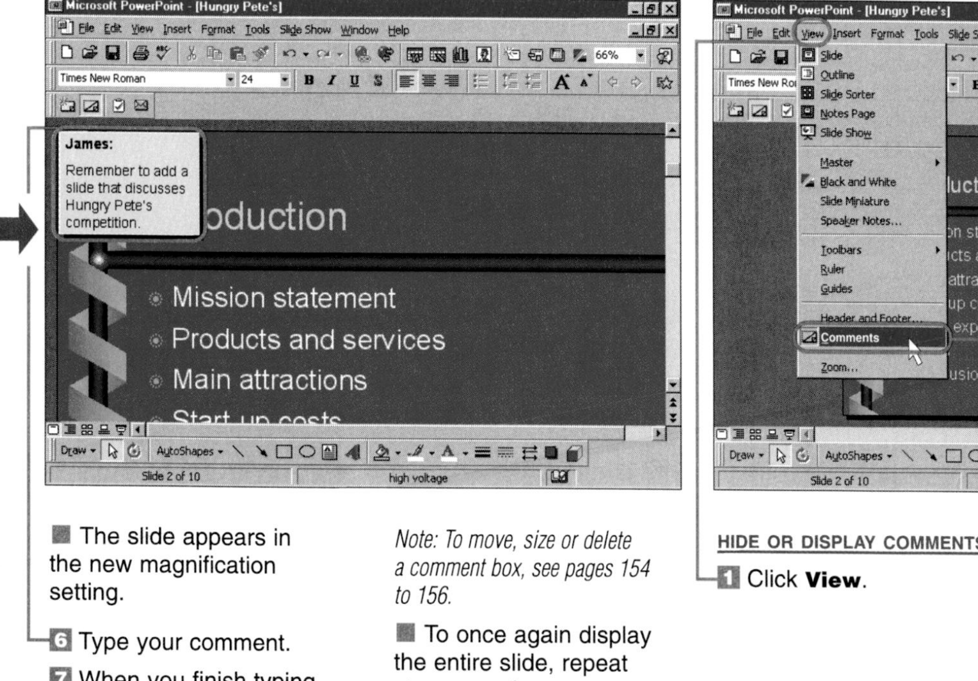

■ The slide appears in the new magnification setting.

6 Type your comment.

7 When you finish typing your comment, click outside the comment box.

Note: To move, size or delete a comment box, see pages 154 to 156.

■ To once again display the entire slide, repeat steps 4 and 5, except select **Fit** in step 5.

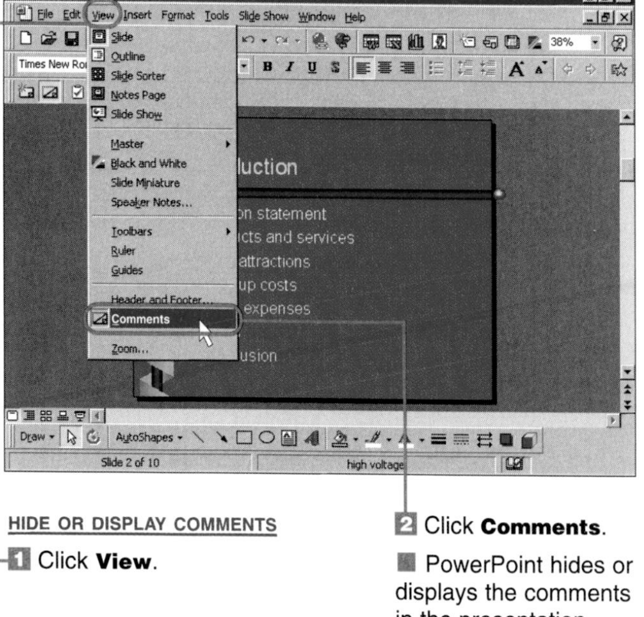

HIDE OR DISPLAY COMMENTS

1 Click **View**.

2 Click **Comments**.

■ PowerPoint hides or displays the comments in the presentation.

CREATE SPEAKER NOTES

You can create speaker notes that contain copies of your slides with all the ideas you want to discuss during your presentation.

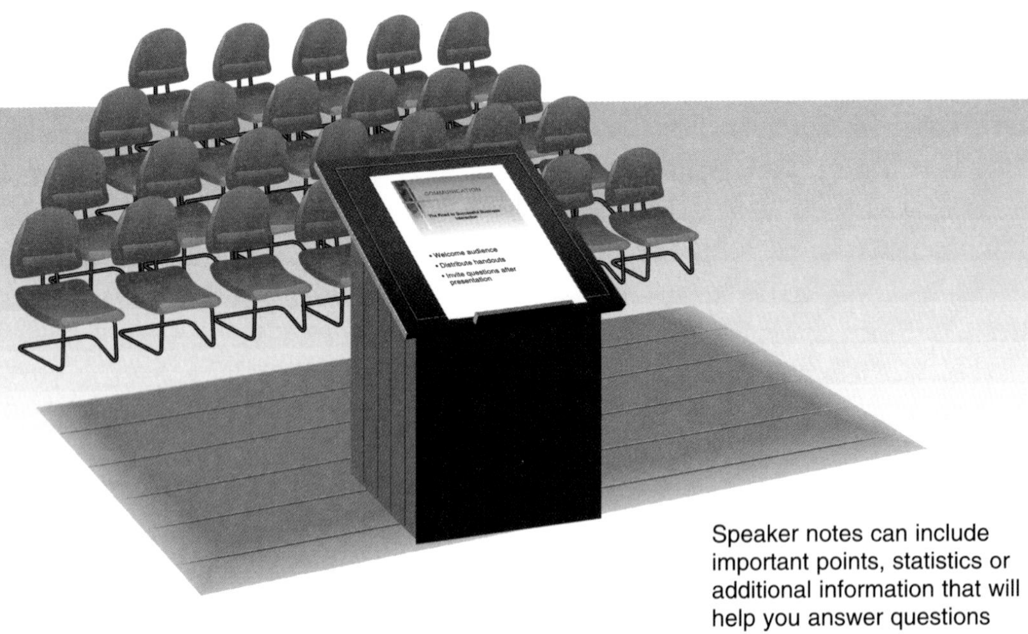

Speaker notes can include important points, statistics or additional information that will help you answer questions from the audience.

CREATE SPEAKER NOTES

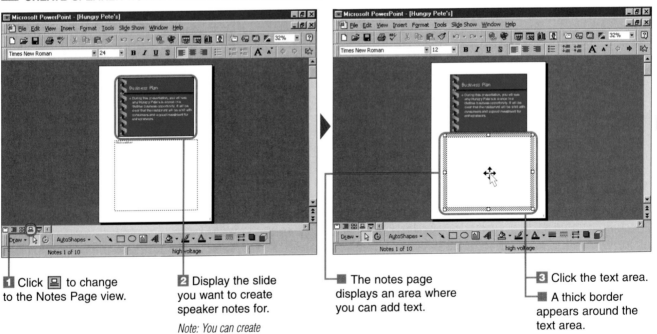

1 Click [icon] to change to the Notes Page view.

2 Display the slide you want to create speaker notes for.

Note: You can create speaker notes for any slide in the presentation.

■ The notes page displays an area where you can add text.

3 Click the text area.

■ A thick border appears around the text area.

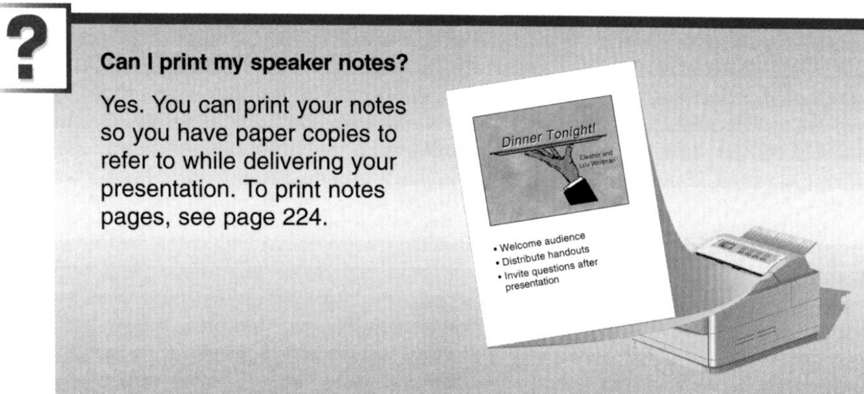

Can I print my speaker notes?

Yes. You can print your notes so you have paper copies to refer to while delivering your presentation. To print notes pages, see page 224.

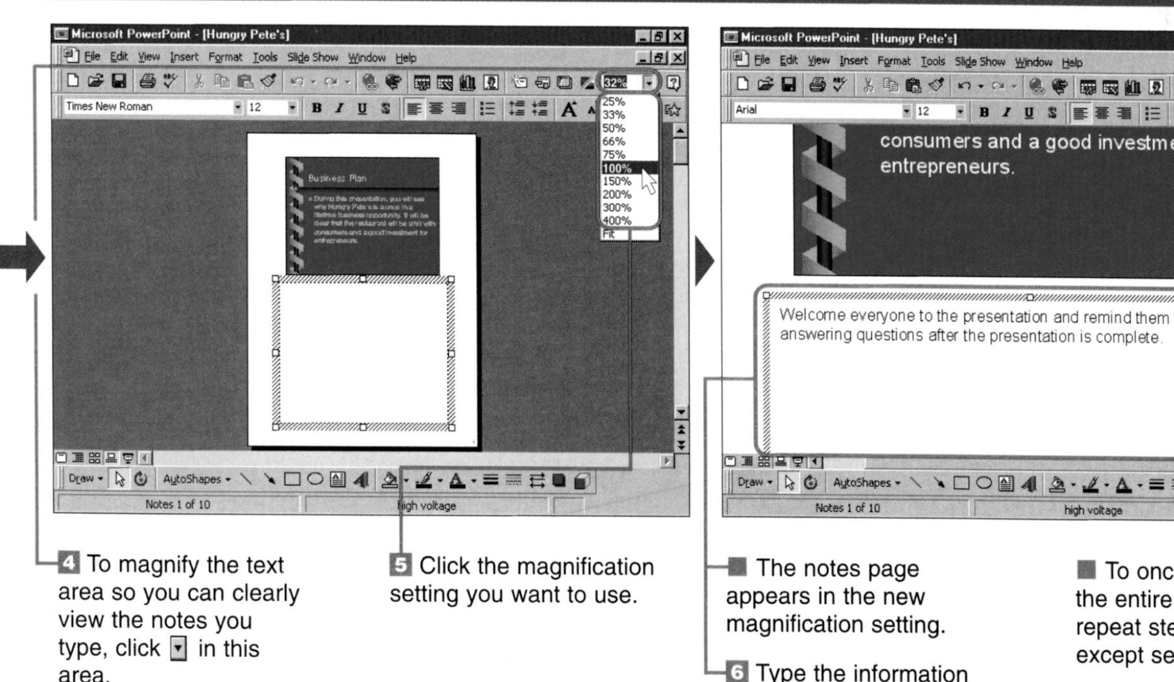

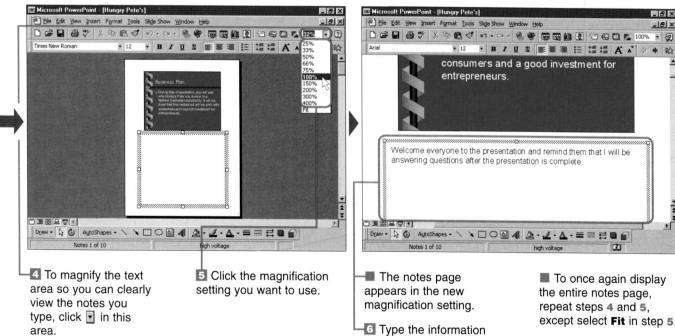

4 To magnify the text area so you can clearly view the notes you type, click ▾ in this area.

5 Click the magnification setting you want to use.

■ The notes page appears in the new magnification setting.

6 Type the information you want to discuss when you display the slide during the slide show.

■ To once again display the entire notes page, repeat steps **4** and **5**, except select **Fit** in step **5**.

SET UP A PRESENTATION FOR PRINTING

Before printing your presentation, you can specify how you want to output the presentation, such as on paper, 35mm slides or overheads.

You can also specify the orientation you want to use when printing your presentation.

SET UP A PRESENTATION FOR PRINTING

1 Click **File**.

2 Click **Page Setup**.

■ The Page Setup dialog box appears.

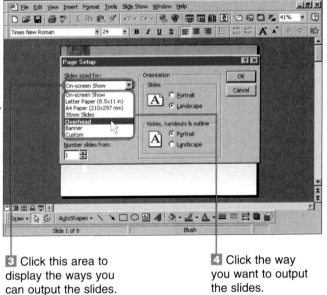

3 Click this area to display the ways you can output the slides.

4 Click the way you want to output the slides.

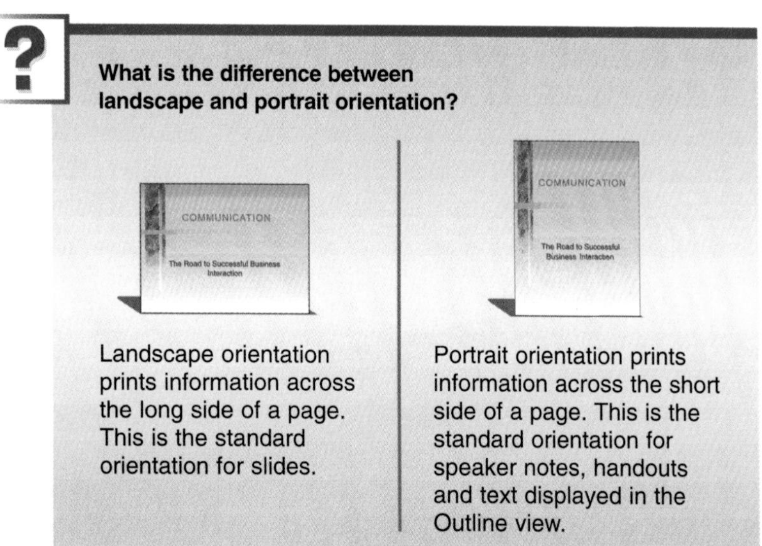

What is the difference between landscape and portrait orientation?

Landscape orientation prints information across the long side of a page. This is the standard orientation for slides.

Portrait orientation prints information across the short side of a page. This is the standard orientation for speaker notes, handouts and text displayed in the Outline view.

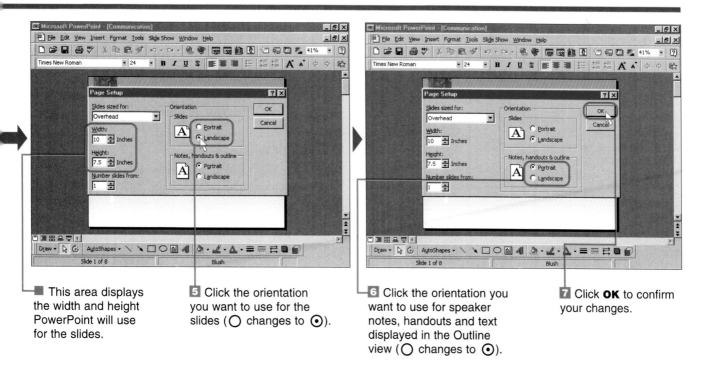

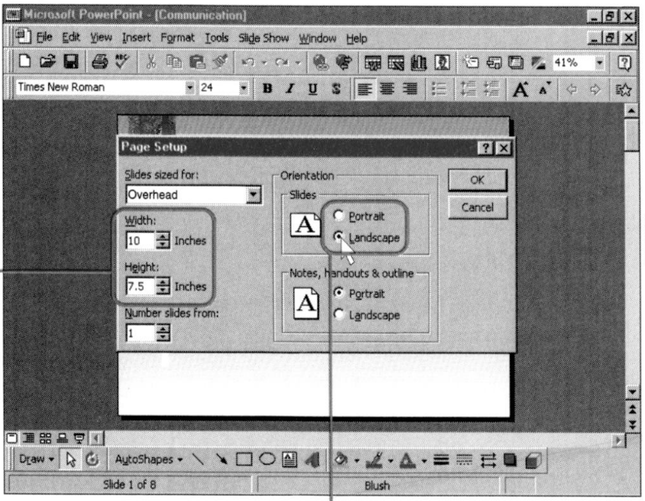

■ This area displays the width and height PowerPoint will use for the slides.

5 Click the orientation you want to use for the slides (○ changes to ⊙).

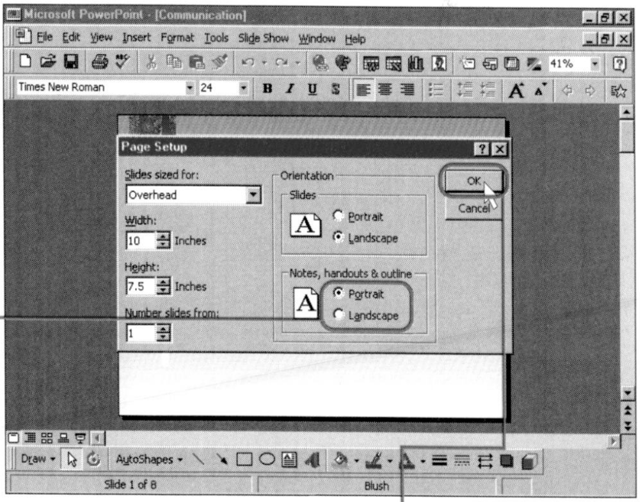

6 Click the orientation you want to use for speaker notes, handouts and text displayed in the Outline view (○ changes to ⊙).

7 Click **OK** to confirm your changes.

PRINT A PRESENTATION

You can produce a paper copy of a presentation for your own use or to hand out to the audience.

PRINT A PRESENTATION

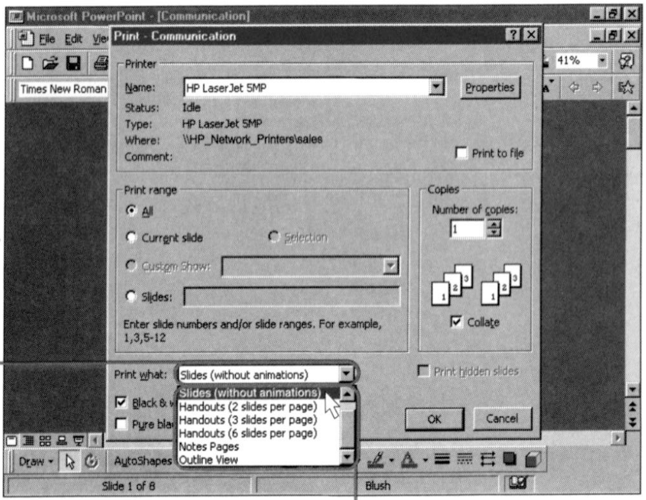

1 Click **File**.

2 Click **Print**.

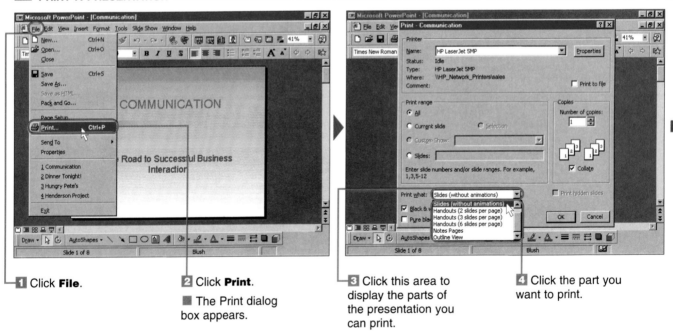

■ The Print dialog box appears.

3 Click this area to display the parts of the presentation you can print.

4 Click the part you want to print.

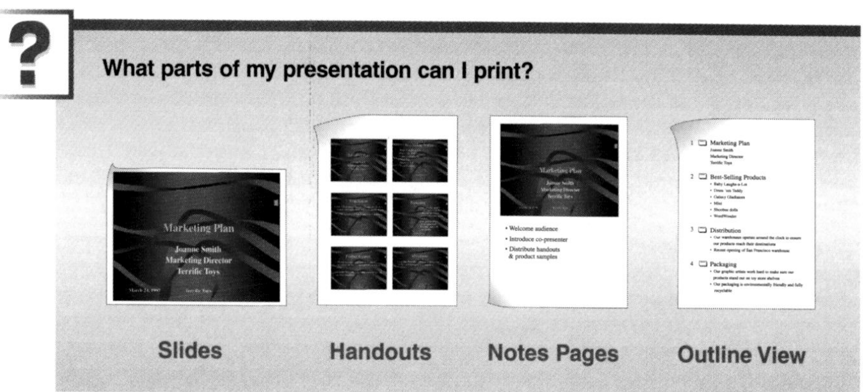

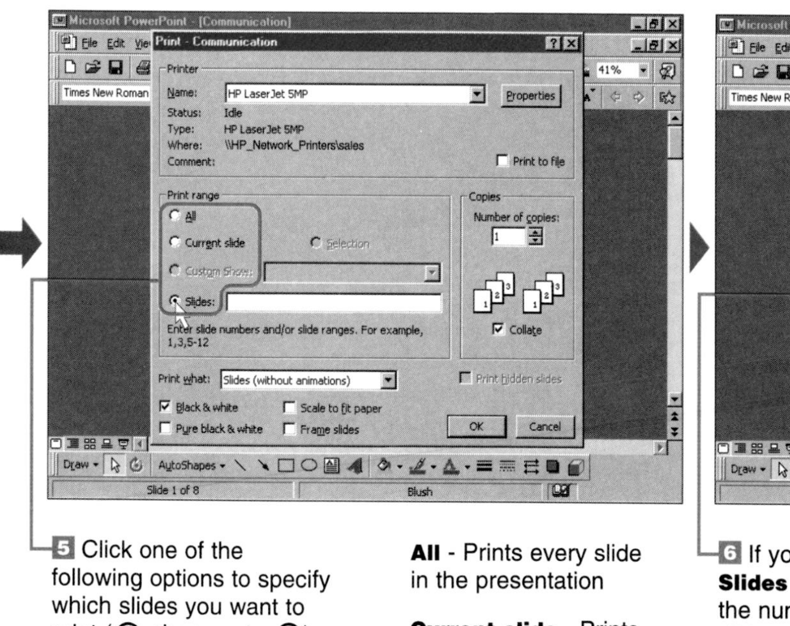

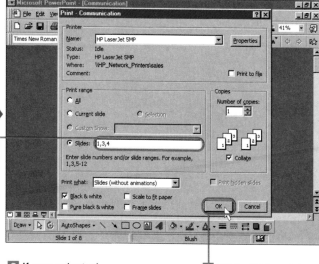

5 Click one of the following options to specify which slides you want to print (○ changes to ⊙).

All - Prints every slide in the presentation

Current slide - Prints the selected slide or the slide displayed on the screen

Slides - Prints slides you specify

6 If you selected **Slides** in step **5**, type the numbers of the slides you want to print (example: 1,3,4 or 2-4).

7 Click **OK** to print the presentation.

WORK WITH A PRESENTATION IN MICROSOFT WORD

You can work with your presentation as a Microsoft Word document. This gives you more flexibility when creating and printing handouts or speaker notes for your presentation.

To perform this task, you need Microsoft Word installed on your computer.

WORK WITH A PRESENTATION IN MICROSOFT WORD

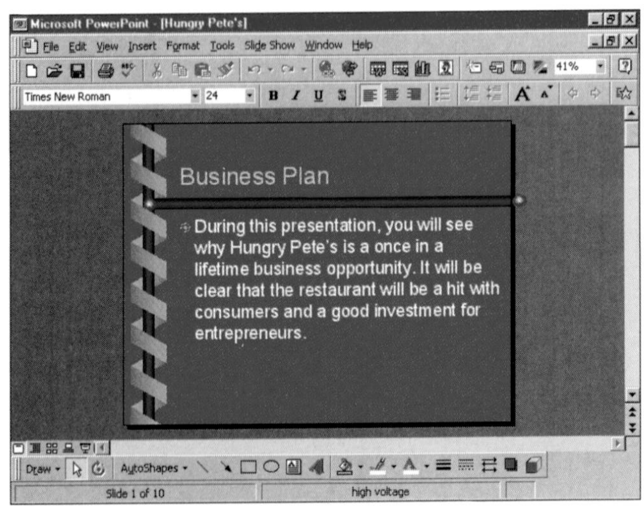

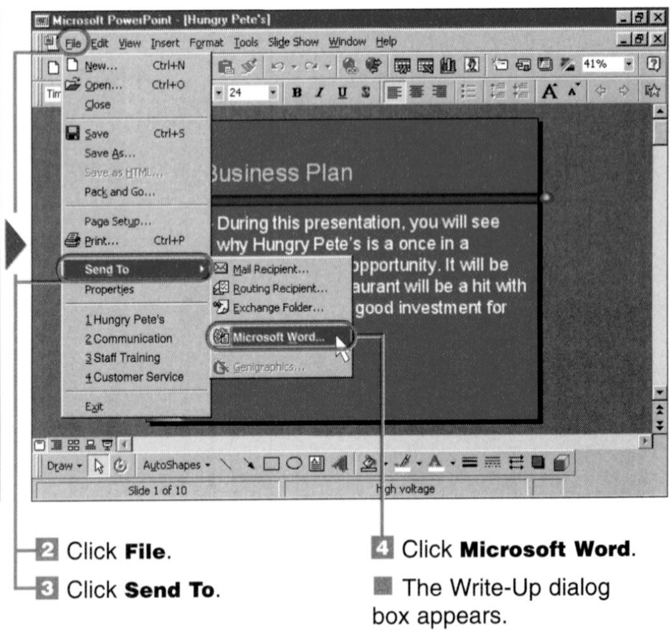

1 Open the presentation you want to work with as a Microsoft Word document. To open a presentation, see page 22.

■ If you plan to print the Microsoft Word document on a black-and-white printer, you should display the slides in the presentation in black and white before performing step 2. For more information, see page 211.

2 Click **File**.

3 Click **Send To**.

4 Click **Microsoft Word**.

■ The Write-Up dialog box appears.

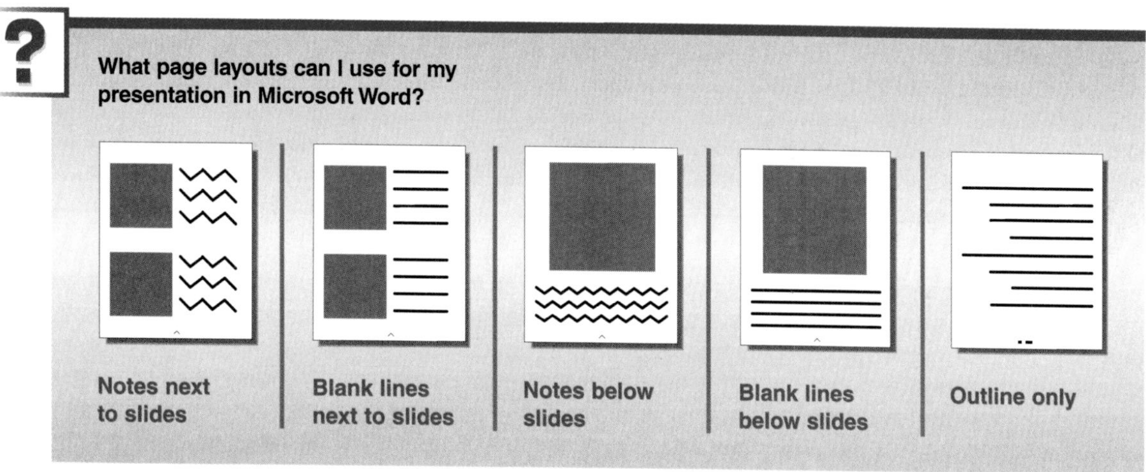

?
What page layouts can I use for my presentation in Microsoft Word?
Notes next to slides
Blank lines next to slides
Notes below slides
Blank lines below slides
Outline only

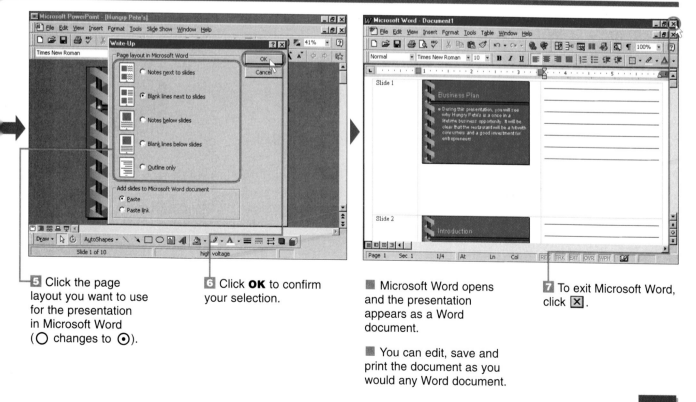

5 Click the page layout you want to use for the presentation in Microsoft Word (○ changes to ⊙).

6 Click **OK** to confirm your selection.

■ Microsoft Word opens and the presentation appears as a Word document.

■ You can edit, save and print the document as you would any Word document.

7 To exit Microsoft Word, click ☒.

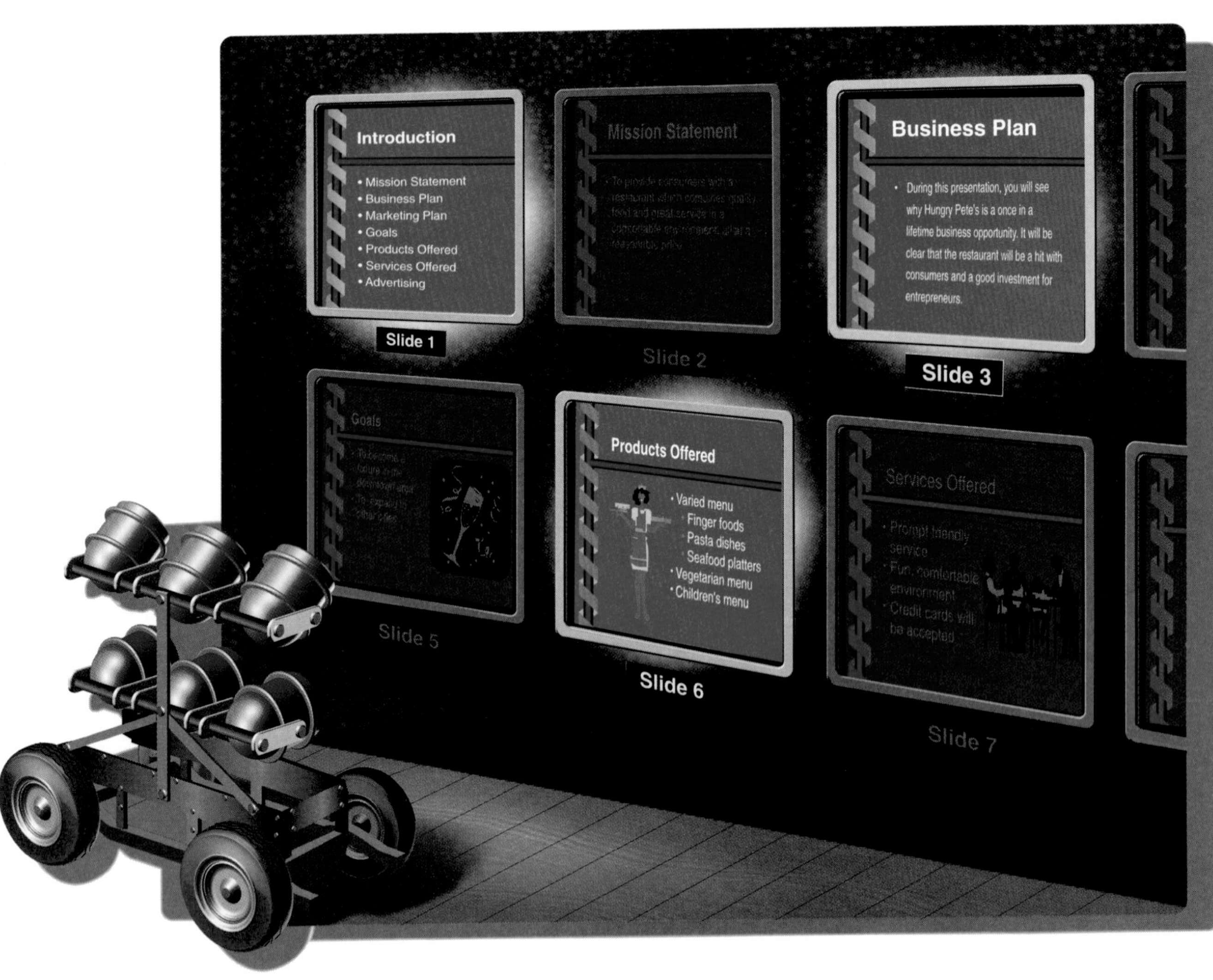
Introduction
• Mission Statement
• Business Plan
• Marketing Plan
• Goals
• Products Offered
• Services Offered
• Advertising
Slide 1
Mission Statement
Slide 2
Business Plan
• During this presentation, you will see why Hungry Pete's is a once in a lifetime business opportunity. It will be clear that the restaurant will be a hit with consumers and a good investment for entrepreneurs.
Slide 3
Goals
Slide 5
Products Offered
• Varied menu
Finger foods
Pasta dishes
Seafood platters
• Vegetarian menu
• Children's menu
Slide 6
Services Offered
Slide 7

CHAPTER 11

Deliver a Presentation

Are you ready to deliver your presentation? This chapter shows you how to set up, rehearse and deliver your presentation.

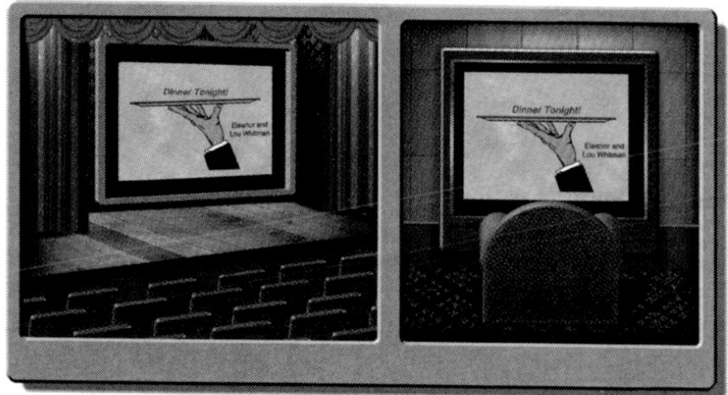

SET UP A SLIDE SHOW

You can specify how you want to present a slide show on a computer. For example, you can deliver the slide show yourself or allow other people to browse through the slide show on their own.

SET UP A SLIDE SHOW

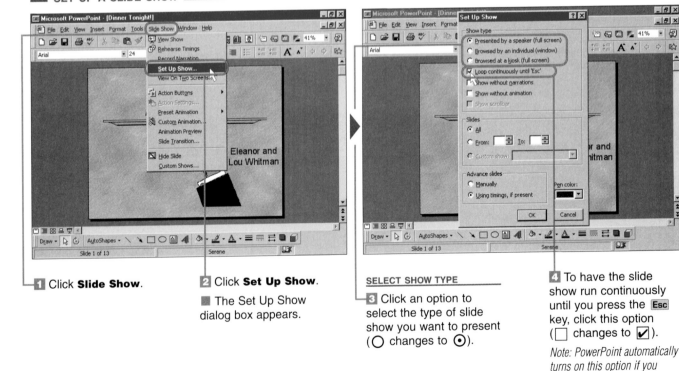

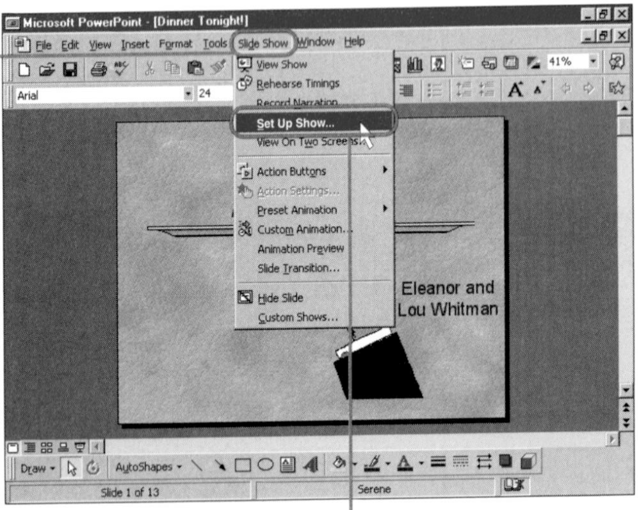

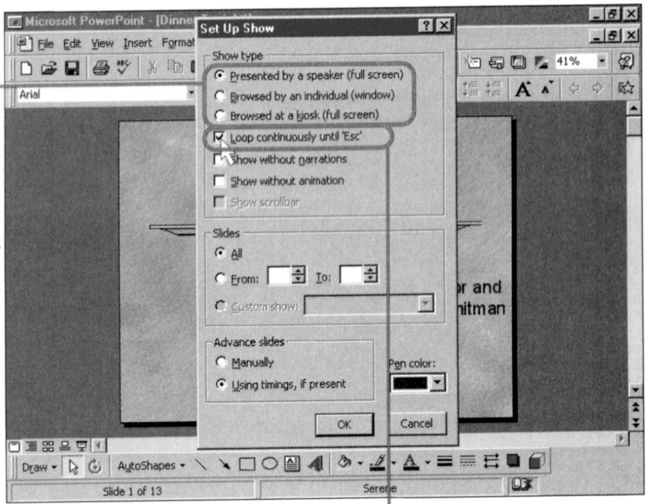

1 Click **Slide Show**.

2 Click **Set Up Show**.

■ The Set Up Show dialog box appears.

SELECT SHOW TYPE

3 Click an option to select the type of slide show you want to present (○ changes to ⊙).

4 To have the slide show run continuously until you press the Esc key, click this option (☐ changes to ☑).

*Note: PowerPoint automatically turns on this option if you selected **Browsed at a kiosk** in step **3**.*

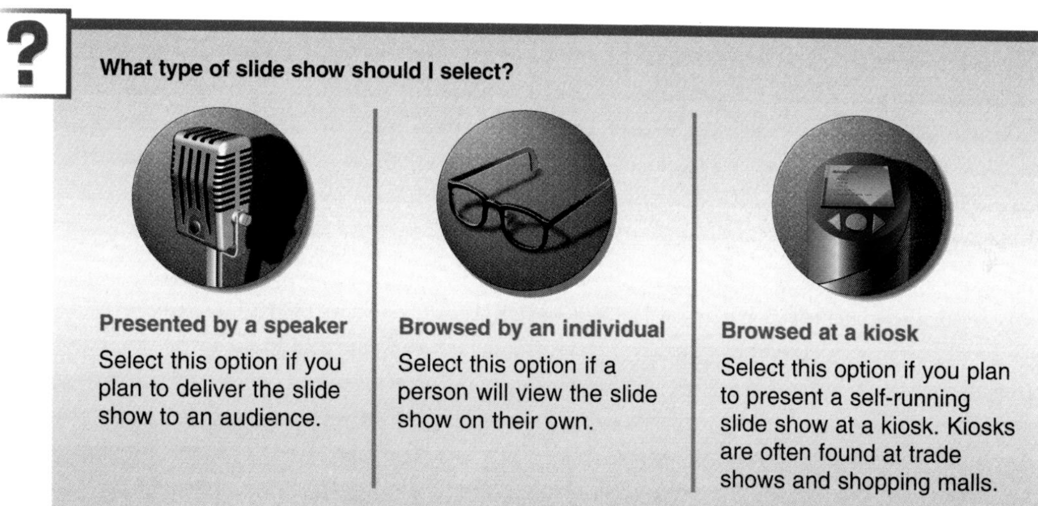

? What type of slide show should I select?

Presented by a speaker

Select this option if you plan to deliver the slide show to an audience.

Browsed by an individual

Select this option if a person will view the slide show on their own.

Browsed at a kiosk

Select this option if you plan to present a self-running slide show at a kiosk. Kiosks are often found at trade shows and shopping malls.

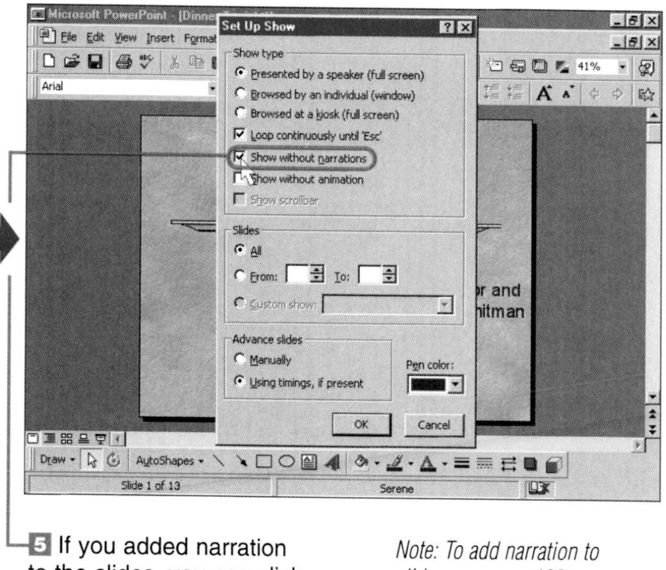

5 If you added narration to the slides, you can click this option to run the slide show without the narration (☐ changes to ☑).

Note: To add narration to slides, see page 182.

6 If you added animations to the slides, you can click this option to run the slide show without the animations (☐ changes to ☑).

Note: To add animations to slides, see pages 192 to 201.

CONTINUED

SET UP A SLIDE SHOW

You can select which slides you want to display during the slide show.

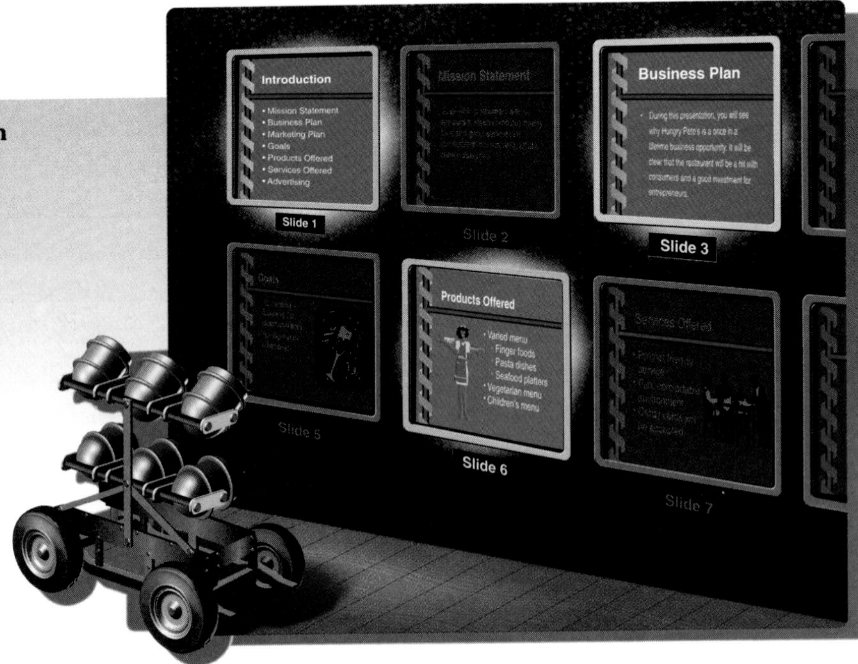

SET UP A SLIDE SHOW (CONTINUED)

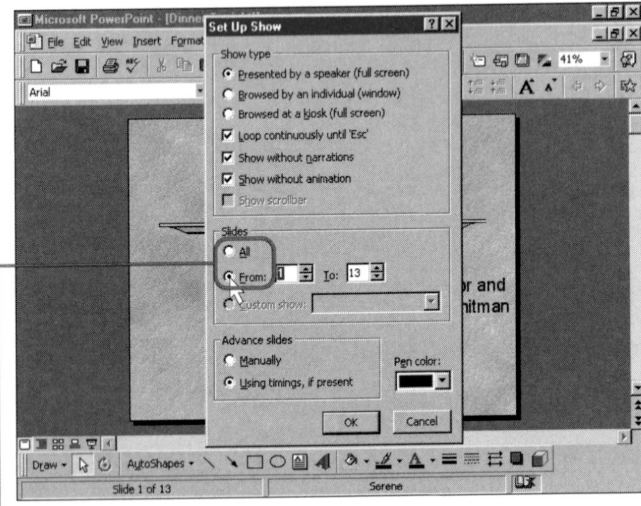

SELECT SLIDES

7 Click an option to specify which slides you want to present during the slide show (○ changes to ⊙).

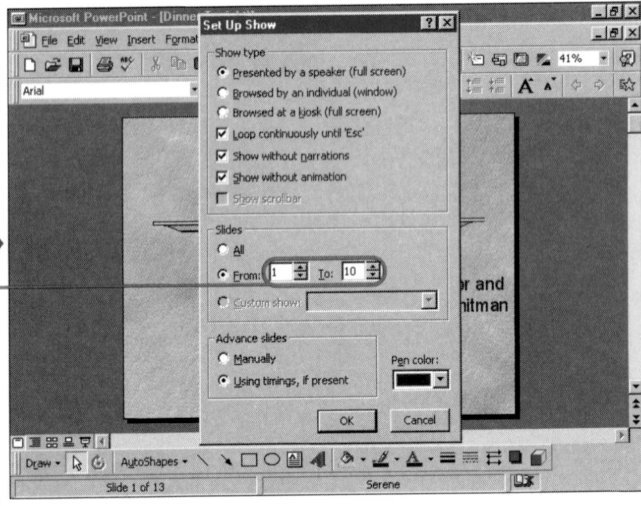

8 If you selected **From** in step 7, type the number of the first slide you want to display. Then press the Tab key and type the number of the last slide you want to display.

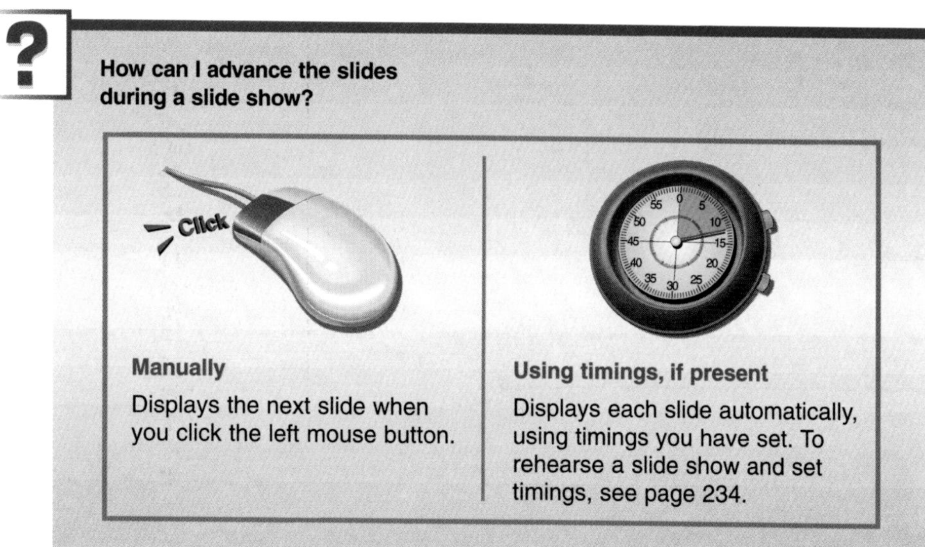

? **How can I advance the slides during a slide show?**

Manually

Displays the next slide when you click the left mouse button.

Using timings, if present

Displays each slide automatically, using timings you have set. To rehearse a slide show and set timings, see page 234.

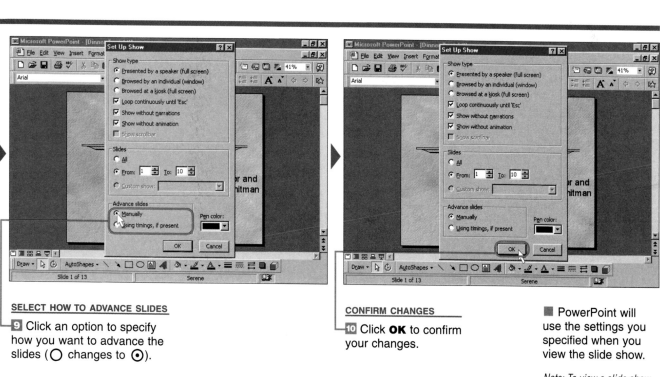

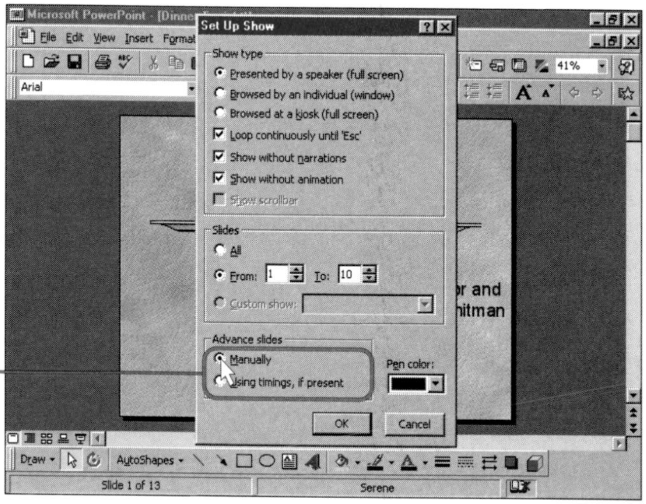

SELECT HOW TO ADVANCE SLIDES

9 Click an option to specify how you want to advance the slides (○ changes to ⊙).

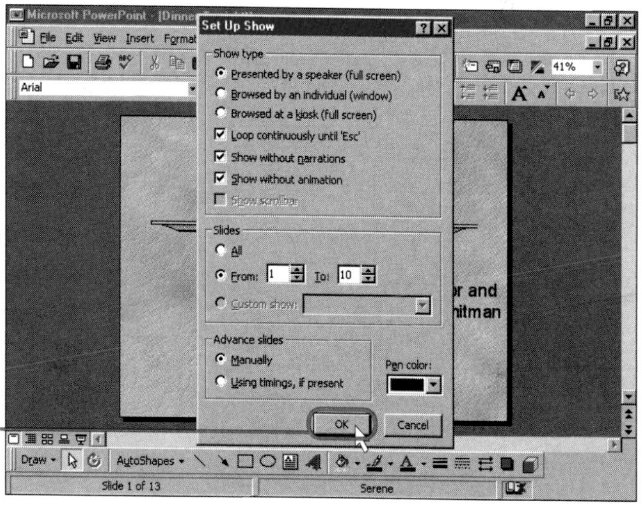

CONFIRM CHANGES

10 Click **OK** to confirm your changes.

■ PowerPoint will use the settings you specified when you view the slide show.

Note: To view a slide show, see page 238.

REHEARSE A SLIDE SHOW

You can rehearse your slide show and have PowerPoint record the amount of time you spend on each slide.

REHEARSE A SLIDE SHOW

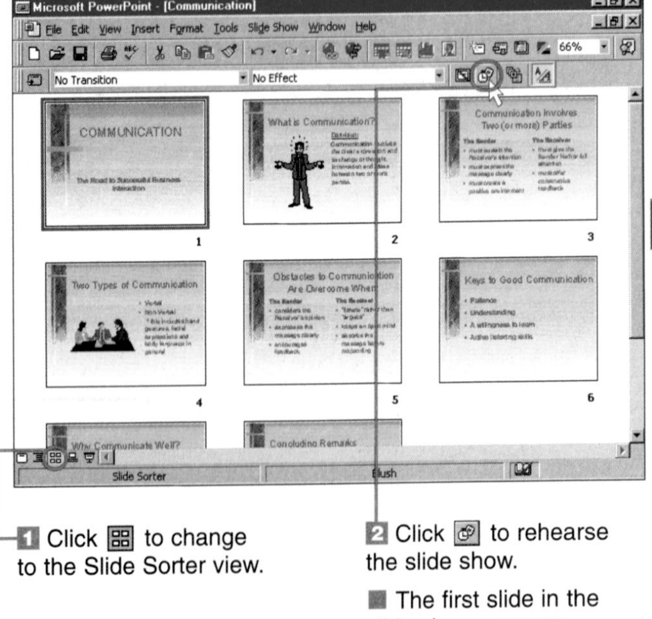

1 Click ▦ to change to the Slide Sorter view.

2 Click ⧉ to rehearse the slide show.

■ The first slide in the slide show appears.

■ The Rehearsal dialog box displays the total time you spend rehearsing the slide show and the time you spend rehearsing the current slide.

?

How does PowerPoint use the timings I record?

PowerPoint can use the recorded timings to advance your slides automatically during a slide show. This is useful if you want to set up a self-running slide show for a kiosk. Kiosks are often found at trade shows and shopping malls.

If you do not want PowerPoint to advance your slides automatically, see page 230.

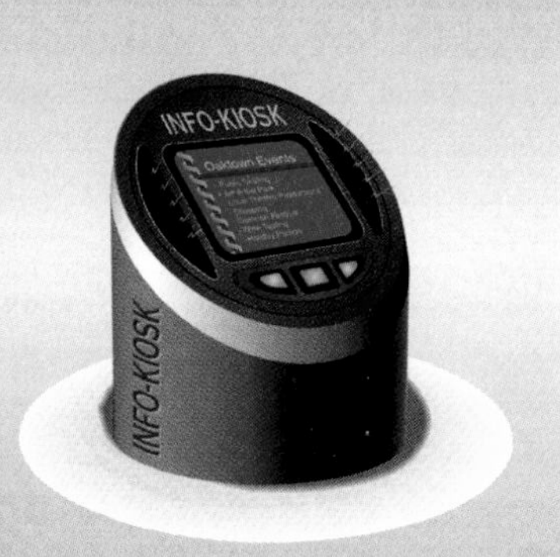

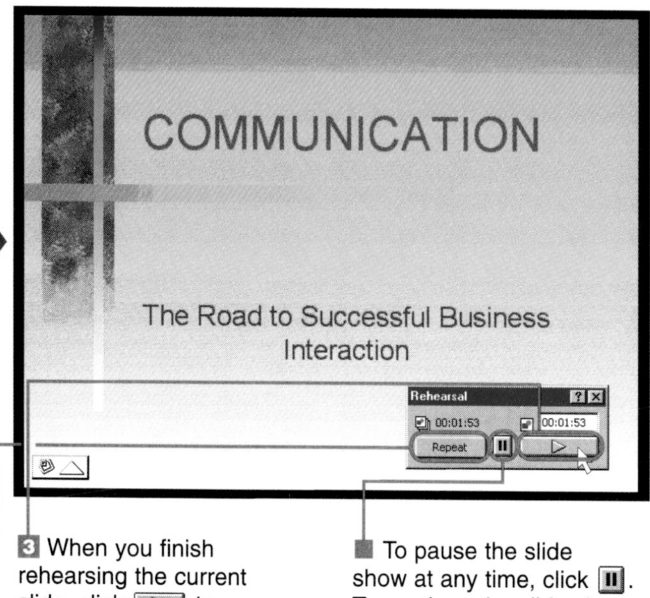

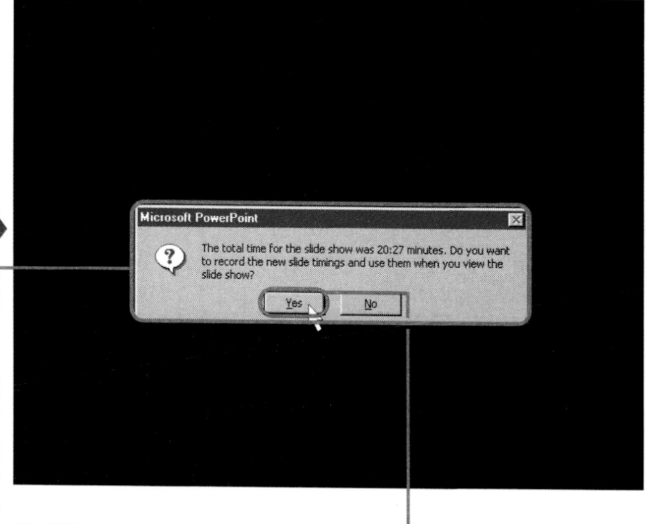

3 When you finish rehearsing the current slide, click ▷ to display the next slide.

■ If you make a mistake and want to reset the timer for the current slide, click **Repeat**.

■ To pause the slide show at any time, click ⏸. To continue the slide show, click ⏸ again.

■ When you finish the slide show, a dialog box appears, displaying the total time for the slide show.

4 To record the time you spent rehearsing each slide and use the timings when you later view the slide show, click **Yes**.

CONTINUED

REHEARSE A SLIDE SHOW

When you finish rehearsing your slide show, you can review the time you spent on each slide to determine if you have set an appropriate pace for your presentation.

REHEARSE A SLIDE SHOW (CONTINUED)

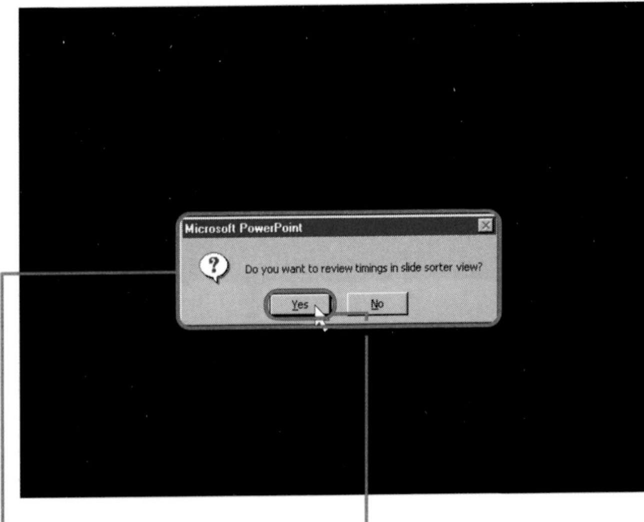

■ A dialog box appears, asking if you want to review the timings in the Slide Sorter view.

5 Click **Yes** to review the timings.

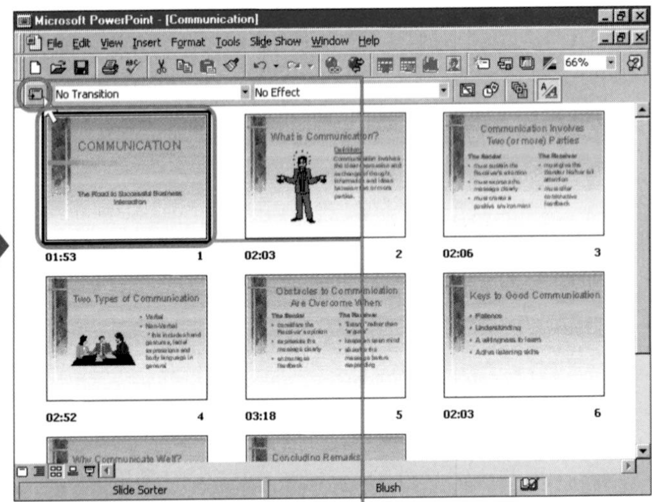

■ The time you spent rehearsing each slide appears below the slides.

CHANGE SLIDE TIMINGS

1 Click the slide you want to change the timing for. A black border appears around the slide.

2 Click .

?

Why would I want to change the slide timings?

Changing the slide timings is useful when you want a slide to appear during a slide show for a longer or shorter time than you originally rehearsed. You may also want to change the slide timings to ensure your presentation runs for a specific length of time.

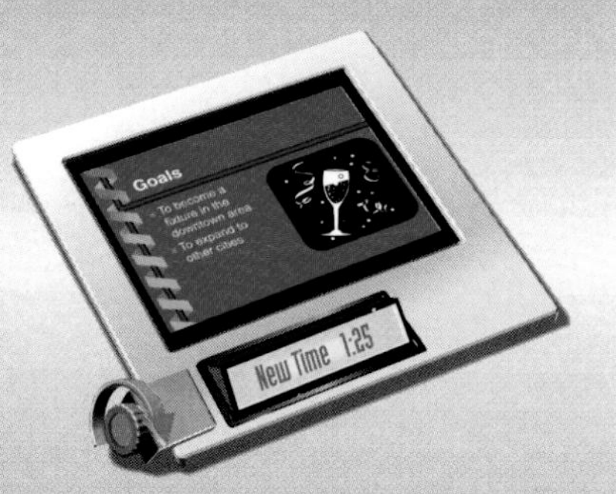

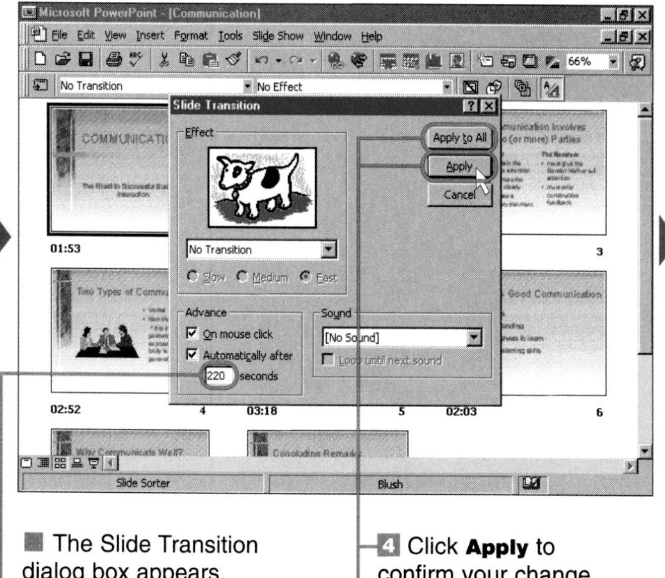

■ The Slide Transition dialog box appears.

3 Double-click this area and then type the number of seconds you want the slide to appear on your screen during the slide show.

4 Click **Apply** to confirm your change.

■ To use the timing for all the slides in the slide show, click **Apply to All**.

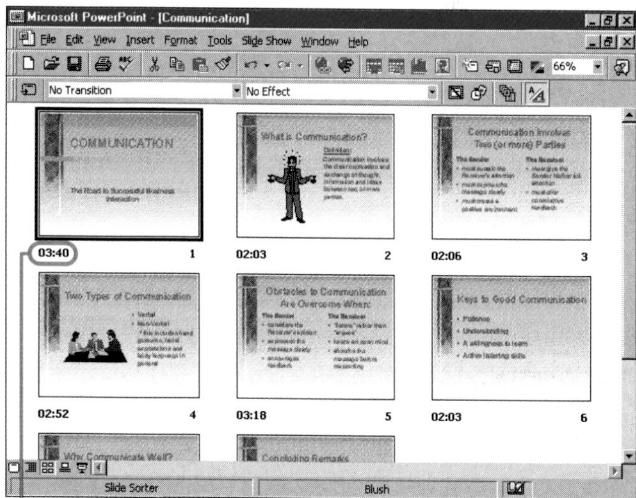

■ The slide displays the new timing.

VIEW A SLIDE SHOW

You can view a slide show of your presentation on a computer screen.

VIEW A SLIDE SHOW

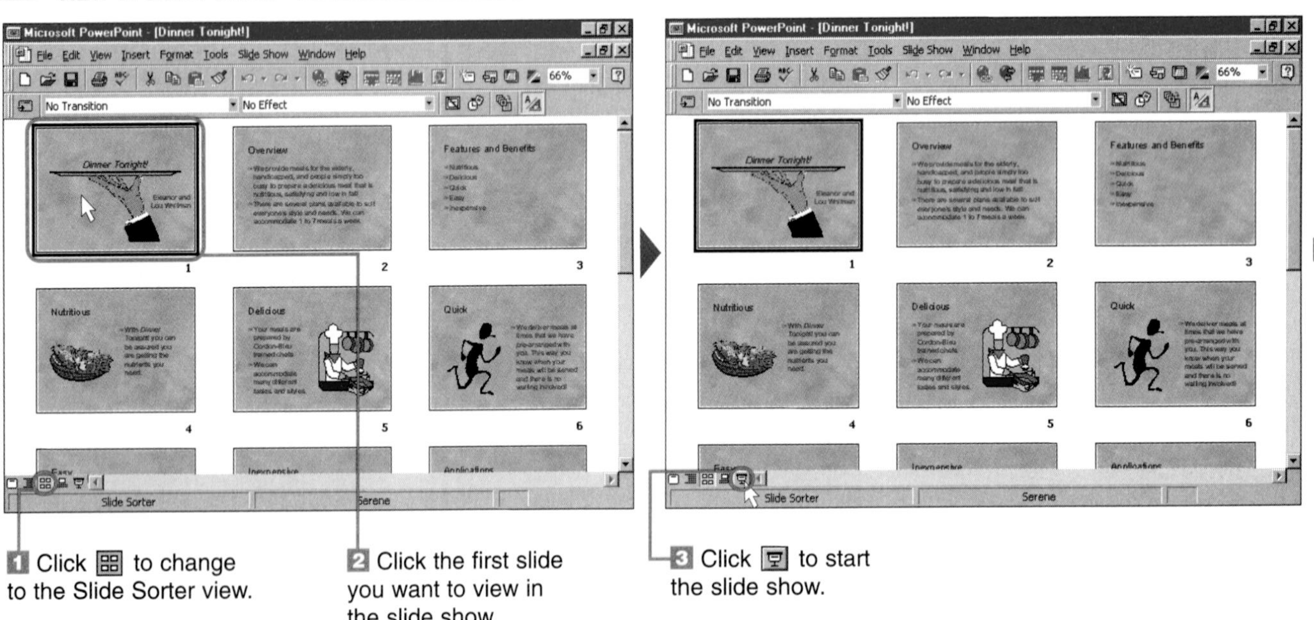

1 Click to change to the Slide Sorter view.

2 Click the first slide you want to view in the slide show.

3 Click to start the slide show.

How can I use my keyboard to move through a slide show?

Task	Press this key
Display the next slide	Spacebar
Display the previous slide	Backspace
Display any slide	Type the number of the slide and then press Enter
End the slide show	Esc
Turn the screen black	B
Turn the screen white	W

Overview

We provide meals for the elderly, handicapped, and people simply too busy to prepare a delicious meal that is nutritious, satisfying and low in fat!

There are several plans available to suit everyone's style and needs. We can accommodate 1 to 7 meals a week.

■ The first slide fills the screen.

Note: You can press the Esc key to end the slide show at any time.

4 To display the next slide, click the current slide or press the **Spacebar**.

■ To return to the previous slide, press the Backspace key.

■ The next slide appears.

■ Repeat step 4 until you finish viewing all the slides in the slide show.

CONTINUED

VIEW A SLIDE SHOW

During a slide show, you can instantly display any slide in your presentation. You can also draw on the slides to emphasize information you are presenting.

VIEW A SLIDE SHOW (CONTINUED)

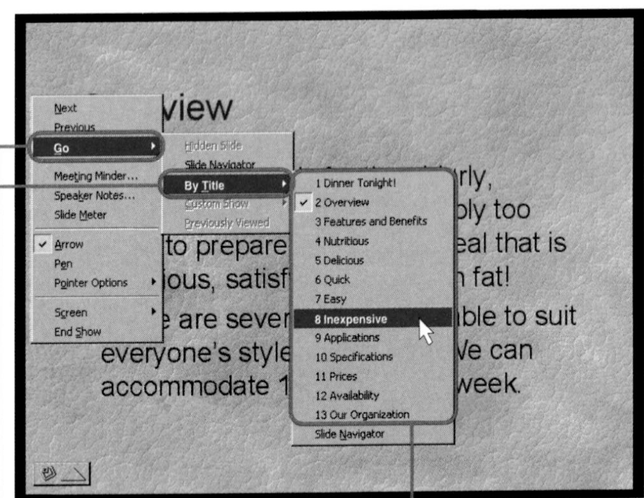

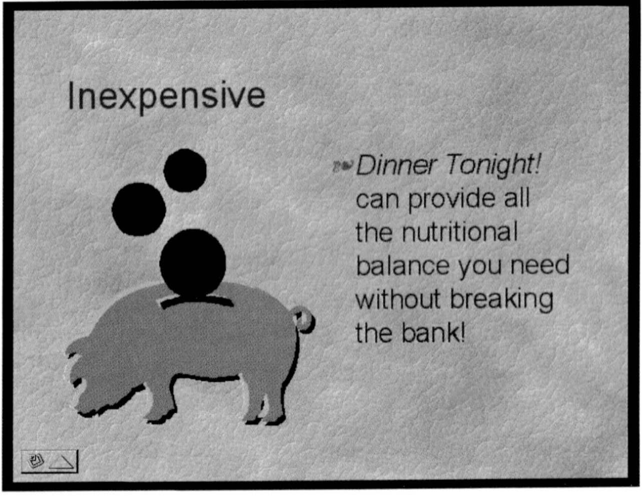

DISPLAY ANY SLIDE

1 Right-click the current slide. A menu appears.

2 Click **Go**.

3 Click **By Title**. A list of the titles for the slides in the presentation appears.

4 Click the title of the slide you want to display.

Note: A check mark (✔) appears beside the title of the current slide.

■ The slide you selected appears.

Will the lines I draw during the slide show remain on my slides?

No. Lines you draw during a slide show are temporary and will not appear when the slide show is over.

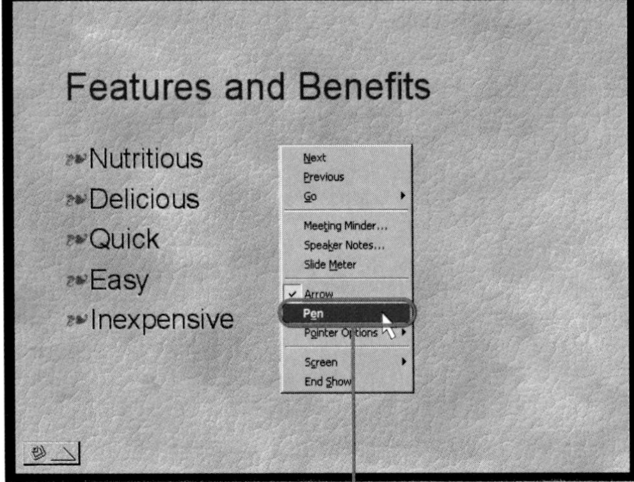

DRAW ON A SLIDE

1 Right-click the slide you want to draw on. A menu appears.

2 Click **Pen** to activate the pen.

Note: You can also press and hold down the Ctrl *key and then press the* P *key to activate the pen.*

3 Position the mouse where you want to start drawing on the slide.

4 Drag the mouse to draw on the slide.

■ To erase all the drawings on the slide, press the E key.

Note: You cannot use the mouse pointer when the pen is activated. To display the next slide, you must press the ***Spacebar****.*

USING THE SLIDE METER

You can use the Slide Meter to help you monitor your progress during a slide show. The Slide Meter compares your timing to the timings you recorded while rehearsing your slide show.

To rehearse your slide show and record timings for the slides, see page 234.

Before using the Slide Meter, you must set up the slide show to advance the slides manually. For more information, see page 230.

USING THE SLIDE METER

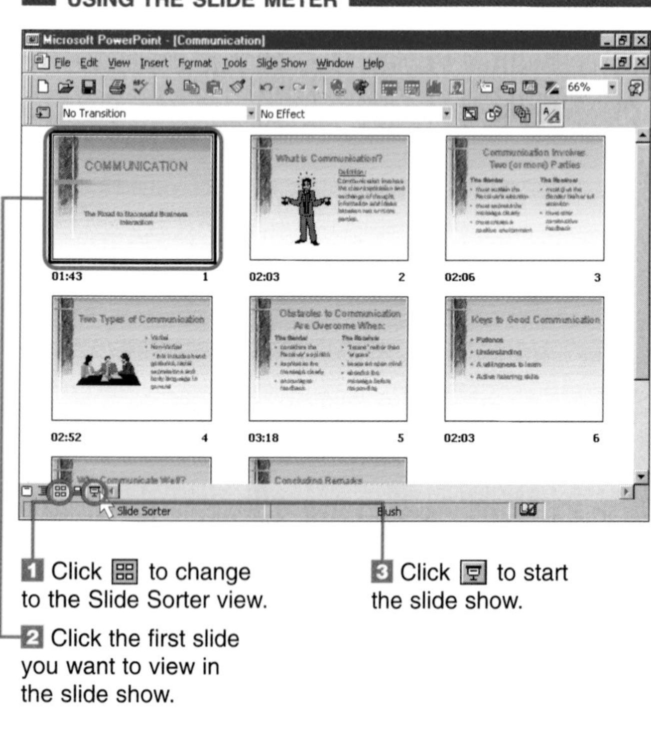

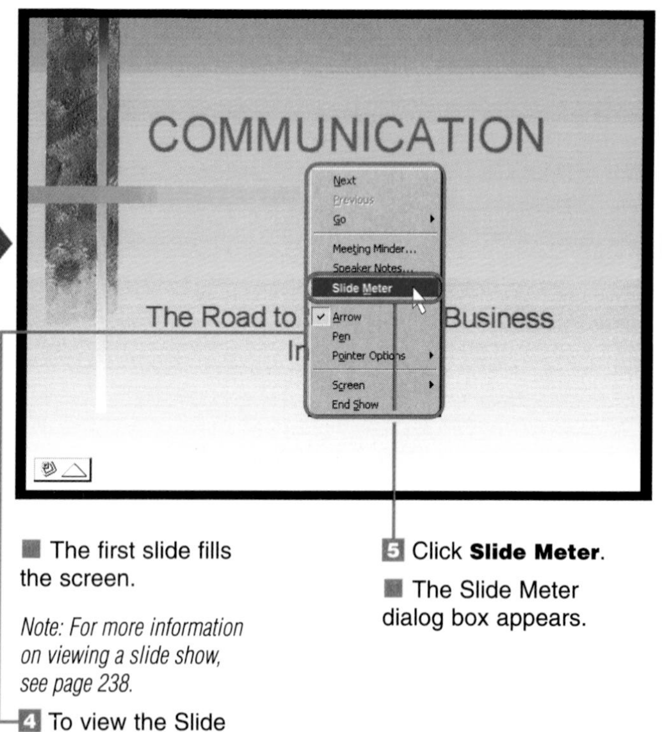

1 Click ▦ to change to the Slide Sorter view.

2 Click the first slide you want to view in the slide show.

3 Click ▣ to start the slide show.

■ The first slide fills the screen.

Note: For more information on viewing a slide show, see page 238.

4 To view the Slide Meter, right-click the slide. A menu appears.

5 Click **Slide Meter**.

■ The Slide Meter dialog box appears.

?

When would I use the Slide Meter?

You may want to use the Slide Meter to help you determine when you are speaking too quickly. You may also want to use the Slide Meter when the speed at which you deliver a presentation is important. For example, you may need to deliver a presentation within a time limit.

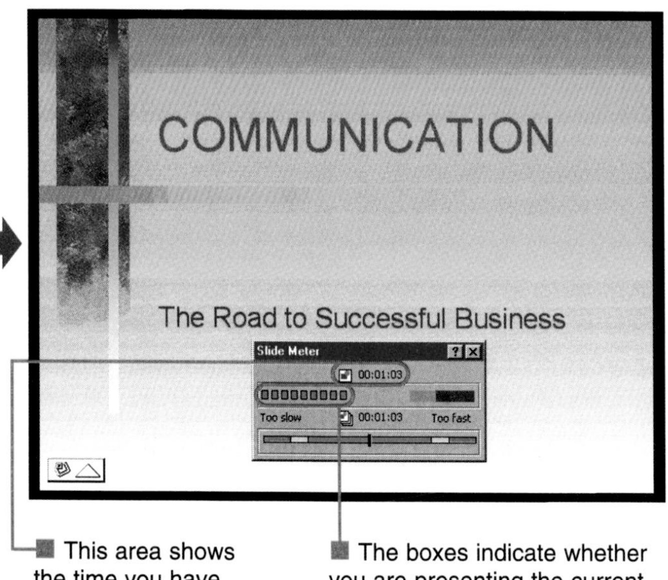

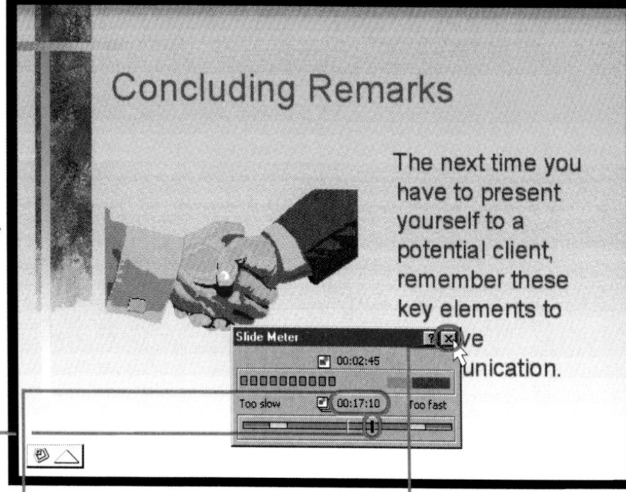

■ This area shows the time you have spent presenting the current slide.

■ The boxes indicate whether you are presenting the current slide too slowly or too quickly compared to the rehearsed time for the slide.

■ Within rehearsed time

■ Beyond rehearsed time

■ Far beyond rehearsed time

■ This area shows the total time you have spent presenting the slide show.

■ The position of the black bar (❙) indicates whether you are presenting the slide show too slowly or too quickly compared to your total rehearsed time.

6 If you no longer want to display the Slide Meter dialog box, click ☒ to close the dialog box.

USING MEETING MINDER

You can record meeting minutes during a slide show to take notes on important ideas discussed during the presentation. You can also record action items to help assign tasks related to the presentation.

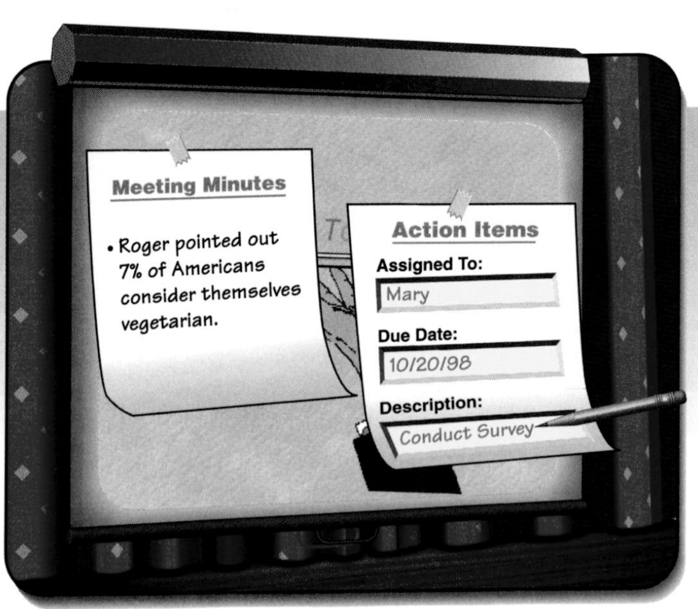

RECORD INFORMATION IN MEETING MINDER

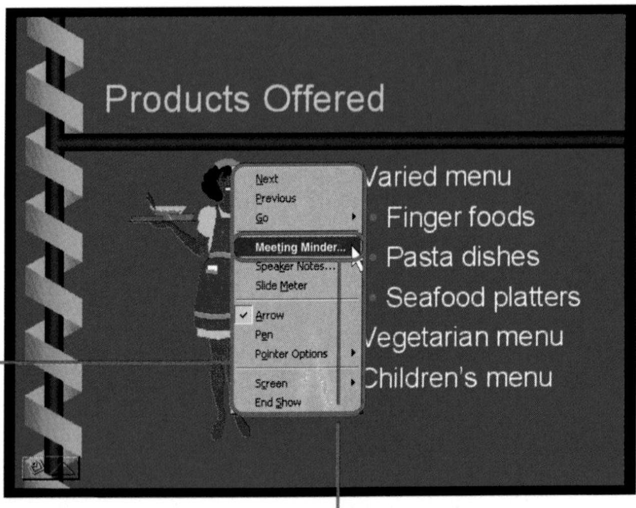

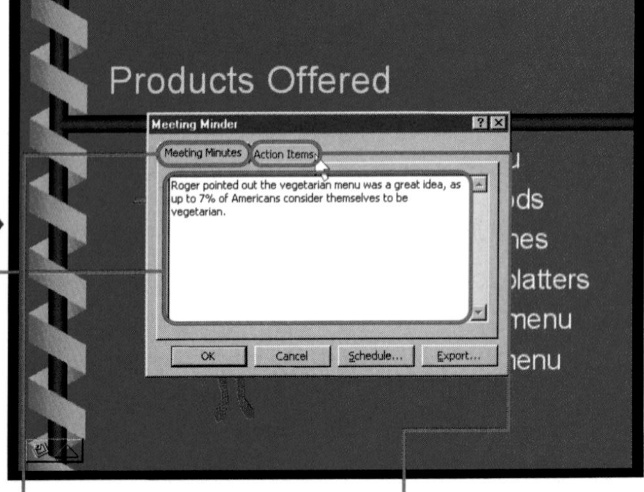

1 During the slide show, right-click a slide on your screen. A menu appears.

Note: To view a slide show, *see page 238.*

2 Click **Meeting Minder**.

■ The Meeting Minder dialog box appears.

3 To record meeting minutes, click the **Meeting Minutes** tab.

4 Type the meeting minutes in this area.

5 To record an action item, click the **Action Items** tab.

?

Where can I view the action items I recorded?

PowerPoint creates a new slide at the end of the slide show listing the action items you recorded. This lets the audience review the action items and take note of the items that are their responsibility.

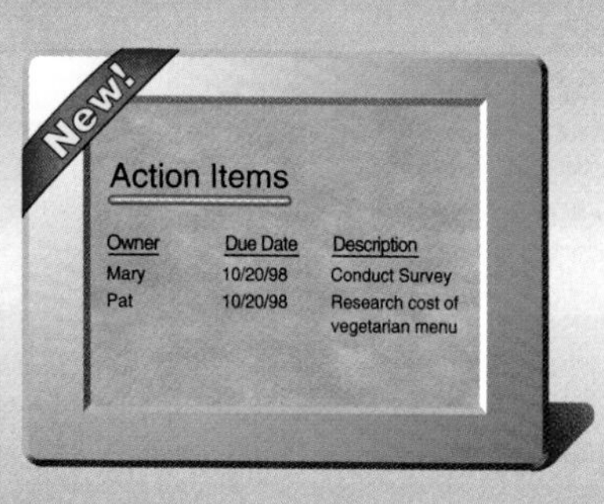

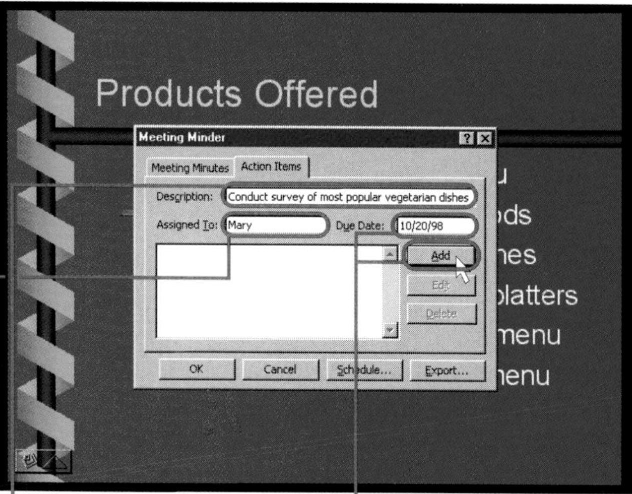

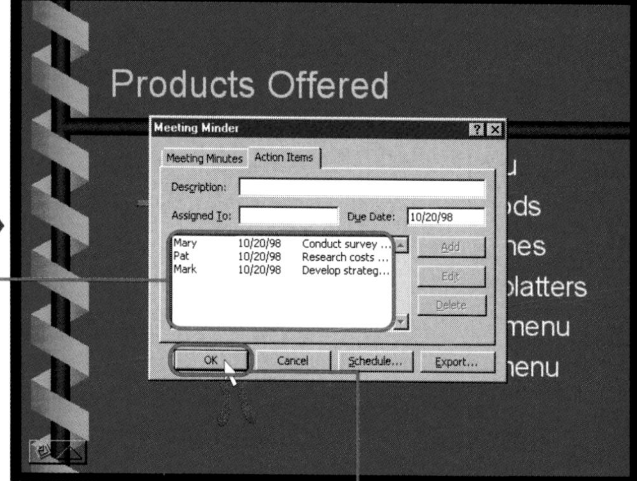

6 Click this area and type a description for the action item.

7 Click this area and type the name of the person you want to assign the action item to.

8 To specify a due date for the action item, double-click this area and type the date.

9 Click **Add** to record the action item.

■ The action item appears in this area.

10 Repeat steps 6 to 9 for each action item you want to record.

11 When you finish recording meeting minutes and action items, click **OK** to close the Meeting Minder dialog box.

Note: To redisplay the dialog box at any time during the slide show, repeat steps 1 and 2.

USING MEETING MINDER

After you finish viewing a slide show, you can send the meeting minutes and action items you recorded to Microsoft Word.

To perform this task, you need Microsoft Word installed on your computer.

SEND INFORMATION TO MICROSOFT WORD

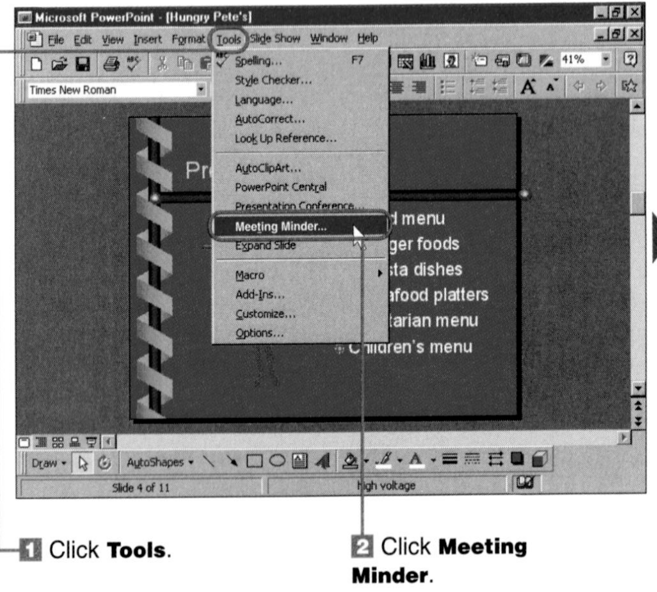

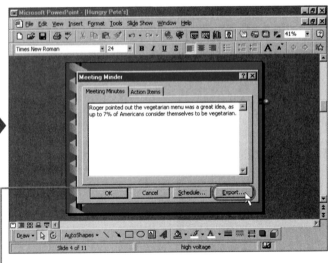

1 Click **Tools**.

2 Click **Meeting Minder**.

■ The Meeting Minder dialog box appears.

3 Click **Export** to send the meeting minutes and action items to Microsoft Word.

■ The Meeting Minder Export dialog box appears.

?

Why would I want to send meeting minutes and action items I recorded to Microsoft Word?

Sending meeting minutes and action items to Microsoft Word allows you to edit and format the information as a Word document. You can then print the document and hand it out to the audience or save the document for future reference.

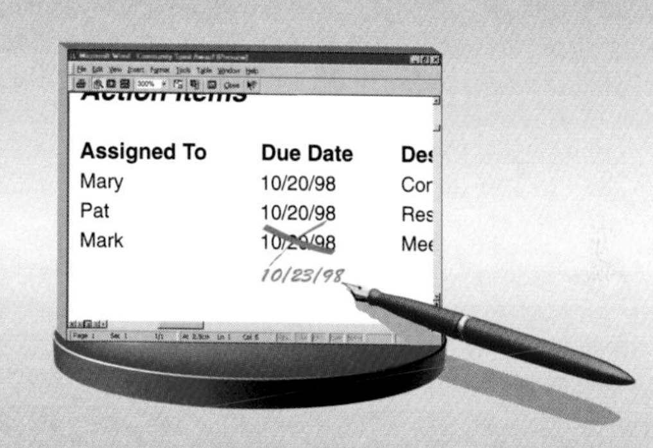

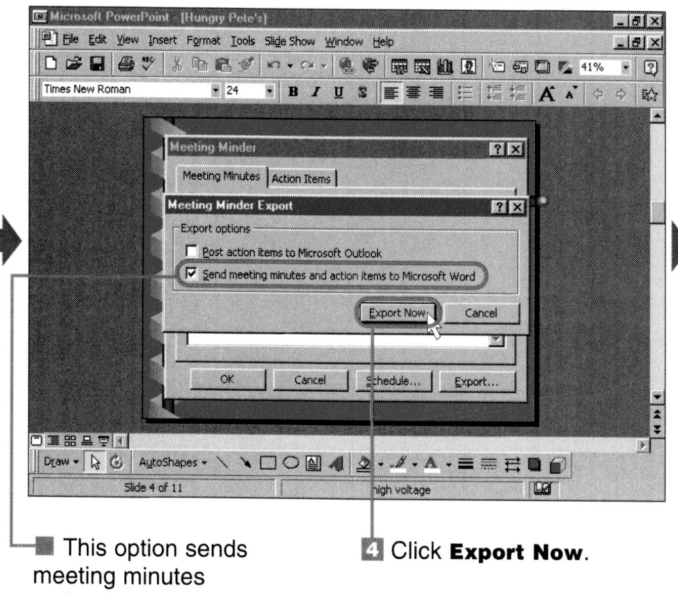

■ This option sends meeting minutes and action items to Microsoft Word.

4 Click **Export Now**.

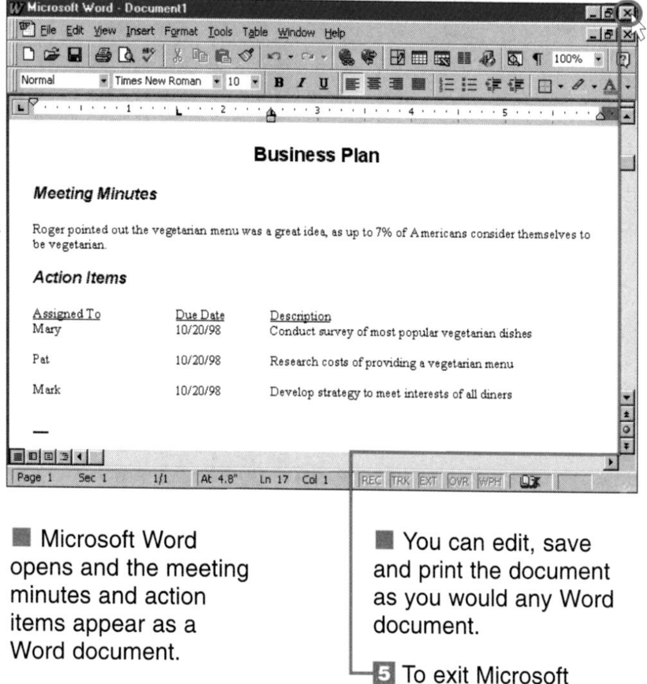

■ Microsoft Word opens and the meeting minutes and action items appear as a Word document.

■ You can edit, save and print the document as you would any Word document.

5 To exit Microsoft Word, click ☒.

CREATE A CUSTOM SLIDE SHOW

You can create a custom slide show that includes only some of the slides in a presentation. This is useful if you want to customize your presentation to suit specific audiences.

CREATE A CUSTOM SLIDE SHOW

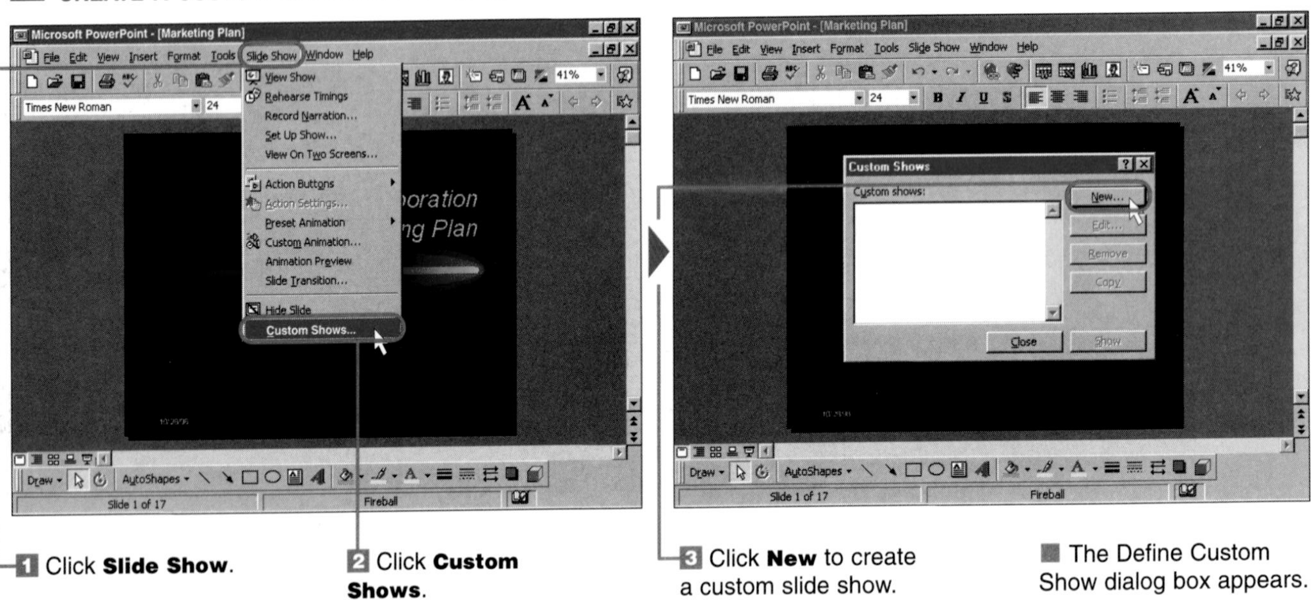

1 Click **Slide Show**.

2 Click **Custom Shows**.

■ The Custom Shows dialog box appears.

3 Click **New** to create a custom slide show.

■ The Define Custom Show dialog box appears.

?

Can I create several custom slide shows from one presentation?

You can create several custom slide shows from a presentation containing all of your ideas and information. For example, you may want to use a presentation about a new product to create a detailed custom slide show for the sales department and a shorter custom slide show for the executive committee.

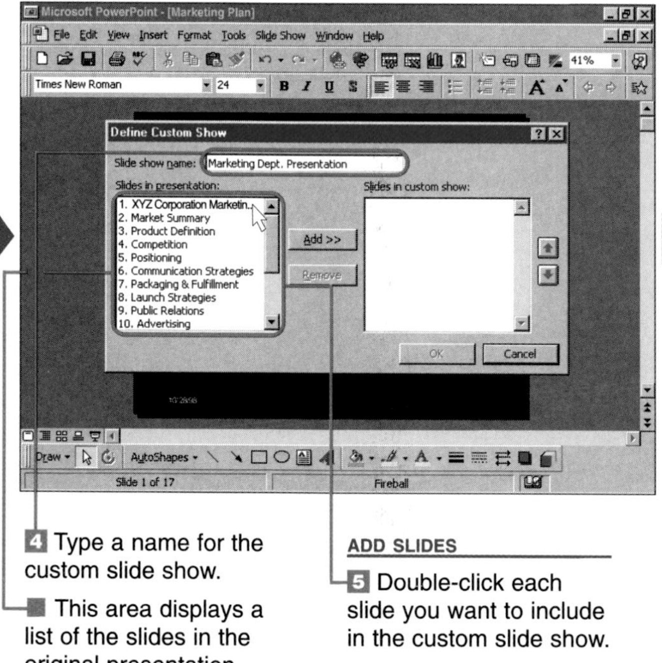

4 Type a name for the custom slide show.

■ This area displays a list of the slides in the original presentation.

ADD SLIDES

5 Double-click each slide you want to include in the custom slide show.

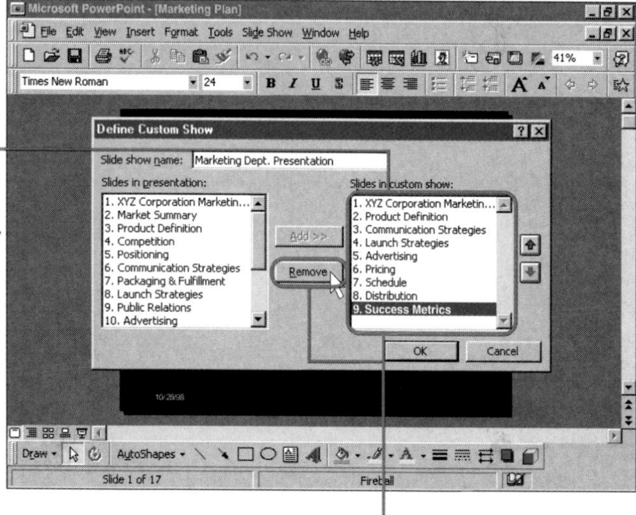

■ Each slide you selected appears in this area.

REMOVE SLIDES

6 If you accidentally added a slide, click the slide in this area.

7 Click **Remove** to remove the slide.

CONTINUED

CREATE A CUSTOM SLIDE SHOW

By default, slides you add to a custom slide show will appear in the order you added them. PowerPoint allows you to rearrange the slides into an order you prefer.

CREATE A CUSTOM SLIDE SHOW (CONTINUED)

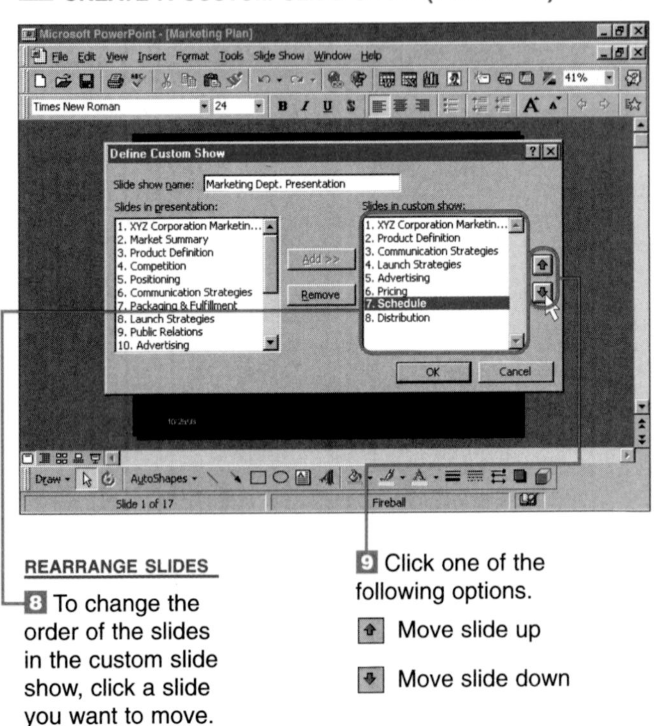

REARRANGE SLIDES

8 To change the order of the slides in the custom slide show, click a slide you want to move.

9 Click one of the following options.

- Move slide up
- Move slide down

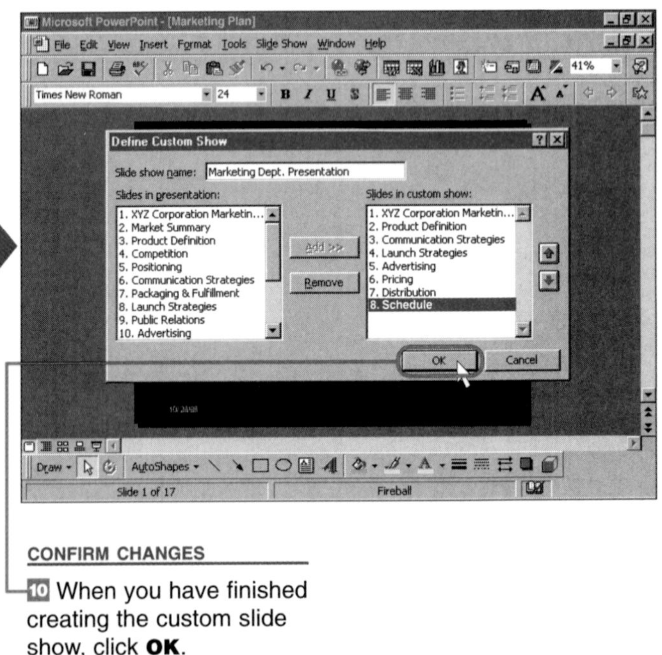

CONFIRM CHANGES

10 When you have finished creating the custom slide show, click **OK**.

?

How do I make changes to the slides in a custom slide show?

When you make changes to the slides in the original presentation, the slides in the custom slide show automatically display the changes.

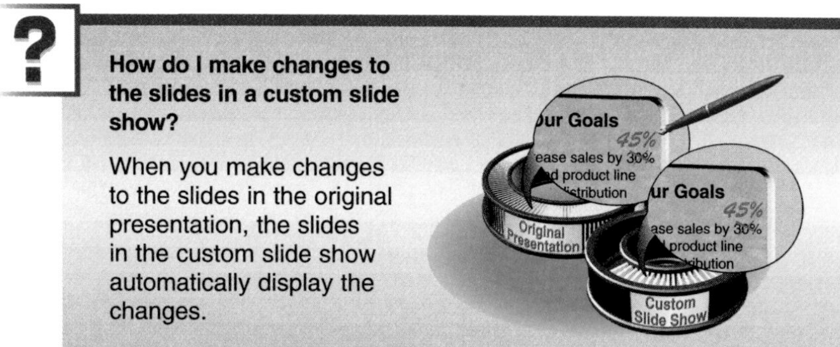

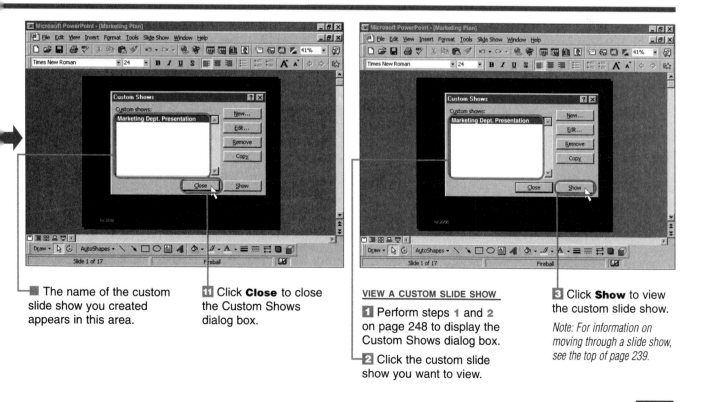

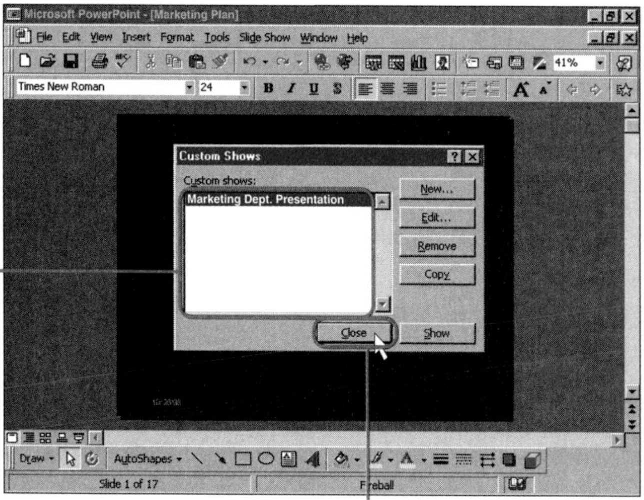

■ The name of the custom slide show you created appears in this area.

11 Click **Close** to close the Custom Shows dialog box.

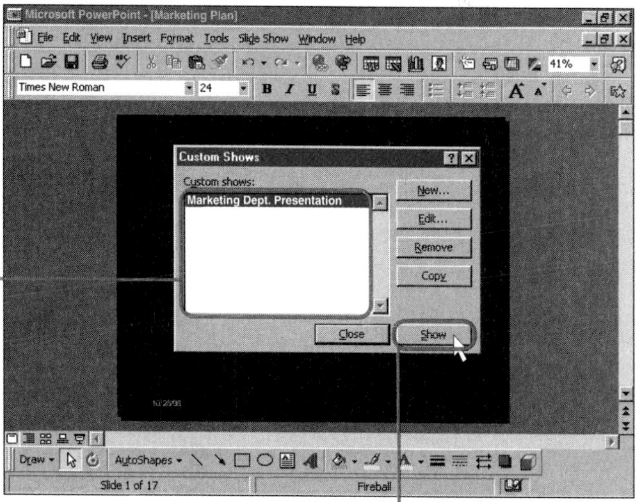

VIEW A CUSTOM SLIDE SHOW

1 Perform steps 1 and 2 on page 248 to display the Custom Shows dialog box.

2 Click the custom slide show you want to view.

3 Click **Show** to view the custom slide show.

Note: For information on moving through a slide show, see the top of page 239.

VIEW A SLIDE SHOW ON TWO SCREENS

You can control a slide show from one computer screen while your audience views the slide show on another computer screen.

Viewing a slide show on two computer screens allows you to deliver your presentation from a notebook computer while your audience views the slide show on a computer with a larger monitor.

VIEW A SLIDE SHOW ON TWO SCREENS

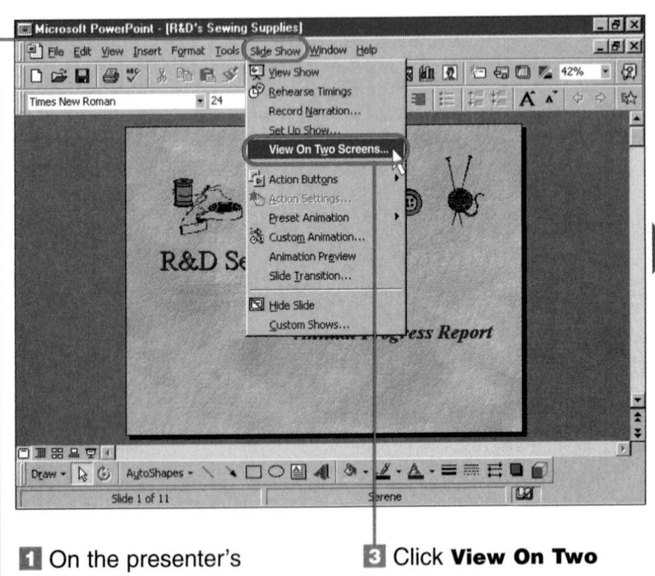

1 On the presenter's computer, open the presentation you want to view on two screens. To open a presentation, see page 22.

2 Click **Slide Show**.

3 Click **View On Two Screens**.

■ The View On Two Screens dialog box appears.

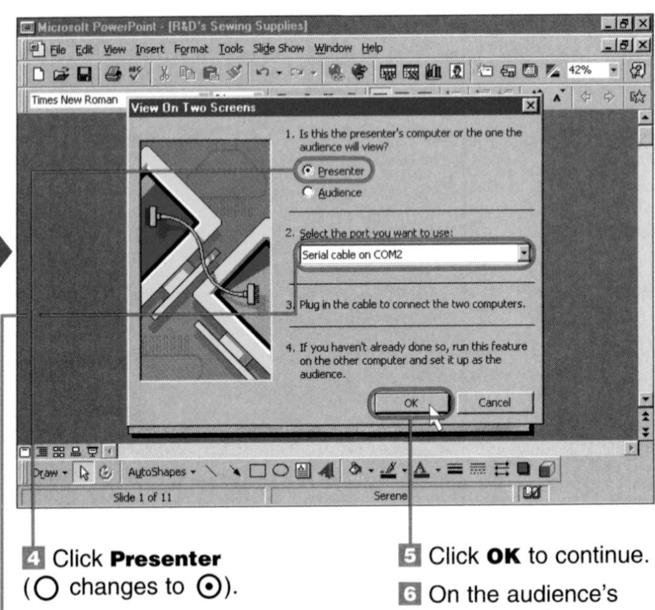

4 Click **Presenter** (○ changes to ⊙).

■ This area displays the port used to connect the two computers. You can click this area to change the port.

5 Click **OK** to continue.

6 On the audience's computer, perform steps 2 to 5, except select **Audience** in step 4.

How do I connect two computers to view a slide show on two screens?

You need a null-modem cable to connect the two computers. You can purchase this type of cable at most computer stores. Plug one end of the cable into an available COM port on the presenter's computer. Then plug the other end of the cable into an available COM port on the audience's computer.

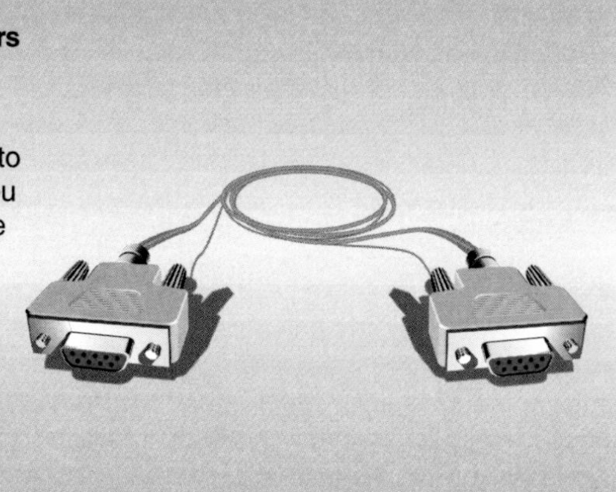

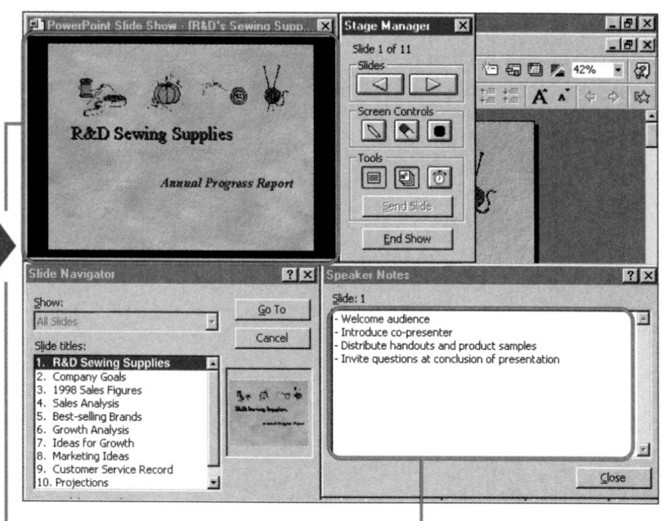

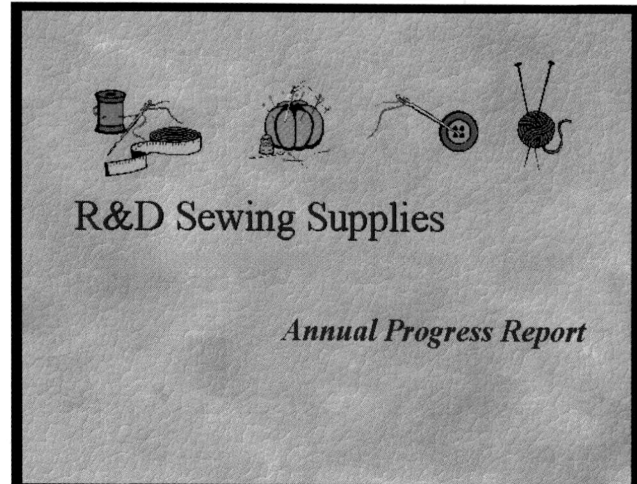

■ Once the computers are connected, the presenter's screen displays the first slide of the slide show and tools for delivering the slide show.

■ The slide shown in this area will fill the audience's screen.

■ This area displays the speaker notes for the current slide.

■ The audience's screen displays the first slide of the slide show.

CONTINUED

VIEW A SLIDE SHOW ON TWO SCREENS

The presenter's screen displays many tools that help you deliver your presentation.

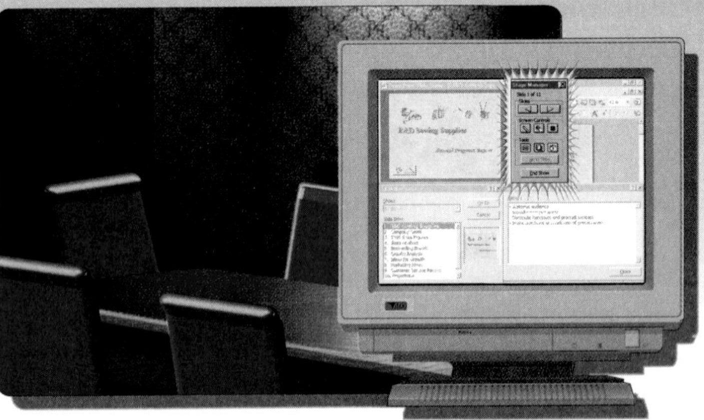

If your presentation contains sounds or movies, you must copy the sound or movie files to the C:\Program Files\Microsoft Office\Office folder on the audience's computer.

The sounds or movies in the presentation must also be set to play automatically. For more information, see page 186.

VIEW A SLIDE SHOW ON TWO SCREENS (CONTINUED)

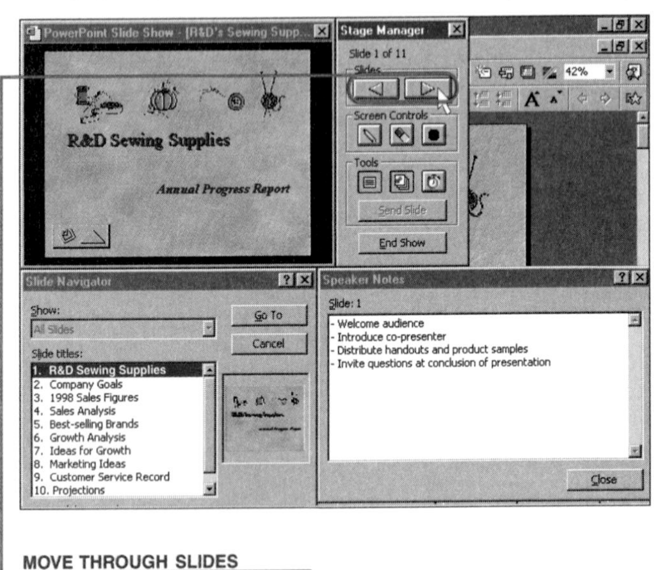

MOVE THROUGH SLIDES

1 Click one of the following options.

◁ Display previous slide

▷ Display next slide

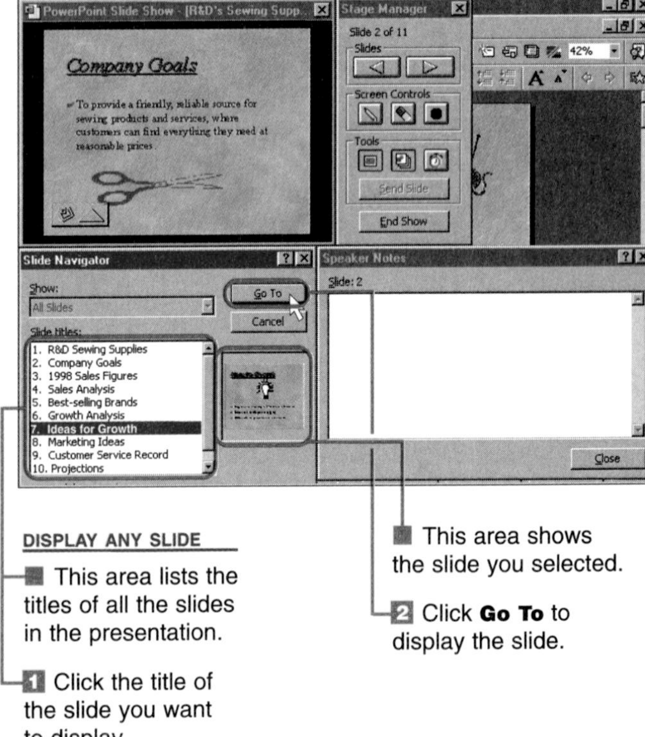

DISPLAY ANY SLIDE

■ This area lists the titles of all the slides in the presentation.

1 Click the title of the slide you want to display.

■ This area shows the slide you selected.

2 Click **Go To** to display the slide.

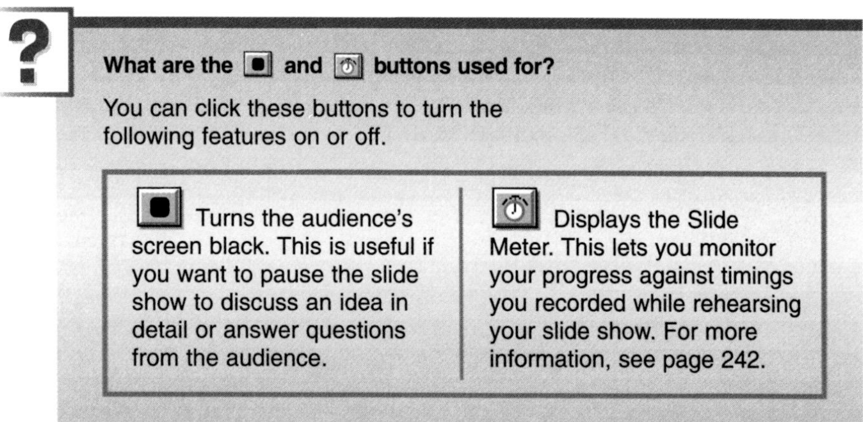

What are the and buttons used for?

You can click these buttons to turn the following features on or off.

Turns the audience's screen black. This is useful if you want to pause the slide show to discuss an idea in detail or answer questions from the audience.

Displays the Slide Meter. This lets you monitor your progress against timings you recorded while rehearsing your slide show. For more information, see page 242.

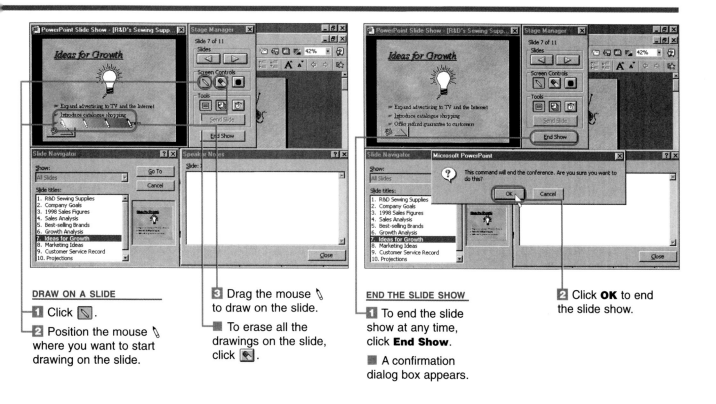

DRAW ON A SLIDE

1 Click .

2 Position the mouse where you want to start drawing on the slide.

3 Drag the mouse to draw on the slide.

■ To erase all the drawings on the slide, click .

END THE SLIDE SHOW

1 To end the slide show at any time, click **End Show**.

■ A confirmation dialog box appears.

2 Click **OK** to end the slide show.

USING THE PACK AND GO WIZARD

You can use the Pack and Go Wizard to package your presentation onto a floppy disk and transport it to another computer.

PACKAGE A PRESENTATION

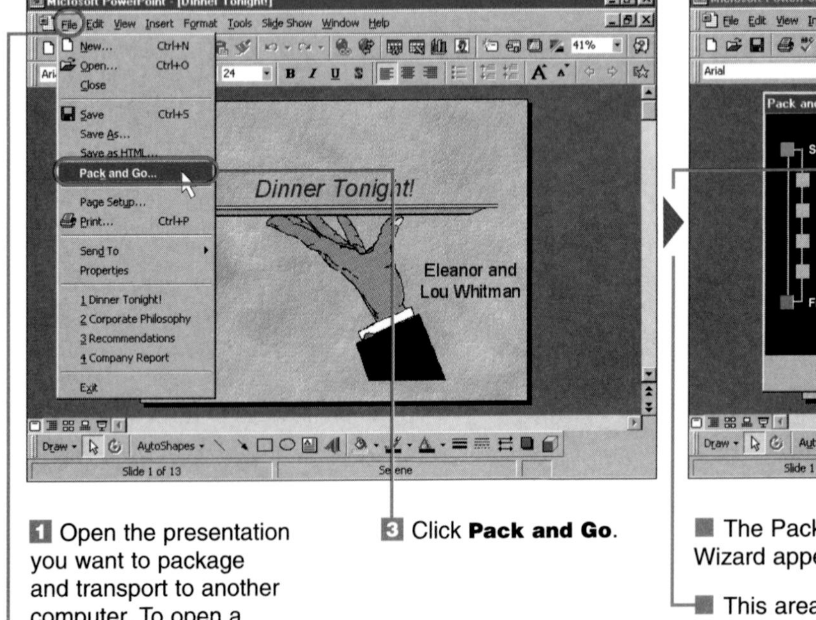

1 Open the presentation you want to package and transport to another computer. To open a presentation, see page 22.

2 Click **File**.

3 Click **Pack and Go**.

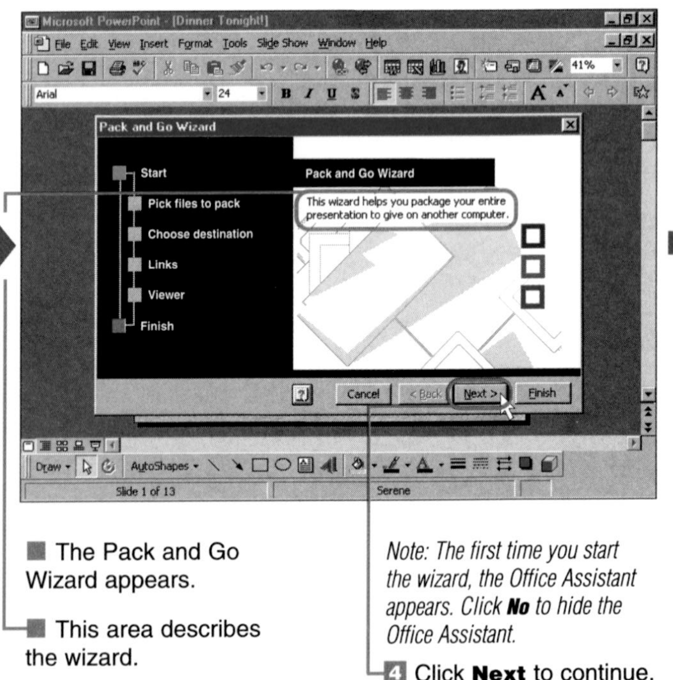

■ The Pack and Go Wizard appears.

■ This area describes the wizard.

*Note: The first time you start the wizard, the Office Assistant appears. Click **No** to hide the Office Assistant.*

4 Click **Next** to continue.

Why should I use the Pack and Go Wizard instead of simply copying my presentation to a floppy disk?

The Pack and Go Wizard efficiently packages your presentation and all the files associated with the presentation, such as sound or image files. You should use the Pack and Go Wizard to ensure that you have all the files you need to deliver your presentation on another computer.

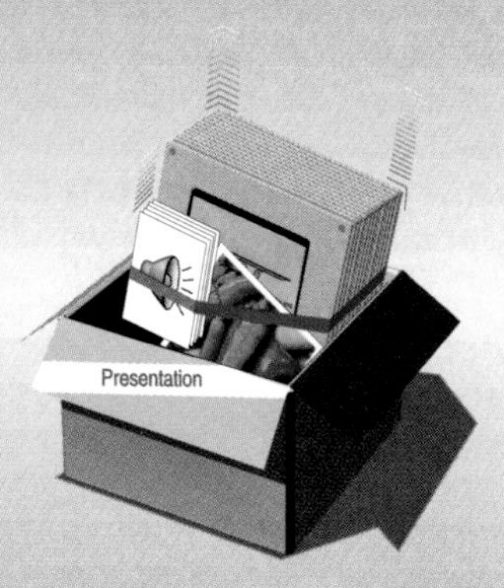

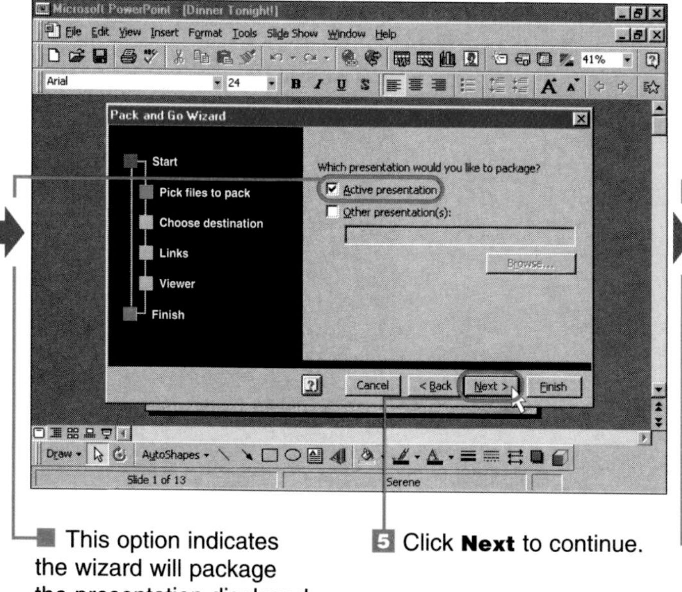

■ This option indicates the wizard will package the presentation displayed on your screen.

5 Click **Next** to continue.

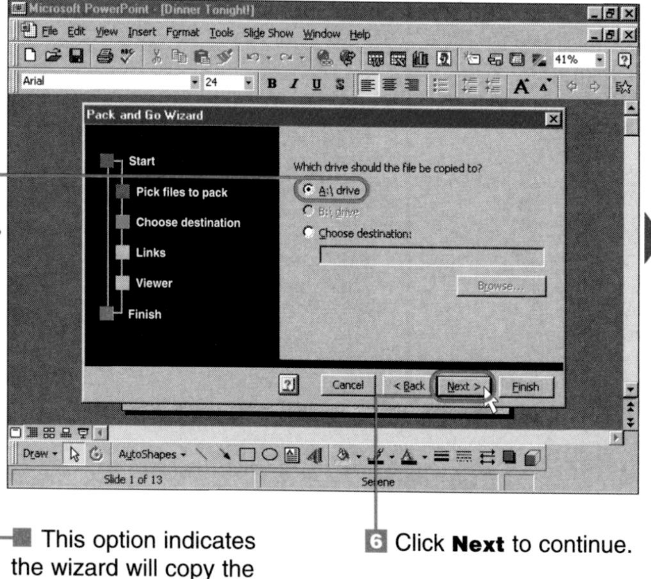

■ This option indicates the wizard will copy the presentation to your floppy drive.

6 Click **Next** to continue.

CONTINUED

USING THE PACK AND GO WIZARD

The Pack and Go Wizard compresses, or squeezes, your presentation so you can easily transfer the presentation from one computer to another.

PACKAGE A PRESENTATION (CONTINUED)

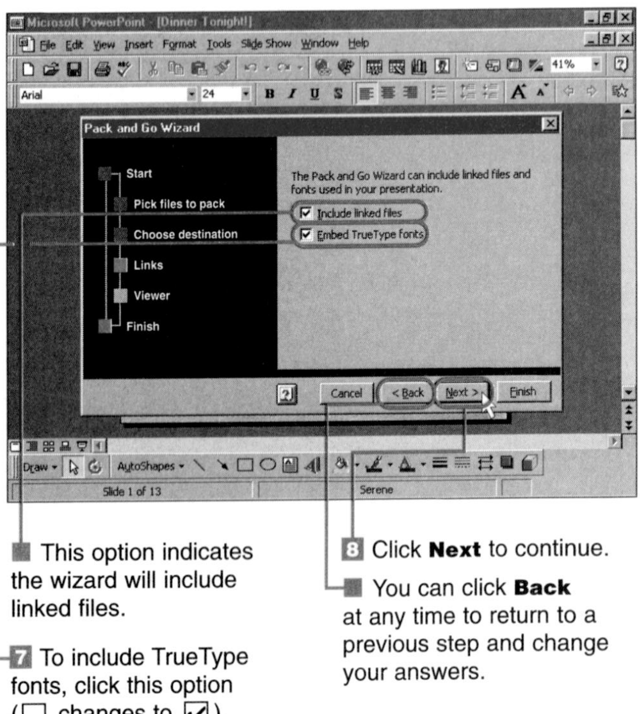

■ This option indicates the wizard will include linked files.

7 To include TrueType fonts, click this option (☐ changes to ☑).

8 Click **Next** to continue.

■ You can click **Back** at any time to return to a previous step and change your answers.

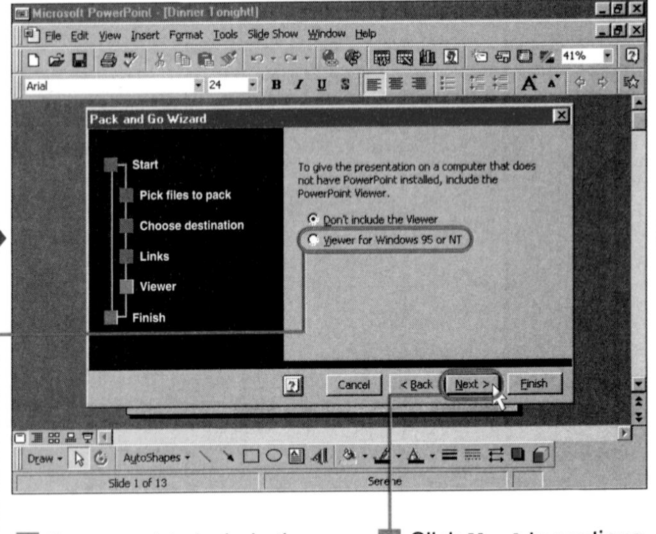

9 If you want to include the PowerPoint Viewer, click this option (○ changes to ⊙).

Note: If you chose to include the PowerPoint Viewer, insert the CD-ROM disc you used to install PowerPoint into your CD-ROM drive.

10 Click **Next** to continue.

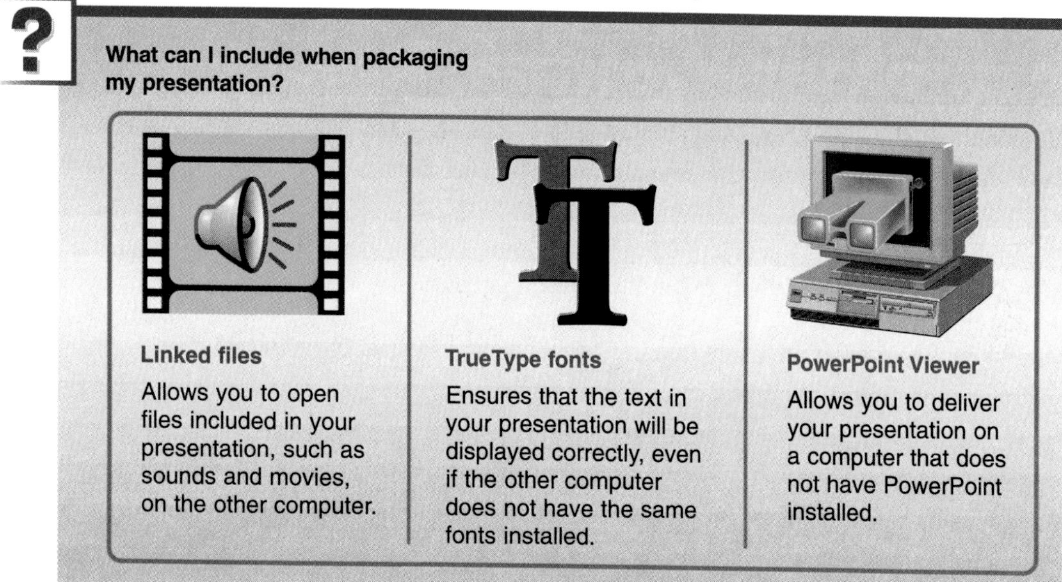

What can I include when packaging my presentation?

Linked files

Allows you to open files included in your presentation, such as sounds and movies, on the other computer.

TrueType fonts

Ensures that the text in your presentation will be displayed correctly, even if the other computer does not have the same fonts installed.

PowerPoint Viewer

Allows you to deliver your presentation on a computer that does not have PowerPoint installed.

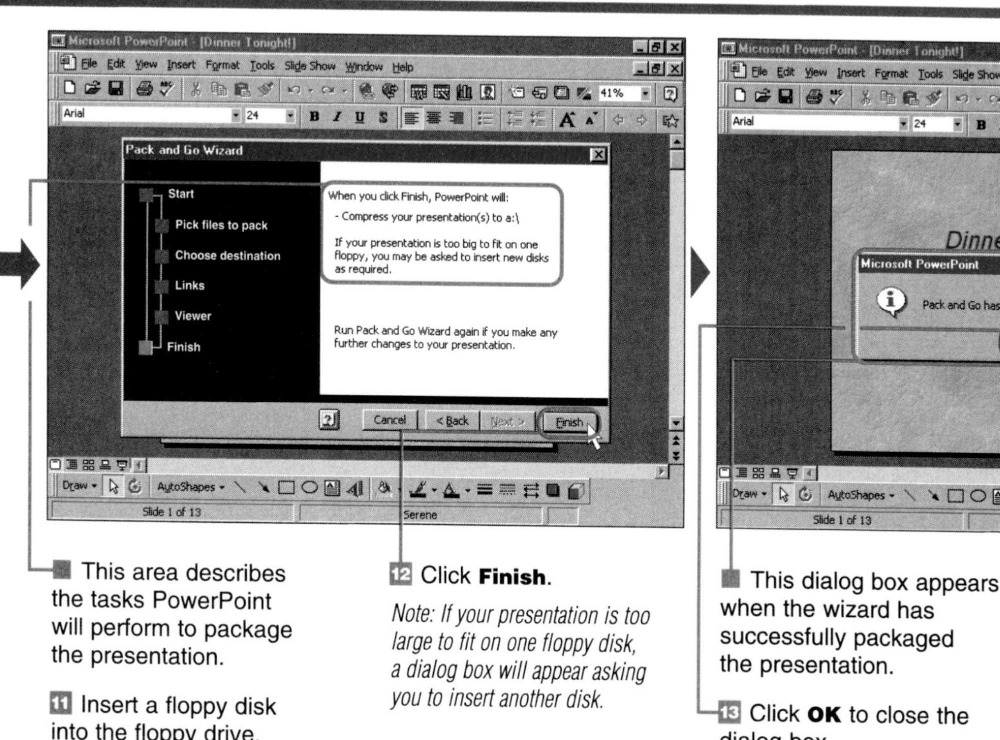

■ This area describes the tasks PowerPoint will perform to package the presentation.

11 Insert a floppy disk into the floppy drive.

12 Click **Finish**.

Note: If your presentation is too large to fit on one floppy disk, a dialog box will appear asking you to insert another disk.

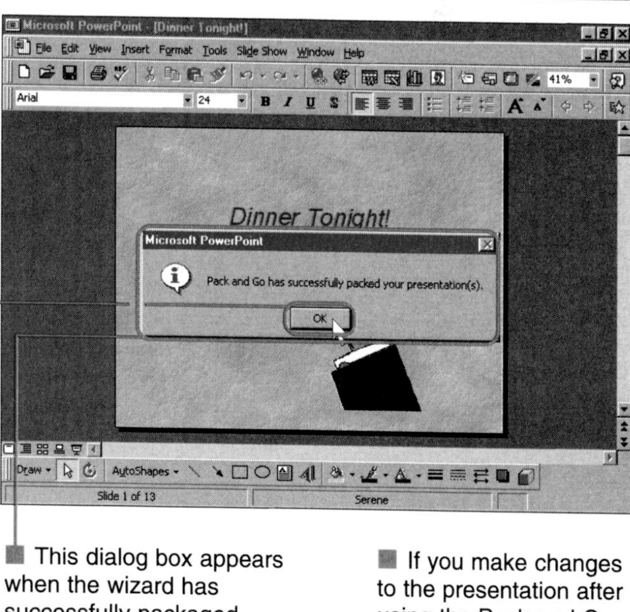

■ This dialog box appears when the wizard has successfully packaged the presentation.

13 Click **OK** to close the dialog box.

■ If you make changes to the presentation after using the Pack and Go Wizard, run the wizard again to update the package.

USING THE PACK AND GO WIZARD

When you arrive at your destination, you can unpack your presentation on the computer you will use to deliver the presentation.

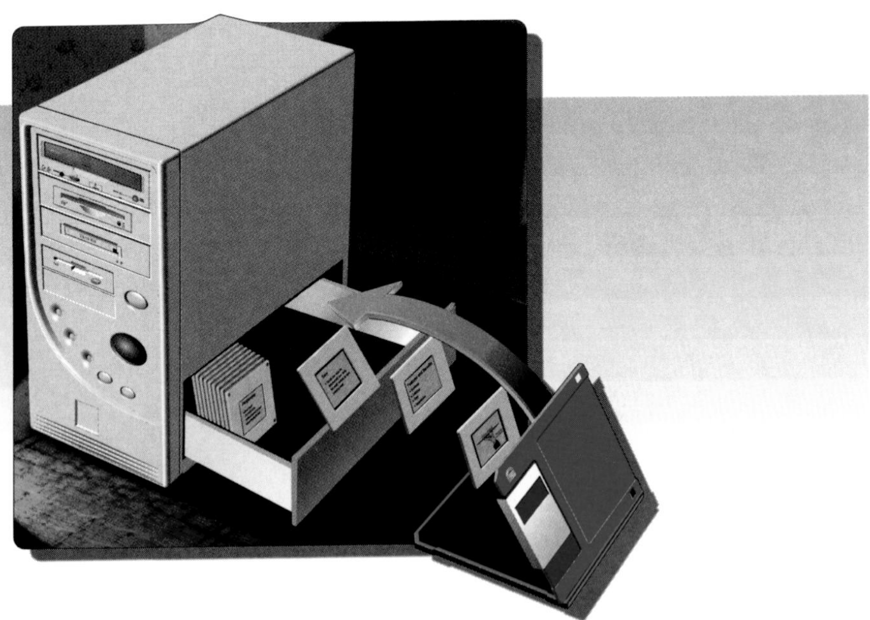

UNPACK A PRESENTATION

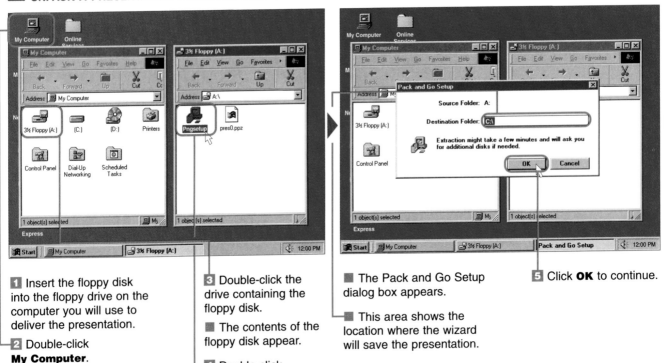

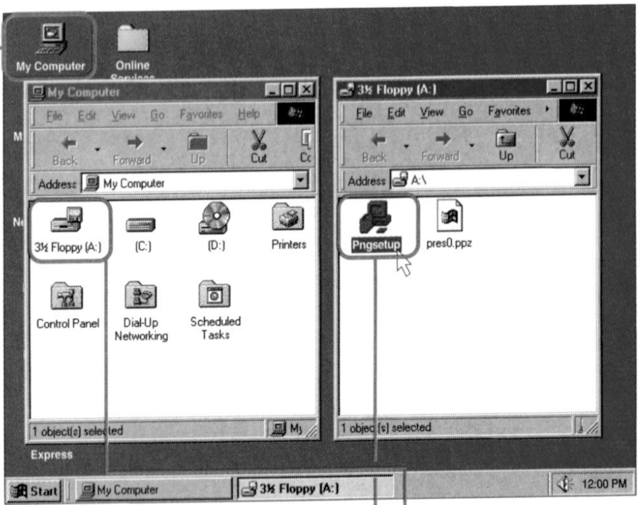

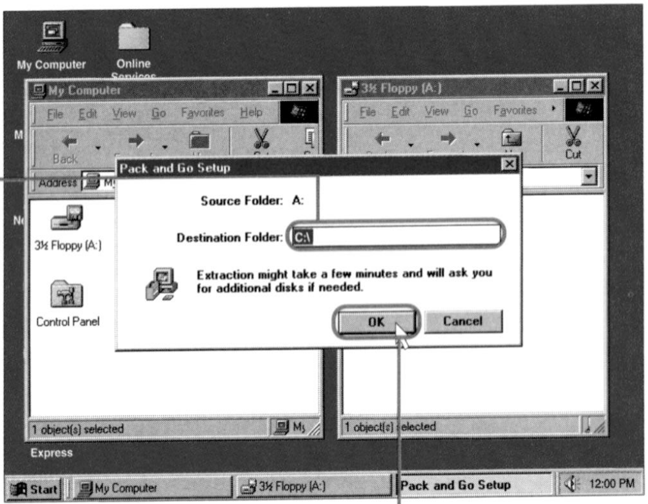

1 Insert the floppy disk into the floppy drive on the computer you will use to deliver the presentation.

2 Double-click **My Computer**.

■ The My Computer window appears.

3 Double-click the drive containing the floppy disk.

■ The contents of the floppy disk appear.

4 Double-click **Pngsetup**.

■ The Pack and Go Setup dialog box appears.

■ This area shows the location where the wizard will save the presentation.

5 Click **OK** to continue.

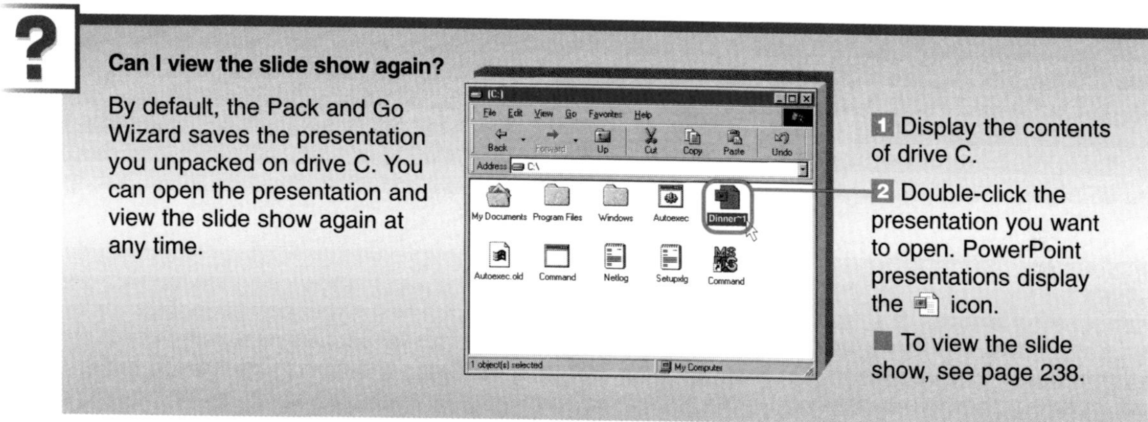

?

Can I view the slide show again?

By default, the Pack and Go Wizard saves the presentation you unpacked on drive C. You can open the presentation and view the slide show again at any time.

1 Display the contents of drive C.

2 Double-click the presentation you want to open. PowerPoint presentations display the icon.

■ To view the slide show, see page 238.

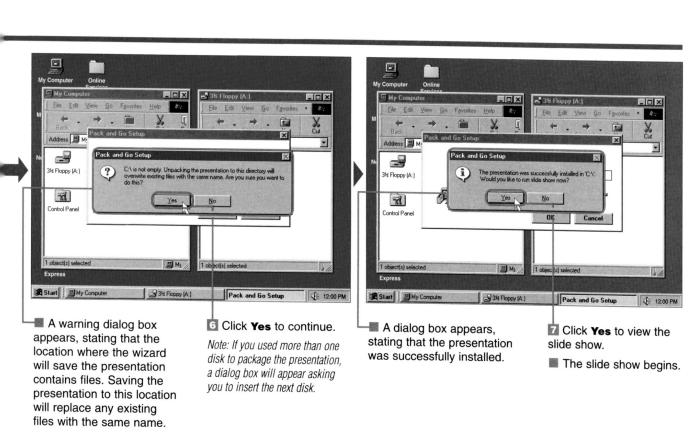

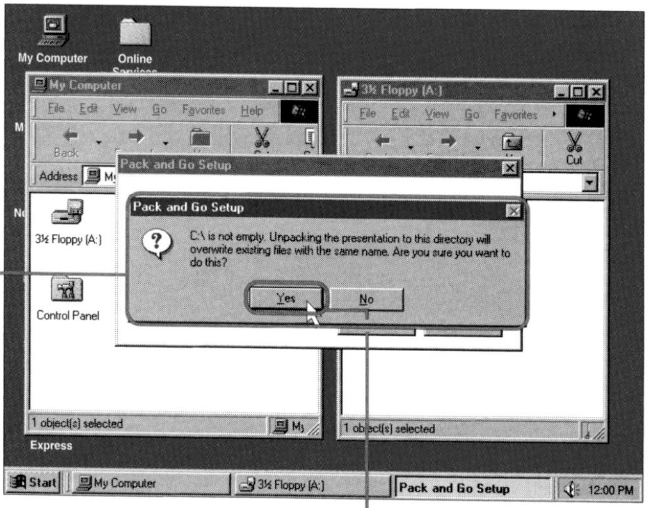

■ A warning dialog box appears, stating that the location where the wizard will save the presentation contains files. Saving the presentation to this location will replace any existing files with the same name.

6 Click **Yes** to continue.

Note: If you used more than one disk to package the presentation, a dialog box will appear asking you to insert the next disk.

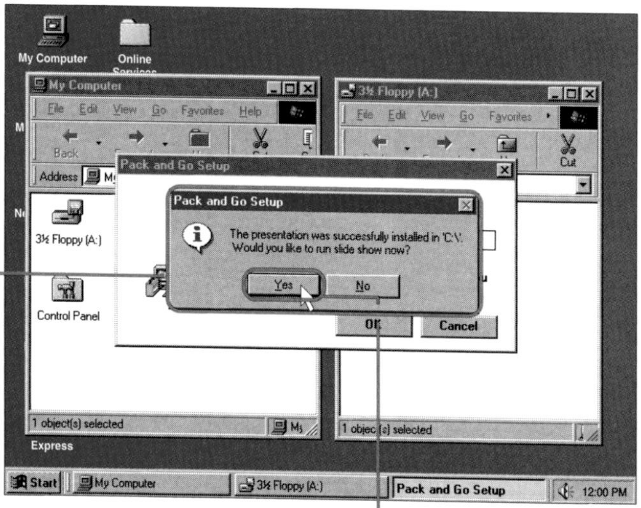

■ A dialog box appears, stating that the presentation was successfully installed.

7 Click **Yes** to view the slide show.

■ The slide show begins.

Discovery CHANNEL ONLINE
BOB'S Music BIZ
Click Here
Someone in Time
Solve a Mystery
AUSTRALIA
EXPEDITIONS
SPIDERS
NAME THAT SPIDER CONTEST
FEATURE STORIES
EXPEDITIONS
MIND GAMES
Let's Meet at Cleopatra's Place
HDD
RESET

CHAPTER 12

PowerPoint and the Internet

Are you wondering how PowerPoint can help you take advantage of the Internet? In this chapter you will learn how to display a Web page, create hyperlinks and save a presentation as a collection of Web pages.

DISPLAY THE WEB TOOLBAR

You can display the Web toolbar at any time. The Web toolbar allows you to access information on the Internet, your company's intranet or your own computer.

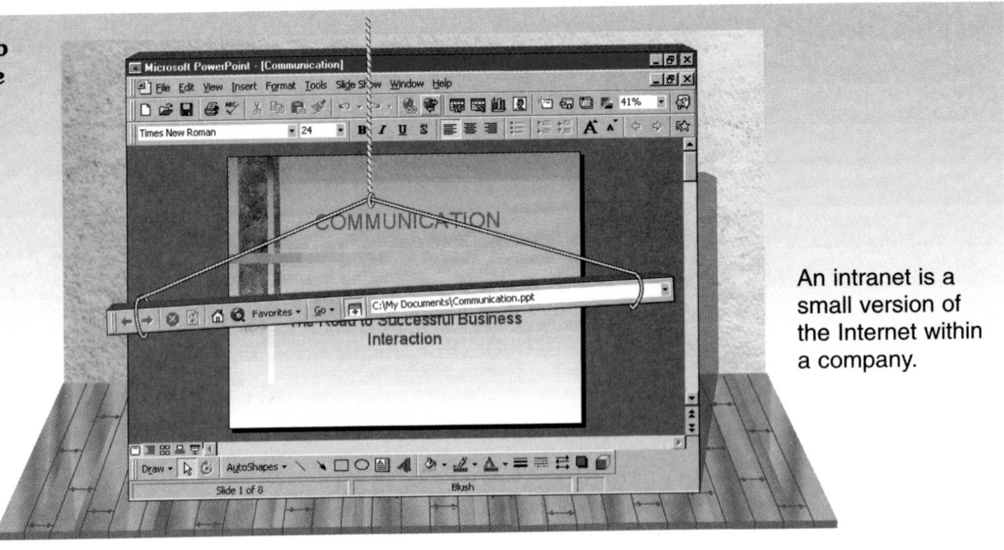

An intranet is a small version of the Internet within a company.

DISPLAY THE WEB TOOLBAR

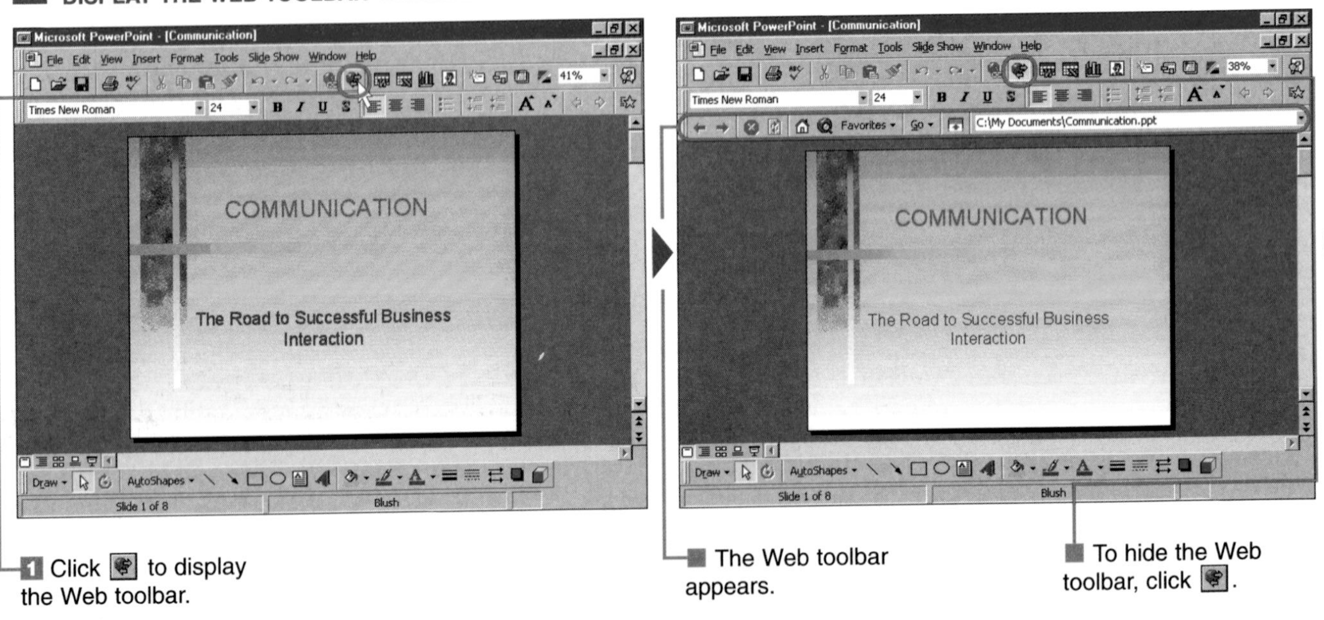

1 Click [icon] to display the Web toolbar.

■ The Web toolbar appears.

■ To hide the Web toolbar, click [icon].

?

How can the Internet help me prepare my presentation?

The Internet allows you to access information on every subject imaginable. You can review newspapers, magazines, academic papers and government documents to help you prepare your presentation. You can also use the Internet to find sounds, movie clips, clip art images and pictures for the slides in your presentation.

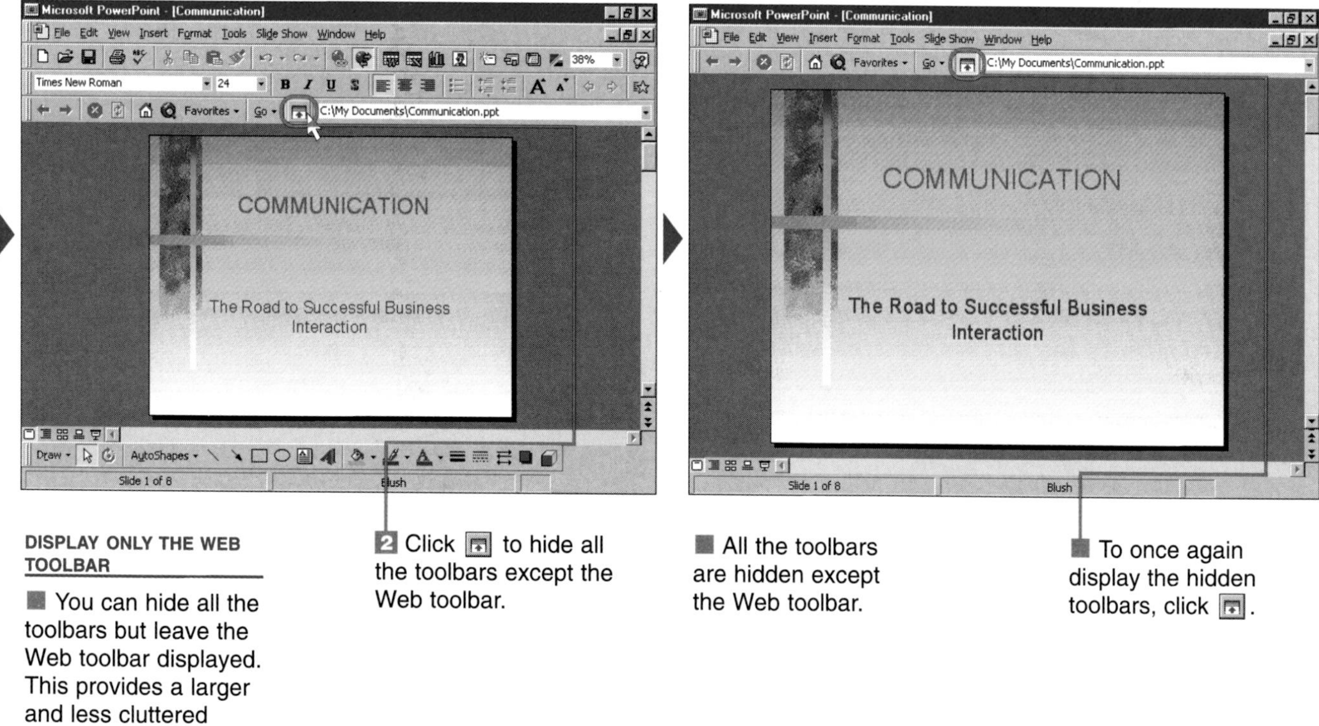

DISPLAY ONLY THE WEB TOOLBAR

■ You can hide all the toolbars but leave the Web toolbar displayed. This provides a larger and less cluttered working area.

2 Click ▣ to hide all the toolbars except the Web toolbar.

■ All the toolbars are hidden except the Web toolbar.

■ To once again display the hidden toolbars, click ▣.

DISPLAY A WEB PAGE

While working in PowerPoint, you can quickly display a Web page of interest.

DISPLAY A WEB PAGE

1 Click [icon] to display the Web toolbar.

2 Click this area and type the address of the Web page you want to open (example: www.maran.com). Then press the Enter key.

Note: A dialog box may appear, warning you about security issues. Click ***OK*** *to open the Web page.*

■ Your Web browser opens and displays the Web page.

Note: If you are not currently connected to the Internet, a dialog box may appear that allows you to connect.

DISPLAY THE START OR SEARCH PAGE

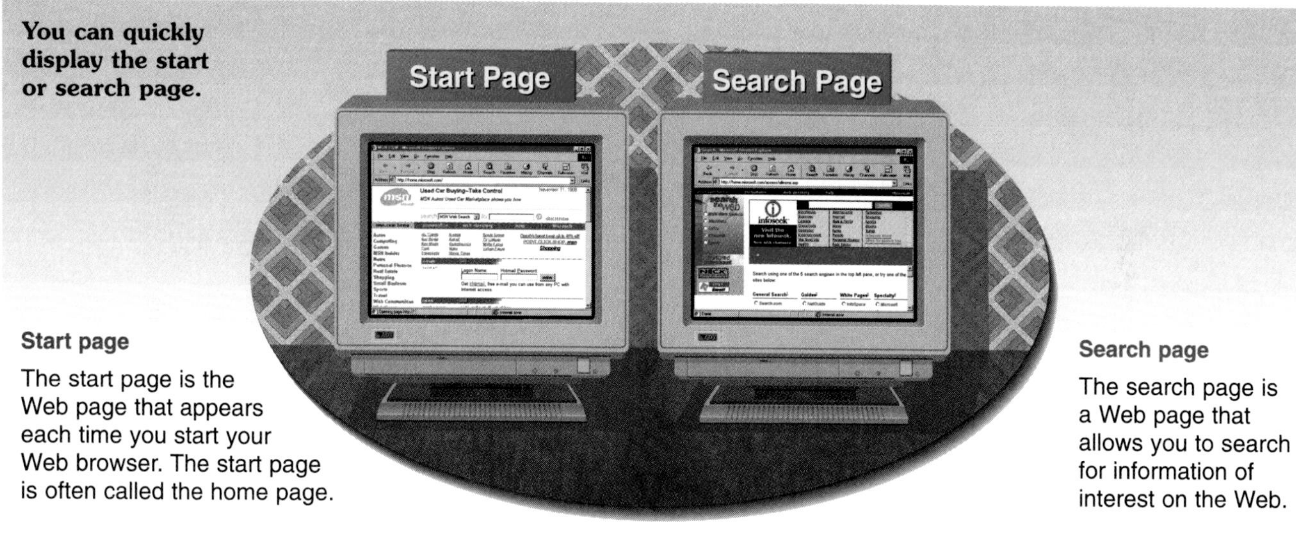

You can quickly display the start or search page.

Start page

The start page is the Web page that appears each time you start your Web browser. The start page is often called the home page.

Search page

The search page is a Web page that allows you to search for information of interest on the Web.

DISPLAY THE START OR SEARCH PAGE

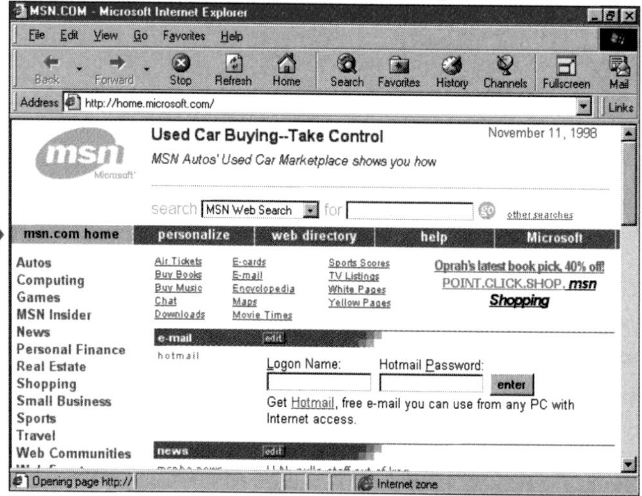

1. Click [icon] to display the Web toolbar.
2. Click one of the following options.

[icon] Displays start page

[icon] Displays search page

*Note: A dialog box may appear, warning you about security issues. Click **OK** to open the page.*

■ Your Web browser opens and displays the page you selected.

Note: If you are not currently connected to the Internet, a dialog box may appear that allows you to connect.

ADD A PRESENTATION TO THE FAVORITES FOLDER

You can add a presentation you frequently use to the Favorites folder. This allows you to quickly open the presentation at any time.

ADD A PRESENTATION TO THE FAVORITES FOLDER

1 Open the presentation you want to add to the Favorites folder.

Note: To open a presentation, see page 22.

2 Click [icon] to display the Web toolbar.

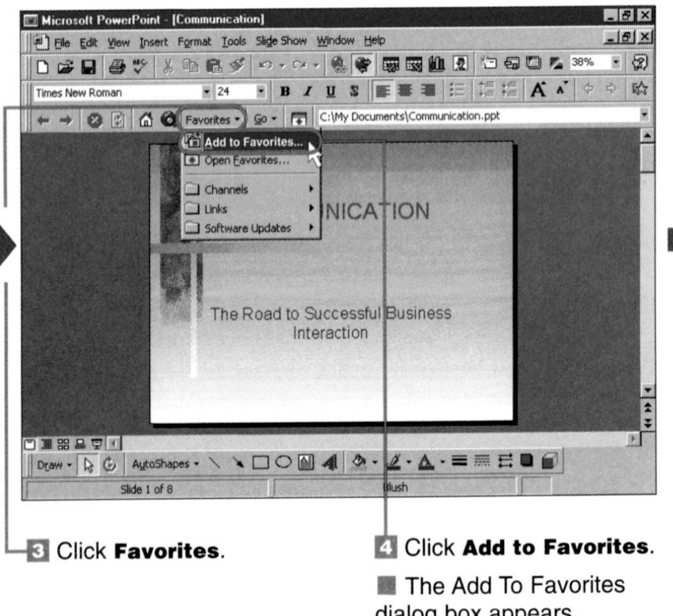

3 Click **Favorites**.

4 Click **Add to Favorites**.

■ The Add To Favorites dialog box appears.

When I add a presentation to the Favorites folder, does the location of the presentation on my computer change?

No. PowerPoint places a shortcut to the original presentation in the Favorites folder. The original presentation does not change its location on your computer.

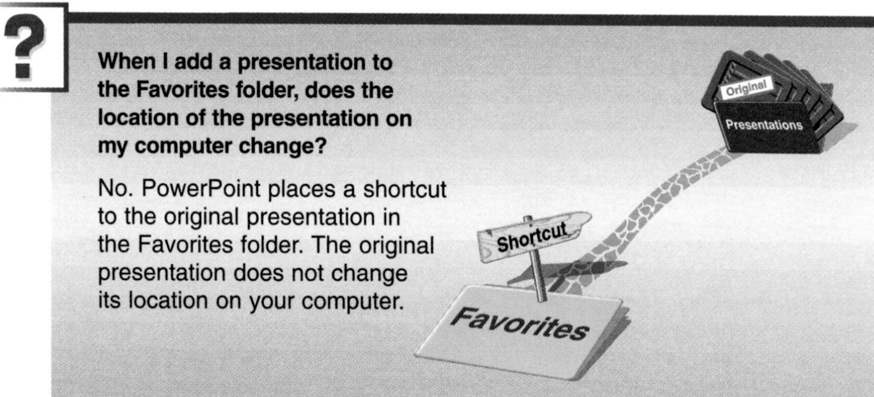

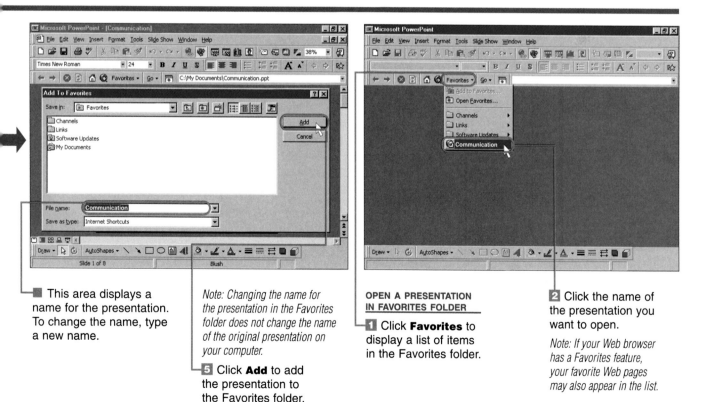

■ This area displays a name for the presentation. To change the name, type a new name.

Note: Changing the name for the presentation in the Favorites folder does not change the name of the original presentation on your computer.

5 Click **Add** to add the presentation to the Favorites folder.

OPEN A PRESENTATION IN FAVORITES FOLDER

1 Click **Favorites** to display a list of items in the Favorites folder.

2 Click the name of the presentation you want to open.

Note: If your Web browser has a Favorites feature, your favorite Web pages may also appear in the list.

CREATE A HYPERLINK

You can create a hyperlink to connect text in your presentation to another document or a Web page. When you select the hyperlink during your slide show, the document or Web page will appear.

CREATE A HYPERLINK

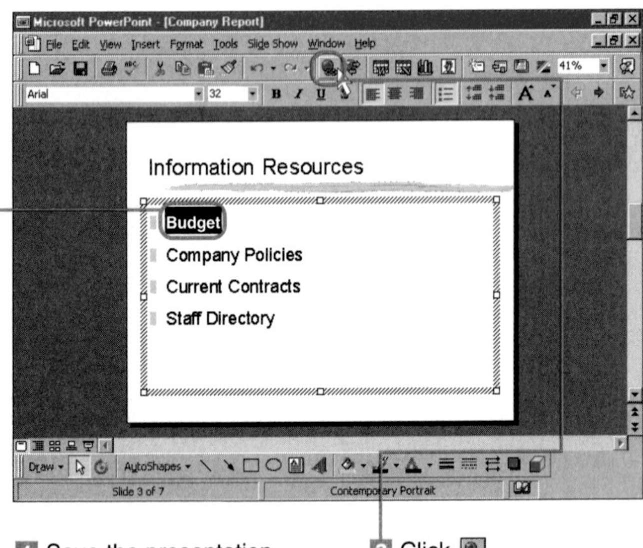

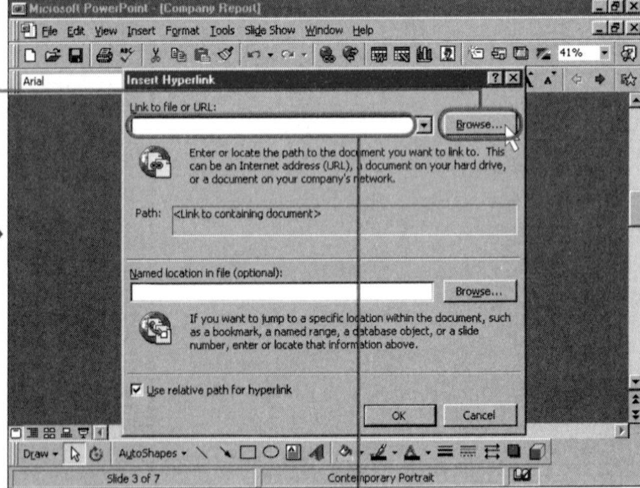

1 Save the presentation you want to contain a hyperlink to another document. To save a presentation, see page 18.

2 Select the text you want to use as a hyperlink. To select text, see page 48.

3 Click .

■ The Insert Hyperlink dialog box appears.

4 To link the text to a document on your computer or network, click **Browse**.

■ The Link to File dialog box appears.

■ To link the text to a Web page, type the address of the Web page (example: www.maran.com). Then skip to step 7.

?

Can I use an object instead of text as a hyperlink?

You can create a hyperlink to connect an object on a slide to a document or Web page. Perform steps 1 to 7 below, except select the object you want to use as a hyperlink in step 2.

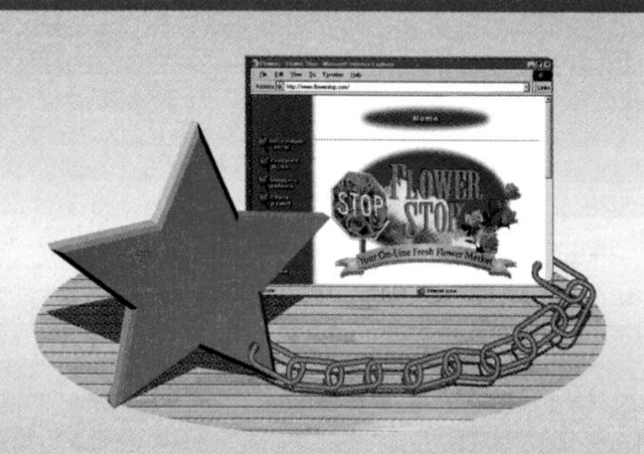

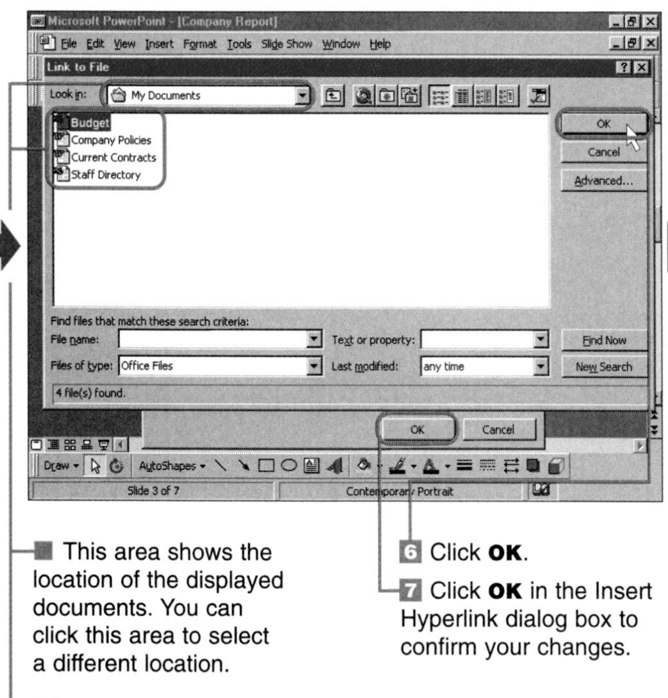

■ This area shows the location of the displayed documents. You can click this area to select a different location.

5 Click the document you want to link to.

6 Click **OK**.

7 Click **OK** in the Insert Hyperlink dialog box to confirm your changes.

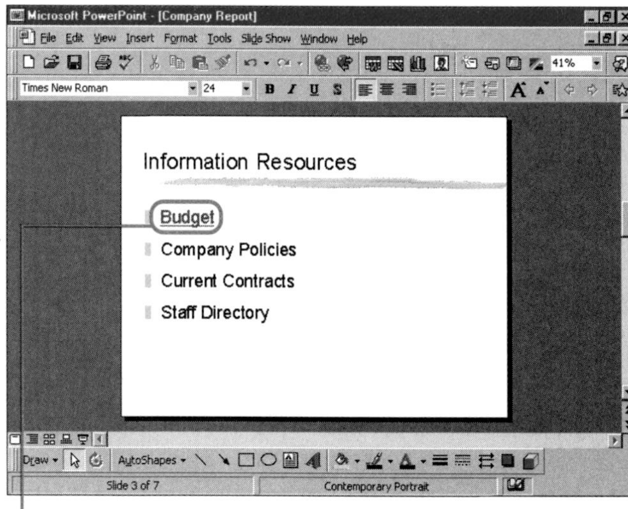

■ The text you selected appears as a hyperlink. Hyperlinks appear underlined and usually display a different color.

■ When you click the hyperlink during a slide show, the document or Web page you specified will appear. To view a slide show, see page 238.

SAVE PRESENTATION AS WEB PAGES

You can save a presentation as a collection of Web pages. This allows you to later publish your presentation on the Web or your company's intranet.

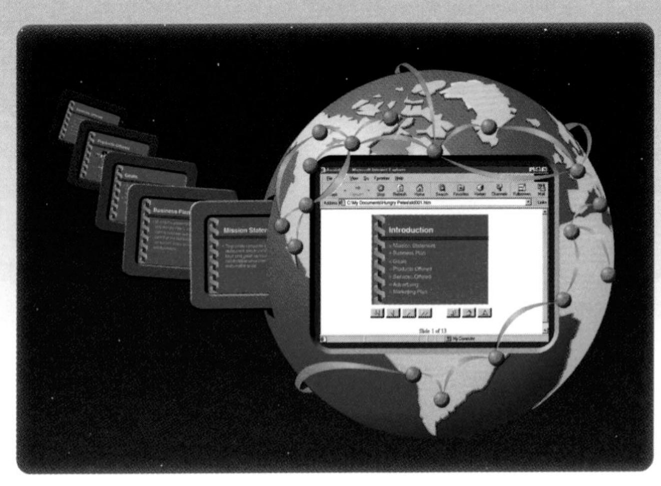

Before you can save your presentation as a collection of Web pages, you need to install the Web Page Authoring (HTML) component from the CD-ROM disc you used to install PowerPoint.

SAVE PRESENTATION AS WEB PAGES

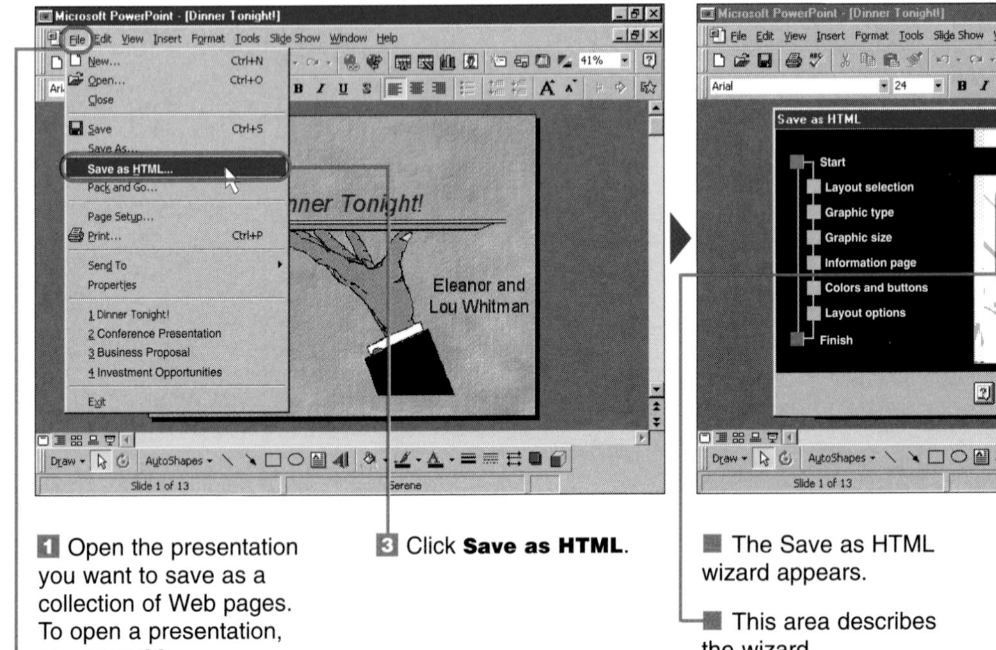

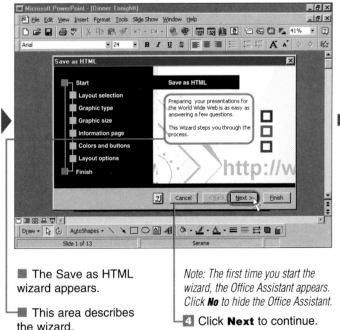

1 Open the presentation you want to save as a collection of Web pages. To open a presentation, see page 22.

2 Click **File**.

3 Click **Save as HTML**.

■ The Save as HTML wizard appears.

■ This area describes the wizard.

*Note: The first time you start the wizard, the Office Assistant appears. Click **No** to hide the Office Assistant.*

4 Click **Next** to continue.

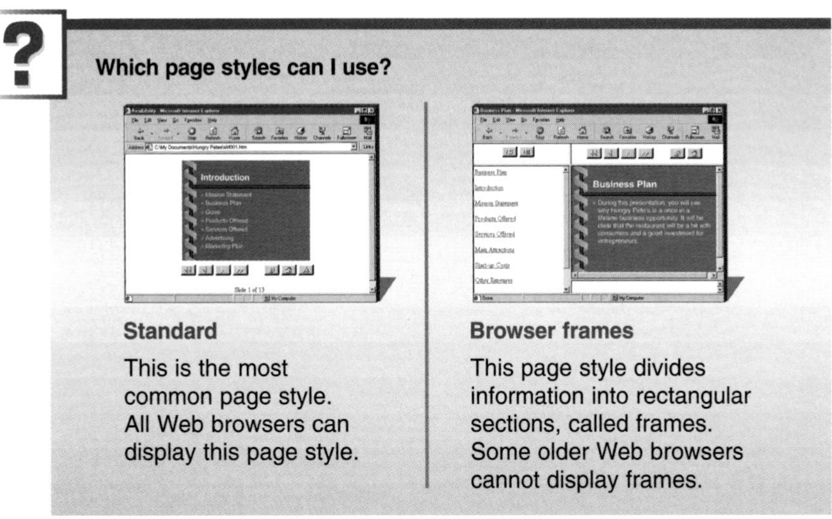

? Which page styles can I use?

Standard

This is the most common page style. All Web browsers can display this page style.

Browser frames

This page style divides information into rectangular sections, called frames. Some older Web browsers cannot display frames.

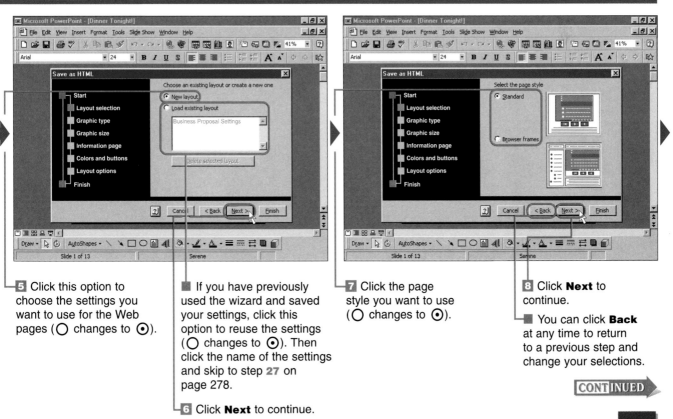

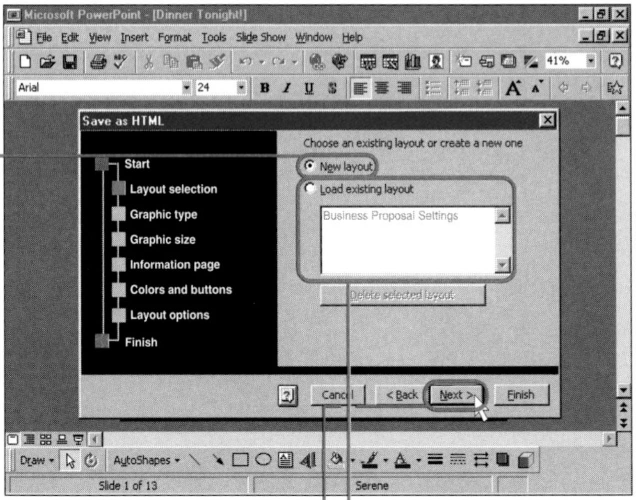

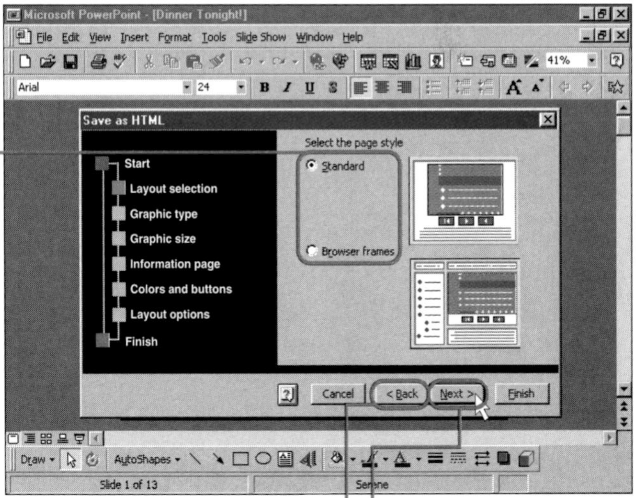

5 Click this option to choose the settings you want to use for the Web pages (○ changes to ⊙).

■ If you have previously used the wizard and saved your settings, click this option to reuse the settings (○ changes to ⊙). Then click the name of the settings and skip to step **27** on page 278.

6 Click **Next** to continue.

7 Click the page style you want to use (○ changes to ⊙).

8 Click **Next** to continue.

■ You can click **Back** at any time to return to a previous step and change your selections.

CONTINUED

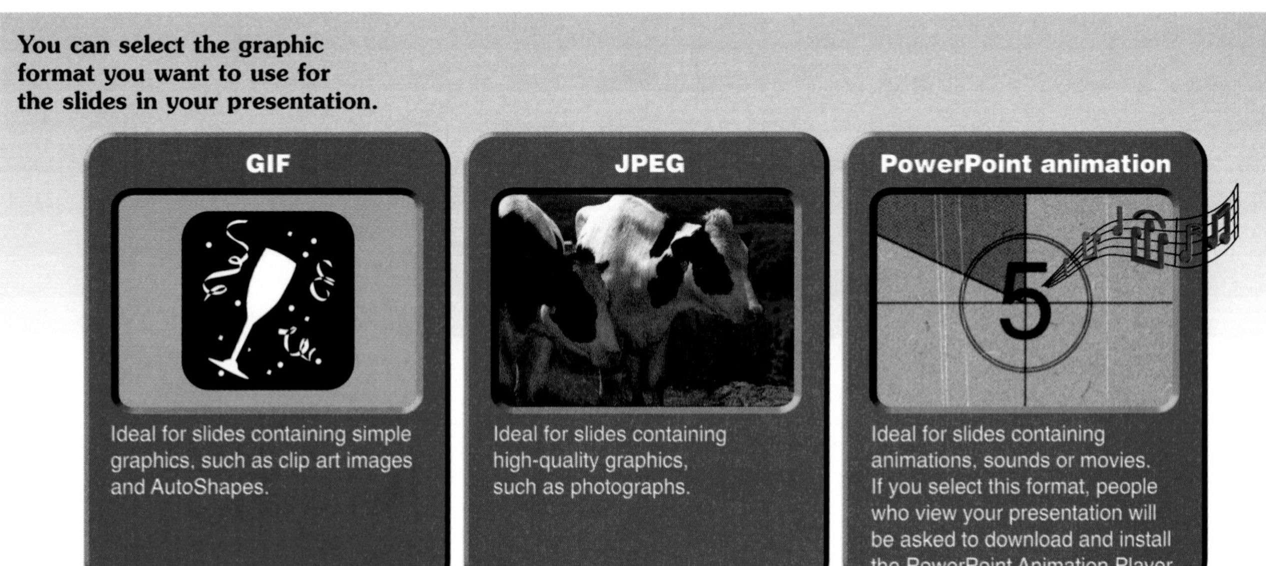

You can select the graphic format you want to use for the slides in your presentation.
GIF
Ideal for slides containing simple graphics, such as clip art images and AutoShapes.
JPEG
Ideal for slides containing high-quality graphics, such as photographs.
PowerPoint animation
Ideal for slides containing animations, sounds or movies. If you select this format, people who view your presentation will be asked to download and install the PowerPoint Animation Player.

SAVE PRESENTATION AS WEB PAGES (CONTINUED)

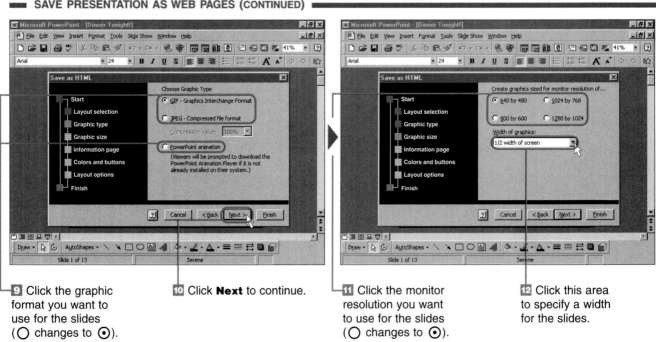

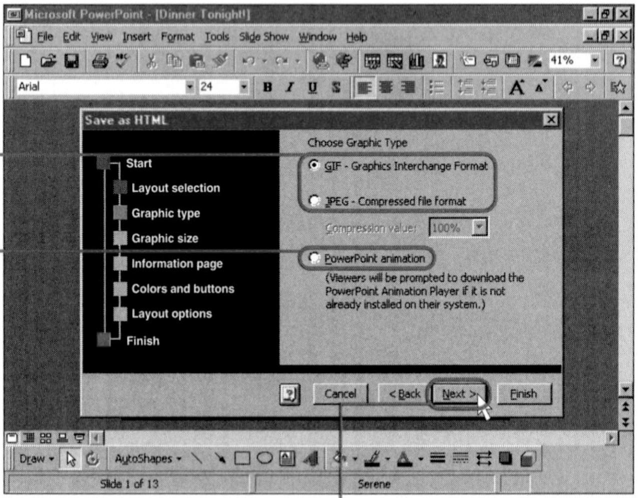

9 Click the graphic format you want to use for the slides (○ changes to ⊙).

10 Click **Next** to continue.

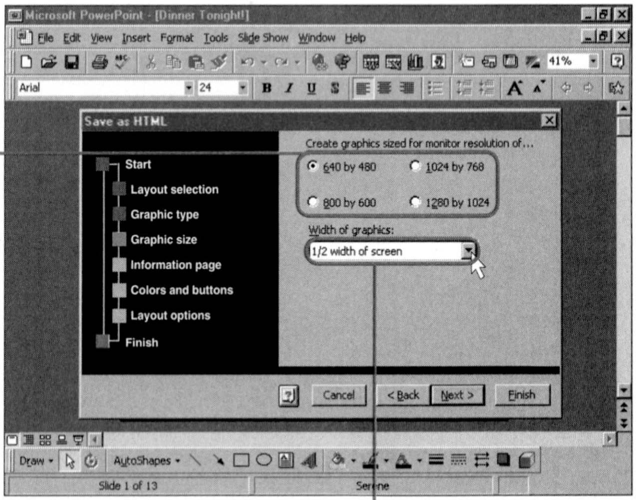

11 Click the monitor resolution you want to use for the slides (○ changes to ⊙).

12 Click this area to specify a width for the slides.

?

What resolution and width should I choose for my slides?

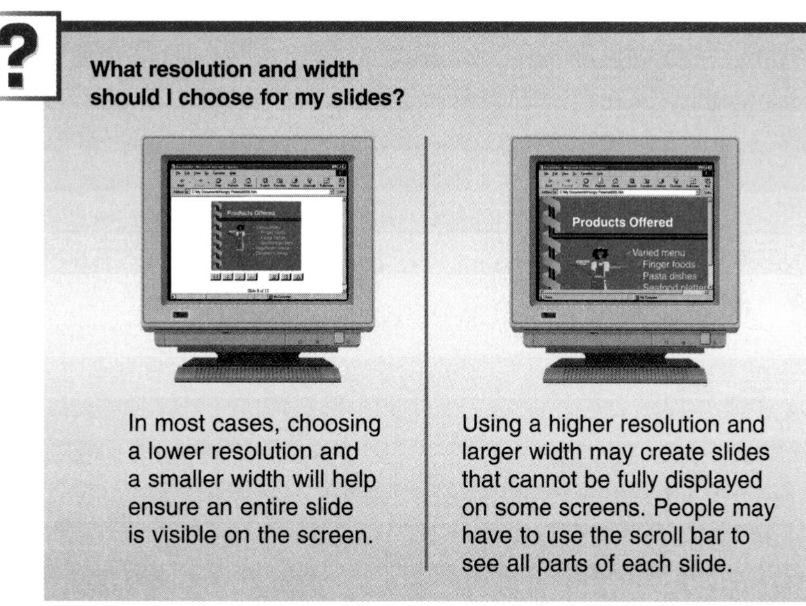

In most cases, choosing a lower resolution and a smaller width will help ensure an entire slide is visible on the screen.

Using a higher resolution and larger width may create slides that cannot be fully displayed on some screens. People may have to use the scroll bar to see all parts of each slide.

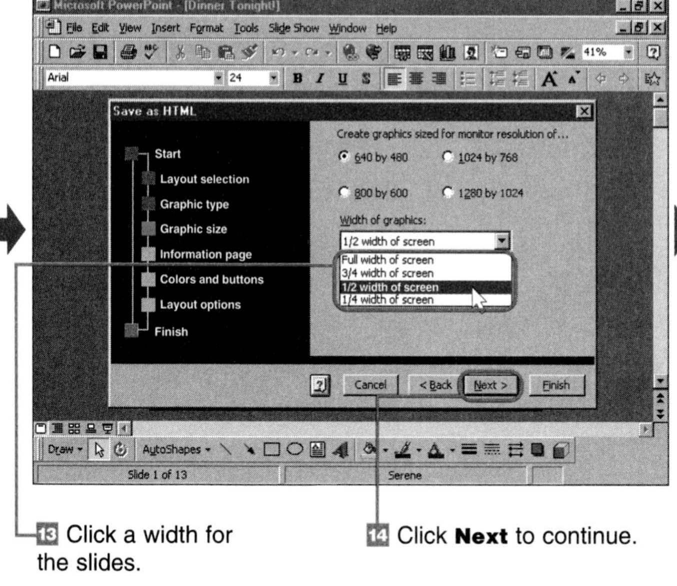

13 Click a width for the slides.

14 Click **Next** to continue.

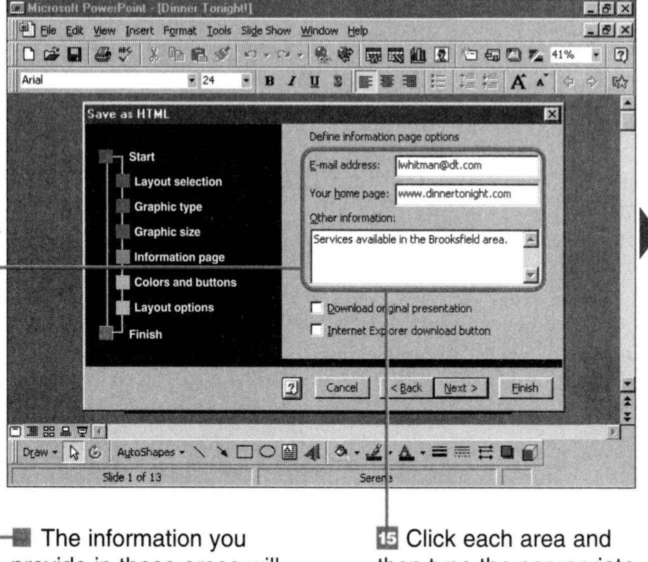

■ The information you provide in these areas will appear on the first Web page of the presentation, called the index Web page.

15 Click each area and then type the appropriate information.

CONTINUED

SAVE PRESENTATION AS WEB PAGES

You can specify the type of navigation buttons you want your Web pages to display. Navigation buttons allow people to move through the slides in your presentation.

SAVE PRESENTATION AS WEB PAGES (CONTINUED)

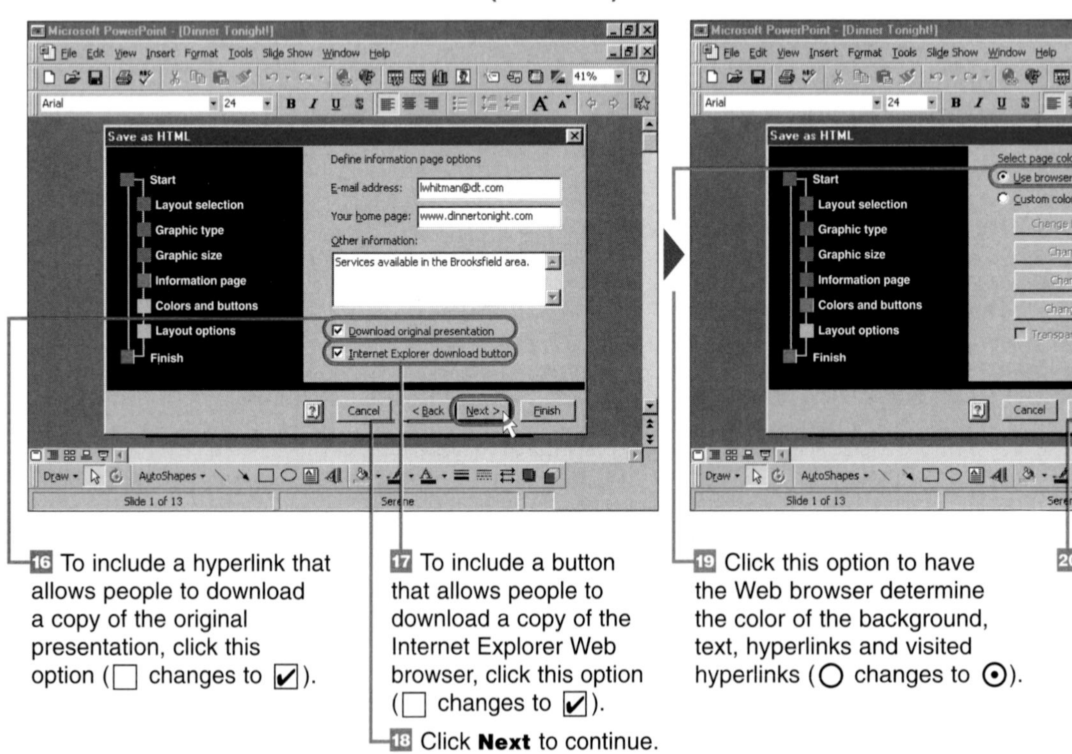

16 To include a hyperlink that allows people to download a copy of the original presentation, click this option (☐ changes to ☑).

17 To include a button that allows people to download a copy of the Internet Explorer Web browser, click this option (☐ changes to ☑).

18 Click **Next** to continue.

19 Click this option to have the Web browser determine the color of the background, text, hyperlinks and visited hyperlinks (○ changes to ⊙).

20 Click **Next** to continue.

?

Why would I want to allow people to download a copy of my original presentation?

Many Internet service providers charge their customers for the time they spend accessing the Internet. If your presentation is long, people may prefer to download a copy of the presentation to their own computer and view the slide show when they are not connected to the Internet.

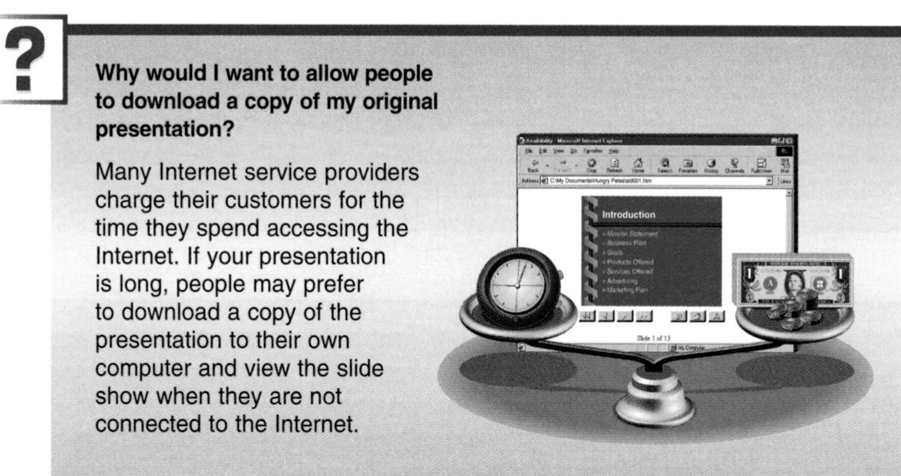

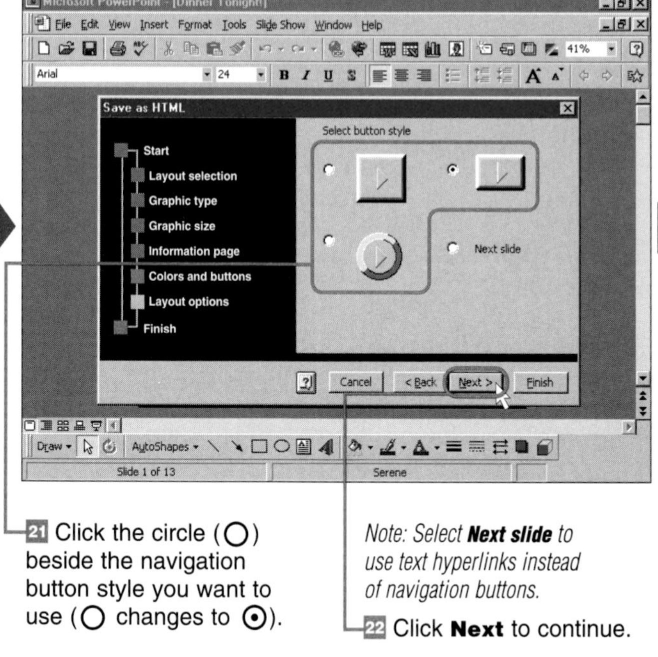

21 Click the circle (○) beside the navigation button style you want to use (○ changes to ⊙).

*Note: Select **Next slide** to use text hyperlinks instead of navigation buttons.*

22 Click **Next** to continue.

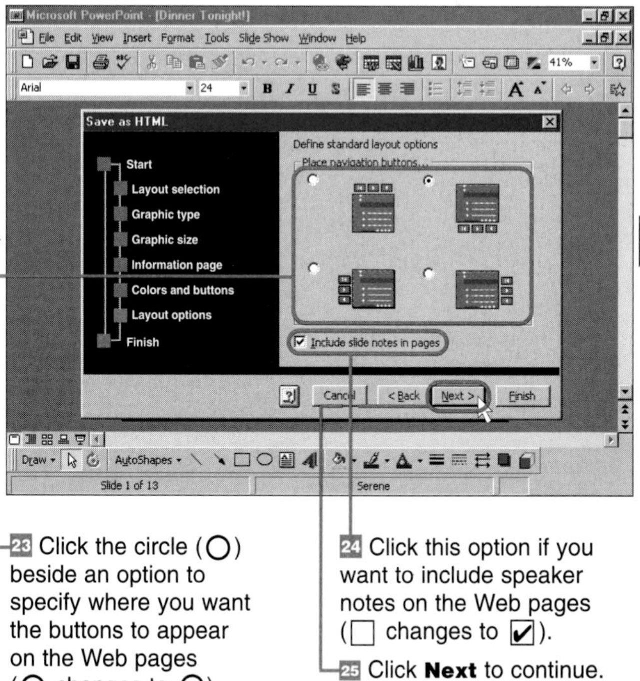

23 Click the circle (○) beside an option to specify where you want the buttons to appear on the Web pages (○ changes to ⊙).

Note: If you chose the Browser frames page style in step 7, these options are not available.

24 Click this option if you want to include speaker notes on the Web pages (☐ changes to ☑).

25 Click **Next** to continue.

CONTINUED

SAVE PRESENTATION AS WEB PAGES

PowerPoint creates a folder on your computer to store your collection of Web pages.

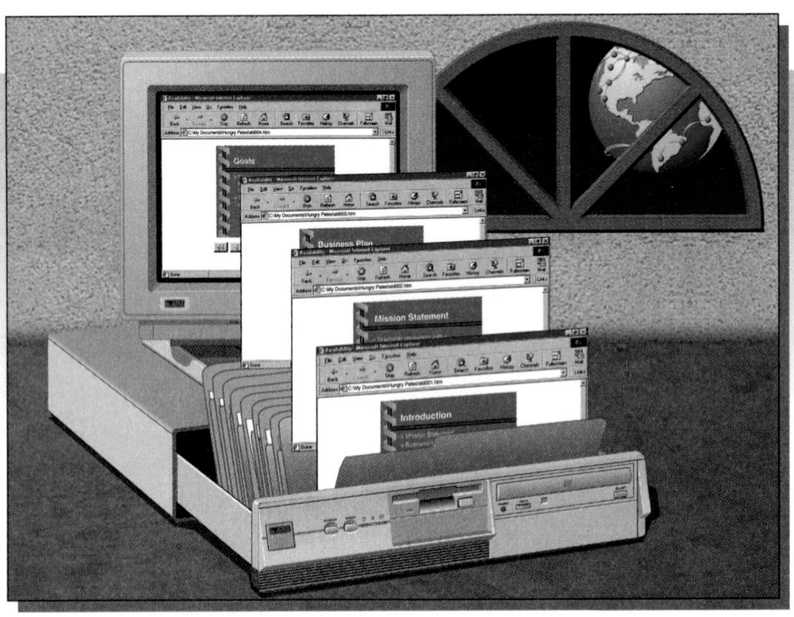

SAVE PRESENTATION AS WEB PAGES (CONTINUED)

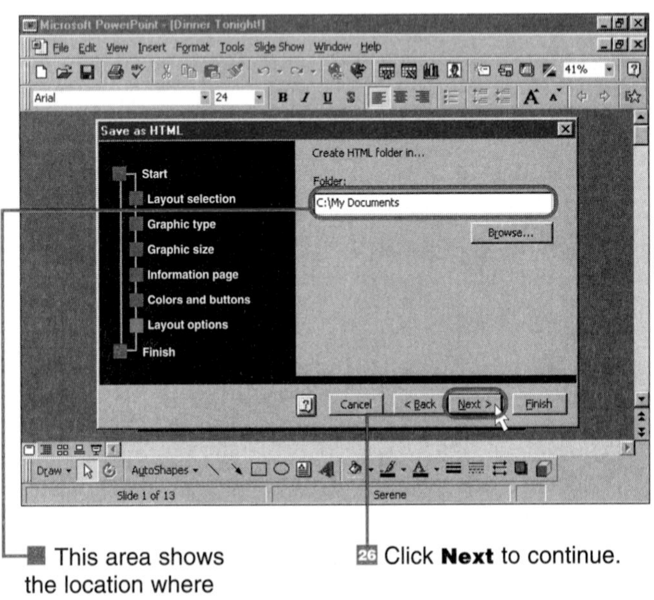

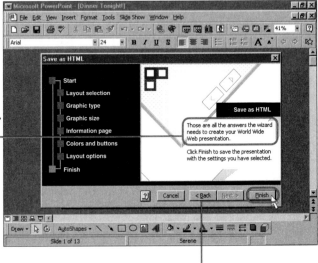

■ This area shows the location where PowerPoint will store your collection of Web pages.

26 Click **Next** to continue.

■ The wizard indicates that you have provided all the information needed to save the presentation as Web pages.

27 Click **Finish** to save the Web pages.

?

How do I publish my presentation on the Web?

After you save your presentation as a collection of Web pages in a folder, you can publish the pages by transferring the folder to a Web server. The company that gives you access to the Internet usually offers space on its Web server where you can publish your Web pages.

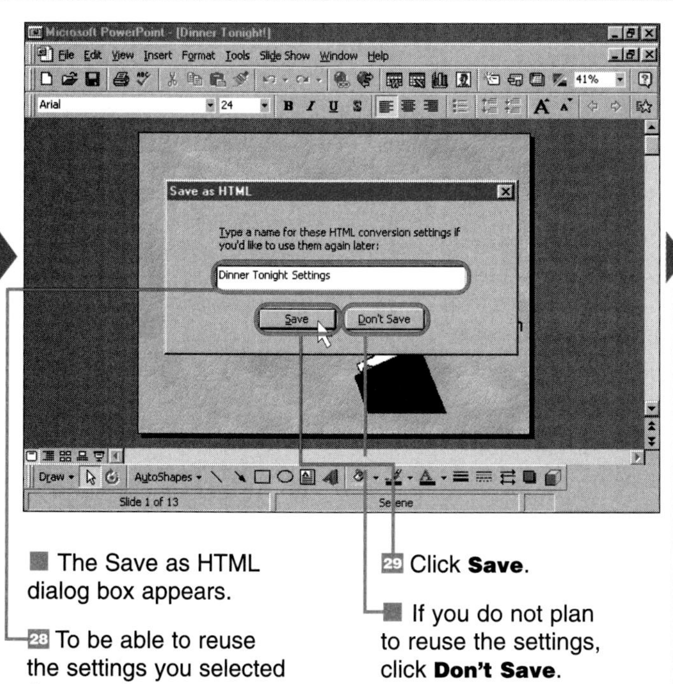

■ The Save as HTML dialog box appears.

28 To be able to reuse the settings you selected the next time you save a presentation as Web pages, type a name for the settings.

29 Click **Save**.

■ If you do not plan to reuse the settings, click **Don't Save**.

■ A dialog box appears when PowerPoint has successfully saved the presentation as a collection of Web pages.

30 Click **OK** to close the dialog box.

■ You can now publish the presentation on the Web.

■ To view the Web pages you saved, see page 280.

VIEW PRESENTATION SAVED AS WEB PAGES

After you save your presentation as a collection of Web pages, you can view the Web pages on your computer.

The index Web page is the first Web page that appears on your screen. This Web page displays a table of contents for your presentation.

VIEW PRESENTATION SAVED AS WEB PAGES

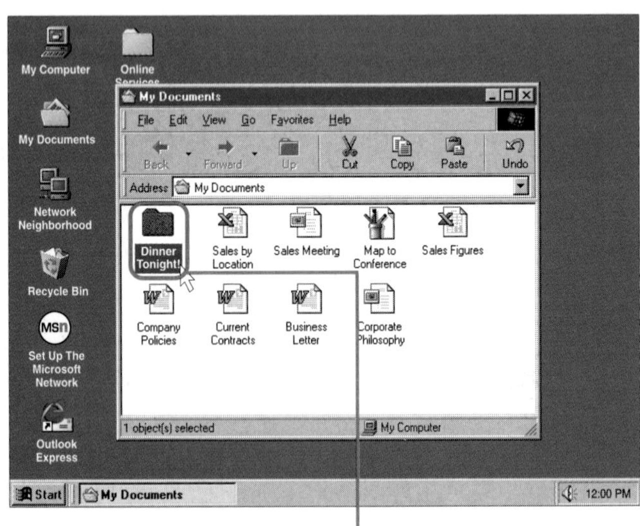

1 Display the contents of the My Documents folder.

2 Double-click the folder containing the presentation you saved as a collection of Web pages.

Note: The folder has the same name as the presentation.

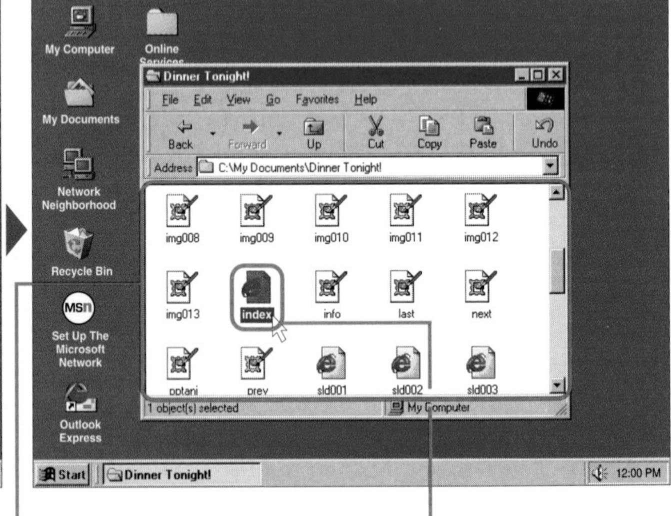

■ The contents of the folder appear, displaying all the files needed to view the presentation on the Web.

3 Double-click the **index** file.

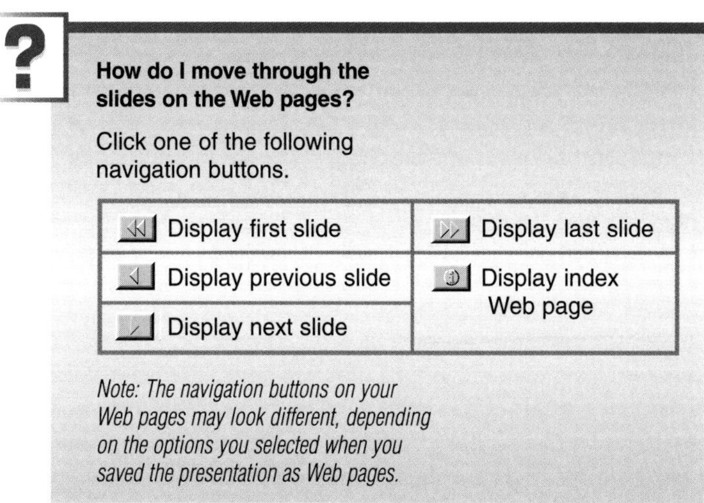

How do I move through the slides on the Web pages?

Click one of the following navigation buttons.

Display first slide	Display last slide
Display previous slide	Display index Web page
Display next slide	

Note: The navigation buttons on your Web pages may look different, depending on the options you selected when you saved the presentation as Web pages.

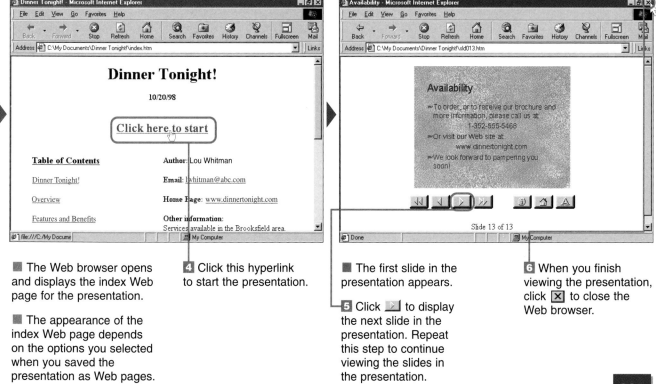

■ The Web browser opens and displays the index Web page for the presentation.

■ The appearance of the index Web page depends on the options you selected when you saved the presentation as Web pages.

4 Click this hyperlink to start the presentation.

■ The first slide in the presentation appears.

5 Click ▷ to display the next slide in the presentation. Repeat this step to continue viewing the slides in the presentation.

6 When you finish viewing the presentation, click ☒ to close the Web browser.

INDEX

D

E

M

N

O

P

R

T

U

V

W

Z

OVER 6 MILLION

OTHER 3-D Visual SERIES

SIMPLIFIED SERIES

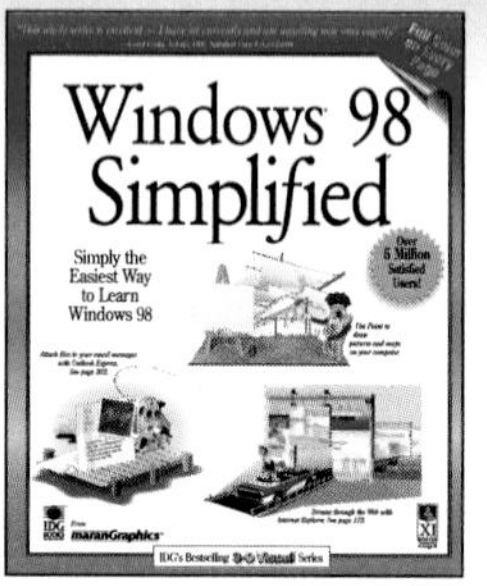

Windows 98 Simplified
ISBN 0-7645-6030-1
$24.99 USA/£23.99 UK

Windows 95 Simplified
ISBN 1-56884-662-2
$19.99 USA/£18.99 UK

More Windows 95 Simplified
ISBN 1-56884-689-4
$19.99 USA/£18.99 UK

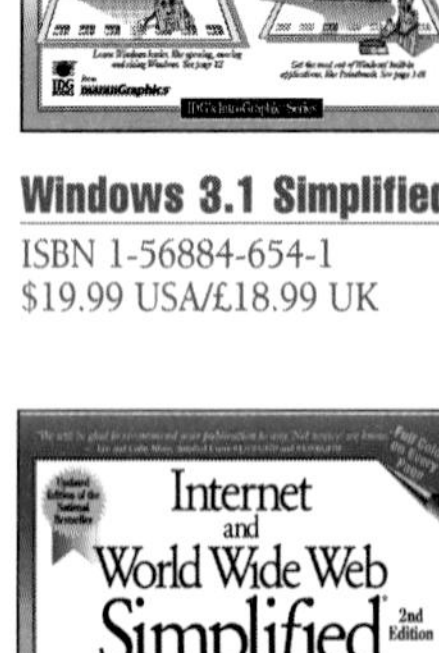

Windows 3.1 Simplified
ISBN 1-56884-654-1
$19.99 USA/£18.99 UK

Office 97 Simplified
ISBN 0-7645-6009-3
$29.99 USA/£28.99 UK

Microsoft Office 4.2 For Windows Simplified
ISBN 1-56884-673-8
$27.99 USA/£26.99 UK

Creating Web Pages Simplified
ISBN 0-7645-6007-7
$24.99 USA/£23.99 UK

World Wide Web Color Yellow Pages Simplified
ISBN 0-7645-6005-0
$29.99 USA/£28.99 UK

Internet and World Wid Web Simplified, 2nd Edi
ISBN 0-7645-6029-8
$24.99 USA/£23.99 UK

POCKETGUIDES

The Proven 3-D Visual Approach To Learning Computers In A Handy Pocket Size.

Windows 98 Visual PocketGuide
ISBN 0-7645-6035-2
$14.99 USA/£13.99 UK

Windows 95 Visual PocketGuide
ISBN 1-56884-661-4
$14.99 USA/£13.99 UK

Word 6 For Windov Visual PocketGuide
ISBN 1-56884-666-5
$14.99 USA/£13.99 UK

FOR CORPORATE ORDERS, PLEASE CALL: 800-469-6616

S A T I S F I E D   U S E R S !

ord 97 Simplified

3N 0-7645-6011-5
4.99 USA/£23.99 UK

Word For Windows 95 Simplified

ISBN 1-56884-681-9
$19.99 USA/£18.99 UK

Excel 97 Simplified

ISBN 0-7645-6022-0
$24.99 USA/£23.99 UK

Excel For Windows 95 Simplified

ISBN 1-56884-682-7
$19.99 USA/£18.99 UK

Excel 5 For Windows Simplified

ISBN 1-56884-664-9
$19.99 USA/£18.99 UK

mputers Simplified, h Edition

3N 0-7645-6042-5
4.99 USA/£23.99 UK

America Online Simplified

ISBN 0-7645-6033-6
$24.99 USA/£23.99 UK

PC Upgrade and Repair Simplified

ISBN 0-7645-6049-2
$24.99 USA/£23.99 UK

The 3-D Visual Dictionary of Computing

ISBN 1-56884-678-9
$19.99 USA/£18.99 UK

WordPerfect 6.1 For Windows Simplified

ISBN 1-56884-665-7
$19.99 USA/£18.99 UK

ALSO AVAILABLE:

Windows 3.1 Visual PocketGuide

ISBN 1-56884-650-9
$14.99 USA/£13.99 UK

Excel 5 For Windows Visual PocketGuide

ISBN 1-56884-667-3
$14.99 USA/£13.99 UK

WordPerfect 6.1 For Windows Visual PocketGuide

ISBN 1-56884-668-1
$14.99 USA/£13.99 UK

Lotus 1-2-3 R5 For Windows Visual PocketGuide

ISBN 1-56884-671-1
$14.99 USA/£13.99 UK

FOR CORPORATE ORDERS, PLEASE CALL: 800-469-6616

S A T I S F I E D   U S E R S !

Teach Yourself Office 97 VISUALLY

ISBN 0-7645-6018-2
$29.99 USA/£28.99 UK

Teach Yourself Windows NT VISUALLY

ISBN 0-7645-6061-1
$29.99 USA/£28.99 UK

Teach Yourself Microsoft Excel 97 VISUALLY

ISBN 0-7645-6063-8
$29.99 USA/£28.99 UK

MASTER VISUALLY SERIES

Master Windows 98 VISUALLY

ISBN 0-7645-6034-4
$39.99 USA/£36.99 UK

Master Windows 95 VISUALLY

ISBN 0-7645-6024-7
$39.99 USA/£36.99 UK

Master Office 97 VISUALLY

ISBN 0-7645-6036-0
$39.99 USA/£36.99 UK

Visit our Web site at www.maran.com

FOR CORPORATE ORDERS, PLEASE CALL: **800-469-6616**

TRADE & INDIVIDUAL ORDERS

Phone: **(800) 762-2974**
or **(317) 596-5200**
(8 a.m. – 6 p.m., CST, weekdays)
FAX : **(800) 550-2747**
or **(317) 596-5692**

EDUCATIONAL ORDERS & DISCOUNTS

Phone: **(800) 434-2086**
(8:30 a.m.–5:00 p.m., CST, weekdays)
FAX : **(317) 596-5499**

CORPORATE ORDERS FOR 3-D VISUAL™ SERIES

Phone: **(800) 469-6616**
(8 a.m.–5 p.m., EST, weekdays)
FAX : **(905) 890-9434**

Qty	ISBN	Title	Price	Total

Shipping & Handling Charges

	Description	First book	Each add'l. book	Total
Domestic	Normal	$4.50	$1.50	$
	Two Day Air	$8.50	$2.50	$
	Overnight	$18.00	$3.00	$
International	Surface	$8.00	$8.00	$
	Airmail	$16.00	$16.00	$
	DHL Air	$17.00	$17.00	$

Subtotal ______________

CA residents add applicable sales tax ______________

IN, MA and MD residents add 5% sales tax ______________

IL residents add 6.25% sales tax ______________

RI residents add 7% sales tax ______________

TX residents add 8.25% sales tax ______________

Shipping ______________

Total ______________

Ship to:

Name ______________________________

Address ______________________________

Company ______________________________

City/State/Zip ______________________________

Daytime Phone ______________________________

Payment: □ Check to IDG Books (US Funds Only)
□ Visa □ Mastercard □ American Express

Card # ______________ Exp. ________ Signature ______________

maranGraphics™